The Killing Time

The Killing Time

Fanaticism, Liberty and the Birth of Britain

DAVID S. ROSS

Luath Press Limited
EDINBURGH
www.luath.co.uk

First published 2010

ISBN: 978-1-906817-04-6

The publisher acknowledges subsidy from

towards the publication of this book.

The paper used in this book is sourced from renewable forestry
and is FSC credited material.

Printed and bound by
MPG Books Ltd, Cornwall

Typeset in 11 point Sabon by 3btype.com

Maps by Jim Lewis

The author's right to be identified as author of this book under the
Copyright, Designs and Patents Act 1988 has been asserted.

© David S. Ross 2010

In memory of John Murchison, sometime Headmaster of Bridgend Primary School, Alness

The Scotch, it is well-known, are more remarkable for the exercise of their intellectual powers, than for the keenness of their feelings; they are, therefore, more moved by logic than by rhetoric, and more attracted by acute and argumentative reasoning on doctrinal points, than influenced by enthusiastic appeals to the heart and to the passions...
                                            SIR WALTER SCOTT, *Rob Roy*

History consists, for the greater part, of the miseries brought upon the world by pride, ambition, avarice, revenge, lust, sedition, hypocrisy, ungoverned zeal, and all the train of disorderly appetites.
      EDMUND BURKE, *Reflections Upon the Revolution in France*

... Calvinism was an active and radical force. It was a creed which sought, not merely to purify the individual, but to reconstruct Church and State, and to renew society by penetrating every department of life, public as well as private, with the influence of religion.
      R. H. TAWNEY, *Religion and the Rise of Capitalism*

The theory that truth is manifest – that it is there for everyone to see, if only he wants to see it – this theory is the basis of almost every kind of fanaticism... Yet the theory that truth is manifest not only breeds fanatics – men possessed by the conviction that all who do not see the manifest truth are possessed by the devil – but it may also lead... to authoritarianism.
      KARL R. POPPER, *On the Sources of Knowledge and of Ignorance*

Scotland is... ideally suited for investigation of the interaction of politics and ideology.
                                        MAURICE LEE, JR., *The 'Inevitable' Union*

There is very little of the bliss of Heaven revealed to us in the world.
      From a sermon by the Rev. James Kirkton, October 13, 1698

Stay, passenger, take notice what thou reads,
At Edinburgh lie our bodies, here our heads;
Our right hands stood at Lanark, these we want,
Because with them we signed the Covenant.
                          Epitaph on a tombstone at Hamilton

Contents

Acknowledgements		ix
Money		x
Foreword: Why 'The Killing Time?'		xi
CHAPTER ONE	Signing Up To Revolution	1
CHAPTER TWO	The Glory of the Covenant	10
CHAPTER THREE	The Generation of '48	23
CHAPTER FOUR	The Covenant – Vainglory and Disaster	28
CHAPTER FIVE	The Usurpation	36
CHAPTER SIX	A Nation of Theopoliticians	42
CHAPTER SEVEN	Boys Growing Up	47
CHAPTER EIGHT	Philosophers and Witches	55
CHAPTER NINE	Owls and Satyrs, and Bangster Amazons	66
CHAPTER TEN	Improvement and Reaction	77
CHAPTER ELEVEN	'I did see the outlaw Whigs Lye Scattered...'	84
CHAPTER TWELVE	*Naphtali* and *Caelia*	94
CHAPTER THIRTEEN	Old Politics, New Practitioners	102
CHAPTER FOURTEEN	Experiences of an Advocate	114
CHAPTER FIFTEEN	The Highland Host	119
CHAPTER SIXTEEN	'Beloved Sufferers'	128
CHAPTER SEVENTEEN	Assassination, Schism, Defeat	134
CHAPTER EIGHTEEN	'Blood Shall Be Their Sign'	145
CHAPTER NINETEEN	'My Lord Advocate Does Wonders'	157
CHAPTER TWENTY	The Tolbooth in Winter	165
CHAPTER TWENTY-ONE	Torture Under Law	170
CHAPTER TWENTY-TWO	The Killing Time	182
CHAPTER TWENTY-THREE	A Carnival of Blood?	190

CHAPTER TWENTY-FOUR	Argyll's Adventure	197
CHAPTER TWENTY-FIVE	Dancing at Holyrood	204
CHAPTER TWENTY-SIX	'… before the Delivery Come'	215
CHAPTER TWENTY-SEVEN	Interregnum	226
CHAPTER TWENTY-EIGHT	The Revolution Settlement	237
CHAPTER TWENTY-NINE	'Dark John of the Battles'	248
CHAPTER THIRTY	A Mirror-Scotland	259
CHAPTER THIRTY-ONE	The Interest of the State	267
CHAPTER THIRTY-TWO	The Perils of Atheism	271
CHAPTER THIRTY-THREE	The Silence of Darien	280
CHAPTER THIRTY-FOUR	Questions of Succession	287
CHAPTER THIRTY-FIVE	An Unruly Parliament	295
CHAPTER THIRTY-SIX	'Forever After'	305
Select Glossary		315
Timeline		319
Notes and References		323
Bibliography		353
Index		362

Acknowledgements

THE DRAFT TEXT WAS kindly read by Dr Barry Robertson and I am grateful to him for numerous helpful criticisms and suggestions. Errors and misjudgements that remain are exclusively those of the author. Most of my research was done in St Andrews University Library, the National Library of Scotland, and the London Library, and I am grateful for their help.

Picture Acknowledgements

Picture sources are noted throughout. Thanks are due to Dundee Art Gallery (Lady Dundee), The Fitzwilliam Museum, Cambridge (fourth Earl of Perth), The Scottish National Portrait Gallery (Viscount Melfort), and the National Trust for Scotland (Earl of Stair). I regret that it was not possible to include the portrait of Lady Errol held on long-term loan by the Scottish National Portrait Gallery.

Money

IN THE 17TH CENTURY, Scotland had its own monetary system, though aligned on that of England, at a set exchange rate of £Sc.12 to one English pound (re-confirmed by an Act of Parliament in 1686). Pounds were divided into 20 shillings (s) and 240 pence (d). The Scottish economy ran on a mixture of money trading and barter. In barter, goods and services were exchanged, or given in return for certain rights, such as tenancy. Value had to be established and agreed, and the basic unit of account was the merk, at a value of 13s 4d (raised to 14s in 1681), or 1s 2d in English money. Scottish visitors to England winced at the exchange rate, but not everything was more expensive. In Edinburgh, in 1642, a 1-lb loaf of rye bread cost 12 pennies; in Southampton, in 1643, a wheat loaf of the same weight cost three-quarters of a penny. The Mint, just off the Cowgate in Edinburgh, produced mostly 'copper' coins. In the reigns of Charles II and James VII, there were four silver coins, ranging from 4 merks to one quarter of a merk in value, and two copper coins, the bawbee, worth 6d, and the bodle or turner, worth 2d. In the text, Scottish pounds are identified as £Sc. English, French, Dutch and Imperial German currency ('rix-dollars') also circulated, as did many ancient Scottish coins going back to the previous century. There were no banks (until the Bank of Scotland was established by Act of Parliament in 1695) and no bank-notes, but bonds and promissory notes were exchanged.

Foreword

Why 'The Killing Time'?

A SPAN OF 70 YEARS is covered in this book, from 1638 to 1707, during which the Scots experienced huge upheavals in every aspect of public life – political revolution, military disasters, civil disorder, abrupt regime changes. From these confrontations, disputes and battles, clouds of myth and propaganda arose and still hang over us. Central to this mythomachia is the role of the 'Covenanters'. In 1638, almost everyone was a Covenanter. Fifty years later, they were a 'Remnant', their great manifesto irrelevant and half-forgotten. In 1685 the government began a draconian campaign against them, which they called, not without reason, 'The Killing Time', and the name has stuck. Seventy-eight persons were summarily executed. Long before that, however, the Covenant's wars had inaugurated a killing time of far more shattering scale. Not even in 1914–18 would such a high proportion of the nation's manhood and youth be slaughtered for a nationally accepted cause. The title, then, warns against our ability to see what we wish to – or have been told to – see in history, but the book takes no side in exploring what the people of Scotland, rulers and ruled, thought and did during those tumultuous years.

England too had its tumults in those decades, emerging vigorous, combative and rich, a nascent world power. Scotland, it seemed, was going the other way, in a national winding-down process. The impression is strong that proud Scotia came to her wedding with John Bull as a somewhat forlorn and needy bride. In exploring this contrast, it does not take long to find that much of what is generally assumed about the period is a travesty of the reality. This book seeks to reveal the era between the National Covenant and the Treaty of Union as it was made by the people who lived through it – rich in passions and disputes, plots and rebellions, personal and communal quandaries, agonies and ecstasies perhaps more intense than anything in the centuries before or after – but also a time of vigorous commercial and industrial development, domestic improvements and civic progress. A trading nation cannot be an introverted one, and Scotland lived by international trade.

Within the wider narrative, it follows the careers of a handful of men, mostly born in 1648–9, to illustrate aspects of personal life as well as the background to power-politics and plots. Their individual stories often intertwine. Two died in battle; two in exile; one was tortured; one was the architect of a notorious official crime. Born into the flow of events in Chapter Three, in Chapter Seven they are growing up, and by Chapter Eight they are beginning to gain reputations. Long before the end, they are shaping the blocks of future history – and myth.

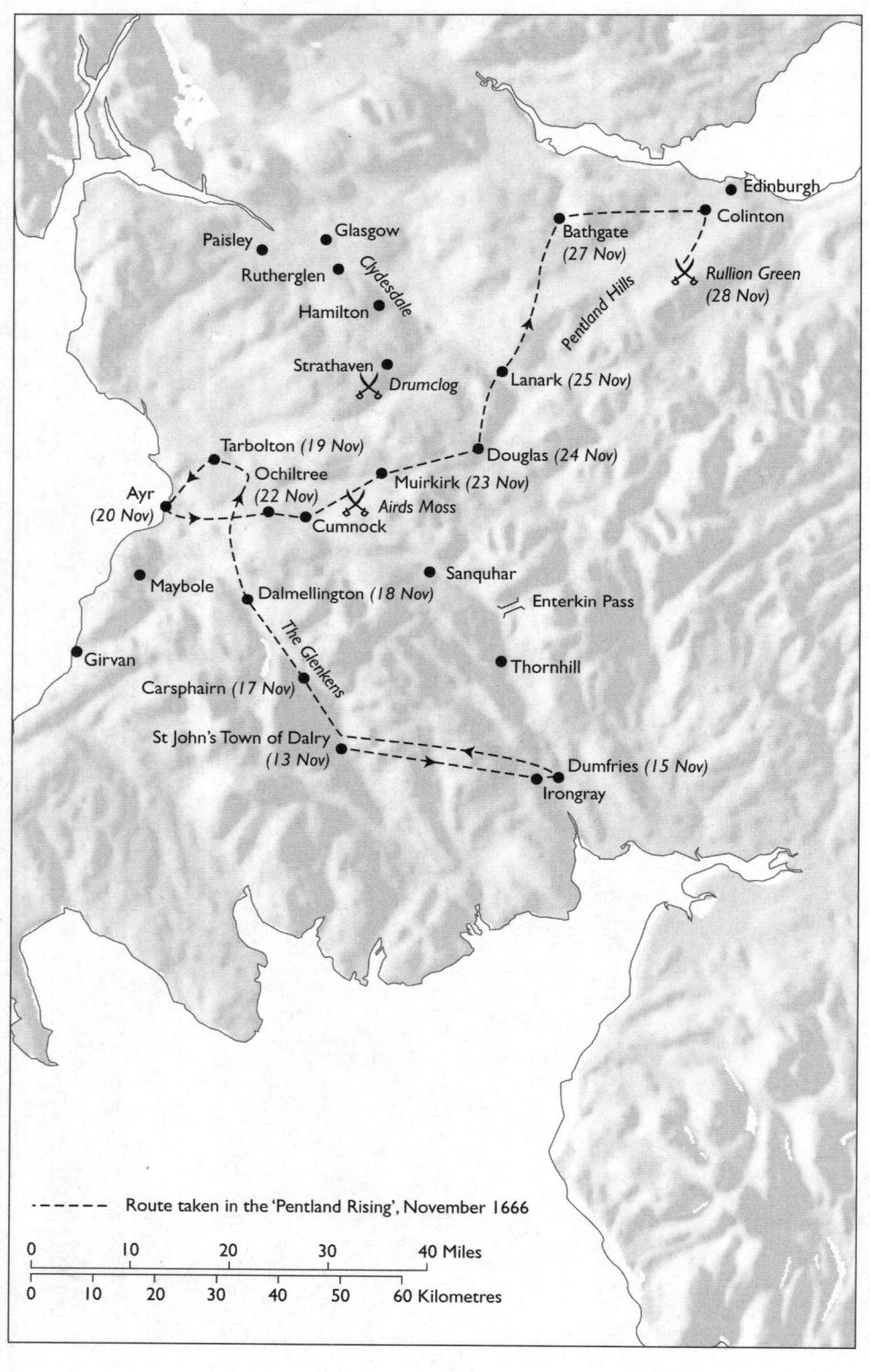

CHAPTER ONE

Signing Up To Revolution

FOR MOST EUROPEANS IN the 17th century, the kingdom of Scotland was as remote and exotic as the Khanate of Crimea. It was one of Europe's poorer countries, best known as a source of mercenary soldiers and wandering pedlars. Visitors were less struck by its poverty – hovels and aggressive beggars were to be found in every land – than by the smells of the towns and the wretchedness of their inns.[1] But Scotland was not on any through route for wealthy travellers. The country maintained five universities, more than in Sweden, Poland, and England together. They did not chafe at the boundaries of modern knowledge. But the cheapest and most portable international commodity is ideas, which often come free and are only paid for later. North-western outpost though it might be, Scotland always drew strongly on the main streams of European thought, and fashioned the results into something very much of its own.

In 1603 its king, James VI, as heir to the English Queen Elizabeth I, had become King of England and Ireland also: monarch of three adjacent but very different nations, in an era when kings really did rule, or were expected to. Suddenly, if not unexpectedly, the Scots were confronted with the ending of their separate monarchy, and a new, ambiguous relationship, neither political union nor separate co-existence, with England. Up to his death in 1625, James managed to hold together what could have been an impossible combination of roles. But the efforts of his son Charles I were much less successful. After 12 years of Charles's triple kingship, England and Ireland were in turmoil, and the Scots mounted a revolution. It was almost bloodless: the only wounds being self-inflicted by people who, not content to use mere ink, wanted to show their feelings in blood. They were putting their names to an impressively titled document, the National Covenant.

Grievances about taxation and property rights went back to the beginning of Charles's reign, but were sharpened by the King's aim to have, if not a single Church in his realms, at least a unified form of religious observance. In June 1636 the government issued a form of guidance for the Church of Scotland, *Canons and Constitutions Eclesiasticall*. Though published in Aberdeen, it was compiled under the direction of William Laud, Archbishop of Canterbury, and much of it came from the Church of England's rule-book of 1604. Intense national and personal feelings were invested in the Scottish Church, the 'Kirk', seen as created by divinely inspired men to serve the country's spiritual needs. Previously, changes to its procedures and forms of worship had been approved by its own Assembly and authorised by the Scottish Parliament. The *Canons* were issued under 'our Prerogative Royal', and commanded by royal authority to be 'diligently observed and executed'. To one 20th-century writer, this was 'a gauntlet flung by royal absolutism in the face of a Church and people reared in a tradition of independence'.[2] In fact the independence was of a distinctly restricted kind, but there is no doubting the resentment caused. When the *Canons* were followed up by a new Prayer Book, imposed in the same arbitrary manner on 23 July 1637, the protests became so widespread and vehement as to create a sense of national resistance. The King was making a crude attempt to force changes in something that most people took extremely seriously – the way in which they publicly worshipped God. Complaints and protests came from parishes throughout the country, and many sent delegates to Edinburgh with messages of remonstration.[3] Many ministers simply ignored the order to use the new Prayer Book; others dared not refuse. The Bishop of Brechin, Walter Whitford, when he placed it on his pulpit lectern in front of a glowering congregation, meaningfully flanked it with loaded pistols.[4]

The sense of crisis swelled. Supporters of the King's innovations or of his right to introduce them were overwhelmingly outnumbered and out-shouted by opponents. Obdurate in response to loyal petitions, Charles I took a high hand, but his proclamations and threats merely fuelled the collective anger. Edinburgh's streets, churches and taverns were loud with debate and protest, and non-residents without business to transact were ordered to leave. Most stayed on. Threats to move the Privy Council and the courts of justice out of the city had no effect. In January–February 1638 the Council and the Court of Session did meet at Stirling, Edinburgh being too disturbed.[5] Banned pamphlets like George Gillespie's *Dispute Against the English-Popish Ceremonies Obtruded on the Church of Scotland* were openly passed around. The Council itself was so divided as to be impotent. Supposedly the executive agency of royal government, it consented to the formation of a parallel and more dynamic authority in December 1637 when the complainers set up their own representative groups of four members from each of the 'estates' of the kingdom: nobles, gentry, burgesses, and the clergy. Taking over the debating chamber of the almost-completed Parliament House, each group sat at its own table, with a fifth for executive officials, and 'the Tables', with no constitutional authority, became the focus of a national state of protest. No hint of concession came from the King, and the Tables and all influential men were bombarded with demands for action. A letter of 4 January 1638 from Samuel Rutherford, minister of Anwoth, Dumfriesshire, one of the most outspoken opponents of the King's policy, to John Campbell, Lord Loudoun, a leading figure among the Protestant aristocracy, blends Biblical metaphor and crude abuse in its exhortations:

> ... your name and honour shall never rot or wither in heaven (at least) if ye deliver the Lord's sheep that have been scattered in a dark and cloudy day, out of the hands of strange lords and hirelings... that by the bringing in of the Pope's foul tail first, upon us (their wretched and beggarly ceremonies) they may thrust in after them the Antichrist's legs, and thighs, and his belly, head and shoulders, and then cry down Christ and the gospel, and up the merchandise and wares of the great whore.[6]

It was to satisfy this hunger for meaningful action that the National Covenant was conceived and drawn up. Loudoun was one of the small group concerned with its planning and launching. Compiled by Archibald Johnston, a 27-year-old lawyer, known as Johnston of Wariston from his small family estate between Edinburgh and the sea, and Alexander Henderson, aged 55, parish minister of Leuchars in Fife, its concept was a brilliant one. In Scotland's somewhat primitive politics, powerful men had often joined together in 'bands' – private or public bonds of commitment to support one another in a particular cause – now the entire nation was invited to join formally in a 'band' with God to obtain the redress of its grievances. Other populations, in Portugal and Catalonia for example, were in revolt against absentee kingship, but no country had ever done such a thing as this.

The idea harks back to the the Old Testament covenants made by the Israelites with their God. Scots in the 17th century felt a close affinity with the Biblical Jews and many yearned for the same direct and unambiguous

Alexander Henderson
Reproduced from Hewison, *The Covenanters*, Vol. 1 (I,9)

dialogue with God. The concept of the covenant had been taken up by both Luther and Calvin in their reformist teachings. Fundamental to Protestantism was the 'Covenant of Grace' – God's offer to sinful humanity. In its most basic form, the individual Christian's obligation, as a sharer in this pact, was to attend the preaching of the Gospel and the administration of the sacraments. Under the name of federal theology, the notion of the personal covenant was elaborated by several eminent Dutch and German scholars in the early decades of the 17th century. To call this document a Covenant thus had a special meaning and resonance, emphasising that it was no earthly agreement, but one made with and under God.

At first there was no great burst of popular enthusiasm. On 27 February 1638 the draft document was read out out first to a gathering of nobles, then to one of ministers, in the hall of the Tailors' Guild, and approved with minor amendments. A final copy, 'a fair parchment above an ellne in squair' was made. On the following afternoon this was displayed in the Greyfriars' Church, and after a religious service, signing began at four o'clock, first by members of the nobility, then lesser barons and gentry. On the 29th, ministers of the Kirk signed it, again in the Tailors' Hall. It was not until 2 March that ordinary citizens had an opportunity to add their names.[7] By then copies were circulating through the country. As the novelty of the idea was absorbed, and the import of the text itself digested, enthusiasm grew each time the much-copied document was re-presented; and in Edinburgh on 1 April, Johnston recorded in his diary that when during a church service, four noblemen present, including the Earl of Montrose, raised their hands in re-affirmation, to 'swear by the name of the living God... there raised such a yelloch... as the like was never seen nor heard of'.[8]

The Covenant not only concentrated a sense of purpose out of a potent but unformed and undirected feeling of national agitation, but also pre-supposed and licensed further action. Phrased in such a way that almost all who were not Roman

Archibald Johnston of Wariston
Reproduced from Hewison, *The Covenanters*, Vol. 1

Catholics (and these were few) could sign it with the sense that here was a statement corresponding to their own feelings, it demanded commitment. Although both Henderson and Johnston were strongly opposed to the presence of bishops in the Kirk (imposed in the reign of James VI), there is no mention of this in the Covenant, since it would have alienated the many episcopalians who signed with the aim of halting what they saw as an attack on their own bishops' authority, or as preliminary steps towards restoring Catholicism. Nevertheless, old Archbishop Spottiswood of St Andrews saw beneath the surface: 'We have been making a tub these 40 years, and now the bottom thereof is fallen out.'[9] The Covenant brought everyone in on an equal basis, and the very first sentence of its 4,000-plus word text shows what that basis is: it is signed 'after long and due examination of our own consciences'. But the promptings of private conscience are stood firmly upon the laws of the land. Beyond a catalogue of the evils of Roman Catholicism and of the virtues of Protestantism: 'God's true religion, Christ's true religion... a perfect religion', its legal-clerical authors invoke the Confessions of Faith approved by the Scottish parliament, particularly the Negative Confession of 1581, and refer to various Acts of Parliament from 1560 onwards. Having established that all Scots are in law and duty bound to maintain this true religion, it turns to their King: 'Seeing the cause of God's true religion and his Highness's authority are so joined, as the hurt of the one is common to both,' no-one shall be considered a loyal subject who fails to accept and profess 'the said true religion'.

Having ingeniously linked loyalty to King with, but subordinate to, loyalty to Kirk, the Covenant reminds Charles of the coronation oath he swore in Edinburgh in 1633, to defend the true religion, its preaching, sacraments and Confession of Faith. Describing itself as 'a general band to be made and subscribed by his Majesty's subjects of all ranks, in obedience to the commandment of God' and 'warranted also by act of council'; it sets out two purposes. Firstly, to defend the true religion; secondly, 'For maintaining the King's majesty, his person and his estate.' Immediately after this it declares that 'the present and succeeding generations in this land are bound to keep the foresaid national oath and subscription inviolable.'

Proclaimed thus as valid for all time, the document examines present dangers to the true religion, 'the manifold innovations and evils, generally

The National Covenant
Reproduced from Hewison, *The Covenanters*, Vol. 1

contained, and particularly mentioned in our late supplications, complaints and protestations... do sensibly tend to the re-establishing of the Popish religion and tyranny, and to the subversion and ruin of the true reformed religion, and of our liberties, laws and estates.'

These innovations, of course, had been made at the direct order of King Charles 1. The signatories swore by 'THE GREAT NAME OF THE LORD OUR GOD' to resist them as errors and corruptions, to the uttermost power that God should give them. The next paragraph commits them to 'stand to the defence of our dread sovereign the King's Majesty... in the defence and preservation of the foresaid true religion, liberties and laws of the kingdom.' It is made even more clear that loyalty to the King is dependent on his 'blessed and loyal conjunction' with the true religion.

In its language the Covenant goes to the heart of the matter: the changes being imposed on Scottish religious observances were violations of legally established practice, and, more importantly, of the divinely inspired spirit of the Confession of Faith. Strongly implicit in its wording is the idea that a King who tampers with this true, indeed 'perfect' religion must be resisted. This stated readiness to take up arms for the defence of 'true religion' was enough to make the Covenant a rebellious document. What made it a revolutionary one was its premise that individual subjects could set their private consciences above their obligations to the King and the State. No government could accept this doctrine.

But Scotland could scarcely be said to have a government. The King was in another country, and preferred to rule by proclamation and decree. His Privy Council in Scotland, composed of hereditary grandees and more recent 'lords of erection', was largely opposed to his policies and methods. The Church was nominally ruled by its bishops but there had always been tension between these royally appointed prelates and the Kirk's visceral desire for the equality of its ministers within a presbyterian system. Presbyterianism meant that each parish had its Kirk Session, or local church court. A group of these formed a presbytery, which in turn combined with others in 13 provincial synods, and finally in a national General Assembly, attended by ministers and chosen representatives. Each gathering elected its own Moderator to serve for a year at a time. By the end of 1637 the supporters of presbyterian church government were overwhelmingly dominant. The bishops were isolated, with scant control over events in or out of the churches, and in the spring of 1638, they abandoned their posts and all but five[10] retreated to England. The people who had formerly been humble 'supplicants' to the King now had for themselves a new title. They were Covenanters.

CHAPTER TWO

The Glory of the Covenant

THE SUCCESS OF THE Covenant lay in the fact that all sections of the community signed up to it, but particularly important was the support of most of the nobility, who for centuries had exercised power and management at local, provincial and national levels. Religious conviction played its part with some, but as a class with limpet-like attachment to position and privilege they were thoroughly exasperated with Charles I, whose policies, fiscal and legal as well as religious, tampered with their traditional rights and powers. Following many new creations by James VI, the aristocracy was a disproportionately large one: by the end of the 17th century, Scotland, with a sixth of England's population, would have almost the same number of earls.[1] It had been easy for them to gang up on a king in Edinburgh; in London, surrounded by far more pomp and circumstance, he was vastly less accessible. The towns, mostly very small but representing in aggregate a high proportion of the country's productivity and wealth, were equally supportive of the Covenant, with the major exception of Aberdeen. Civic leaders and territorial lords were familiar with the process of raising and equipping armed forces, normally on the King's behalf. But now troops began drilling with the intention of marching against the King.

It is unlikely that, after the rejection of previous loyal petitions, the authors of the Covenant thought their stern warning would do the job. Rather it was an ultimatum, informing the King of organised opposition, and it put Charles in a serious quandary. A famous phrase, 'A troop of horse and a regiment of foot had prevented all that followed',[2] perhaps underestimates the spirit of resistance, but underlines the fact that, though the King's reaction was to suppress the Covenant by force, he had no army, and no means of paying for one. His prime source of money supply was the English Parliament, which he had dissolved; and if recalled, was more likely to oppose than to support him. From his immediate circle of courtiers, he appointed the Marquis of Hamilton as Commissioner for Scotland, in the hope that this leading Scottish aristocrat would manage to hold things together while preparations were made for a punitive expedition. But others were making the running; the Scots knew what they wanted, they were arming and it was impossible for Hamilton to set the agenda. He had to report failure and in September, the King reluctantly revoked the use of the new Prayer Book, along with a number of other measures, and agreed to the calling of a General Asembly of the Kirk. In an effort to upstage the National Covenant, Hamilton introduced the 'King's Covenant' – also based on the anti-Catholic 'Negative Confession' of 1581. Loyalists signed, but it was a damp squib.

The General Assembly which opened in Glasgow in November 1638, the first for 20 years, was a fiery event, so much so that Hamilton, as Commissioner, seeing it was packed with pro-Covenant delegates, officially dissolved it. Defying him, it continued to sit in his absence, and on its own authority ordered the abolition of all Charles's attempts to alter the liturgy and the government of the Kirk, deposed the bishops and abolished their offices. Such defiance of royal authority could not possibly be tolerated; and because the Assembly, secure in popular support, was unpunishable, war became inevitable. Charles raised an army, largely made up of untrained conscripts. Luckily for the Scots, mercenary involvement in the campaigns of the Thirty Years' War in central Europe had created a reserve of returned military veterans,[3] and in response to appeals sent by the Tables, others came back to join the cause. Experienced in up-to-date warfare, they included Robert Moray, who had learned military engineering in France and was made quartermaster-general; and Alexander Leslie, aged 58, one of the field marshals of King Gustavus Adolphus of Sweden, who was given supreme command. Leslie applied Swedish methods to improve the old recruiting system, with a 'committee for war' established in every shire, responsible for providing its quota of men – this would prove effective in the years to come.[4]

Episcopalian and Catholic support for Charles in Aberdeen and its hinterland was forestalled by an army headed by James Graham, Earl of Montrose. Leslie's army, as it headed for the Border, had no hostile intention against England,[5] nor against the king's person. Neither side had declared a war, and in this campaign, later known as the first Bishops' War, the kissed-knuckle gesture was successful. The King had to make a treaty with his subjects, the 'Pacification of Berwick' on 18 June 1639, agreeing to a new General Assembly of the Kirk and the election of a new

Parliament. This Parliament confirmed the abolition of bishoprics; suspended the committee known as the 'Lords of the Articles', which had previously presented Parliament with bills which it scarcely discussed before passing them; doubled the number of shire representatives; passed a Triennial Act ensuring that a new parliament must be summoned at least every three years, and accepted the terms of the National Covenant – the document of rebellion was now the law of the land.

With the Covenant ratified by both Kirk and Parliament, the revolution might seem to be complete, except that a vital element was missing. For Charles, who believed that he was appointed King by God, the notion of a Covenanted King ruling by the sufferance of his people was intolerable. Parliament got round this difficulty by infringing the royal prerogative in a most blatant fashion. Until now, no Act could become law until touched with the sceptre by the King or his Commissioner, but this and subsequent Covenant parliaments dispensed with that formality.[6] Quite apart from the need to re-establish his authority, Charles could not allow this to continue – if Scotland could function as a nation in his name while excluding him from involvement, what lesson would England, already deeply restive, take from it?

Though given authority and security by the backing of a majority of the nobility and clergy, and sustained by ordinary people in town and country, the Covenant was not cherished by everyone. In most societies there is a mass of largely indifferent opinion, which may incline for a time towards a new and radical set of ideas, but which tends to swing back to domestic and local concerns, and resents too much disturbance, especially if – as here – it is associated with taxation and military service. And supporters of episcopacy among ministers and congregations had quickly found that the Covenant was being used as a licence to destroy it.[7] With signs of an anti-Presbyterian reaction widening, both General Assembly and Parliament found it necessary in 1639 to enact that acceptance of the Covenant should be enforced 'under all civil pains' on those who had not signed or were backwards in support; and those who refused would be denied any public office.[8] Writing in 1937, a church historian likened the methods of exerting pressure to those of the current Nazi regime in Germany,[9] and many people signed out of conformity or to avoid harassment.

The North-East had to be held down by a combination of armed force and blandishment of rival lords. Opposition sparked armed conflict in Dumfriesshire, where Robert Maxwell, first Earl of Nithsdale, was a Catholic whose castles of Threave and Caerlaverock held out for the King's rule until September 1640. In August 1640, after Charles had managed to put together an army of sorts in England, a second 'Bishops' War' began, and this time the Scottish army entered England, overcame the royal force at Newburn, and took possession of Newcastle and Durham. At Ripon, a temporary treaty was agreed by which the Scots, still proclaiming loyalty to Charles (within the terms of their Covenant), maintained their occupation of six North-Eastern counties, and were due to receive payment of £850 a day for the support of their army, until a final settlement should be ratified by the English Parliament. Invasion and occupation drove forward the political events in England which were to bring Charles I and his London parliament to civil war in 1642.

The Covenant was supreme, and with this came an unfamiliar sense that might be exhilarating to some and sobering to others. For the first time since 1603, Scotland was conducting its affairs from within, as an independent nation. There had to be a national policy, not only for internal matters, but towards England – and towards the King.

National policy required new methods of making and implementing decisions. Unused to managing their own affairs without the topmost tier of royal government, and also maintaining the military occupation of a large English province, the Scots faced the problem of operating – in the King's name – a policy to which the King was squarely opposed. Debate was vehement in both national forums: Parliament, and the General Assembly of the Church. The clergy's exclusion from Parliament was an indication of power-sharing between the two bodies: in many ways the Assembly led and Parliament followed. The temper of the times was shown by the allocation of the rents and property rights of the bishoprics of Edinburgh and Aberdeen to the respective universities; and much of Galloway's to Glasgow University,[10] though various nobles inevitably shouldered up for their shares. But the Covenant governments had no primary interest in commerce or economic reform. Men with experience in public administration were on hand, but found short-term money raising their chief priority. Voluntary or coerced gifts to the cause were soon replaced by systematic taxation. Having found the Scottish Exchequer effectively bankrupt in 1638, successive governments struggled to find money to pay and equip armies.[11] Achievement of their programmes relied on squeezing existing resources and, with no time to build new sources of wealth, circumstances worked against investment in industry or trade. Though the Covenant Movement has been described as 'a revolutionary alliance of the landed and commercial classes intent on redressing constitutional and nationalist grievances in the State as well as upholding the Presbyterian version of the Reformed tradition', there were few Acts to promote commerce and 'improvement'.[12]

Most covenanting Scots were concerned purely about methods of worship and church government in their own country, but the General Assembly – and a majority in the 1639–41 Parliament – had wider aims. If presbytery and a bishop-free constitution were how the 'perfect religion' should be managed, surely it was a duty to God, and a charity to the English, to arrange for the same system in Charles Stewart's southern kingdom. Such holy imperialism was not new to the Church of Scotland; in the previous century, John Knox had had similar thoughts. Apart from sublime duty, there was a pragmatic reason: two forms of official religion under one monarch was never likely to work – certainly not if Charles I were expected to ratify acts such as one of the 1639 General Assembly which called episcopacy 'contrary to the laws of God'.

Archibald Campbell, 8th Earl of Argyll, as an intense young man of 23, had been the only member of the nobility to stay on in the General Assembly which Hamilton had tried to dissolve, and remained the most conspicuous Covenanter. He also had his own clan force at his disposal, which he used, under licence from Parliament's Committee of Estates, to run with fire and sword through the lands of the Earls of Atholl and Airlie, to the east of his own domains, in the summer of 1640. Both of these magnates were seen as anti-Covenant, but Argyll, Gilleasbuig Gruamach, 'Gloomy Archibald' to his Highland enemies, was widely suspected of having his own agenda, on which the first and only item was the extension of Campbell dominion. The place of debate and decision was now the parliament[13] and its executive committees, where the spirit of the Covenant prevailed. Covenanted and militant Scotland, with its army and its enforced unity, held the ring in negotiations with the King and his London Parliament. In June 1641 it had been agreed that there would be consultations on the reform of the English Church, and Charles promised to accept the Acts of the Covenanting parliament in Edinburgh.

Adherents to the Covenant might well feel that God was putting a favourable wind into their sails. Two months later, the King came to Edinburgh, in a bid to restore his authority and prestige. Argyll was made a marquis, and William Dick, the government's chief tax collector and financier, was knighted.[14] Knowing where the Scottish nobility kept its sense of loyalty, he also granted 'pensions' to some Covenant leaders. 'The Incident', discovery of an apparent royalist plot against Argyll, Hamilton and his brother Lord Lanark, wrecked any slender chance of Charles gaining control of affairs, by parliamentary or other means. He left, having gained nothing. The Covenanters remained firmly in charge.

In 1640 came the biggest bout of iconoclasm since the 1590s. Many churches still retained statues and altars, paintings, carved screens, and other religious imagery. Now in 1641 the Assembly, backed by an Act of Parliament,[15] ordered all idolatrous images, crucifixes, and pictures of Christ to be removed from all churches, colleges and public buildings by their owners or else be destroyed. Hammers were taken to rood screens, statues and wayside calvaries, and only semi-superstitious local feeling helped to preserve at least some of the tall carved stone crosses that had stood since the days of the Celtic Church. Illustrated and illuminated books, some of great age, were burned; and lime-wash obliterated wall paintings. Smashing up the humane beauties of the past emphasised the intransigent new spirit of the present.

James Hamilton, 1st Duke of Hamilton
Reproduced from Hewison,
The Covenanters, Vol. 1

Masterful steps were taken. When Catholic rebellion broke out in Ireland in October 1641, the Covenant government approved the raising and despatch of an army of around 11,000 men under General Robert Monro of Ospisdale to oppose the insurgents. This was in conjunction with the English Parliament and with the support of the King. As civil war became imminent in England, Scotland's Privy Council received requests at the end of 1642 for military support both from the King and from the London Parliament. Now a split opened between those who felt the way forward was to procure promises of reforms in England from the King, and those who believed that an alliance with the English Parliament would be more effective. The pro-Parliamentary faction, led by Argyll, more dynamic and more numerous, managed to control events: on 7 August 1643 a deputation of English commissioners came to Edinburgh to discuss a programme of religious reform, and a military alliance against the King. This resulted in the compilation of the Solemn League and Covenant, in effect a treaty between Scotland and England, for the preservation of the reformed religion in Scotland, and for the reformation of religion in England and Ireland in doctrine, worship, discipline and government, 'according to the Word of God and the example of the best reformed churches'. No-one in Scotland doubted where that example was to be taken from. Unlike a conventional treaty, it was intended to be subscribed by both peoples, as a personal commitment. Rather than a proof of democratic ratification, this was intended to display the people's faithful support for the leadership. Signing was done only to a minute extent in England, where some of its backers were cynical about it from the start, regarding it as a carrot to obtain desperately needed military support; but widely in Scotland, where many people viewed the Solemn League as a diplomatic and religious triumph.

But the English Parliament could point to the fact that already in June 1643 it had set up a commission, 'an Assembly of learned, godly and judicious divines'[16] at Westminster to consider reform of the Church of England with a view to obtaining 'nearer agreement with the Church of Scotland and other reformed churches abroad'. Four Scots ministers and three, later seven, elders were sent by the General Assembly as observers and advisers to the proceedings. The Westminster Assembly would gradually founder amidst disputings between Independents and Presbyterians, and the Scots could only look on with increasing glumness, though they did bring from it the *Shorter* and *Longer Catechism*, the *Confession of Faith*, the *Form of Presbyterial Church Government* and the *Directory*,[17] all of which became fundamental documents in the teachings and proceedings of the Kirk. Military arrangements were completed much faster, and by November 1643 a force of 18,000 foot and 2000 cavalry was raised, to assist the English Parliament against the King.

The Covenant government had acted like the large-scale military contractors of central Europe, supplying a complete army for an agreed price, but it was not a wholly mercenary force, and a share of control was retained. To make effective the 'blessed Union and conjunction' of the two countries, specified in the Solemn League and Covenant, a Committee of Both Kingdoms was established in February 1644, with four Scottish commissioners to 21 English, and held responsibility for direction of the Parliamentary war effort until hostilities came to an end in 1646.

These actions were approved by a newly elected Convention of Estates, the first Scottish parliament summoned without a royal warrant, and from which the royalist faction was excluded through the enforcement of an oath of support for the Solemn League which all members had to swear. The effective creation of a 'one-party state' sharpened the rift in opinions and pushed some opposition figures into armed resistance. The Earl of Montrose had signed and fought for the National Covenant, but he had been in correspondence with the King from October 1639, and in August 1640 had formed the 'Cumbernauld Band' with 17 nobles who shared his concerns about Argyll's policies and intentions. In his view the King had done, or promised, as much as the Covenant required, and to support his English adversaries was mere rebellion, as spelled out by the Covenant itself. Charles made him a marquis in 1644. His year of dramatic victories in the Highlands, as the King's Lieutenant-General, beginning with the rout of a much larger government army at Tippermuir on 1 September 1644, coincided with a serious outbreak of plague in Edinburgh, Fife and Angus,[18] and caused the Covenant government to wonder why God was making its task so hard. But Montrose failed to win wider support even when in the summer of 1645 he was, briefly, master of the country. He began steps to restore royal government (under the Covenant) but the defeated government and the Kirk still kept effective control down to local level. Montrose was branded a renegade to the Covenant, and his Scots-Irish shock troops, under the Catholic Alasdair MacColla, were seen as invaders and wild plunderers.[19] Throughout this time the Covenant government had kept its army in England, partly to maintain its agreement with the Parliamentarians, partly to maintain its own bargaining power. A force of around 6,000 was now recalled, commanded by David Leslie (another veteran of the

Swedish campaigns) and defeated Montrose at Philiphaugh, near Selkirk, on 13 September 1645.

Montrose escaped to the Highlands while the victors slaughtered several hundred non-combatants, including women and children, after the battle, at the instigation of the army's Kirk ministers, who saw themselves as extirpating the enemies of God. Every army had its motley support group of wives and concubines, servants, camp-cooks and pot-boys, that would expect rough handling in defeat, but not mass murder. The Covenanters' atrocities after Philiphaugh are well-attested: 'With whole bagage and stufe... there remained now but boyes, cookes, and a rable of rascalls, and woemen with there children in there arms, all those without commiseration were cutte in pieces.'[20] Slaughter and rape had also marked the rampage of Montrose's men when he had allowed them to sack Aberdeen exactly a year earlier. But these civilian corpses left on town doorsteps or piled into the River Tweed were not to be counted in the 'Killing Time', which was yet to come.

For more than a year, the government had been made to look feeble and incompetent in its own backyard, and official vindictiveness continued in new acts of parliament passed to punish Montrose's supporters and exclude them from public life. The rulers were also facing serious setbacks to their wider policy: the growing strength of the English parliamentary army was reducing the Scots' influence and leverage. Scottish military support was no longer vital to the cause; and within the English Parliamentary camp, those who favoured a Scottish-model Presbyterian church were outnumbered by the 'Independents' who wanted no truck with any sort of established church. In May 1646, Charles chose to surrender himself to the Scots army, camped at Newark on Trent. A month later, the defeat of Monro's troops by Owen Roe O'Neill's Catholic army at Benburb in Ireland dented the Scots' military pride (any Irish combatants captured in Scotland by Covenant forces were summarily executed without trial). In the North-East, belated Royalist efforts by the Marquis of Huntly, who had failed to support Montrose, kept sporadic warfare going into 1647.

Lengthy interviews with Alexander Henderson and negotiations with commissioners from both parliaments failed to convert Charles I to Presbyterianism or to produce any generally acceptable settlement, though the Scots found that their terms for reaffirming his crown were milder than those of their English allies. Their army, though considerably reduced in numbers, was still in England, and none of the agreed payment for its services had been received. By the autumn the Edinburgh government's priority was withdrawal and payment, and after much haggling, and against the opposition of Hamilton and his associates, it agreed to accept a down-payment from England of £200,000 against what was due. With no army in England, Parliament could not keep the king, and it voted on 16 January 1647 to hand the protesting monarch over to its English counterpart;[21] and later that month the army began its return across the Border.

During 1647, partly because of the seizure of the King by the English army, and the apparent dominance of Independents over Presbyterians in determining English policy, considerable re-thinking was going on, and the radical-Covenanter group, headed by the Marquis of Argyll, found it could no longer command a majority in the Council or in Parliament. Hamilton (who had been made a duke in 1643), leading what might be called a royalist-Covenant group, was able to effect a drastic change of policy. In October his brother William, Earl of Lanark, had gone with Loudoun to see the King at Hampton Court, and even offered to liberate him and ride for Scotland there and then.[22] At the end of the year, during Charles's curious interlude of semi-confinement in the Isle of Wight, the same two, plus John Maitland, second Earl of Lauderdale, were sent down from the Committee of Estates (the most important of the 'interval committees' appointed to maintain affairs between sessions of parliament).

Loudoun and Lauderdale were both members of the still-extant Committee of Both Kingdoms (which was dissolved by the London Parliament on 3 January 1648), but, operating quite independently of the diplomatic team still working with the English for the honouring of the Solemn League and Covenant, they made what was called 'The Engagement' with the King. In return for military support, Charles pledged himself to honour Scottish Presbyterianism, to try the experiment of Presbyterianism in England for three years, and to give Scottish traders the same rights and freedoms as English ones. He was not required to sign the Solemn League and Covenant. A majority of the Committee of Estates approved the Engagement in February 1648, but the venture caused a furious split in public opinion. To the zealous, it was a sell-out of the Solemn League and Covenant, and also broke the

The Earl of Lauderdale and the Duke of Hamilton
Reproduced from Hewison, *The Covenanters*, Vol. 1

National Covenant by putting loyalty to the King before loyalty to God. For the treasury, it meant the abandonment of any hope of further repayments from England's Parliament. The Engagers' view was that Scotland had got what it wanted from its King and was now bound to support him, and also that a deal with the King was now more likely to achieve the aims of the Solemn League than negotiations with an Independent-dominated London Parliament. But their emergence in power also marked something of an aristocratic revival, motivated by the thought that zeal for the Covenant had gone too far both in domestic matters and in relation to policy towards England, and by resentment at upstart and low-class ministers of the Kirk exercising control over national affairs. Parliament, which resumed in March, accepted the *fait accompli*. For a time it and the Kirk's General Assembly, largely hostile to the Engagement, were in simultaneous session and locked in angry argument. Neither side gave much thought to the fact that the people of England, especially in the North, were heartily sick of the presence and 'brotherly assistance' of Scottish armies; or to how their erstwhile allies might react to the Scots' sudden change of sides in England's increasingly bloody and bitter civil war.

The new army, 15,000 strong, was not hired out: it was that of the Kingdom of Scotland, though payment in due course had been agreed for its 'charge and expense' as well as for any losses sustained. Some barons and burghs declined to co-operate in levying troops. Glasgow Town Council refused to organise a muster, and half its members were imprisoned and a new council imposed.[23] During these years, the country was in a permanent and unprecedented state of military preparedness. Between 1639 and 1651 'the Covenanters raised over a dozen armies ranging in size from 2,000 to 24,000 men;'[24] in 1644, they may have had over 30,000 men under arms. The southbound army easily pushed aside a opposition attempt to block its way at Mauchline Moor, but neither Engagers nor Covenanters rightly estimated the might and effectiveness of the new Cromwellian military machine. Perhaps the generals did; in any case both Alexander Leslie (now Earl of Leven) and David Leslie signed petitions against the Engagement; and the army's titular head, the Duke of Hamilton, was no soldier.

To the unconcealed sour pleasure of the anti-Engagers, who of course saw divine judgement in action, Hamilton's army was defeated on 17–19 August 1648, near Preston, with the loss of some 2,000 dead and many thousands more taken prisoner. With that disaster, and the duke's imprisonment in London (he was executed there in March 1649),[25] the cause of the Engagement was totally lost. Scottish policy towards England and the King was bankrupt. All who were in control of affairs, nobles and ministers, lairds and burgesses, had let their commanding position in the heady days of 1639 slip away, until ten years later they had to wait on events and decisions in England. Thomas Carlyle later condemned their inadequacy: 'Instead of inspired Oliver, with direct insight and noble daring, we have Argyles, Loudouns, and narrow, more or less opaque persons of the pedant species.'[26] Montrose apart, the decade of the 1640s produced no hero-figure, though the problems were intractable enough to inspire, or confound, the greatest wisdom and boldness.

The Engagement was perhaps as much the nobility's effort to seize the initiative in Scotland, as a real attempt to resolve the deadlock over the King's future. An army, largely of Highlanders,[27] was mustered under Lord Lanark, and for a time, things teetered on the brink of civil war with the Covenant faction. Monro's soldiers chased Argyll's men away from Stirling, but Monro was a soldier, not a politician. By September

1648, there was only one theme left in Scotland, that of the strict Covenanters, still with the Marquis of Argyll at their head. Deprived of the chance to enforce Presbytery on England, they concentrated on setting up in Scotland what many regarded at the time, and even much later, as God's Kingdom upon Earth.

CHAPTER THREE

The Generation of '48

IN THAT YEAR OF mixed auspices, 1648, some 40,000 babies were born in Scotland. Many would not survive infancy or childhood,[1] but among those who did were John Graham, first child of the laird of Claverhouse, an estate near Dundee; Richard Cameron, son of a merchant in the little Fife town of Falkland, and John Dalrymple, born in the house of Carsecreuch in Galloway, first son of a 29-year old lawyer, James Dalrymple, who had been admitted to the Bar as an advocate in February of that year. Another was James Drummond, first son of the third Earl of Perth. None was a typical child of a country populated mainly by peasants, using time-wearied methods to scrape a modest living from the land. Ownership or tenure of land, or of town property, made their families part of elite groups whose importance in national life vastly outweighed their numbers. Only the infant Drummond belonged to the nobility, much the smallest social group, but dominant in influence, wealth and prestige. Though great-uncles of the babe had fought on each side at Tippermuir in 1644,[2] the family was identified with royalism and episcopacy, and the third Earl kept a low profile. But his son would become Lord High Chancellor. Two of the mewling, puking scions of the middle order would acquire noble titles – a viscount's coronet hung unseen over the young Graham's cradle; an invisible earl's belt encircled the tiny Dalrymple. In the minds of many Scots, however, Richard Cameron would far outclass the others: his destiny was to become a Saint and Martyr, 'the Lion of the Covenant'.

The following year saw the arrival of a brother for James Drummond, christened John; and the birth of William Carstares, son of the minister of Cathcart, near Glasgow. His parents would have been gladdened to know he would become Principal of Edinburgh University, maybe not so happy about his being confidant to a king, but they lived only long enough to know of his being tortured as a secret agent. Someone also to be involved in that process was a boy of 11 in 1649, George Mackenzie, attending school in his home town of Dundee. His father was a lawyer, Simon Mackenzie of Lochslin, and an uncle was the Earl of Seaforth, chief of the large Clan Mackenzie which dominated a wide tract of Wester Ross. Mackenzie and Carstares came from the same privileged section of society as the others: able to claim the best education their country could give; comfortably-off, but needing to earn an income in order to maintain their condition and its comforts. Fortunately for them, matters had long been ordered in a way that ensured families like theirs both served the needs of the nation, and did well for themselves in the process.

Greyfriars Church, 1640
Reproduced from Hewison, *The Covenanters*, Vol. 1

But what were the needs of the nation? It must be governed, it must have laws and the means of enforcing them, and the duties, rights and responsibilities of the citizens must be understood. Not least, as visible guarantor of laws and rights, and the personification of its existence as an organised state, it needed a monarch. The role of a king had always been central, and even after ten years of virtually republican government, no-one was considering an alternative. In other ways, however, the nature and purpose of monarchy and government were fiercely argued over. Political and military events had moved swiftly in the decade since the Covenant, slashing and scoring deep new lines across the timeless national pattern of rural life and the farming season.

The family of Dalrymple had for some generations been associated with the modest estate of Stair in Ayrshire, but when James Dalrymple married Margaret Ross, daughter of the laird of Balneil, near New Luce, they set up home in Carsecreuch. It was in the far south-west, the tip of a region stretching from Glasgow through Lanarkshire into Ayrshire, Dumfriesshire, and Galloway, which ever since the days of John Knox had been a heartland of Presbyterian commitment, in which the Dalrymples shared. Here the Covenant had been taken to heart as the charter of their beliefs, and some had tried to oppose the Engager army. Now in September 1648, following the collapse of the Engagement, they marched on Edinburgh in the 'Whiggamores' Raid', confident that nothing could withstand them. In fact something did, in the form of a brigade brought over from the army in Ulster, under General Monro (originally intended to supplement the Engager army), with which there was a sharp struggle at Linlithgow on 12 September. But the Whiggamores won through to Edinburgh. Part of the reason for such aggressive resolution, not shown by any other province, may lie in commitment at all social levels to the Covenant: the Earl of Cassillis in Ayrshire, head of the numerous Kennedys, and the Agnews, hereditary sheriffs of Galloway, were staunch Presbyterians. Not all local magnates shared these views, but there was sufficient protection by hereditary justiciars and wielders of power for landowners of a middling sort to feel safe in demonstrating loyalty to the Covenant. There was a much higher proportion of what were later known as 'bonnet lairds' than any other region; in effect farmers with assured heritable possession of their land, whose history and circumstances encouraged independence.[3] In Fife, another province of presbyterian enthusiasm among lairds and tenant farmers, the Earls of Rothes, Wemyss, and Balcarres were not to be relied on in the same way.

Leven, Leslie, and a chastened Loudoun associated themselves with the Whiggamores.[4] Most of the nobility, probably most of the population, had no wish to see the radicals take over government. But soon, the architects of Engagement were compounding with the leaders of the radicals for their lives and estates. Despite the whiggamore support, the new governors had to contend with the fact that the majority of their fellow-countrymen no longer had any enthusiasm for achieving the Solemn League and Covenant, to which all members of parliament re-subscribed on 23 January 1649.[5] And there was a third factor now, the looming shadow of Oliver Cromwell. Argyll, using his credit as an anti-Engager, had asked Cromwell not to cross the border unless invited to do so, but Cromwell, aware of the deep divisions among the Scots, and perhaps unsure as to who really held power now, entered Edinburgh on 4 October 1648, and made it clear that he too claimed a voice in the country's affairs. To those who had supported the Engagement, he was a military conqueror whose power rested on guns and pikes, but he and the restored Covenanter government saw each other as potential allies. At this time, he wanted no more from Scotland than to ensure that the King's supporters were kept from power. All Engagers were excluded from Parliament, which continued to sit with only Covenanter and Whiggamore members. This latter name, soon shortened to 'Whig' was, like so many political labels, first a term of derision used by their enemies. It derives from the Scots verb 'to whig', meaning jog along.[6] 'Whig!' or 'Whiggam!' was a drovers' call to keep cattle on the move. The implication may have been one of cattle thieves.

Meeting in January 1649, this Parliament was guarded by English soldiers. Only 16 members of the nobility, compared to 56 in the preceding session, took part[7] – making it the most 'popular' parliament, in one respect, yet held. It proceeded to pass the Act of Classes. This notorious legislation, modelled on an Act of January 1646 designed to punish supporters of Montrose, specified four different classes of person who were to be excluded from any public office, however modest. Prominent Engagers and those who had supported Montrose's campaigns were banned for life; lesser Engagers, together with other persons who had been previously censured for their support of the King, or for 'malignancy' – a term embracing everything from acceptance of bishops to outright Catholicism – were excluded for ten years; sympathisers with the Engagement, or those who had failed to protest against it when opportunity presented, for five years; and finally a non-political class, persons guilty of immorality or neglect of family worship, for one year. For these last, readmission to eligibility required a certificate of acceptance from their local Kirk Session, the lowest of the Church courts.

By this means the radicals, ardent, vengeful and insecure, conscious both of their mission and of the weight of opinion against them, hoped to make a basis on which to teach the country what to believe and how to behave. At the request of the General Assembly, Parliament also abolished (9 March 1649) in favour of the kirk sessions, the right of patronage in the Church, by which each parish church's 'superior', who might be the burgh council, or the laird, or a member of the nobility, had had the right to nominate a new minister when a vacancy occurred. But it also passed the 'Act Anent the Poor' on 1 March: not many legislatures in the mid-17th century were trying to remedy the plight of tenants impoverished through 'the guiltines and sins of your lordships and such as rule in the land'.[8] Grain prices had doubled since 1646 and many people were suffering hunger and hardship. For a time, Parliament was the glove clothing the hand of the Kirk. No-one was too great to escape inspection and discipline; even Loudoun, now Lord Chancellor of Scotland, was compelled to do public penance in the East Church of Edinburgh for his part in the Engagement.

CHAPTER FOUR

The Covenant: Vainglory and Disaster

JUST AS THIS NEW regime was getting under way, the Scots were shocked to learn that Charles I's trial had ended in his death sentence. The trial had been a purely English affair, and commissioners sent to London with an official protest were rebuffed.[1] The King was executed on 30 January 1649. Following the Engagement, most people felt the country no longer had a formal quarrel with him; and for the English to kill him was an outrage. Even the ultras of the 'Kirk Party' had not threatened Charles's life, though some who had long given up hope of him probably felt relief. But if they had not trusted the King, they did not trust Cromwell either, and even less his Independently inclined colleagues, who were hostile to the Solemn League and Covenant. England might make itself a republic, but the Scots had the opportunity to make a new start with a legitimate and Covenanted King. The reign of Charles II, not just over Scotland but over 'Great Britain, France and Ireland' was speedily proclaimed in a traditional ceremony at the Market Cross of Edinburgh, though with a new qualification: he must subscribe to the National Covenant and to the Solemn League and Covenant.

In a small coda to the King's execution, some of his art collection, auctioned off by the new government, turned up in Edinburgh, having been bought by the Earl of Lothian, whose Calvinism (he had accepted Charles's surrender at Newark) did not preclude connoisseurship. His sister, Lady Elizabeth Carr, wrote to him:

> I have gott some of your pictures from Mr Geldrop, and am in daily expectation of the rest. What I have is two old men and a great pictur (I think of Venus and Adones) with two little picturs... and another of a king sitting by a seaside &c., with three other picturs, with strange antique creatuures in them. They hang up in a roume in our new house in Queen Street.[2]

Scotland's diplomatic commissioners to the English Parliament were briefly imprisoned in London, but in March 1649 a new team was sent to the 19-year-old Charles Stuart at his small court of exile at The Hague in Holland. Their secretary was James Dalrymple, valuable no doubt for his knowledge of law and legal history. His abilities impressed the royal advisers, but Charles had no intention of accepting the terms on offer: Ireland might yet rally to him, and he was also hearing other voices from Scotland. Perhaps the Marquis of Montrose might win that country for him without conditions of any kind.

It was March 1650 before Montrose landed in Orkney, with the King's commission. The venture lasted only a few weeks. People in the far north felt little connection with the politics of Edinburgh, but the Covenant had reached them, and Montrose found almost no support before his defeat at Carbisdale on 27 April and his subsequent capture as a fugitive by Macleod of Assynt. Irish royalism was already crushed by Cromwell. Charles II's involvement with Montrose's last campaign was an awkward factor, not really explained away by the assertion that the commission, of 22 February 1649, predated his negotiations with the government delegates. Doubts that Presbyterians already held about his character and sincerity were intensified. Dalrymple informed him of Montrose's execution during a second set of negotiations in May, at Breda in Holland, where he was again Secretary. Charles's options had run out: he either had to repudiate the Scots, or accept their terms and the tutelage in Presbyterian doctrines that was part of the package. The reluctant king finally put his name to both Covenants on board ship off Spey Bay on 23 June, and, even less willingly, signed a document in August condemning the religion and crimes of his parents. In Edinburgh, the hard-liners, still triumphant from Montrose's death, were flexing their muscles and finding much to do; as the lawyer John Nicoll noted non-committally in his diary:

> Much falsit [falsehood] and scheitting [scheming] at this time was daily detected by the Lords of Session, for the quhilk [which] there was daily hanging, scourging, nailing of lugs, and binding of people to the Tron, and boring of tongues; so that it was a fatal year for false notaries and witnesses, as daily experience did witness. And as for adultery, fornication, incest, bigamy, and other uncleanness and filthiness, it did never abound more than at this time.[3]

The policy of the Scots, however reasonable in their own context, was not acceptable to republican England. Charles II's prime aim was always to

James Graham, Marquis of Montrose
Reproduced from Hewison, *The Covenanters*, Vol. 2

regain the Stuarts' English crown, and Scotland was his mounting post. The Covenanter Government knew this perfectly well, but was willing to help him, with the Solemn League and Covenant as its price. Cromwell returned north as Lord General with an English army, and punitive intentions. During August 1650 he did his best to bring the Scots army, commanded by David Leslie, to battle, but Leslie was in no hurry. His army, the second large force to be mustered in two years, was half as numerous again as Cromwell's at 23,000 men, but through application of the Act of Classes, many experienced men had been rejected.[4] A committee of parliament and a commission of the Kirk Assembly, this latter including Mr John Carstairs (whose son would adopt the spelling of

Carstares), accompanied his manoeuvrings, until on 3 September the Scots left a strong position on Doon Hill above Dunbar to form up facing the English at the foot. Cromwell said 'The Lord hath delivered them into our hands.' Early next day he attacked, with 'The Lord of Hosts!' as his men's war-cry. The Scottish slogan was 'The Covenant!' but it did not prevail. More than 3,000 Scots were killed and around 10,000 surrendered. Leslie's tactics are hard to explain; Royle[5] suggests he felt Cromwell's army was sufficiently weakened by sickness. In a letter after the battle to Argyll,[6] the general blamed his officers: '... wee might have as easily beaten them, as wee did James Graham at Philiphaugh, if the officers had stayed by theire troops and regiments...' in what may be a hint against the Act of Classes. The kirkmen, however, interpreted the defeat as a divine signal that they had not been severe enough in their purgings, and the army not sincere enough in its prayers. Some considered it God's judgement on the King: 'It concerneth the King to consider if he has come to the Covenant and joined himself to the Lord upon politic grounds, for gaining a crown to himself rather than to advance religion and righteousness[7]...' John Carstairs was among those wounded in the battle: stripped by looters, he only survived by feigning death, and was taken with other prisoners to Edinburgh. Eventually freed as part of an exchange of prisoners, he returned to his wife and infant son with his convictions unchanged, but with a distaste for active involvement in non-religious matters.

The political and military situation was fluid: the radical Covenanters were still in government but they, as well as the royal cause, had suffered a heavy blow. Shaken by defeat, the Committee of Estates found its control disintegrating. Four armies were present: the Government's own defeated army; a separate muster of Whiggamores in the south west, under the nominal control of the Committee of Estates; a royalist force, the 'Northern Band' in the Highlands, under the command of John Middleton, a capable officer who had led the cavalry in the Engager invasion and was now a committed royalist; and the English army led by Cromwell. The national army, regrouped after Dunbar but ill-provided with arms, ammunition and supplies, lay in straggling and dispirited encampments between Stirling and Falkirk. One army was enough to guzzle the resources and sap the morale of a countryside on which it lived like an aggressive parasitic growth – with four in different parts of the country, hardship and deprivation were most people's lot. On 3 October

1650, Charles II broke away from his mentors at Perth, intending to join the Northern Band, only to be brought back and chided for his defection. A letter from the Committeee of Estates instructed Lord Lothian, Sir Charles Erskine and James Sword that: 'Yow shall show how much wee are greived and amazed with his Majesty's sudden and unexpected behaviour.'[8]

This ill-organised, failed coup, 'the Start', was nevertheless a turning-point. After it, the humiliated and angry Charles was treated less as a pupil and brought more into the councils of the regime. It could not afford to break with him, 'for by this time it was only the claim to be acting in the king's name that allowed it to remain in power'.[9] With this, the political claim of the National Covenant was in collapse. The subjection of King to Kirk might be proclaimed, but could not be enforced. The conservative aspect of the Covenant itself, and the conservatism of the Scottish political class, were revealed. The only way forward for the Covenanters was to dump hereditary monarchy and establish some form of theocratic rule. But the King was in the Covenant even if the converse were not true; and even if they had considered such a drastic policy, they were in no position to realise it. It was becoming steadily more apparent that the strict Covenanter party was being squeezed out of power.

With their relationship with Cromwell in tatters, and the King in sulky opposition, they had no base beyond their own faction. They could no longer command a majority in the Committee of Estates, nor prevent it from taking decisions which they strenuously opposed. What most of the Committee most wanted was to procure national unity, and an Act of Indemnity was extended to the Northern Band on 29 October 1650. For their part, the militant Whigs drew up the 'Western Remonstrance', in the name of God and the Covenant, and sent it from Dumfries to the Committee of Estates on 17 October. Unmoved by government overtures, they refused to support the King until he should publicly repent of past misdeeds and throw off his malignant advisers. Their message was rejected by the Committee of Estates on 25 November. In December the Act of Classes was watered down by a 'Public Resolution' to allow former Engagers into the army; and some Engagers with a good Presbyterian record, like the Earl of Lauderdale, were allowed back into Parliament. Scotland's parliament was no longer a one-party assembly: there were the Resolutioners who would abandon the Act of Classes, and the ultras, strong in the south-west, who, from the tone and content of successive missives, received the name of Remonstrants, though to the indifferent public they remained Whiggamores.

Meanwhile Cromwell enforced the surrender of Edinburgh Castle in December and made it his headquarters. Also, on 1 December his colleague Lambert defeated the Whiggamore force at Hamilton, depriving the 'Western Association' of the leverage they had exerted on the government through allies like Johnston of Wariston. Against this confused background, Charles II was crowned King of Scots in the church at Scone, on 1 January 1651, in the last enactment of a traditional ceremony whose origins were lost in time and Gaelic myth. Suitably modified for the times, it had neither druids nor their episcopal successors, nor any anointing, but there was a sermon of prodigious length from the Rev. Robert Douglas,[10] and a renewal of the Covenants. The Marquis of Argyll was stage-manager, and the King received the crown from his hands. Gilbert Burnet notes that there was talk about Charles marrying Argyll's daughter Anne.[11]

All this might have seemed hardly more than play-acting, with the great Regicide abroad in the land, but Cromwell's illness in the spring of 1651 slowed the pace of events. A bloody battle at Inverkeithing on 20 July marked another English victory, over an army composed largely of Highlanders, and left Fife in Cromwell's hands. St Andrews castle and cathedral were destroyed. But Cromwell had no mandate to take over the government, and there were intensive comings and goings between the various headquarters. Parliamentary committees met in both Perth and Stirling, with debate focusing on whether the Act of Classes should be fully repealed, or not. Finally, it was repealed on 2 June, showing how far opinion had swung towards the royalists,

Archibald Campbell, Marquis of Argyll
Reproduced from Wodrow's *History*, Vol I

and on the following day the Western Remonstrance was formally condemned. In July the Remonstrants acquired a new name, the Protesters, after most of their delegates walked out of the General Assembly in protest when the Kirk accepted the withdrawal of the Act of Classes.

A strange and fatal decision was taken, or acquiesced in, by the Scottish leaders at the end of July 1651, though Argyll and Loudoun dissented from it. The English army was advancing on Perth, the *de facto* capital, which it captured on August 2, and Cromwell was clearly bent on completing his military conquest. Defence of the realm might have seemed to be a vital need. But the army, of around 15,000 discouraged, ill-equipped, shedding deserters, was marched away, with Charles II at its head, to secure England for the King. Cromwell has been credited by some writers as 'forcing' this move, but a letter of his notes that: 'This present movement is not out of choice on our part, but by some kind of necessity.'[12] One modern writer feels that David Leslie's only option was 'to march rapidly into England and rally royalist support'[13] – another says that they had no illusions about their chance of success.[14] It was a desperate gamble.

Now the active pro-royalist element, including Middleton, was in control. Much had changed from the previous year, when Scotland's leaders would not let the King be with the army, 'for they were afraid he might gain too much upon the soldiers'.[15] Only three days behind, Cromwell followed in pursuit, leaving sufficient forces behind under General Monck to continue the capture of remaining strong points. England showed no enthusiasm for having its monarchy restored by a Scottish army, especially one still – ostensibly – proclaiming the Solemn League and Covenant. Royalists stayed at home and the hoped-for rush of support for the new King was a bare trickle. Far into England, at Worcester, on 3 September, they were defeated, with 2,000 killed and most of the rest captured. Few managed to struggle home through hostile country. General Leslie was a prisoner and Charles II a fugitive. It was the third shattering defeat inflicted by Cromwell on the Scots in three years, and with it, what might be called the First, or Ruling, Covenant Period came to an end.

Among the people, the Covenant ideal was still widely supported. Only one thing shows shows its popular appeal more than the way in which, again and again, large armies were raised in its support; and that is the toleration of the appalling national sacrifice that was exacted. Edward M. Furgol estimates the total number of casualties for the period between 1639 and 1651 at 47,000 – as he says, 'a horrific figure for a nation of a million souls'.[16] The 'fencible' population liable for military service, formed of males between 16 and 60, during these years was literally decimated. Hacked and bloodied corpses were left strewn and heaped by the thousand on every battlefield, to be stripped by looters. They did not die for national independence, or defending the land against invasion, but for an ideology. Many more were prisoners. The toll of sons, brothers, and fathers who did not come back measured the price, and the value, of the Covenant to the Scots.

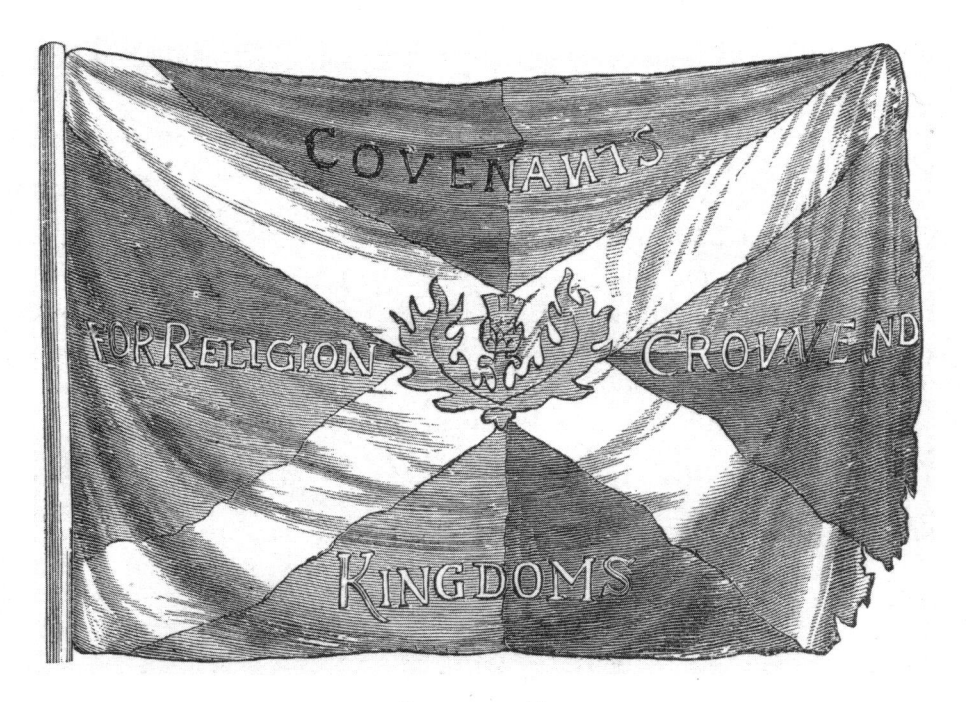

Covenanter Flag
Reproduced from *Cassell's Old & New Edinburgh*

CHAPTER FIVE

The Usurpation

GOD'S PUNISHMENT MIGHT BE again claimed by the Protesters, but they were in no condition to assume government. Most of the Committee of Estates had been captured by Colonel Alured at Alyth on 28 August 1651, and efforts by Loudoun to reconvene a remnant were hopeless. The vacuum of power was filled by the only body which could enforce control, the English army; which did so on an *ad hoc* basis until a final settlement should be made. By December the parliamentary government in England switched from its initial policy of annexation, to political union in 'one nation';[1] and on 24 December a Declaration relating to the settlement was published. Eight English commissioners sat at Dalkeith from mid-January to the end of April, receiving representations and delegations, explaining their own intentions, and making arrangements for administration and law enforcement. A Tender of Incorporation was produced, intended to be signed on behalf of all shires and burghs, though about a third of the shires and more than half the burghs did not do so. In September 1652, following delegate meetings in Edinburgh, 21 Scottish deputies journeyed to London, to find themselves very much on the sideline in the debates relating to union. Fighting was still going on in the western Highlands, and in the North-East under the Marquis of Huntly and the Earl of Balcarres. For a time, before the Cromwellian grip tightened, bands of 'moss-troopers' fought guerrilla-style in hill areas: 'They sallied down in small parties, and surprised and cut off such of the English as were detached in small commands, or that plundered the country... They provided themselves in arms and horses, at the expense of the English, and the country willingly afforded them provisions.'[2] The Marquis of Argyll had deserted Loudoun's efforts to convene a rump of the Estates, and made his own peace with the English, somewhat cloyed by the energetic participation of his son Lord Lorne in a new royalist campaign. Encouraged by the exiled King, Macdonald of Glengarry set about mobilising royalist clans in early 1653, with a Lowlander, William Cunningham, ninth Earl of Glencairn as general, and much of the Highlands relapsed from English control during that year.

On 16 December the Council of State in London proclaimed the Protectorate, under Oliver Cromwell, as the Commonwealth of England, Scotland and Ireland, and an Instrument of Government for Scotland was drawn up, providing for 30 members to attend the Parliament at Westminster, when summoned. A formal Ordinance of Union was published on 12 April 1654, enacting that the people of Scotland should be 'made equal sharers with those of England in the present settlement of peace, liberty and prosperity, with all other privileges of a free people'. The Instrument of Government defined the supreme legislative authority of the Commonwealth as residing in 'one person, and the people assembled in Parliament; the style of which person shall be Lord Protector of the Commonwealth'.[3] Assuring freedom of religion, apart from 'popery and prelacy', the document made no mention of the Solemn League and Covenant. In the years which followed, whatever benefits the Commonwealth and Protectorate brought, there was never any doubt that the union was imposed from outside and preserved by military occupation. Andrew Hay noted in his diary[4] that: 'because it was told me that Scotland was 20 yers in Edward I of England his peaceable possession of the time of competition betwixt Baliol and Bruce, and that that tyme was very like to this tyme, I did read in Buchanan the whole story...' John Barbour's *Brus* and 'Blind Harry's' *Wallace* also reminded people of what had happened from 1296 when Edward I attempted to make Scotland into a military province. However different the circumstances, the comparison was discomfiting.

In early 1654, the military manoeuvrings and skirmishes in the Highlands were becoming more intensive. In February, General Middleton landed from Holland at Tarbat Ness, to assume overall command of a royalist force officered by squabbling, duelling chieftains and lords, and the delayed English response came in April when supreme command of the English army, and of the Scottish administration, was taken over by General George Monck.

With a reinforced army, Monck commanded a vigorous and destructive stategy that left many Highland settlements in ruin with stripped fields. His rapid marches kept Middleton and his men on the move to avoid a battle, but eventually caught between Monck's army and a force led by Colonel Thomas Morgan, they were scattered rather than routed at Dalnaspidal, in the southern neck of Drumochter Pass, on 17 July. 'An unhappy rencounter' it was called by Sir James Turner who came over from Bremen to join the royal side but arrived too late for the battle. Turner, an experienced soldier, soon came to the view that the King's affairs 'were all out of frame' and 'hereupon I put on a resolution to get out of Scotland as soon as I could'.[5] But he would come back in due course. Monck continued his harassing and scorched-earth campaign, and arranged for prisoners to be shipped to Barbados. Middleton was isolated with a few hundred armed men as, one by one, his supporters made terms with Monck, and in April 1655 he sailed to the Continent. Relative peace in the Highlands was assured by new strong-points, a fort at Inverlochy and a citadel in Inverness, commanding opposite ends of the Great Glen. As the presbyterian Argyll had already done, Highland magnates of contrary views, like the episcopalian Ewen Cameron of Lochiel, found it equally possible to make accommodations with the Commonwealth government.[6]

Quiescence of extreme groups on both sides was assured by the pike and the bayonet. The causes of Covenant and King, briefly united, now half-separated, went quiet. 'The only sanction of Oliver's rule beyond the Tweed was the presence of the English army,' wrote G. M. Trevelyan.[7] Gradually its size was reduced from 20,000 at the time of the Highland campaigns to around 12,000.[8] Its cost was still enormous, and only partly paid for by the Scottish taxpayers, whose contribution in 1659 was £72,000 out of a total exceeding £270,000.[9] With varying degrees of reluctance and protest, shire officials and burgh councils accepted the reality of power, or were replaced by more compliant councillors. In 1654, 21 Scottish members were elected, or appointed, to the Commonwealth Parliament, and by 1656 the number had risen to the statutory 30, of whom 19 were army officers or government officials.[10]

Commonwealth government cut across the established model of social and economic life. 'It is the interest of the Commonwealth of England to break the interest of the great men of Scotland, and to settle the interest of the common people upon a different foot from the interest of their lords and masters' observed one of Cromwell's officers, Colonel John Jones, in November 1651.[11] But presbyterian nobles like Lothian found it easy to adapt, though in London he was short of cash: '... for no Scotts men will lend money heere, and Inglishmen desyre not to have money to lift in Scotland.'[12] Gilbert Burnet thought that Scotland flourished under the Commonwealth,[13] but he was a boy of 15 in 1658, albeit observant and already an M.A. of Aberdeen, and he also quotes the Presbyterian minister Robert Baillie, writing in November 1658, who observed that: 'The country lies very quiet; it is exceeding poor; trade at nought, the English have all the money'. At that time, the government's entire revenue from Scotland, including the army 'cess' and new customs duties and revenues from former crown lands, was £143,652.[14] The terms of the enforced union included freedom of trade within the Commonwealth. This has been called the 'freedom of the English merchants to exploit Scottish markets',[15] but such would always have been the likely result of a move desired by successive Scottish governments. No provision was made for widening Scotland's foreign trade, and there was little, if any, economic expansion. Feudal legacies like the courts of regality were abolished and replaced by baron courts on the English manor court model, but it does not seem that anything was done by the Commonwealth to redeem the bonded workers of the coal-pits and salt-pans.

Most of the adult population were supporters of the exiled King and in favour of a Presbyterian Church which did not aspire to dominate the civil government. A substantial proportion had no objection to union with England as such, provided the terms and conditions might be agreed and not imposed.[16] The two Covenants were by no means forgotten, but with Parliament non-existent, no king, and no General Assembly of the Kirk permitted after 1652 (an attempt to hold one in July 1653 was swiftly terminated by the English military), both were dead letters.

The imposition of the Commonwealth put new strains on loyalties. Almost everyone had signed up to the National Covenant, with its oath to the King; now a king who had signed the Covenant was in exile. Many ministers continued to pray publicly for Charles II. Cromwell's assumption of supreme power made him Lord Protector of Scotland – could a man of honour declare loyalty to the Usurper? Some, like Sir Thomas Urquhart of Cromarty, the translator of Rabelais, and Robert Moray, the erstwhile quartermaster-general, who defected to the King and was knighted in 1643, chose exile; but they were committed royalists (and in Sir Thomas's case, never remotely a Covenanter) and of enough substance and prestige to be welcome at Charles's jovial table. As godly men themselves, in broad sympathy with its theology, the colonels and commissioners of the Commonwealth wanted to come to an understanding with the Scottish Church, as well as ensure that it did not become a network of sedition. Aspects of the Protester faction appealed to them – its discipline, the sobriety of its ministers in public and their enthusiasm in the pulpit corresponded to their own sense of what was proper and desirable in a sect and its pastors. In addition, they knew the Protesters were profoundly suspicious of the exiled King. The banners of the Covenants did not wave above his court, and tales in plenty came back from France about a scandalous lifestyle. But Protesters remained resentful of official interference in the Church and angry about the way in which the Solemn League and Covenant had been dumped by the English. Resolutioners, more varied in their views from almost-Protesters to supporters of episcopacy, were suspect because of the loyalty which most of them gave to the absent king. Meanwhile, despite overtures from the Resolutioner side, and occasional meetings to explore the possibility, it proved impossible for both camps to unite. The hard-line view brought a premature end to a conference held in Edinburgh on 1 June 1650, when the Resolutioners pleaded for bygones to be forgotten. Among the Protesters, John Carstairs was ready to agree, but James Guthrie and Johnston of Wariston refused: the nation must be purged before any reconciliation was possible.[17]

An oath of allegiance from a man taking public office was a normal thing, and the advocates practising at the Scottish Bar were required to take the 'Tender or Oath of Allegiance to Commonwealth and Abjuration of Royalty'. This was something James Dalrymple felt unable to do, and he withdrew from the Bar and his lucrative practice. He was not alone, and in order for the new Supreme Court, which had replaced the Court of Session, to function, the 'Tender' was laid aside by the pragmatic English. Even when Dalrymple accepted the office of a judge, in June 1657, at the request of General George Monck, he was excused the 'Tender' and took a lesser oath, '*De Fideli Administratione Officii*', binding him only to exercise his office faithfully. Father and son, the Dalrymples had a quality, not unknown among the Scots, but regarded by most with a mixture of bafflement, anger and envy, of chilly efficiency, of managing events while keeping at a distance from them, and an ability to rise to the top in successive and very different governments, without apparently compromising themselves. But Dalrymple was typical in serving the Protector. Even Johnston of Wariston, joint author of the National Covenant and arch-Protester, accepted membership in the upper house of Cromwell's

Parliament, and presided over the short-lived Committee of Safety, though he later regretted it until, literally, his last moment. James Dalrymple's glacial self-righteousness did not seem to encompass regret.

During 1655 a Scottish Council was established, of ten members, only two of them Scots, with an Anglo-Irishman, Roger Boyle, Lord Broghill as its President for the first year. His diplomacy and firm moderation were at least as important as his military back-up in setting up a basis for co-operation with most Resolutioners and even the less extreme Protesters in maintaining civil and church affairs. In August 1656, General Monck resumed overall responsibility for government. Nothing illustrates the tenor of Scottish life in the last three years of the Commonwealth so clearly as the fact that the elements of 'history', as typified by times before and yet to come, are generally lacking: no tumultuous Assemblies or Parliaments, no battles, no invasions, no riots – little more than the small change of daily existence. An English visitor to Glasgow in 1656 noted 'store houses and ware houses stuft with merchandize, as their shops swell with foreign commodities',[18] and the largely agrarian society got on with its seasonal practices and pursuits. Even in the ravaged parts of the Highlands, new crops could be grown and harvested. Monck himself, presiding as the Lord Protector's vice-gerent over his system of Justices of the Peace, law-courts, garrisons, patrols, spies and informers, in reporting to the Council of State often had little to say other than that 'things are quiet and well'.[19] His successor might often have envied such calm. The Rev. Robert Law later commented that during the Protectorate the ministers were compelled to preach the Gospel and not 'preach up parliaments, armies, leagues, resolutions, and remonstrances'.[20]

CHAPTER SIX

A Nation of Theopoliticians

ALL SCOTS, BAR A FEW, were agreed on the need for their Church to be established as the sole national Church, into which all citizens were born, and under whose dispensations they lived and died. Only this could guarantee and legitimise its centrality in the life of the country, its structure, and its relationship to civil government. It also prevented the rulers from setting up something different. To the Protesters in particular, establishment confirmed the Church's right to maintain a critique of the government, and encouraged the idea of civil government as a sub-department under religious supremacy. Consequently the Commonwealth policy of toleration of almost all Protestant sects was a permanent annoyance.

Here was a vital difference between Scottish and English attitudes. In England, religious dissent had welled up in opposition first of all to a state Church committed to episcopacy and royal control, and then to any established Church at all. A welter of sects and movements had arisen, proclaiming a wide range of ideas but all clinging to the ideal of non-interference by the state in religion. Scotland had been accustomed to the converse, intervention of religion in the state's affairs; and not even Cromwell could dent the Kirk's role in national life. Its structure was robust enough to withstand both the internal struggle between Resolutioners and Protesters, and the external pressures of anti-Establishment sects and governors. Despite the banning of a General Assembly, it was well capable, from the parish kirk-session up, of maintaining its hegemony over belief and loyalty, and of crushing any breakaway tendencies that might compromise its power and challenge its articles of faith. Few Scots adopted Quakerism, Brownism[1] or any of the other movements on offer via English soldiers and their preachers, and the astrological credulity of many Independents did not catch on. Anti-occupation feeling may also have helped them to resist these seductions. Only in Aberdeen did a locally influential community of religious Independents appear;[2] but there the episcopal-royalist tradition was strong, and with the presbyterian monolith casting less of a shadow, a variety of sects could bloom. One consequence of the Kirk's control was absence of the freedom of discussion that prevailed for a time in England, where Ranters and Seekers reduced God to a universal principle, and Diggers and Levellers refuted the whole basis of a hierarchical, property-owning society. Subversiveness of this kind had almost no public existence, and decades would pass before some of its effects were seen north of the border – except for the case of Alexander Agnew.

In 17th-century Scotland, 'practically everyone was interested in theology'.[3] Anyone who publicly rejected the existence of God, or of divine influence and involvement in daily life, would have been considered crazy at best, and at worst might be condemned as a blasphemer and hanged. This was the fate of Agnew, a tramp executed at Dumfries on 21 May 1656. His crime was to have denied the existence of the Holy Ghost and the divinity of Christ, and to have ridiculed the notion of human souls.[4] Atheism was anti-human. In moments of God-doubting 'melancholy', a man like Johnston of Wariston contemplated atheism with despair and terror, and felt driven towards suicide.[5] Commitment to God could exclude even the pleasures of a country walk in spring: 'In going about the fields, I found the heart apt to rise with carnal delight in fields, grass, wood, etc. This I desired the Lord to guard me against, that such decaying, corruptible, poor comforts steal not away my heart,' wrote Alexander Brodie in May 1656.[6] Vibrant, demanding, striking deep into everyday life, the presence of the religious spirit is the most significant difference between the Scots of now and those of 10 or 11 generations earlier, whose motivations and actions cannot be understood without keeping this high-tension current in mind. A vital generating force was the doctrine of election, a tricky piece of theology which poised humanity's free will against God's omniscience, arguing that it must already be known to God who those were who would be admitted to heaven, and who would not: in other words, the Elect, and the Damned. The old Roman Church had preached the value of good works towards achieving salvation; for the Calvinist there was only divine grace.

Hell-fire was a real and threatening concept to the Scots, and this in its own way powerfully sustained the religious sense. Luxuriant descriptions of infernal torments were not confined to the preachings of the extremists. Scottish ministers generally '... delighted in telling their hearers, that they would be roasted in great fires, and hung up by their tongues.

They were to be lashed with scorpions, and see their companions writhing and howling around them. They were to be thrown into boiling oil and scalding lead. A river of fire and brimstone, broader than the earth, was prepared for them; in that, they were to be immersed; their bones, their lungs, and their liver, were to boil, but never be consumed. At the same time, worms were to prey upon them, and while these were gnawing at their bodies, they were to be surrounded by devils, mocking and making pastime of their pains. Such were the first stages of suffering…'[7] Equally real was the Devil, and ministers who had encountered him personally, and seen him off, were particularly esteemed.[8] A dog, a raven, a strange noise – anything slightly odd or eerie, could be the Evil One. No wonder that one country schoolmaster felt perpetually haunted: 'If any thing had given a knock, I would start and shiver, the seeing of a dog made me afraid, the seeing of a stone in the field made me afraid, and as I thought a voice in my head saying, "It's Satan".'[9]

Not everyone, of course, lived out the taut, sometimes paralysing religious intensity of Wariston, Brodie, and many others. In the ship of Presbyterianism, there were the officers who knew where the vessel was going and how it should get there. Most others were content to understand that the venture would ultimately find gold, and to give it varying degrees of loyal service and personal commitment. But some on board demanded a more challenging course which required greater effort from all hands. In this theology-steeped country, there was little difference in actual doctrine between people who were at one another's throats. Within the Kirk, all were Calvinists. Dispute centred on what appeared quite practical concerns of how it should be organised. Should it have bishops and dioceses – or equal presbyteries with elected moderators? Was it superior to the civil government? Should the King have the right to convene and dismiss General Assemblies? Was not maintenance of the National Covenant a binding commitment? These issues seem far removed from the central principles of religious belief, yet they bitterly divided the nation and provoked decades of civil unrest, repression and bloodshed.

For those who denied the role of bishops, and upheld the Covenant, it was a religious issue and a matter of personal conscience, just as it had been in 1638; to those who considered bishops were essential, or acceptable, and who opposed the Covenant or thought it no longer relevant, the issue was a political one about civic duty and loyalty to the Crown. Religion and politics were knotted so tightly together, that 'theopoliticians' might best describe the hostile camps. After the 'troubles' began, one side represented itself as sustainers of true religion, while the other would insist that 'no Man in Scotland ever suffer'd for his Religion'[10] – that is, the 'martyrs' were deservedly punished as law-breakers and rebels. But the martyrs knew they were embroiled in an increasingly political struggle, about power; and their opponents felt equally strongly that religious truth, as well as the traditions of ecclesiastical and secular government, was on their side.

The purity and freedom of God's perfect Kirk, as the organisation which conserved the covenant of grace between the individual and God, seemed vital to the Protesters; if it were broken, that crucial pact was in jeopardy. A complex range of assurances was required to give an individual person the sense of being in a state of grace, and the removal of any element might mean a tumble towards damnation. For the believer, there could be no higher stake. Furthermore, to demonstrate one's own trustful repose in that divine grace, it did not seem wrong to display confidence, certainty, even intransigence, even intolerance. Why tolerate what you firmly believed to be against the will of God? Was that not a sin? With this sense of ideological certainty and necessity borne in mind, many of the attitudes and actions of the time can be seen to be logical, if not sympathetic or very Christian behaviour as understood (by most) today.

English Puritans governed Scotland in the 1650s, but Protestantism, even Calvinism, and Puritanism were not automatic partners, though Calvinists admired the puritan ideal of character and conduct, emphasising sobriety, seemliness, civic order, and punctual and honest discharge of duties and responsibilities. The Reformed Kirk had a puritan streak from the beginning, but it was not permeated by a puritan spirit, and some traditions were irresistibly strong. Weddings and funerals were festive events which might last for several days, and the wealthier the family, the more important it was to put on a good show – even the grave Dalrymples lived up to this; and the cost of a good funeral send-off might absorb a year's income. Eight dozen bottles of wine, 'not to speak of potations of ale' were consumed at the funeral of John Grierson, in the family of the Whiggamore-hunting Laird of Lagg.[13] In the Highlands, 2,700 on foot and horseback accompanied the funeral of the eighth Lord Lovat in 1672.[14] Wine was only for the rich, but ale, locally or home-brewed and not very alcoholic, was the staple drink at all times of day.

The majority of the population were peasant families: '... around 1660 most of rural Scotland was still recognisably a peasant society',[15] and as a result of closeness to the soil, communal work in the fields, the unavoidableness of other people's bodily functions, an economy based more on barter than on cash, rural conservatism, and a certain vigour of temperament, a tradition of earthiness, ribaldry and popular entertainment was kept up in words, dance and music. At this time it was largely oral, but chapbooks and verse collections early in the next century would draw heavily on its themes and its bubbling reservoir of crude rustic fun, as well as on the more austere and classic forms of the North-East and border ballads. An aspect of this crops up in the raciness and homely phrasing of many sermons, which – to the fury of ministers – were mercilessly exposed in *The Scotch Presbyterian Eloquence Displayed*, an anthology published in England in 1692, which went through several editions.

CHAPTER SEVEN

Boys Growing Up

THE GENERATION OF 1648–9 was growing up in an occupied country, whose tensions and divisions were repressed and covered up by military government. For children, the normalities of life were hardly different to those of previous years. Schools varied from the one-teacher parish schoolroom to the town grammar schools and the High School of Edinburgh. Edicts of both Church and Parliament had required every parish to have a school, and most though not all did, if only in the schoolmaster's house or yard. Normally he was also session-clerk and precentor of the parish church, and usually a licentiate of the Kirk, a minister-in-waiting, not yet ordained. Village schools taught reading, writing, arithmetic and singing, to boys – it was only in the homes of the well-off that girls might get some formal education, from a tutor. The cleverer and more ambitious pupils would also be taught Latin. The grammar schools provided a more complex five-year course, which, once the children had mastered the three Rs, included in Edinburgh, the *Rudiments* of Despauter (a Flemish grammarian of Latin), the Syntax of Erasmus, Corderius and Cicero, then later more Cicero, some Terence and Ovid, followed by Buchanan's Latin Psalms, Virgil, and Horace. As a change from learning by rote, morality plays might be performed: in 1655 Alexander Brodie saw the children of Forres 'act and personate the two great vices of prodigality and covetousness'.[1] In the final year Rhetoric would be taught, probably from Quintilian's first-century AD *Institutio Oratoria*. Naturally, all pupils were required to be word-perfect in the *Shorter Catechism*. Facility of expression in Latin verse and prose was expected; and fluent Latin taken for granted by the time the boys got to university. In addition, most burghs except the smallest and poorest maintained a song-school, whose chief purpose was to impart the music and tunes of the '13 common tunes' of the metric psalms, though some also gave instrumental teaching.

Some ministers specialised in teaching and kept small boarding-schools. Young Carstares was sent to one of these, at Ormiston in East Lothian, run by the Rev. Mr Sinclair; a highly regarded establishment, where only

Latin was spoken and which taught 'Many young gentlemen of the chief families of Scotland'.[2] These ministerial boarding schools had been going for a hundred years, and James Melville recorded from 1563 how the boys were taught archery, golf, and fencing, as well as running, jumping, swimming, and wrestling. Carstares, Richard Cameron in Falkland, John Dalrymple and the others would all be taught the same curriculum, with such additional elements as the master chose to impart. These might include history, an important subject because the history of recent years included the memorable events of the Covenants; that of the past hundred years included the Reformation and the Union of the Crowns; and that of earlier ages included the foundation and justification of Scotland as an independent kingdom. For those with access to books, apart from classical authors, there were histories such as George Buchanan's *Rerum Scoticarum Historia*, and, more entertaining, the 16th-century poems and plays in Scots of Sir David Lindsay, which imparted a spirit of irony and satirical humour as well as a sturdy sense of the country as a 'Commonweal' in which all classes should play a fair part. No general literature of any sort was published in the Commonwealth period, but Lindsay's *Works* were reissued four times between 1665 and 1696, and two long poems full of patriotic and national feeling were also widely read: 'Blind Harry's' biographical poem of Wallace had five editions between 1661 and 1699, and Barbour's *Brus* had two in the same period.[3]

Richard Cameron's family appears to have been of moderate Presbyterian leanings; as the site of a royal palace, Falkland was likely to be well-disposed to the King. Like a complex cell, the typical Scottish burgh was very small, only a few hundred people, but with a fixed internal structure, ruled by a council with the provost as its head, and having separate guilds for merchants (the upper class) and craftsmen (more numerous, at a lower social level but still superior to those with no skills or workshops). Oligarchy rather than local democracy ruled: a retiring council nominated its successors, and the council chose the burgh's commissioner to Parliament. In the larger burghs, the Government regularly sought to control nomination of the provost, something sharply resented by the local gentry, as Graham of Claverhouse would later discover. Often the provostship of a town would run in the same family for generations.

Young Graham lived in a grander milieu than Cameron. His grandfather had been a tutor (guardian) to the Marquis of Montrose, of very recent memory, a kinsman venerated within the family. His father kept out of the maelstrom of national politics: by family tradition he was a King's man but his attitude to the Engagement was lukewarm.[4] He died in 1652 and the boy and his younger brother were brought up by their mother, with the support of her brother David Lour, Earl of Northesk, not at Claverhouse, but in the more secluded house of Glenogilvie, in the northern slopes of the Sidlaw Hills. Hunting, hawking, shooting and fishing were basics of country life for land-owning families, to keep the larder stocked as well as for sporting pleasure; and every boy would learn to ride as soon as possible. Claverhouse, from which the family took its territorial appellation, was closer to Dundee, and when John was 12, the boys were entered on the town's burgess rolls, to emphasise the family interest in its affairs. But there were also lands in Perthshire, on the edge of wild country. The Drummonds, on the south side of Strathearn, also bordered the Highlands.

That vast area, half the country, with a third of the population, was a place of wonder and mystery, legend and menace, with different customs of behaviour and dress, and a different language. Here, and even more so in the Hebridean islands, as far out as St Kilda, a traditional way of life had taken its own course while for 400 years the rest of Scotland had followed a trend of social and economic development broadly in line with other North Sea countries. The most vital difference was in language, since Gaelic, known as 'Irish' or 'Erse', remained the speech of the Highlanders, though through the 17th century, many became bilingual or spoke some essential Scots-English. The Lowland Scots' ignorance of the *Gaidhealtachd* and its ways was profound, laced with contempt and more than a tinge of fear; almost a kind of racial hatred except that all shared the same set of mingled racial origins. Rob Roy MacGregor, Jacobite, cattle-rustler and drover, was a kinsman of the academic and peaceful Gregorys,[5] and there were thousands of similar relationships. In a single generation, a Highland family could be assimilated into the Lowland mainstream, if it came south, shed its plaids, and adapted its language. Scotland carried the Highlands like a bad conscience, an unstable uncle shut in an upstairs room – something inflicted on it by nature and history. But even here was one of the country's contrary aspects, reaching out from the dim past, compelling an almost mystic sense of national identity. It was in the Highlands that the old song had begun: among those glens and mountains the Gaelic-speaking Scots had first mastered the Picts and then extended their rule over the old Cumbric south-west and the newer Anglian south-east, and an awareness of this still lingered. The oldest arcana of nationhood were not in Edinburgh or St Andrews, but at the lost site of King Bridei's fort near Inverness, at the rock of Dunadd in Argyll, and on the isle of Iona.

Nobody from south or east of the Highlands went there unless they had good reason. But there were many links. Highlanders of both sexes emerged to do seasonal work, or to be servants, torch-bearers, messengers, body-guards and chair-carriers in the bigger towns. A modern biographer of Graham awards him a Highland nanny complete with stock of folk-tales;[6] Professor Terry thought it unlikely that he had more than the slightest knowledge of Gaelic.[7] George Mackenzie, at a similar social level, had a closer connection with the Highlands. But George's boyhood home was Dundee, second town in importance and wealth at this time,[8] where the family lived in his grandmother's house – her father, Sir Alexander Wedderburn, a scion of an important local dynasty, had been town clerk. There is no evidence from James Drummond's or George Mackenzie's life and writings that they had any command of, or interest in, Gaelic and the Gaelic tradition; in this they were typical of educated Lowlanders of their time.

William Carstares was brought up in an atmosphere of Protestant piety and Presbyterian politics. His father, siding with the Protesters but refusing to take an extreme position, was well-regarded by both sides and by the Cromwellian commissioners. Leading Presbyterian ministers were characterised by Gilbert Burnet, not an over-friendly observer, as 'men all of a sort' who have '... a small circle of knowledge in which they are generally well-instructed... generally proud and passionate, insolent and covetous. They took much pains among their people to maintain their authority',[9] but John Carstairs was not a man of spiritual pride. In 1655 he became minister of Glasgow's Inner High Church, which occupied the choir of the one-time cathedral. His wife had a constellation of relations among the Renfrewshire gentry and their son had frequent sojourns in the country. The Dalrymples had houses in Ayrshire and Galloway, but Carsecreuch was the main home. John was the eldest of nine children and, as his father was in Edinburgh for much of the time, he would certainly have been considerably influenced by his mother, characterised by Sir Walter Scott as 'an able, politic and high-minded woman, so successful in whatever she undertook that the vulgar and superstitious ascribed her power to necromancy and a compact with the Evil One'.[10] Little is known in detail about the childhood of any of these or any other individuals of the time; it was not considered an important stage of life. A boy from the middle or upper ranks of society, once he had shed the frocks of infancy and assumed breeches, was expected to acquire an education, a belief in and understanding of religion as practised by his own family, with the appropriate code of morals; some dexterity with sword and bow; and not least a sense of honour – national, family, and personal. This was not a simple matter of pride or boy-scoutish sincerity. Honour embraced prestige but also duty, and might impose unpalatable tasks and burdens.

In 1650 George Mackenzie enrolled at Aberdeen University. As young Graham would also be, he was an admirer of Montrose and had written verses in his honour. He boarded with other boys near the college, at a quarterly rate of £Sc40. It was perhaps typical of the times that his father had to borrow money to pay his university costs;[11] the exactions of war taxes, the depression of trade, the brief looting of Dundee by Montrose's men in 1645, and a more intensive rampage by Monck's army in 1651, all were drains on the family purse. George transferred to St Andrews in 1653 as a student of St Leonard's College, of which his mother's father had been Principal, and graduated as a master of arts there on 13 May 1653. Five years later, John Graham began his studies at St Andrews at the tender age of ten (the precocious Gilbert Burnet had been sent to Aberdeen University even before his 10th birthday) and graduated on 27 July 1661. He is the only one of whom we get a description as an undergraduate. Thomas Morer, then a regent at the university, wrote of him much later: 'At St Andrews, in his minority, he was admired for his parts and respects to churchmen, which made him dear to the archbishop of that See, who ever after honour'd and lov'd him…'[12] Richard Cameron from Falkland was also a student at St Andrews, matriculating on 5 February 1662 and graduating in May 1665. His father is said to have borrowed £40 to pay for his studies.[13] James Drummond and his brother John attended St Andrews at that time, but it is unlikely that, other than sitting in the same lecture halls, they had any personal contact with Cameron. Will Carstares, despite having a great-uncle in St Andrews who promised to look after him and keep him well away from the 'occasions to divertisements' offered by Edinburgh,[14] did become a student in the capital, matriculating in 1663 and graduating in 1667. No record survives of John Dalrymple's education, though it is likely that he attended his father's alma mater of Glasgow.

Of the universities, three had been established before the Reformation; the two newer ones, Marischal College, Aberdeen's second university (they competed vigorously to attract the most promising students from the North-East), and the 'Town's College' of Edinburgh, were post-Reformation foundations. In the mid-17th century all, of course, were Protestant institutions, but shared in the divisions of the time. St Andrews, the oldest and most conservative, was perhaps considered too much of an episcopalian stronghold by John Carstairs, but for Richard Cameron, in any case not yet touched by the iron that later would enter his soul, it was his local university as it was for young Claverhouse. Aberdeen's episcopalian leanings[15] would not have bothered the Mackenzies. Among the mountains of Kintail, many of their clan still held to the Catholic faith, and Catholic priests moved with comparative freedom.

All the universities followed the old system of attaching each undergraduate to a regent, who assumed responsibility both for teaching and for pastoral care, and supervised their still-juvenile charges throughout the normally four-year course. Students, identified by their scarlet gowns, were classified in three groups, Primars, who were of noble birth, Secondars, sons of gentlemen, and Ternars, from the rest of the community; and their treatment was not on an equal basis: St Andrews allowed 'leave to noblemen and gentlemen's sons to go to Cowper [Cupar] races for a day or two', but Ternars had to stay in college and work.[16] Better-off students could afford a set of golf-clubs; all could take part in wild ball games, and archery, still supposedly an official requirement, was practised. Apart from these there were inevitable 'divertisements' and high jinks, battles between first- and second-year students, or between students and town boys. Discipline was sometimes strict – according to the hostile evidence of later pasquil writers, James Dalrymple wielded the tawse as a regent at Glasgow – but a tradition of boisterousness was preserved in these all-male institutions.

Regents were recent graduates, of particular merit (James Dalrymple served for seven years; resigning, as the statutes required, on his marriage in 1643 but re-elected the same day) and were expected to teach several subjects, under the aegis of specialist professors. Aristotle loomed large in the curriculum, which was still medieval in content: 'pure scholasticism'[17] of the kind that had been mocked by Erasmus more than a century earlier. Students spent much time copying things down and learning by rote. Greek was taught, and sometimes Hebrew. Aberdeen Town Council paid 400 merks in 1643 to Mr John Row for 'setting furth ane Hebrew dictionar' which he dedicated to the Council. Hebrew was required for study of the Old Testament, Greek for the New as well as for the secular philosophy of Plato and Aristotle. Among intellectuals with a bent for humane learning alongside theology, the doctrines of Neo-Stoicism, already rather old-fashioned in Europe, were something of a cult. More advanced new learning was regarded with deep suspicion: Descartes, whose major works were all published by 1644, was viewed as an atheist, but his ideas could not be ignored. In the universities of Scotland, despite the work of Copernicus and, more recently, Galileo,[18] the earth remained fixed at the centre of the cosmos. Against this dull background moved a few luminary figures, harbingers of things to come; among them James Gregory[19] who invented a reflecting telescope in 1661, did pioneering work in optics and geometry, and was Professor of Mathematics at St Andrews from 1668 to 1674.

Protestant theology was the bedrock of these institutions, but it did not produce distinguished or enterprising scholarship. Samuel Rutherford, who died in 1661, was the only divine with an international reputation. From his travels in Europe, Alexander Brodie observed that other Protestant churches 'exceeded us in zeal, love, fervency, suffering for Christ';[20] and on inquiring what foreign divines thought about Scotland's religious disputes, he got 'Nothing but matter of humiliation'.[21] Scotland was not an intellectual power-house of Calvinism or any other creed or philosophy. A few professors had embarked on modest reforms of the stuffy and stultifying teaching system. Robert Leighton, appointed Master at Edinburgh in 1653, deplored the antique method of 'disputations' or 'justifications' by which students tested each other's knowledge and understanding, and perhaps found its aggressive style all too appealing in some cases: 'as if disputing was the end of learning, as fighting is the design of going to war; hence the youth, when they enter the school, begin disputing, which never ends but with their life'.[22] Leighton would later get more than a bellyful of this arguing style.

Only two careers devolved directly from the acquisition of a university degree: the Church, and teaching (the two, as we have seen, closely interlinked). Medicine, on the verge of becoming a separate discipline, required private tuition from a practising physician. None of the universities taught law, and George Mackenzie, following his father into a legal career, took a well-beaten trail to France to study law at Bourges,[23] returning to Scotland in 1659. James and John Drummond both studied law at Angers in France, and John Dalrymple's law studies were probably also in France. Richard Cameron returned to Falkland where he was appointed as schoolmaster and session-clerk. William Carstares pursued his studies in Holland, intending to follow his father into the ministry. John Graham took none of these options, but returned to Glenogilvie, where, though still a minor, he was laird, and had to learn the practical details and responsibilities of a landowner. Learned professions or pursuits had no appeal for him; like many other scions of the landowning gentry, he was going to be a professional soldier.

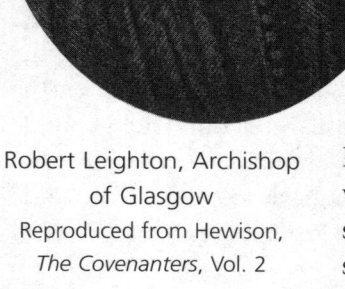

Robert Leighton, Archishop of Glasgow
Reproduced from Hewison, *The Covenanters*, Vol. 2

CHAPTER EIGHT

Philosophers and Witches

SCOTLAND PLAYED A PASSIVE role in the restoration of its monarchy. Following the death of Oliver Cromwell, and the abdication of his son Richard in May 1659, the three countries of the Protectorate required a new dispensation. The lack of a head of state and the obviously temporary nature of government arrangements in London super-heated the excitement among those who favoured a return to the traditional monarchy, and Monck's military-legal machine swiftly moved to check possible pro-Charles activity. All prominent royalists had to pay a bond of engagement or face imprisonment. No-one attempted a *coup d'état*. For future developments, the decisive move indeed came from Scotland, but the army that began its march south from Coldstream on the first day of 1660 was an English one. In withdrawing most of the occupying force, Monck made due provision for administration and defence, appointing commissioners on behalf of the Commonwealth in the burghs and shires, and leaving garrisons in Edinburgh, Stirling and Dumbarton castles and the forts. The shire commissioners elected the royalist Earl of Glencairn (released on sureties from Edinburgh Castle in 1659) as their president, but there was no sense of a royalist tide running, and Monck gave no clue as to his intentions. A Scottish army did not exist, and shires adjacent to the Highlands were permitted to raise forces for internal defence. Conscious of critical events going on elsewhere, and powerless to intervene, the Scots could only wait and absorb the waves of news and rumour that came week by week with mails and travellers from England. Excitement or alarm must have greeted the news in early March that the London Parliament had reconfirmed the Solemn League and Covenant and ordered that the Church in England be reorganised on presbyterian lines – but this Parliament was a spent force (it was dissolved on 16 March) and its acts were unenforceable and irrelevant. Parliamentary elections were held in England in 25 April, producing the strongly royalist Convention Parliament. It was an exclusively English affair, and the Scots could draw their own conclusions from that – the

Commonwealth union was effectively dead. On 8 May, Charles II was formally proclaimed King of England, and most Scots celebrated the restoration.

George Monck was known in Scotland as a sound Presbyterian; Charles II had signed the Covenants. With the King's call to London, Covenanters could allow themselves a sliver of hope that the grace of a Presbyterian God might yet descend on their 30-year-old sovereign. The Usurpation was over, and all patriots could be glad of that while waiting to see what the new regime would do. Open royalists and ex-Engagers who had not compromised themselves were jubilant. For some who had served the Commonwealth, there was uncertainty about how they would be viewed; Charles had already offered an Act of Indemnity to be passed by England's parliament, letting almost everyone except living regicides off the hook, but there was no word of anything similar for Scotland. Alexander Brodie, who had served as a judge under the Commonwealth, resolved to go to London and try to obtain the royal grace, 'for albeit I might, and was willing, to be under the King's displeasure (if it seemed good to the Lord so to exercise me) yet the Lord commands and allows me to seek the removing of it by all lawful means, as far as is possible'.[1] At least one of Charles's senior English advisers, Edward Hyde, Earl of Clarendon, reflected on whether the Scots might not prefer a continued union, 'But the King would not build according to Cromwell's models.'[2] No Scot is recorded as proposing to maintain the union, and Scotland resumed its status as a self-governing nation under the King – up to a point. For three years a Committee for Scotland would sit in Whitehall, with four permanent English members. In August 1660 the Committee of Estates formed in June 1651 was recalled as the nucleus of a new administration in the old mode, and a Parliament, convened by royal command, was elected and began to sit in January 1661.

Charles retained disagreeable memories of his 'ancient kingdom' and of the way his royal self-esteem had suffered at the hands of the Presbyterian ministers in 1650–1. Among those who had suffered on his behalf, and might now claim their reward, was Lauderdale, now 34. A descendant of Queen Mary's great Secretary, Sir John Maitland of Thirlestane, loyalty to the Stuarts since 1647 had enabled him to live down his earlier Covenanting sympathies. Captured at Worcester, imprisoned in the Tower of London, he then attended Charles in exile. Big, red-haired, crudely humorous – once, to divert the King, he had danced in front of him wearing woman's petticoats – well-read, highly intelligent and strongly emotional, this man, who was to become effective ruler of Scotland for nearly 20 years, has had a bad press, at least since Gilbert Burnet's memoirs, though Burnet's acidic account of him is sometimes self-contradictory. Very much wanting to be the King's right-hand man for Scotland, Lauderdale did not intend to let inconvenient principles get in his way. One historian dismissed him as 'a palace minion;'[3] his biographer noted that while in prison, he read Hobbes's *Leviathan*: 'After the Restoration, his standpoint was unadulterated Hobbesianism: he was an egotist after Hobbes's own heart. Self-protection, which Hobbes identified with the Law of Nature, became his guiding rule of life.'[4] The duke, as he later became, has not left his own justification, but, although he profited mightily from his various offices, he was not entirely motivated by greed and ambition, and was remembered in the Presbyterian memoir of Robert Law as 'a man very national'.[5] He thought himself the best man for the job, and none of his contemporaries proved him wrong. The problem which bedevilled his administration was that the wishes of his indolent but obstinate master and those of a sufficient number of Scots were impossible to reconcile, and he was not equal to the task of harmonising the two.

Appointed Secretary of State in 1660, Lauderdale remained at court, and the foremost figures in Scotland were John Leslie, seventh Earl of Rothes, Lord President of the Privy Council, the Earl of Glencairn as Chancellor, and John Middleton, who had been made an earl in 1656, as Commander-in-Chief and Commissioner to Parliament. The Privy Council was restored in July 1661. Rothes was an adherent of the good life, which to him meant wine, women, and carousal, but he had more political guile, and a better grasp of affairs, than Glencairn; Middleton, 'once a pikeman in Hepburn's regiment in France',[6] soon found politics too subtle a game. All were content to follow or anticipate the desires of the King and of what Burnet refers to as 'the herd of the cavalier party',[7] who had emerged as commissioners (members) of the new Parliament after carefully managed elections,[8] 'full of revenge' and with the hope of seeing the estates of the collaborators broken up and divided among the loyalist nobility. Of these domains, none was vaster than the Marquis of

Argyll's, and many, including Middleton, felt that circumstances owed them a piece of those lands. But though the Marquis was a prisoner in Edinburgh Castle, his eldest son, Lord Lorne, with a royalist record, agitating to reclaim the forfeited estates, was an obstacle to these ambitions. Among former collaborators, it was better to have had the favour of Monck, now Duke of Albemarle, than Cromwell's. James Dalrymple slipped into the post of a judge of the reinstated Court of Session in February 1661, taking the courtesy title of Lord Stair, and acquiring a knighthood. He opted for the Court of Judiciary, which dealt with civil cases. 'I never did medle in any criminal court' he wrote later[9] – preferring the toils of property law, inheritances, rights and sub-rights, he was also far-sighted enough to be aware that the civil law remains the same, while crimes can be defined, and re-defined, by kings and parliaments.

New men appeared on the political scene, some of them young, like George Mackenzie, recently back from France, admitted to the Scottish bar in 1659; others were men of experience who felt that their talents and ideas suited the times. Prominent among these was the minister of Crail in Fife, James Sharp, 42 years old in 1660, who had been a moderate Resolutioner and had gained a reputation among the clergy as a capable negotiator on behalf of the Kirk moderates. Their leader, the 72-year-old Robert Douglas, regretfully noted the rise of 'a new upstart generation, who bear a heart-hatred to the Covenant' and 'have no love to Presbyterial Government, but are wearied of that yoke, feeding themselves with the fancy of Episcopacy…';[10] ironically, he was writing to Sharp who was himself wearying of 'that yoke'. Even those who believed Presbyterianism to be the proper thing might welcome the more easygoing social style of the Restoration. Failure of its imperial dream had taken much of the shine off militant Presbyterianism, and its domestic climate, far more concerned with fasts and repentances than feasts, with its intrusive inquiries and punitive repression, sustained by snoopers and informers, keeping the hangmen and their acolytes busy with whip, hammer and nails, and the 'jougs' or stocks well filled, was stifling and offensive to some, at least. As Douglas sadly surmised, aversion to the manner of presbyterian rule was a significant element in maintaining episcopalian sympathies. But among stricter Presbyterians the Restoration brought a resurgence of enthusiasm for the Covenant that the King had forsaken – the second Covenant period, the Years of Unavailing Struggle, was beginning.

John Leslie, Earl, later Duke, of Rothes
Reproduced from Dalton, *The Scots Army*

George Mackenzie got into the centre of activity by becoming a junior advocate in the defence of the Marquis of Argyll, who had failed to make his peace with Charles, and now stood accused of a range of offences, grouped under three main heads, from the handing over of Charles I to the English Parliament to collaboration with the Cromwellian Usurpation. In so intensely political a trial, the defence team had nervously sought assurances that their best efforts on their client's behalf would not be misinterpreted as disloyalty to the King. The overture was refused, but the defence was conducted with spirit and resolution, aided by Argyll's own dignified and skilful self-justification against the crude blustering of the King's Advocate, Sir John Fletcher. Mackenzie made the bold but true point that virtually everyone had shared Argyll's alleged offence of compliance with the Occupation, if only by paying taxes to it. Nevertheless, the verdict was inevitable: Argyll, who had in 1650 seemed to hold the future of Scotland in his hand, was condemned to execution.

Advocacy in the courts was robust and conducted with few scruples. Fletcher's tirade against Argyll as 'an impudent villain' in open court was typical of a style combining insult and abuse with Latin tags and references to abstruse legal sources going back to Justinian. Excessive nicety in legal exchanges was hardly to be expected in a country whose universities practised the rough dialectic of justifications and where the tradition of flyting, the competitive exchange of sustained verbal abuse in verse, was much appreciated (the favourite, *The Flyting of Montgomery and Polwarth*, was re-published three times between 1665 and 1688).[11] Mackenzie felt it was 'undeniable that the Scottish Idiom of the British tongue is more fit for Pleading than either the English Idiom or the French Tongue; for certainly a Pleader must use a brisk, smart and quick way of speaking... Our pronunciation is like ourselves, fiery, abrupt, sprightly, and bold.'[12] He made himself a master of the style, but he was not considered the greatest courtroom advocate of the age; Sir George Lockhart of Carnwath, around eight years his senior, was generally awarded this distinction. Rivalry between these two, personal and political, makes a minor counterpoint within the pattern of events from 1661 onwards.

But Mackenzie had other talents. He had already written the first novel published in Scotland, *Aretina, or The Serious Romance*, dedicated 'To all the Fair Ladies of this Nation'. It is noted as 'Part One', but there was not to be a Part Two, or any sequel. Very much in the fantastic French mode of the time, with the lovely Aretina and her passionate suitor Philarites, and full of hags, hermits, knights, ladies, emblematic skulls and cannibal savages, it has one major difference. Almost a quarter of its 432 pages recount the history of 'Lacedaemon', a thinly disguised

Britain. This long interpolation, covering from 1603 to the Restoration, with Cromwell as Autarchus, Charles II as Theopemptus, Montrose as Oranthus, Argyll as Phanosebus, 'a man of deep reach', must have been written at speed. Excitingly topical, as well as, literally, novel, it shows Mackenzie as a literary innovator.[13] His efforts also included at least one play, now lost,[14] but hardly anyone followed his example: the last four decades of the 17th century were a barren time for Scottish letters.

Mackenzie's literary-contemplative side is also revealed in his lifelong interest in philosophy. University would have made him familiar with Neo-Platonism, seeing a spiritual union behind every aspect of matter, and which had long before branched into alchemy and a diversity of occult themes. But he was specially attracted by the ideas and ideals of Neo-Stoicism, a school of life rather than of academic study, elaborated by 16th-century thinkers, chiefly the Flemish scholar Justus Lipsius, from elements of ancient pagan Stoicism and modern Protestantism. Since the Reformation, three generations of Scottish scholars, poets and men of action had been impressed by it. Most of its expounders taught in continental universities but the presence of Scottish students ensured a steady homeward transference of their ideas. Among the teachers, too, were many Scots emigrés with networks of family and academic friends. Never more than a mild cult among the most literate, but influential in forming attitudes, Neo-Stoicism harmonised with the strand of Protestant thought which put emphasis on each person's own perception of how life should be led.

But it was backward-focused, trying to reconcile two sets of ideas, one which had been in existence for 1,600 years; the other for a mere century or so. Calvinists believed in Original Sin and Redeeming Grace; a Neo-Stoic Calvinist also considered the world to be a corrupt place, and supreme virtue to lie in retirement from it and resignation to the will of God. But when the world could not be ignored, it was permissible to deal with it on its own base terms; involvement was impossible without getting one's hands dirty. Neo-Stoicism prided itself on its understanding of how things worked: George Mackenzie called 'right reason' his one talent, and applied it in his work of 1663, *The Religious Stoic*.[15] He is against 'Fanatics of all Sects and Sorts' and has no time for the luxury of conscience: '... such as think they have a Church within their own breasts, should likewise think their heads are steeples, and so should provide them with bells'. To Mackenzie, religion and belief in God are a natural condition and 'so should all conspire to that exterior uniformity of worship which the laws of his country enjoin'. His argument is important in as far as it sustains his own later persona of 'Bluidy Mackenzie' – his church is a department of state, and accepted formulas of worship, along with practical charity and compassion, are what it requires, not heaven-gazing, dubious inspirations, and wild sermonising. He has no particular problem with heretics: '… it fares with heretics as with tops, which, so long as they are scourged, keep foot and run pleasantly, but fall as soon as they are neglected and left to themselves' – so long as they do not break the law of the state, in which case, 'of all others they should be most severely punished'.[16]

Philosophers like Spinoza and Hobbes were leaving such ideas far behind, but in Scotland, where the intellectual appetite was only slowly acquiring a taste for the bolder novelties of modern thought, they still offered a welcome mental refuge from the disputes and depressing experiences of real life, and laid a few garlands of humane learning and classical scholarship over the stark lineaments of Knoxian theology. Its emphasis on reason made Neo-Stoicism one of the intellectual forces that were gradually encouraging a greater open-mindedness.

Yet, if new abstract philosophy was giving Scotland the go-by, in that country, behind the labels of 'fanatic', 'malignant', 'persecutor', 'Whiggamore', laced with Biblical invective, hot pamphlets and jeering pasquils, a long, hard and thoroughly practical struggle was going on between two irreconcilable views of power, authority, and responsibility. One, royal absolutism, was an idea of the time. The other seems in some ways strangely modern: government in the name, not of a king, but of a set of ideas to which everyone was expected to conform without question. Its effects had been seen at various times between 1638 and 1650, under the regimes of those who considered themselves the interpreters and guardians of the official ideology. They demanded that everyone accept and live by those ideas, or suffer expulsion from public life, or worse punishment. For they claimed to themselves a sanction which the anti-religious ideological tyrannies of the 20th century could not command – the power to dictate the nature of a person's existence after death. God's perfect Kirk believed that it held 'the Keys of St Peter' in wardenship, and exclusion from its sacraments also meant exclusion from heaven, forever.

Ministers making an excommunication did so with all the dread formality of a medieval Pope pronouncing an anathema. For a nation seething in such a crucible, even the excitements of Descartes' *cogito*, and the range of speculation opened up by his method, may have seemed pallid and academic. But the Scottish struggle was intellectually sterile, a battle of two dead ends. It would be resolved from outside, and with no happy synthesis.

In the 1660s the reasonableness of Neo-Stoicism helped Mackenzie to take a less primitive view of witchcraft than most of his compatriots. Appointed a Justice-depute, on the junior bench of the Court of Session, in late June 1661, he and two colleagues were sent to try suspected witches in East Lothian. Belief in the existence and powers of witches was deeply entrenched, hardening periodically into phases of manic witch-hunts, accompanied by savage examination, torture, ludicrous trials and horrible executions. The English commanders of the Occupation had been startled by the extent and fervour of witch-chasing, and clamped down on it, with a resultant surge of cases in the early years of the Restoration. When he came to write his *Laws and Customes of Scotland in Matters Criminal*, Mackenzie had to include a chapter on the laws and procedures relating to witches, but stated that, '... it requires the clearest relevancy, and most convincing probation... I condemn, next to the witches themselves, these cruel and too forward judges who burn persons by the thousand as guilty of this crime.'[17]

Thirty-five commissions were issued by the Privy Council in 1662, to every shire, authorising witch trials and executions. Over 380 cases were examined; the most in any one year apart from 1650 when there had been over 400 (between 1560 and 1730 only two other years had more than 100 recorded witchcraft cases). Mackenzie's thousands seem an exaggeration, but at least 1,337 people were executed as witches between 1597 and 1730.[18] Witch-hunting killed far more victims than the pursuit of recalcitrant Presbyterians, and the Covenanters were among the most zealous witch-burners. Through the 1660s the Kirk was active behind the drive; witchcraft was a sin that always appeared to be on the increase. A thousand years had passed since St Columba inveighed against the people's clinging to superstitions and charms, and their appeal was as strong as ever. Severe persecution had gone on since a Protestant parliament in 1563 had prescribed the sentence of strangulation at the stake, followed by burning. That might be almost a merciful release for the victim, after the ordeals of a witch-trial. Suspects were put in the hands of 'witch-prickers' whose aim was to procure confessions. Once the suspect had been stripped naked, any birthmarks or deformities exposed would be claimed as of satanic origin. Various parts of the body were stabbed with needles for 'devil's mark' – supposed areas of numbness or from which blood did not readily flow – and they were subjected to prolonged deprivation of food and sleep. Sleep deprivation was an officially acknowledged treatment to encourage prisoners to give evidence or confession: supposed to need sanction from the Council, it was often used without permission being asked. As Mackenzie noted,'this usage was the ground of all their confessions'. Human agents were not always needed – the 'witch's bridle', an iron collar fixed round the head, with sharp prongs reaching into the mouth, forcing it to be kept open, was used in some places. Every form of abuse which those with a little power could inflict on the completely helpless was employed, giving legal opportunities to the most vicious members of a community.

In a monograph published in 1685, *Satan's Invisible World Discovered*, George Sinclair, Professor of Philosophy at Glasgow, describes the burning of Helen Ellis in Culross: 'She was carried to the place of execution in a chair by four men, by reason her legs and belly were broken.' The explanation was that her guards left her with her feet in the stocks, while they went to smoke a pipe. The devil came in, took her out of the stocks, and flew off with her. She said, 'Oh God, where are you taking me?' whereupon he let her drop from the height of the steeple. Sinclair's correspondent adds, 'I saw the impression and dimple of her heels'.[19] One can only surmise as to what really happened in this ugly episode, and what part was played by the guards. But the general attitude was not one of cynical brutality or vicious relish, rather of fascinated horror. Sinfulness, the people were told, was their natural condition, the Devil was always round the corner; and many unfortunates were sacrificed to relieve a wider sense of guilt. Sexual crimes were often associated with necromancy, especially in the more infrequent cases of male witches, who were usually also accused of incest, buggery, or bestiality.[20] In the late 1670s, witch-pricking was still rife, and the Privy Council was issuing commissions to investigate witchcraft into the next century.

For Mackenzie's judicial foray into West Lothian, the Privy Council decreeed that the property of persons found guilty was to be divided among the judges. 'Witches' were rarely beggars or paupers, and a cottage (turf hovel though it might be), with grazing rights and a cow or two was not be sneezed at. This procedure of allocating fines and forfeited estates was standard; although the action was taken in the name of the Crown, it was normally a Crown servant or active loyalist who benefited. Mackenzie did not remain a judge for long, resigning in December 1663; he had married in 1662, and practice as an advocate brought in more money than the salary and perquisites of a junior judge. His first wife, Elizabeth Dickson, was daughter of a judge of the Court of Session; before her death around 1669 she would bear three sons, two of whom died very young; and two daughters.

CHAPTER NINE

Owls, Satyrs, and Bangster Amazons

AS A GENERAL, the Marquis of Argyll was ineffectual, and fled from several battles before their end. But he was steadfast in awaiting and suffering his public execution in Edinburgh on 27 May 1661. One of those he invited to attend on him in the Tolbooth was John Carstairs, who preached to him 'in the prison, the last Sabbath of his life'.[1] The city's prison, usually a place of hard rigour, could also afford informalities. Argyll was able to exchange farewells with a fellow-prisoner also under sentence of death, James Guthrie, minister of Stirling, a leading Protester. Outside, the 'Maiden' was waiting to behead him. In a last address, he proclaimed his belief in the Covenant.

Guthrie had had the temerity to write, with nine other ministers and two laymen, to Charles II at the Restoration, reminding him of his obligations under the Covenant. To execute a minister was something new, but apart from writing a book, *The Causes of God's Wrath upon the Nation*, highly critical of Charles's attitude to the Covenant, Guthrie had offended in another way not listed on his 'dittay' or indictment sheet. At the episode of the 'Start' he had excommunicated Middleton, and the new Earl, though he had been readmitted, 'weeping and blubbering', to the embrace of the Kirk and a presumed state of grace, had not forgiven the humiliation.[2] Replying to Parliament on 10 April 1661, after the reading of his 'process', Guthrie said: '... it is not the extinguishing of me, or of many others, that will extinguish the Covenant and work of Reformation since the year 1638. My blood, bondage or banishment will contribute more for propagation of these things, than my life or liberty could do, though I should live for many years.'[3] On the eve of his execution he had a last treat, some cheese, which he had avoided because of kidney gravel, but 'I hope I am now beyond the hazard of the gravel'.[4] Gilbert Burnet, who saw him hanged, noted that 'he spoke an hour upon the ladder, with the composure of a man that was delivering a sermon'.[5]

The Maiden
Reproduced from *Cassell's Old & New Edinburgh*

Custom allowed these last words from the brink of eternity. Not many of those hanged for conventional crimes may have supposed themselves to be destined for heavenly bliss, but Guthrie set a pattern for his many successors, treating the ugly, earthbound finality of the gallows as a launch-pad for immortality, as if an invisible cone of divine grace and promise funnelled downwards on the tall grim posts, the double ladder, the rope. Condemnee and executioner climbed the ladder together, and when the victim gave the sign that he was ready, the hangman thrust him off. To the Martyrs and their supporters, it was only dead flesh that swung and twitched, while the living soul rose to the eternal splendours. An edifying death not only promoted the cause, it justified the life, the beliefs, the struggle.

While the royal government was still new, the moderate Presbyterian party in the Kirk sent James Sharp as its representative to London. With Lauderdale as Secretary of State their hopes were perhaps more realistic than those of Guthrie on the extreme wing, but Lauderdale quickly stopped recommending Presbyterianism for Scotland when he saw the King was hostile to it. Charles's alleged comment that it was no religion for a gentleman[6] echoes the resentment of the nobility at the power exercised by Kirk ministers. Middleton assured the King that episcopacy 'was desired by the greater and honester part of the nation'.[7] Indeed, the new regime lost little time in making its programme clear. Johnston of Wariston, impeached at the same time as Argyll, was able to escape to the continent. He was condemned to death in his absence. Other uncompromising Protesters were rounded up and put on trial. Robert McWard, minister of the Outer High Church in Glasgow, was banished,[8] and removed to Holland where for many years he would be the prime figure of a vocal and influential exile group of hard-line Covenanters, urging defiance from across the North Sea. Meanwhile, from London Sharp maintained a flow of reassuring messages to his colleagues, none of which mentioned that he was becoming ever more deeply involved in proposals to reintroduce bishops to the Scottish Church.

After the nine years of Usurpation, preceded by the brief, heady rule of the ultra-Presbyterians, and the great days of the Covenant (to some an era lit by nostalgia), the nation became aware that a huge attempt was going on to obliterate the events of that entire period, and to return affairs to how they had been, or were assumed to have been, before all the time of troubles began. If it occurred to anyone that the pre-1638 set-up was the framework on which the troubles began to blaze, they kept the inopportune thought to themselves. Under the King the land was to be administered by his chosen members of the nobility; and the Kirk was going to be governed by a hierarchy of deans, bishops and archbishops, appointed by the King. The 'Cavalier Parliaments' of 1661–63, spurred on by Middleton, passed the necessary legislation, much of it combined under the umbrella of the 'Act Rescissory' of March 1661 which simply declared all parliaments and their legislation since 1633 to be of no standing, null, void. Scotland's erstwhile glory, the National Covenant, was condemned as an illegal document, and attempts to make public bonds of any kind were forbidden. The status of the Solemn League and Covenant was made clear when copies were publicly burned in London and other places on 29 May 1661. But to expunge three tumultuous decades was of course impossible. In any case, the new regime was not wholly backward-looking. A Council of Trade was set up in 1661, to regulate, improve and advance trade, navigation and manufactories, and a series of acts was passed with the intention of encouraging commerce and industry. These were necessary responses to the English Parliament's Navigation Act of 1660, which protected the rights of English shippers and traders against all foreigners, including Scots – renewed national independence had its price.

The bishops were duly installed in November 1661 – with James Sharp, to the astonishment, fury and imprecations of his Presbyterian ex-colleagues, at their head as Archbishop of St Andrews. His explanation that he had accepted the role only in order 'to moderate matters' persuaded few.[9] In setting bishops to rule the Kirk (Orkney, Caithness, Ross, Moray, Aberdeen, Brechin, Argyll, The Isles, Dunkeld, Dunblane, St Andrews,

Glasgow, Edinburgh, and Galloway), the King was not only following his own views but was strongly pressed by his English advisers, the Earl of Clarendon and Archbishop Sheldon of Canterbury, who remembered the time when Scottish divines had been loud in London about the imminent purifying of the Anglican Church into Presbyterian form. Sheldon insisted that the first of the new Scottish bishops should be reconsecrated as priests in Westminster Abbey. For those who still clove to the Solemn League and Covenant, this English involvement was a grotesque reversal of their aspirations, and to all Presbyterians it was an additional affront – which however benefited their cause by giving it a patriotic colouring. At first the new bishops played little part in state affairs, though they were restored as an Estate of Parliament in May 1662.

Under the new government, useful Commonwealth systems, like the efficient tax-collecting methods, remained in place. Nor could memories be blotted out, or the spread of undesirable ideas prevented, though of course the administration tried to achieve the latter. In November 1661 a number of 'seditious and scandalous books' were publicly burned in Edinburgh, including 'Archibald Campbell's Speech'. Printing without official warrant was forbidden, and on 5 December James Mein, keeper of the letter office, was granted liberty to publish the *Diurnal Weekly*, 'for preventing of false news'.[10] In fact a propaganda war in words and print was just beginning, and each side would constantly accuse the other of spreading false news.

A general goodwill was felt towards the King, especially among the nobility, who had been sidelined during the Commonwealth, and now rallied to the new spirit of royalism and hoped to benefit. Most of them aged over 40 were likely to have signed the National Covenant, but much had happened since 1638, and those who still supported its ideas would quickly learn to be discreet about their views. Many other people were satisfied with the new order of things, others – the majority perhaps – probably did not greatly care. The Usurpation had provided an uneasy stability, but now, it was to be hoped, stability was possible along with legitimacy and a restoration of national institutions. Few people would have followed Guthrie to the gallows in 1661; after all, there had been bishops before, and unlike 1638 there was no alien Prayer Book being thrust upon them (yet), or an English order of public worship; kirk sessions and the presbyterial structure were not abolished. This was not a concession but a necessity: the kirk sessions administered the poor law, supervised education, and, not least, maintained a degree of discipline in the community.

Led by Gilbert Burnet (a stout episcopalian who preferred to live in England but like many expatriates, liked the idea of Scotland staying properly 'Scottish') historians of the time, and later, depicted both Parliament and government as conducting their proceedings in an alcoholic haze. Their disapproval reflects a relaxation in official attitudes, as Commonwealth-style puritanism, if still a way of life for many people, no longer formed or coloured state policy, or needed to have lip-service paid to it. Rothes might be a notable bottle-man, but was not without culture, and plays were staged in the 'real tennis' court at Holyrood Palace, which was used as the Chancellor's official residence. They included *Marciano*, a tragi-comedy put on 'by a company of gentlemen' on St John's Night 1663.[11] Its author was William Clerke, an Edinburgh lawyer, so Mackenzie was not quite on his own in the field of letters. There were more opportunities for open rather than furtive enjoyment. The tiny, and always closely watched, publishing industry produced a few flowers as the ice age receded. It is perhaps a coincidence that George Mackenzie's pioneering novel appeared in 1660, but in the following year, Forbes's *Cantus, Songs and Fancies* was published in Aberdeen, the first printed collection of popular verse and music – a second edition came in 1666 and a third in 1682.[12] But popular sentiment is shown in the demand for what was by far the most frequently reprinted work – a stream of editions flowing from the handful of presses – the *Psalms of David*, in metrical form. Another glimpse of life in Restoration Edinburgh comes from a sermon preached by the Rev. William Thomson in the Old Church, on 29 December 1661, bemoaning the turning over of the Bible to cabaret-type exhibitions: '... for will ye but stand at the close-heads, they proclaim their wickedness, when they call on passengers, saying: "Walk in, gentlemen, and ye shall see a new piece of work; ye shall see there Adam and Eve, Cain and Abel, walking in a lively manner, to see how they were created naked, and then deceived by the serpent."'[13]

As Government intentions in the Restoration became clear, a substantial minority was left feeling cheated and angry, and fearing that worse things, in their terms, were to come. For them, Argyll and Guthrie were martyrs, and McWard the herald of a struggle that would have to be re-fought. By mid-1662 Parliament had passed the Act of Conformity, imposing 'the Book of Common Prayer, Sacraments, Rites and Ceremonies'.[14] Action was taken against ministers who preached against the imposition of bishops. John Carstairs was one, deprived of his Glasgow ministry, and colleagues 'of seditious carriage' came from widely separated districts – Ancrum, Aberdeen, Inveraray, among others. Some, including Donald Cargill, of the Barony Church, Glasgow, were sent 'north of Tay' in internal exile. One of the most vehement, John Brown, minister of Wamphray, was banished and went to join McWard in Holland. By the middle of 1663 about 270 ministers had been deprived of their livelihoods, from a total of 926 parish incumbents. More than half were in the south-west, but they also included Robert Douglas, leader of the moderate Presbyterians, who had been offered the bishopric of Edinburgh, but invoked God's curse on his one-time friend Sharp. Before long, some of them were holding services in the open air. 'Conventicling' in private houses had existed on a small scale since James VI's time[15] among those who clung to the forms of Knox and Melville – now it became widespread. Official proclamations in November 1663 forbade all such meetings and ordered all heads of families to make sure members conformed to the law.

Without direct intention, the lines of confrontation were being drawn up. Hastiness and greed on the part of Glencairn, Middleton and Rothes, anxious to rush the new programme through to show their zeal and effectiveness to the King; and jealous self-interest on the part of Lauderdale, who mistrusted these colleagues far more than he disliked such men as Douglas and Carstairs, formed one side, supported by a wide constituency of episcopalian-royalist sympathisers. Through the English Occupation, the National Covenant, like the Crown and Sceptre,[16] was effectively buried but not forgotten, and now that the brief flicker of hope at the Restoration was extinguished, those who felt pledged to the Covenant had to reassert it, or abandon it. Presbyterian ministers, once accustomed to see their authority drive the business of the state, had lost their temporal but not their spiritual power under the Protectorate – now they were being compelled to become subordinates in a Church ruled by the state. For men who considered themselves covenanted with God in his perfect Kirk, there was a great deal more at stake here than spiritual pride. To an un-doctrinaire figure like Sir Robert

Heavenly and earthly defenders of the Light of Truth: title page vignette from Kirkton's *History*, first used in *Zion's Plea* by Alexander Leighton (1630)

Moray, 'Wariston and the ministers: and their opinions and ways, were mad and dangerous.'[17] Among elders and laymen, many felt reluctant to take sides, and some found it hard to decide. Alexander Brodie, torn between Presbyterian principles, desire to keep his estate intact, and respect for the law, had a deeply uncomfortable interview with Bishop Murdo Mackenzie of Moray on 28 May 1662: '... with reluctance. I professed that the change was against my will; but God having suffered it to be brought about, the King and laws having established it, I was purposed to be as submissive and obedient and peaceable as any'.[18] This did not stop Brodie from allowing conventicles and living in a permanent fret about the evils of the time and his own sinfulness.

Only one man really strove for a time to reconcile the factions and to win over the people to a reasoned tolerance, and he got neither thanks nor results for his pains. Robert Leighton, Master since 1653 of Edinburgh University, had reluctantly allowed himself to be made a bishop in 1661, at the age of 50, deliberately taking the most impoverished see of Dunblane. He kept his distance from Sharp, attending Parliament only when church affairs were under discussion. Leighton, strongly attracted by the meditative and mystic aspects of religious belief, had a sense, quite modern for his time, that there were many ways to God and that a specific type of church organisation, or form of worship, was not a pre-requisite in the matter. A church historian notes rather sniffily that he 'was scarcely a theologian at all',[19] but if Leighton had been a theologian in the sense intended, he would have been another faction-fighter like his father (author of *Sion's Plea Against the Prelacy*, condemned to whipping, ear-cropping and nose-slitting in Charles I's England). He had abandoned the Presbyterians in despair at their intolerance and narrowness of vision, but without becoming an adversary. Gilbert Burnet, a disciple and admirer, says that he 'had generally the reputation of a saint, and of something above human nature in him',[20] and a historian from the other camp concedes that he was 'very much superior to his fellows'.[21] Leighton's urge was for solitary study, away from the rage of controversy on 'the useless debates and contentions that abound in the world'.[22] Unlike the retreat commended in George Mackenzie's literary and considered Neo-Stoicism, this arose from a genuine religious passion. While Sharp set out to exalt the authority of the bishops, in parallel to the autocratic style of the government, Leighton tried to harmonise his own role with that of the presbyteries in his diocese and to make it easy for stiff-necked Presbyterian ministers and elders to accept him as a colleague rather than a superior. His approach was criticised by Sharp, who deprecated 'parting by own consent with the rights of the episcopal order'.[23]

The outed ministers had to be replaced with qualified men who were willing to work under the episcopal dispensation. A large stock was available, of university graduates who were working as school teachers, private tutors, session clerks, and precentors, in parishes up and down the country. Suddenly to these ill-paid men a change in status and salary was available: to some perhaps it was a chance to fulfil their vocations and work for their beliefs. A furious propaganda storm arose with the appointment of these 'curates'. They were inexperienced as parish ministers and perhaps some were opportunists ready to take an oath of allegiance to episcopacy in order to get a career. Leighton wrote of them contemptuously as 'a great many owls and satyrs'.[24] Whatever their talents, two things wrecked any chance of success. They were imposed on parishes which had not chosen them, and the deprived ministers, despite being forbidden to come within 20 miles of their former parishes, remained a formidable and antagonistic presence. Many of the curates came from 'north of Tay', regions traditionally friendly to episcopal rule. A presbyterian sneer[25] that northern gentlemen could no longer find lads to keep their cows is of interest today only as the first recorded reference to cowboys employed in posts for which they had no qualification. Efforts were made to attract able men: Gilbert Burnet records that though only 19 in 1662, he was urged by Glencairn in person 'to go into any of the vacant churches that I liked'[26] (he desisted), but the introduction of the curates was a major step towards civil disruption. Conventicles became more frequent, and a sense of defiance grew stronger. Looking back on events, Sir George Mackenzie marked this episode as the real start of the 'troubles': 'Blam'd by all wise and good men, as tending to irritate a country which was fond of its ministers.'[27]

In an age when only males were formally educated and held public offices, it is not easy to assess the full part played by women. But from the legendary stool-hurling by 'Jenny Geddes' in 1637, when the Prayer Book was first read in the cathedral of St Giles, it is evident that they had a powerful role in the Covenanting and Presbyterian section of the community. From 1662, with the great majority of the nobles and gentry backing government policy, support of presbyterianism was a popular cause in the real sense of the word. Since the greatest number of outed ministers had been in the south-west, it was there that the curates were most numerous, and the consequent unrest greatest. In Irongray and Kirkcudbright, women led demonstrations against curates, even when these were supported by troops. The Irongray leader, Margaret Smith, was sentenced to be shipped to the Barbados plantations, 'but she told her tale so innocently, that our lords were ashamed to execute it'.[28] Normally, the only women who appeared in courts of law were those excluded from or peripheral to the community, as suspected witches, or through disorderly behaviour, but these women were at the centre of local life. The Council quickly got over its reluctance to proceed against them, and whippings, imprisonment, brandings and transportation became regular punishments. With an edge of male prejudice, Kirkton calls these woman a 'rabble' and the term 'bangster Amazons' comes from this time, to describe women agitators.[29]

The more the Covenanting cause sank to parish and family level, the greater became the importance of women within it. The fervency of the preachers may have played a part; perhaps also the greater democracy of a movement to which adherence was becoming a matter of family or individual choice. For women of the land-owning class, punishments were normally imprisonment or attempts to fine them or their husbands. The latter, with more to lose by way of property in fines and forfeitures, often allowed their wives to house outlawed preachers, or attend conventicles; often, too, the wives acted on their own initiative. Margaret Dalrymple, Lady Stair, was by no means untypical at a time when, with their husbands often away, the wives of lairds or lords ruled their own homes in formidable style. Their activities were well-known to the authorities. When John Graham of Claverhouse began his police operations in 1678 by destroying a new presbyterian meeting house disguised as a barn, he wrote to his commander-in-chief that: 'So perished the charity of many ladies.'[30] According to one Covenant chronicler, even Rothes's wife was a covert sympathiser who gave refuge on occasion to fugitive non-conformers.[31] Without the active sympathy and support of very many women, at all levels of society, the cause of Presbytery would have been lost between 1662 and 1688.

Confronted with protest and disorder, even on a relatively modest and localised scale, the executive headed by Glencairn, Middleton and Rothes reacted crudely and bluntly with repressive measures. It also became increasingly obsessed with proving and enforcing loyalty at every level. In 1661 Sir James Dalrymple, a valuable man, had found it possible to become a judge without signing any declaration that showed him in favour of episcopacy – and hence of royal control of the Church. Sir James had signed the Covenant like everyone else, but in 1651 he had also put his name to one of the documents of Remonstrance.[32] In 1664 he resigned his position as a judge rather than sign a declaration of loyalty that embraced episcopacy. The outcome was a summons to the court of Charles II in London, where Sir James was permitted to sign a declaration which emphasised his loyalty to the King, with his own reservations on matters relating to the governance of the Kirk.[33] Armed with this and the support of Lauderdale, he was restored to his seat in the Court of Session, which cannot have given pleasure to the trio of earls who considered themselves in charge of affairs. In June he was made a baronet. Between his audience with the King and his return to Edinburgh in late May, he spent five weeks in France, accompanied by his eldest son John, then aged 16: a visit perhaps in the interest of John's legal studies.

CHAPTER TEN

Improvement and Reaction

AN ENGLISH HISTORIAN, SOMETHING of a Scot-baiter, described Scotland at this time as not merely politically, economically and socially backward, but inert, stifled by religiosity.[1] But in the politics of the time, religion was not an optional side-dish but – for good or ill – central on the plate of daily life, and the educated laymen, and women, of Scotland were, in this sense, among the most highly politicised populations in the world. The political dimension was very real. Andrew Melville had bluntly informed King James VI in 1592, that in Scotland there were two kingdoms, and James's was the inferior one.[2] Among the Scots the conviction remained that the Kingdom of God had an earthly province in their 'perfect Kirk', whose rights no terrestrial king should challenge, and whose remit ultimately included the fate of that king if he should step beyond God's path, as defined by the Kirk. Reinforced by the National Covenant, in that idea lay the core of all the long bitter dispute which was re-inflamed by the reintroduction of bishops in 1662.

The concept of a constitutional king was perfectly familiar in the 17th century, but its very existence prompted counter-arguments for royal absolutism. Louis XIV of France, 26 in 1664, could already say, '*L'état, c'est moi.*' Not only parliaments, where they existed, could feel threatened, but all corporations, churches, social goups and classes that possessed traditional rights and liberties. England's civil war, in which Scotland had so confidently and disastrously embroiled itself, had been fought around such a conflict of interests; and Charles II, despite struggles with the Westminster Parliament, never went as far in England as he did in Scotland to rule by proclamation, force of arms, and state-managed terror tactics. Scottish laws allowed him far more latitude than did those of England.

Absolute monarchy, a centralised dictatorial kingship, was not only a philosophical idea, most recently elaborated in England by Thomas Hobbes in *Leviathan* (1651), and an aristocratic reaction against the way in which people of 'the meaner sort' were increasingly seeking to manage or influence state affairs, but to some extent a response to the new problems of governing a country whose economy was beginning to diversify and in which industry was increasingly an employer of labour, a consumer of resources and a source of wealth. In Scotland, a small government organisation, centred on the accepted role and authority of the king, had relied on the realm's territorial magnates to maintain order, administer justice, and provide the bulk of the national army when called upon. Such dependence had often been precarious, and even in the time of Charles II's grandfather, a faction of powerful men could possess themselves of the king's person and try to dictate policy for their own purposes. Charles himself had experienced something similar in the hands of the Covenanters, and he was well aware that they did not represent the entire nation.

Parliament House, Edinburgh, in the 17th Century
Reproduced from *Cassell's Old & New Edinburgh*

By the middle of the 17th century, the old system was, apart from its inherent weaknesses, incapable of sustaining the state. In a trend already 100 years old, the basis of aristocratic power had shifted, from numbers of dependants and fighting men to the productivity of land and sea, yielding resources, contributed by tenants and sub-tenants in lieu of cash, that had to be converted into money, which could then be invested in new ventures. A 'Guinea Company of Scotland', for trading to Africa, was founded in 1636, though it was a failure.[3] In 1637 Lord Lorne had set up salt-pans at Machrihanish in Kintyre, with locally mined coal as fuel, and the Earls of Sutherland had already done the same at Brora.[4] Throughout the century, efforts were being made, in the *Gaidhealtachd* as well as the Lowlands, to exploit the country's range of natural resources, to establish and improve markets, and to upgrade the methods of financial transaction. Timber, fisheries, coal, salt, cattle, grain and flax were vital sources of individual livelihoods and of proprietors' wealth, and the landowners, however preoccupied by other issues, could not afford to ignore their management. In the early 1700s, even as he was grappling in London with constitutional problems, the Earl of Seafield was in constant touch with his chamberlain back in Banffshire about grain prices.[5]

'Improvement' in commercial and industrial methods incorporated its own forward drive, revealing new potentials for wealth-building. New technology in pumping enabled deep coal mines to be sunk in Fife and Lothian, and wagonways were laid to carry coal to new or extended harbours in places like Dysart and Port Seton. In the same areas, the boiling-out of coarse salt from sea-water was an important industry. Glasgow and Edinburgh merchants were involved in the growing West Indies sugar trade, and small factories, such as soap and glass works – products indicative of social development – were being set up. The chain of activities involved in the cottage-based wool and linen industries needed management and social stability. Addiction to tobacco, chewed, smoked in pipes, but mostly snuffed, was spreading through the population, creating wealth along the supply-line. Increase in money transactions had enabled the Covenanter Government to levy its innovatory excise of January 1643. Now a substantial new issue of copper and silver coins was made, with 23 million (mostly low value) struck between 1663 and 1686. Indeed the Mint well exceeded its authorised issues. But foreign trade required gold, and no gold coins had been produced since 1642.[6] Obstruction by more powerful competitors (not only English) often frustrated Scottish enterprise or forced it along devious routes: 'The idea was to infiltrate the empires of England and other powerful European states at the level of the individual merchant, soldier, official and investor' – Professor Devine calls this 'imperialism by stealth',[7] though it may have been seen as hardly better than parasitism at the time. Smuggling was also a growth industry, often run by syndicates of local lairds.

Agriculture, by far the most important economic activity, was still practised in ways increasingly seen by the modern-minded as inefficient and insufficiently productive. Improvement began with the planting of trees and orchards around the lairds' houses, and the extension of gardens. Parliaments after 1660, reflecting the concerns of landowners, provided for enclosing of common land, and regulation of the grain trade with Ireland. Much of the impetus came from the 'new' nobility whose titles dated from after 1603, and their extended families. They had no great landholdings, but their land was usually of the more fertile kind, and to maintain their comforts and status they had to consider how to make soil and people productive on their behalf. The conclusions were not necessarily socially progressive: they were responsible for the reintroduction of serfdom, when in successive acts of parliament between 1606 and the end of the century, the status of the colliery and salt workers, men, women and children, was reduced to make them the property of the mine and salt-pan owners. The collier 'became a piece of mining equipment that could be bought, sold and inherited by his master'.[8] Though their children were theoretically born free, the practice of 'arling', pledging of the child's future bondage for a small gift, ensured a continuing supply of bonded labour. In some important fishing districts, like the Tay estuary, controlled by the Earl of Errol, boatmen were also forced into this condition;[9] and an Act of Parliament of 1663, noting that 'vagabonds and idle persons do yet so much abound', authorised the owners of factories to press such people into service.[10] No public protest was made about this revival of medieval practice: 'church and state alike saw it as a simple and admirable way out of an economic dilemma'.[11] Discipline and punishments in these closely policed small industrial communities were brutal. In a – very small scale – anticipation of the gulag-type system, convicted religious dissidents were occasionally sold to the coal-owners, though it was more usual to send them across the Atlantic, or sell them to recruiters for foreign armies.

For government too, management of new processes required new procedures. Historical writing's focus on politics, religion and rebellion obscures the degree to which the parliament, the Council and the judiciary saw their real business in matters of land-ownership and sale, landlord-tenant disputes, inheritance settlements, customs revenues, granting of trading and manufacturing licences, the rights of burghs, fixing of prices for all sorts of goods, adjudicating in trade disputes, and the taxing of new commodities. These were perpetual concerns. A lengthy list of export items and the duty (in ounces of silver bullion) payable on them, made for Parliament in June 1661, includes whisky in 10-gallon barrels, drinking glasses by the gross, night-caps likewise, paper by the 40 reams, plaiding by the 100 yards, and oysters by the 20,000, as well as animal horns, skins, wool, coal and other products and materials.[12]

All this made a centralised administration essential, along with a cadre of officials to cope with the increasing work-load and to keep proper records. Normal practice allowed men in power to allot official posts to their relations and associates, and these men in turn could use their positions for personal gain. Lauderdale secured charge of the Mint for his brother Charles Maitland, Lord Hatton, and later also the customs collections, and deployed his patronage in many less lucrative appointments. Since government had to expand, this seemed the most natural and workable method – here again Scotland was simply copying the practice of countries like France and England, where the mechanisms of capitalism were being worked out. 'Corruption' was not seen in quite the same light as today. 'Compliments' to judges of the court of session, whether as money or gifts of wine or fine cloth, were expected, and, coming from both sides in civil cases, were supposed not to affect their judgement. If not done to excess, these things were permissible (though, as John Graham would discover, the fluidity of the rules could be hardened against an official who fell from grace).

Hand in hand with the state's increasing emphasis on information-gathering in commercial matters went its urge to monitor and control public life. But all sorts of limitations – traditional practice, wayward loyalties, personal interests, inefficiencies, and the age-old ability of the 'robbers' to anticipate the 'cops' ensured that the Stuart monarchy was never as absolute as it wished to be.

The hand of central government was lightest in the Highlands and Islands, though it could fall weightily there on occasion. After the Restoration, the garrisons and courts of Monck's time were removed, and earls, chiefs and lairds resumed their sway. Most were supporters of the new regime in any case. The administration's attitude was inconsistent: most of all it wanted to ensure the Highland shires paid their full share of taxes,[13] and it inherited old Lowland prejudices against the customs and speech of Gaeldom. Yet it needed friends to maintain a sufficient degree of law and order to enable tax collection and guard against the spread of conventicling. A committee was set up by the Privy Council in July 1661 to monitor Highland activities, and named chiefs were required to appear each 1 October to report on the good order of their dependants. With most estates heavily encumbered by debt, many were reluctant to make these visits for fear of arrest by their creditors. In as far as this combination of *laisser-faire* and periodic demands for accountability had a general effect, it was to encourage the process by which patriarchal chiefs and their clan *fine*, or elite, were becoming conventional landlords. The resulting tensions and resentments were exacerbated by the activities of certain small clan groups, notably in Lochaber and the adjoining region stretching down through Glen Coe to the old MacGregor territory. Squeezed and vulnerable between the encroaching Campbell powers of Argyll and Glenorchy, they fended for themselves by short-lived alliances, cattle raids and protection rackets. Often they allied themselves with 'cateran' gangs of no territorial base, who were out-and-out bandits. Just how troublesome they were is not easy to gauge, but undoubtedly their enemies and victims made the most of it in complaining. It was always easy to represent the Highlands as more lawless and unruly than the reality. In August 1667 the Earl of Atholl was authorised to set up an Independent Company[14] of militia in order to watch the foothills, and such bands were to be the government's main resource in policing the region south of the Great Glen.

Reactionary politics accompanied the moves towards commercial expansion. Following the re-installation of the bishops as an estate of Parliament, in 1663 the Lords of the Articles were re-established, on the old basis: the bishops chose 8 nobles, the 8 nobles chose 8 bishops, and these 16 then chose 8 from the burgesses and from the shire commissioners. With a parliamentary attendance normally varying between 150 and 190, the 32 'Articles' were the only members allowed to discuss legislation until a bill had been framed and presented.

By July 1663 the scale of conventicles was such that the Government felt compelled to take further action: new laws imposed a schedule of fines on people who failed to attend worship in their own parish churches: a quarter of a year's rent for noblemen or heritors (property owners), a quarter of their moveable possessions for tenants, farmers, and burgesses. Normally, such fines would have been levied by the landowner, but too many of the gentry were known to be openly or covertly sympathetic with the non-conformers for that to be a realistic option. Instead, troops were used, under the command of Sir James Turner, the hard-riding, hard-drinking veteran (son of a Kirk minister), who had campaigned in the Highlands with Leslie in 1647, and appeared briefly in the anti-Cromwell campaign of 1654. He never signed the Covenant, even though he notes in a comment with chilling modern reverberations, 'I would have made no bones to take, swear and sign it, and observe it too; for I had then a principle, having not yet studied a better one, that I wronged not my conscience in doing anything I was commanded to do by those whom I served.'[15] To Burnet, 'he knew no other rule but to obey orders'.[16] When sober and off-duty, he was also a man of culture and wide reading – not an untypical combination of qualities for the time (or later). Turner had to account to the Privy Council for what he had collected, and his expenses; it was March 1665 before his accounts for 1663 were cleared.[17] Military enthusiasm for catching defaulters and hunting down conventicles sharpened local hostility to the 'curates' who often passed information to Turner's officers. In addition to paying fines, the better-off inhabitants had to provide free living quarters, stabling and food for the troopers and their horses, as there were no barracks. This first escalation of government action against the non-conformers did not succeed in stopping conventicles or even reducing their frequency; the area was wide, the number of dragoon troops small, and the capacity of the people for contumacity great.

CHAPTER ELEVEN

'I did see the outlaw Whigs Lye Scattered'

THE UNEASY ALLIANCE BETWEEN the executive earls in Edinburgh and Lauderdale in Whitehall fell apart in 1662 with the 'billetting affair', a wheeze of Middleton and the other Sir George Mackenzie. A cousin of the advocate, six years older, known as Mackenzie of Tarbat from his Ross-shire home, he was more politician than lawyer, a usually adroit operator who made one of his rare slip-ups here. An act of indemnity for Scotland, removing the threat of trial for those on the wrong side in the 'troubles' was at last being drawn up. Middleton convinced the King that Parliament should be allowed to exclude from indemnity the 12 persons deemed to be least deserving of it: these were to be selected by a ballot, each member naming 12 persons. By dint of heavy persuasion, it was ensured that the name of Lauderdale – one-time Covenanter – was high on the final list of the dirty dozen. The plan blew up when Lauderdale got advance warning of it and complained to the King. Middleton and Tarbat, having sped to London with their ballot result, got an icy reception, and the scheme was dumped. Another enterprise of Middleton's, an act compelling people to purchase their indemnity, at a total cost exceeding £Sc1,000,000, also had to be abandoned. In March 1663 Middleton was deprived of his Scottish posts and eventually despatched to govern Tangier. Rothes became Commissioner to Parliament, and Lauderdale continued as Secretary of State. In June, Lord Lorne was released from imprisonment, and on 16 October he was confirmed as ninth Earl of Argyll, with the (heavily in the red) Campbell patrimony restored.

Scotland could have no foreign policy, as this was in the hands of the King, conducted in his own and England's interests, in that order. The Council invoked the ancient Franco-Scottish alliance in a letter to Charles of September 1663, informing him that, 'in the year 1558, when the dolphin of France was married to Mary, then queen of Scotland, there was a reciprocal naturalization of the subjects of either kingdom, ratified and recorded here in parliament'.[1] Scottish merchants had been having troubles with French tax-farmers and customs collectors, and on grounds of their special status under the old treaty, the King was asked to graciously intercede with His Majesty of France on their behalf. He did nothing.[2]

Under Rothes, the bishops took more part in affairs, particularly the two archbishops, Sharp in St Andrews and Alexander Burnet in Glasgow (not a relation of Gilbert Burnet the memorialist). At the beginning of 1664 a Court of High Commission was set up, to try anyone suspected of offences against the discipline and order of the Church. It was empowered to levy fines, half to go to 'pious uses',[3] half to finance its own costs; and to order imprisonment and internal exile, as far away as Shetland. This new body was very busy, and took a good deal of 'the ordinary work of persecution'[4] off the Privy Council, which however still dealt with more prominent offenders. Sharp wanted a role in the executive, preferably as Chancellor, and maintained his own line of communication to London, with a stream of complaints about Glencairn, the actual holder of that office. When Glencairn died in 1664, however, Rothes was given the chancellorship, which satisfied Sharp 'who governed Lord Rothes, who abandoned himself to pleasure',[5] according to Gilbert Burnet. But Gilbert was among Sharp's many enemies. Archbishop Burnet, whose diocese reached into the south-west, was primarily concerned to step up the level of campaigning against the dissident Presbyterians.

Those people on whom the Council spent so much time were identified en bloc as 'Phanatiques,' whose actions, because they transgressed laws made against them, laid them open to charges of sedition. 'Fanatic', a 16th-century borrowing from Rabelais's French, has a root meaning 'of the temple', thus God-driven. But now it became a label for determined dissidence. Fanatics are always other people. The public good, historical precedent, formal expression of the constitution of the state – these produced the King's policy; its opponents, therefore, were wild people, of distorted belief and mentality. The more they resisted coercion, the more they were seen as fanatical. Surviving testimonies are from those who appeared before the Council, or whose words are recorded by contemporary diarists and historians, who tended to be the leaders or the most committed in their views. Ordinary people who tramped miles to listen, who stood in the cold while the voice of the preacher rose and fell on the wind, who sang their psalms to the hilltops – foot-soldiers of a small and forlorn crusade (who considered the sign of the Cross as a totem and therefore wicked) – what moved them? Loyalty to a deprived minister? Indignation that a bishop should govern their presbyteries? Protest against an earthly king interfering with what properly concerned only the ministers of God? Fear that the Westminster Catechisms would be taken from them? Perhaps a lingering zeal for the Solemn League and Covenant and the conversion of England and Ireland?

A Field Communion
Reproduced from Anderson, *Ladies of the Covenant*

Such questions are not rhetorical: we know from Gilbert Burnet's personal experience[6] that the folk of the south-west knew their Bibles and argued from the scriptures with skill and force: they felt themselves to be the latter-day People of the Book. He also noted that they had acquired a taste for salty controversy and politics in their religion: they 'loved to hear the ministers preach to the times, as they called it'.[7] And a culture of hatred was already a generation old in the 1660s, among children who had been brought up to regard 'Malignants' as loathsome, as if there were something vile and unclean inside them. But that there was a genuine feeling of grievance, a real wish to preserve important things seen to be under threat, cannot be doubted. Something precious and pure, personal as well as communal, was perceived within the rites of the Presbyterian Kirk.

Originally the whole nation – as it seemed – had rallied to the Covenant, but now only a handful of the nobility were still true to it and the rest preferred to keep in with the King and enlarge their 'pensions' or their commercial interests. Many churchmen were also seen as backsliders, and the withdrawal of so many men of position and influence left an angry sense of abandonment among the rank and file. Government policy baffled them as much as they baffled the government: loyal by nature, they were happy to give the King his due, in harmony with their beliefs; and it was the King who had started the troubles. Matters were exacerbated by the repression policy. It did not accord with the grain of people stubborn by nature and conscious of possessing things hard-won and worked for, to give in simply because a lieutenant of dragoons, backed up by muskets, forced them to pay a fine for an action they considered lawful and no business of his. For those who had lost large sums or seen their lands taken away, there was the thought that if they persisted, a change of policy and regime might come about – under the King – and they would be able to claim restitution (after 1688, many were able to do so). Also there was a question of honour: having been compelled to hand over his coin, goods or home to a political and personal adversary, no man could retain his self-respect, or the community's esteem, if he then joined, or gave acceptance to, that other's cause. Each time a fine was paid, or the roughness of the troops endured, the pattern of resistance was reinforced. Some people proved willing to face death for the cause, not only in the hot hazard of battle, but facing the cold inevitability of the gallows or the musket barrels – in them, belief and commitment had become a condition of mind which transcended eveything else. The price of their beliefs was set by their enemies, not by themselves, and, fatalistically or otherwise, they were ready to pay it. Long before the 'Killing Time', Samuel Rutherford had reminded them of whom he saw as their great exemplars: 'Christ, the prophets, and apostles of our Lord, went to heaven in the note of traitors, seditious men, and as such turned the world upside down...'[8] Day by day, the relationship between dissidents and government slipped hopelessly into a mire of done deeds, hard resentments, accusations and counter-accusations, and propaganda which becomes accepted fact on each side.

One of the first heavy shots in the propaganda war was fired in 1665 from Holland by John Brown, with *An Apologeticall Relation of the Particular Sufferings of Faithful Ministers and Professours of the Church of Scotland*. More concerned to stiffen the backbones of the nonconformers than to win new recruits, it sets the form and tone for books to come, recording the persecutions of the Presbyterians and setting out their 'testimony'. Promptly banned by the authorities, it was circulated and read clandestinely. For a people with respect for books and learning, here was their book, with their names and places, their stories, just like the Israelites of old; and the printed words gave their cause a sense of objective authority.

For three years the stagnant impasse would continue, bringing to those involved misery, exasperation and suffering as well as moments of excitement, comradeship and exaltation. The majority of the nation, sympathetic or not, were not involved. Some of the outed ministers had had churches in Edinburgh, Glasgow and other towns, but agitation was largely confined to south-western country districts. This is not to say that the towns did not harbour a strong and occasionally vocal Presbyterian element, but the citizenry whose ancestors had run with the Protestant storm in 1560 and whose fathers had been full of the Covenant in 1638, did not turn out for the sake of Presbytery when the opportunity arose late in 1666. Most people lived their own lives, like John Graham, the young laird of Claverhouse, among his kinsfolk in Forfarshire, or Richard Cameron, teaching the schoolboys of Falkland how to do sums and sing in tune.

In many ways the 1660s were a good time, with food cheap, and trade generally, if modestly, on the increase; though external war sometimes interfered. Glasgow's burgesses began the construction of a deep-water harbour at Port Glasgow, to develop their Atlantic trade. England's war with Holland in 1664–67 made commerce with Scotland's main trading partner very difficult, and at one point, Rothes was sufficiently concerned about the country's finances and lack of circulating money to consider publishing the national accounts, if they could be seen only by Scots merchants, 'that our poverty might not be blazed through the world'.[9] John Nicoll recorded that, 'Upon the 12 February 1666 new wine came out of France to Leith, both strong and stark, the like whereof has not been seen these many years bypast, but at a very dear price, sold at two merks the pint, by reason of the great danger they had by sea, being compassed with Hollanders, as also in respect that the King of France had denounced [declared] war with England and Scotland.'[10] But the rebuilding of London after the Great Fire, and English naval expansion, improved the market for Scottish timber.[11] Although there were a couple of hard winters, no famine was recorded, and the plague that beset London and parts of England in 1665, to the unseemly satisfaction of some Scots,[12] had less effect in Scotland. Steps were taken to counter it: the Council decreed that no-one should be allowed to enter Scotland from affected places without a 'testimonial' of health.[13]

Further forays by Sir James Turner in the south-west, in March 1666, mulcted the non-conformers of some £Sc50,000[14] apart from the costs of quartering his troops. The official collector and receiver of fines was Sir William Bruce, a financier of talent, even genius; later the principal tax farmer, contracting with the Government to collect a fixed sum, and entitled to keep the surplus, enabling him to pursue his prime interest, in contemporary architecture and gardens. In 1665–66 there had been political in-fighting between Sharp and Rothes, and Lauderdale; the archbishop demanding more punitive action against dissidents, while Lauderdale managed to close down Sharp's detested High Commission, which in its zeal had perhaps been stepping too close to the Privy Council's prickly sense of its own authority.

With England at war with Holland, and rumours of invasion rife,[15] it was now decided to set up a standing army. Two regiments of foot were raised in the summer of 1666, making around 3,000 men with the existing forces, and six new troops of horse. The only previous standing army, under the Commonwealth, had been paid for by general taxation, but it was intended to defray the high cost of the new force through the fines it would levy on the dissidents. As before, an experienced general was found from among mercenary officers who had served European potentates, in this case Thomas Dalyell, of a West Lothian landed family, a royalist who had fought at Worcester, and subsequently in the Polish wars of the Russian Tsar Alexei I. Hale and vigorous for his 67 years, a touch of cavalier eccentricity was shown by his long, white beard, which he had (allegedly) sworn never to trim again after the execution of Charles I, though he also nourished a more sinister reputation for violence in dealing with 'Turks and Tartars'. Some pro-Presbyterians have seen the raising of this army as a deliberate provocation, but after several years of ineffectual repression, the Government had to step up its campaign. The field preachers had become more vehement and their supporters more militant. If the spirit of dissent were to spread more widely, things could very quickly get out of control.

McWard and Brown had been trying to promote a Presbyterian rising in the summer of 1666.[16] But their efforts had no direct link with the flash-point that came on 15 November, when a group of Dumfriesshire lairds and tenants, some of whom had been involved in a fracas with troopers at Dalry in Galloway two days earlier, resolved to strike at Sir James Turner before he struck back at them. Surprised in his nightgown at Dumfries with only a handful of troops, Turner was made a prisoner. With no thought of a general rising and certainly no plan for one, the raiders paused at the Cross of Dumfries to drink the King's health. Rothes was in London, and the Council, headed in his absence by Sharp, made hasty preparations against what they took to be a rebellion. Express messengers were sent to the King, and to loyal nobles; Dalyell was instructed to march with all available men to Glasgow; the bridge at Stirling and river ferries were guarded to prevent Presbyterian sympathisers from coming south. Turner's captors, debating whether to shoot him or not, found themselves on a slippery slope. They had seen their action as a loyal protest against military oppression; now to extend it into rebellion was the only option other than disbanding and waiting arrest. On the 21st, an official proclamation denounced the rising and said nothing about indemnity for any who surrendered. The leaders appealed for support, with mostly discouraging results, but by the 22nd they had enough men to form something resembling an army, with officers in charge of companies, under the command of an experienced soldier, Colonel James Wallace.

They resolved to march towards Edinburgh, in the hope of gaining further numbers on the way. The days were short, it was cold, and rain fell almost incessantly, making the going along rutted tracks very difficult. At Douglas, a council of war seriously considered dispersal, but one of the reasons offered for giving up, the suddenness of it all, was turned in the opposite sense – surely it was a sign from God? With God on their side, even a small force might work great things. Had He not even stayed the sun's motion to help the children of Israel? Numerous outed Presbyterian ministers were with them, including John Carstairs, reportedly a reluctant attender, opposed to the venture, in the company of his more militant brother-in-law, William Mure of Caldwell.[17] But it was decided to go on, and a cause was proclaimed, the restoration of the Covenants. Still squabbling about Turner's fate, they squelched on through the sodden countryside.

Edinburgh was 'all in arms against them: Sir Andrew Ramsay, the provost, very active; not ane advocate almost but he is in his bandileers';[18] even the judges of the Court of Session had formed a somewhat slipshod platoon. It was very different to the city's tame acquiescence in the Whiggamore Raid of 1648. To most people, the Whigs and their actions had been something of concern only to the Government; now they were on the march, an active threat to civic well-being. Rumours, officially sponsored or spontaneous, exaggerated their number and ferocity, and suggested that a Dutch invasion fleet was coming to support them. Even those who sympathised with their beliefs thought the enterprise was doomed, and kept within doors. At its greatest, the army of the Covenant may have reached about 3,000, but in the course of another dismal night of rain and sleet, at Bathgate, resolutely ignored by the inhabitants, around half of them straggled away. Next day, the residue pressed on, as far as Colinton, west of Edinburgh, from where they could glimpse the power of the state: the embattled castle and the outlying defenders. Dalyell, they knew, was advancing from the west. The Duke of Hamilton, whose own called-up men had earlier dispersed a band which had hoped to join the Covenanters, sent an emissary to plead with them to give up, in the hope of an indemnity, and Wallace sent messages to him and to Dalyell, indicating that they would accept terms of surrender if their grievances would be considered. Dalyell forwarded his letter to the Council, and got a firm reply from Sharp: '... all they can expect is... if they lay should down their arms, and come in to your excellency within the time appointed, they might petition for mercy.'[19] Nothing having been agreed, Dalyell maintained his advance, and the Covenanters, barely 900 of them, retreated along the eastern flank of the Pentland Hills.

On 28 November, at Rullion Green, they paused to regroup and to continue parleying.[20] But Dalyell went straight in to attack, and though the Covenanters' cavalry made a fight of it, the resolve of Wallace's foot soldiers, ill-armed and exhausted, collapsed before the musket-fire of the regulars. Turner, still a prisoner, saw it all, and heard 'Mr Welsh and Mr Semple cry out loudly and very often, 'The God of Jacob! The God of Jacob!' I asked them [his guards] what they meant. They answered, Could I not see the Lord of Hosts was fighting for them?'[21] Turner said they could pistol him if all was not over within a quarter of an hour. Darkness was coming on, and most of the insurgents fled into the night; about 50 had been killed and another 50 were captured. Dalyell's losses were negligible. Wallace left the scene with John Welsh, and took refuge in Holland, as, probably, did John Carstairs.

So ended the unintentional 'insurrection', the closest thing to a popular revolt Scotland had yet seen. No lord added the lustre of his name to it, and none of its leaders were men of national standing. Although the ministers were quickly drawn to it, its immediate origin lay in the resentment against fines and the aggressive methods employed by troopers to enforce payment or obtain quarters, food, and drink for themselves. Its Covenanting label was adopted only after the rising had started. The Whiggamores' isolation and lack of organisation were apparent, and popular reaction outside their own community was jeering contempt, as in a contemporary verse on 'The Covenanters' Army at Rullion Green':[22]

> '... I did see the outlaw Whigs
> Lye scattered up and down the rigs,
> Some had hoggars, some straw boots,   [footless stockings]
> Some uncovered legs and coots,   [ankles]
> Some had halbards, some had durks,   [daggers]
> Some had crooked swords like Turks,
> Some had slings, and some had flails,
> Knit with eel and oxen tails,
> Some had spears and some had pikes,
> Some had spades which delvit dykes...'

Their own justification, in homely bardic style, was seen in an inscription later set above the buried bodies:[23]

'A Cloud of Witnesses lie here,
Who for Christ's interest did appear,
For to restore true Liberty,
O'erturned then by tyranny:
These Heroes fought with great renown,
By falling got the Martyr's crown.'

Sharp, still acting President of the Council, pushed forwards prosecution of the prisoners on capital charges, despite their claim, apparently backed by Dalyell,[24] that they had been granted quarter on the battlefield and so their lives should not be at hazard. For their defence the Council accorded them the not inconsiderable figures of Sir George Lockhart and Sir George Mackenzie with two others. Mackenzie put the case for clemency, as they had been granted quarter on the field of battle: pointing out that if it were now denied, no-one would trust a guarantee of quarter again, and many lives would be lost unnecessarily.[25] But on the score that the prisoners were participants not in a just war, but merely an act of sedition, and so were not subject to accepted rules of war, they were condemned, and ten were hanged at the Cross of Edinburgh on 7 December. The right arms they had raised at Lanark, to salute the Covenant, were cut off and sent to that town to be exhibited.[26] A special commission was issued on 5 December empowering the Duke of Hamilton, the Marquis of Montrose and 21 other notables, any three making a quorum, to hold courts in any shire, burgh or place to try those who had been involved in the rising, or had supported them in any way, and to inflict the full penalty of the law. Some were hanged in Glasgow as a result, and it was here that the custom began of ordering drum-rolls to make final speeches inaudible, if they were 'seditious'.[27] About 30 men were hanged; the others, around 50, were transported to Barbados. A massive round of finings and forfeitings also ensued, with Sir William Bannatyne said to be worse in Galloway than Turner had been in Dumfries-shire.[28] Mure of Caldwell's estate was forfeited and awarded to General Dalyell. Mr Carstairs's name appeared on the list of those forfeited.

CHAPTER TWELVE
Naphtali and *Caelia*

LATE IN 1667 A NEW book was published in support of the Covenanters' cause, bringing the *Apologeticall Relation* up to date. Though immediately banned, and publicly burned, it was widely read. Its title, *Naphtali*, shows a more sophisticated touch than Brown's, referring to the Book of Genesis in which Jacob described his son Naphtali as: '... a hind let loose; he giveth goodly words', and its anonymous authors were James Stewart of Goodtrees, aged 32, son of a former Provost of Edinburgh, who 'did the reasoning', and James Stirling, minister of Paisley, who wrote the historical part.[1] The rising had a backlash for Sir James Turner, who, by his own account, was made a scapegoat with the excuse that 'my severity, or at best my indiscreet zeal, had occasioned the commotion'. To his indignation, *Naphtali's* records of the fines he had exacted, which he claimed were wildly exaggerated, and other accusations, were officially quoted against him. In his memoirs, he explained why he would not produce his written instructions: 'this I was sensible of, that the showing them might wrong my lord chancellor [Rothes], and do me no good, for I was told I was liable to punishment for giving obedience to illegal commands.'[2] Turner was eventually deprived of his commission, though exonerated from the charges of excessive fining and misuse of the money. He became a retainer of the Duke of Hamilton, showing one of that nobleman's problems: in his 'tail' there were men whose views ranged from Turner's indifference to religion but sturdy royalism, to others' strong presbyterianism and suspicion of the king.

George Mackenzie also had leisure to write, and his flow of publications suggests an ambition to become Scotland's moral philosopher. He took no side as yet; another essay, *Solitude Preferred to Public Employment*, was suitably dedicated in 1665 to John Lindsay, Earl of Crawford, one of the few overt pro-Presbyterians in high office, who had just resigned from the Privy Council on which he had been Treasurer, while *Moral Gallantry* was effusively dedicated in 1666 to the dissolute Rothes. In 1667 came *A Moral Paradox: maintaining That it is*

Sir George Mackenzie of Rosehaugh, in 1665
Reproduced from Lang, *Sir George Mackenzie*

Much Easier to be Virtuous than Vitious. To be wicked, Mackenzie explains, requires effort and brings opprobrium and trouble, whereas virtuous behaviour demands less effort and expense, and incurs no trouble. His argument would not have gone down well with the dissident Presbyterians, for whom the course of virtue, as they saw it, was involving heavy expense and serious personal trouble.

In 1665 he had made a modest increase to his emoluments by becoming Advocate for the burgh of Dundee, at an annual retainer of £Sc46, but his income was increasing year by year, and he bought the estate of Rosehaugh, in the Black Isle of Ross-shire, in 1668–69; from now on, in the Scottish manner which accepts that people come and go, but the land remains, he was Mackenzie of Rosehaugh, or just 'Rosehaugh'. With good cultivable land, and offshore fishing grounds, it may have been a sensible investment, but it also secured him a base in Mackenzie country and made him more of a figure to his fellow-clansmen than as a mere Edinburgh advocate he could ever hope to be.[3] He was already Sir George, having gained a knighthood at some time in the mid-1660s: perhaps the dedication to Rothes had been useful. His first wife died around this time, as had two of his five young children, and in 1670 he remarried. His new wife, Margaret Haliburton, was the daughter of a Lowland laird, of episcopal, and later Jacobite, sympathies.

Perhaps for her (as Andrew Lang surmised) he wrote a poem of 510 lines, *Caelia's Country House and Closet*,[4] in 1668. But it is far more than a lover's tribute: Mackenzie displays his familiarity with some of the intellectual vogues of the time, from its invocation to Friendship, as the Neo-Platonic ideal union of kindred souls, onwards. The room-by-room tour of the house is a reminder of the 'art of memory', in which the interior of an idealised building is used as a prompt for consecutive memories; by this century the technique was well-endowed with symbolic and esoteric values. There are hints, if no more, of Francis Bacon's prescription for the ideal house and garden. Caelia's garden, with its avenue of orange trees, a resident hermit of strict vegetarian principles: 'No murder'd Beast does in his Bowels groan', and an 'artificial rock', is a creation of the baroque era, instruction concealed within ornament. And the scientific spirit of inquiry is there: among the 'rarities' of her closet are a glass-sided clock, amber, corals and shells, the latter a wonder of 'sporting Nature':

'Which tho' most Glorious are but the Cells
Which it with Ease doth for poor Worms provide'

It is not great poetry, but it was a notable effort to introduce a new aesthetic and promote a morality based on reason in a country where most intellectual discourse focused on a sterile religious controversy. Mackenzie sent a copy of it to John Evelyn in London. They had been corresponding ever since Sir Robert Moray had introduced the Englishman to the essay on Solitude.[5] One may guess that Mackenzie was keen to show that the finer points of modern thought could be found among writers – and readers – north of the River Tweed. He is again a lone sailor beating against the literary, or anti-literary wind, and *Caelia* did not inspire others into verse. *Naphtali* was much more widely read and influential. But *Caelia* indicated where the future lay.

At this time, Thomas Sydserf, son of the Bishop of Orkney, was putting on dramas in the 'tennis court' at Holyrood, like his own *Tarugo's Wiles: Or the Coffee-House*, in 1668.[6] An enterprising media man, Sydserf had also published a news-sheet in London in 1661, *Mercurius Caledonius*, with news of Scottish affairs. Rothes was his patron, and such plays would not have been approved of in the Carstairs circle. *Naphtali* would have been respected, but *Caelia's Country House* would have seemed crassly materialistic, and scandalous in its praise of Charles I. William was a student in Edinburgh, where more accessible diversions included street entertainments by acrobats, rope-walkers, and musicians. Wild animal shows, including elephants, were also popular.[7] His father, summoned to appear before the Privy Council in 1664, had absconded to Ireland, where fugitive Presbyterians could count on a welcome among the Ulster Protestants, and was leading an unsettled life, moving between Ireland, Argyll and Ayrshire.

Sir James Dalrymple would have cared for neither *Caelia* nor *Naphtali*. He continued to act as a judge in Edinburgh while his wife, in Galloway, was making little secret of her sympathy with the conventiclers. As a senior judge, Sir James was a 'privileged attender' of Parliament, where he and his colleagues had a table between the King's Commissioner's throne and the seats for commissioners from the burghs.[8] He could address the house, but could not vote, this being reserved to the elected commissioners from shires and royal burghs, and the other two Estates: the clergy in the persons of the bishops, and the higher nobility. Scotland's parliament was dismissed by R. H. Story as 'except perhaps the Polish Diet, the most turbulent and impotent legislature in the world',[9] but modern studies of its work show that though lacking many of Westminster's hard-won rights and freedoms, and often merely the obedient creature of the current regime, it sometimes acted as a genuine forum for the nation; and that, from 1640, when the number of shire representatives was doubled, 'a Scottish Commons clearly emerged'.[10] Sir James took the Parliament seriously and would later become an influential shire commissioner himself, but in 1660–63 its role was much reduced compared to the 1640s, more akin to the obedient, 'decent and comely' assembly of the Estates that King James VI had worked to form. Elected – in the case of burgessses and shire commissioners – by a tiny minority of the male population, seated by estate in the single great chamber of Parliament House, it had no cohesive parties, only transient flows of opinion and shifting pressure groups clustered around leading figures. No parliament was summoned between 1663 and 1669, and the Lauderdale-Rothes combination ruled through the Privy Council.

Lord Lauderdale, in Gilbert Burnet's view, was content to let his colleagues overreach themselves at last and suffer dismissal, whatever damage they did in the meantime. Sometimes he helped things along, as when he enabled the King to discover that Sharp while acting President had sent a message of bland reassurance to the court, at the same time writing to an English nobleman to say all was by no means well.[11] Sharp's credit with Charles was gone, though he remained in his church post. While the Pentland Rising showed a failure of official policy, its ineffectual nature perhaps helped to reduce the level of government anxiety, and in 1667 an indemnity was offered to participants, requiring only an oath not to take up arms against the King again – but they did not consider themselves to have done this. Official concern about invasion may have prompted the policy: in April 1667 a Dutch naval attack in the Firth of Forth was alarming but unsuccessful, and Scottish privateers from East Coast ports were busy bringing in captured vessels in a short-lived but lucrative boom of licensed piracy.[12]

Official efforts were also being made to gather in weapons and remove many of the horses owned by the countrymen, and the aftermath of Rullion Green saw the Privy Council's first use of torture in three decades, in pursuing interrogations. The bulk of the new army was disbanded in August, to be replaced by county militias which would only be called up if required, and a further indemnity was proclaimed in October, embracing all but some 52 named persons, 'guilty of horrid and heinous crimes of rebellion, treason, and lese-majesty in the highest degree' and, in defiance of Scots law, courts were permitted to sentence them to death *in absentia*. That month a reshuffle of the Council saw Rothes deprived of his Commissionership and other posts, but he remained Chancellor: a position of responsibility and honour but with less opportunity for self-enrichment. Sharp's influence was correspondingly reduced, and eroded further by the appointment of allies of Lauderdale, John Hay, second Earl of Tweeddale, and Alexander Bruce, second Earl of Kincardine. Both were supporters of Presbyterianism, but not of dissidence or civil disobedience. A kindred spirit, though of broadly episcopalian sympathies – more precisely 'a non-sectarian personal Christianity'[13] – was Sir Robert Moray, who had been depute Secretary of State since 1663, and who came up in 1667 in order to send back confidential reports to Lauderdale. Moving in both court and literary-scientific circles in London, and 'a most excellent man of reason and learning' according to Samuel Pepys,[14] Moray had been a founder of the Royal Society in 1660, and presided over its first formal meetings. One of the few genuinely selfless men in public life, he came much closer than George Mackenzie to exemplifying a Neo-Stoic view.

These were men of intellectual bent, but of a practical sort, interested in machines and business as well as ideas, and familiar with scientific method as set out by Francis Bacon, who drew a distinction between religious faith, based on revelation, and philosophical ideas, based on experiment and reason. Bacon's philosophy makes another of the underlying strands of thought that, slowly and patchily, were irradiating intellectual life and laying a modest foundation for things to come. Such men saw the civil unrest as a distraction which could surely be settled by reason and goodwill. They were more concerned – not exactly selflessly in the cases of the earls – with economic progress and the expansion of trade. Kincardine presided over the coal and salt industry of the upper Firth of Forth, and Tweeddale was in charge of customs revenue collecting.

James Sharp, Archbishop of St Andrews
Reproduced from Wodrow's *History*, Vol I

Archbishop Sharp, always the prime hate-figure of the Presbyterians, was fired at in July 1668 as he emerged on to an Edinburgh street, but the shot missed, wounding the Bishop of Orkney, who was with him. The would-be killer, James Mitchell, a minister who had been in the Pentland Rising, simply walked away, and was not caught and arrested until 1674. The incident did not disrupt the new policy of moderation, and for a time, it seemed possible that the troubles were being brought to an end. A conscientious effort was begun to reconcile dissident Presbyterians with the Kirk in its episcopal form. Archbishop Burnet, who complained that 'the gospel was banished out of his diocese the day the army was disbanded'[15] was compelled in 1669 to resign, and the archbishopric of Glasgow was put under the charge of the pacific Leighton as Commendator (he became Archbishop in 1672). Leighton was keenly aware that no question of doctrine separated the dissidents from fellow-Calvinists who accepted, or tolerated, the bishops. If the difference were purely a matter of forms, surely a means of reconciliation could be found. His solution was a scheme known as comprehension, or accommodation, which sought to draw the deposed ministers back to the Kirk by limiting the powers of bishops and allowing ministers to be reinstated if agreeing to accept the bishop's role 'for the sake of order'.[16] His willingness to accept that bishops could not countermand the decisions of provincial synods, and could be censured by the assembled ministers at a synod, was not shared by his fellow-bishops, nor by the King, and the Government's own policy was different. Under it, notices of Indulgence could be issued to the deposed clergy, allowing them to return to their churches under certain conditions, without having to renounce their commitment to a full presbyterian settlement. The first Indulgence, announced in June 1669, though seen at the time, and later, as 'an artful attempt to sow dissension among the Covenanters',[17] nevertheless brought back 42 ministers.

The official aim was that as these men died off, they would be replaced by 'orthodox' episcopalians. But the unyielding element of the Presbyterians ensured that the policy was only partially successful. McWard and Brown sent over a relentless stream of letters and pamphlets condemning Indulgence and insisting on the Covenant as the bedrock of their beliefs. As a result, opposition was kept up against both 'indulged' and episcopalian ministers. Hoping to gain popular acceptance for his 'accommodation' scheme, Leighton recruited a team of six apostles of moderation and compromise, to tour the south-west and speak directly to the people. One of these was Gilbert Burnet, now 24, newly appointed Professor of Divinity at Glasgow. He was impressed by the country folk's knowledge and their capacity for argument, but they did not come in great numbers to hear him, and 'as soon as we were gone, a set of these hot preachers went round all the places in which we had been... They told them, the Devil was never so formidable, as when he was transformed into an angel of light.'[18]

Leighton also convened conferences with the Presbyterians, in the hope of applying reason to the problem by mutual concessions, but was bluntly told by one of them, the Rev. John Guthrie, at Paisley in December 1670, that, 'We judge it but the effect of the wisdom of the flesh and to smell rankly of a carnal politic spirit to halve and divide the things of God for making peace among men.'[19] This was the decisive factor: to Guthrie and his colleagues, the Covenant was a 'thing of God' and not negotiable. To Leighton, it was only a human document drawn up in circumstances that no longer applied. His case was not helped by the Assertory Act passed by Parliament in 1669 which affirmed the King's supremacy in all matters ecclesiastical, causing distress to the more committed episcopalians as well as confirming one of the Presbyterians' great objections. Both wings condemned such 'Erastianism', the reduction of the church to a department of state. The ultra-Presbyterian case was buttressed, for them, and exposed in its full menace, for their opponents, by the publication of a new book by the part-author of *Naphtali*, James Stewart, *Ius Populi Vindicatum* ['The Law of the People Vindicated']. He prudently fled to Holland on its publication, as the text recommended the hanging of the bishops and indeed requested the King not only to reaffirm the 'holy Covenants' but to make a new covenant, 'that whosoever will not seek the Lord God of Israel shall be put to death, whether small or great, whether Man or woman'.[20] The hecatomb required by this demand remained Stewart's personal ideal; but his approval of 'the call' of divine inspiration to strike down enemies of the Covenant helped to make this a tenet of the extremists.

CHAPTER THIRTEEN

Old Politics and New Practitioners

IN 1669, THE GENERATION of '48 came of age, and John Graham was made a Commissioner of Excise, and Justice of the Peace, in Forfarshire – his first public appointments. Agitation was not strong there, and though the local militia had been called out at the time of Rullion Green, it was stood down without seeing action. William Carstares was studying divinity at the University of Utrecht. Richard Cameron was still content to teach in Falkland, under a 'curate' as parish minister. What John Dalrymple was doing is not recorded, but it is likely that he was at home, managing the family estates. Two years before, when travelling in England, he was said to have been a witness of the incursion of the Dutch fleet into the Medway, and to have lent valuable assistance in preventing an English man of war from being blown up.[1] The story has no proof, but he appears to have gained his knighthood in 1667 at the precocious age of 19.

The first full Parliament since 1662 met in October 1669, with Lauderdale himself officiating as King's Commissioner. Apart from the Assertory Act, his list of bills included the appointing of commissioners to negotiate a treaty of full union with England. Charles II set the union proposal rolling, and it was enthusiastically backed by Lord Tweeddale. A tax was imposed on salt imported for fish curing, which had previously been exempt, and the raising of a substantial new militia force of 22,000 men was approved. All met strong opposition, and the salt tax was procured only after a challenged count and by the casting vote of Rothes, the Chancellor. Prominent in the opposition was George Mackenzie, sitting as commissioner for the shire of Ross, whose speeches so infuriated Lauderdale that he tried to find a technical means of debarring the 'factious young man'.[2] Mackenzie objected that the union proposal had been insufficiently considered and debated, and was angrily interrupted by Tweeddale. Sir James Dalrymple was in favour, and was one of the commissioners duly sent to discuss the details of union at Somerset

House in London. But on 14 November 1670 the King informed them that it was 'not feasible; but that he would take another time to it'.[3]

1669 had been a tragic year for Dalrymple's family. In August his daughter Janet had married Dunbar of Baldoon, a young laird of sound presbyterian credentials, but very soon afterwards, she died. From this sad but not exceptional turn of events arose an extraordinary set of stories and rumours. It was said that the marriage had been forced by the bride's mother and that Janet's heart was already given to Lord Rutherford. After the wedding, the couple were locked in their bedroom (a standard precaution to prevent pranks by the guests), and later shrieks were heard from inside. When the door was opened, the groom was found 'weltering in his blood', with Janet in a state of madness exclaiming, 'Tak' up your bonnie bridegroom!' Another version had it that she was the one to be stabbed, and the husband was found sitting in the chimney piece, laughing hideously. The story was turned into a novel by Sir Walter Scott, subsequently dramatised by Donizetti as *Lucia di Lammermoor*. The Dalrymples' biographer[4] concluded that there was no truth in these lurid accounts except perhaps for the unwilling nuptials: arranged marriages were so frequent as to be the norm among landowning families. Other tales flourished; another daughter, who married the Earl of Dumfries, was said to be a witch, able to fly through the air. Central to it all is the bride's mother, 'who enjoyed the reputation of a witch during her lifetime, and long after'.[5] Why should such wild libels be made against the highly respectable family of Stair? Sir James's capacity to retain high office under regimes of opposite views did not go unnoticed; the family was known to have Presbyterian sympathies and the episcopalian-royalist (and later Jacobite) pasquil-writers, completely without scruple, found them fair game, all the more so because of Sir James's cleverness and perhaps his own awareness of it. He was said to have a wry neck, though portraits show no sign of it. Gilbert Burnet thought him false and cunning; to George Mackenzie, who knew him better, he was 'a gentleman of excellent parts, of an equal wit and universal learning; but most considerable for being so free from passions, that most men thought this equality of spirit a mere hypocrisy in him... But that which I admired most in him was, that in ten years' intimacy I never heard him speak unkindly of those that had injured him.'[6]

The reality of witchcraft, of course, was taken for granted. In a notorious case in April 1670, Major Thomas Weir, commander of the Edinburgh City Guard, a prominent Presbyterian, famous for extempore prayer, made public confession of a whole string of necromantic activities, committed along with his sister, Jean. They included driving from Edinburgh to Dalkeith in a fiery coach with Satan at the reins. Incest and bestiality were also included. Weir, who may have long been leading a double life, appears to have undergone a mental breakdown. He suffered the prescribed execution for a witch, and his sister was hanged a few days later. *Satan's Invisible World Discovered* quotes Jean Weir as saying on the scaffold: 'There are many here this day, wondering and greeting for me; but alas! few mourn for a broken covenant.'[7] The hangman had to struggle with her to prevent her from stripping naked, so keen was she to exaggerate her shame. Satanic witchcraft was the shadow-runner at the heels of religious fervour. The episode makes one wonder how many others sought illicit thrills and semi-occult excitements, with ritualistic and sexual aspects, in furtive gatherings whose existence, suspected or hinted at, helped to spread a wider feeling of spiritual danger and unease. Fear, guilt and complicity must have affected many lives in that time when religious enthusiasm ran so high. The Evil One seemed often very close,

Edinburgh Tolbooth
Reproduced from *Cassell's Old & New Edinburgh*

potent, and easy to yield to. Preachers' vehemence against witchery kept up a vicious reciprocity between these complementary and mutually antagonistic sets of beliefs.

Lauderdale returned with relief to London at the end of 1669, having written to his royal master, after the proroguing of Parliament, that 'Never was King so absolute as you are in poor old Scotland.'[8] But undesirable things were happening. The limited success of the first Indulgence, and the failure of Leighton's 'Accommodation', together with the relaxation of the campaigns against non-attenders at church and those who attended conventicles, led to an increase in the number and size of the preachings and communions conducted by the non-conformers, mostly at this time in barns and houses.[9] Often only a handful of people may have attended, but big names among the field preachers, like John Welsh the former minister of Irongray (grandson of the fiery preacher John Welsh who had married John Knox's daughter: it was not only belted earls who walked proud in their lineage), could attract hundreds. High on the Government's wanted list, such a man had the lure of reputation, the human interest of the fugitive, the authority of inspiration in words of prophecy and doom, the lustre of personal sacrifice, and the charisma of one who trod a narrow path with God. Curiosity helped to swell the numbers, but there was no doubting the commitment of most who came along.

Forced into inconsistency, the Government used the parliaments of 1671 and 1672 to increase the penalties, imposing fines on landowners on whose ground conventicles were held, and making death the penalty for preaching in field conventicles. An Act of 1672 making 29 May, the King's birthday and restoration day, into one of national thanksgiving, violated a long-held Kirk tenet, that 'no human authority hath power to appoint constant returning anniversary holydays'.[10] A hint of the heart-searchings caused among some of the Presbyterians by the offer of Indulgence comes from a letter of August 1672 written by some 20 ministers to Sir James Dalrymple, who had been appointed Lord President of the Court of Session and a Privy Councillor in the previous year and in whom they had as much confidence 'as in any at the board',[11] asking that any new Indulgence (it was much touted about that Lauderdale at this time had one in his pocket) should be free of 'straitening ingredients and conditions' which would make its acceptance difficult. Sir James is recorded as giving them very kind assurances that he would do all in his power for them. He was an exemplary Lord President, unbribable, impartial and prompt in action at a time when judges often delayed uncomfortable or tricky decisions, or swapped cases to assist their own friends or clients; and in December 1676 the Town Council of Edinburgh ordered the rent of his town flat to be paid from town funds not only for his life, but for all his successors in office.[12]

In 1672 Sir John Dalrymple was admitted to the Scottish Bar. Back in 1641, in the second Bishops' War, Sir James had briefly captained a troop of horse. His grandson John would be a British Field Marshal, but none of his five sons were military men. John Drummond became a soldier, commissioned captain in the foot guards in 1673.[13] He stayed in Scotland, but for many other young men, warfare in Europe gave a welcome prospect of earnings and excitement. Scotland's reservoir of mercenary soldiers was being heavily tapped in 1672–73, following Charles II's combination with Louis XIV of France to make war on the United Provinces and the Spanish Netherlands. Lord George Douglas and Sir William Lockhart both commanded Scottish regiments in the French service, and it was one of these, probably Lockhart's,[14] that the 24-year-old John Graham joined. He gained experience as a junior officer, but there was no major battle in this campaign. Among other Scottish officers then serving in France was Hugh Mackay of Scourie, from the far north-west of Sutherland, some eight years older. On England's withdrawal from the French alliance in February 1674, both men, independently of each other, removed themselves to the Dutch side, joining the forces of William, Prince of Orange, Stadholder of the United Provinces, who had unfinished business with King Louis. The international battlefront moved southwards between France and the German imperial states, and both gave distinguished service, presumably feeling more comfortable under a Protestant flag. A well-established but unsupported Jacobite legend claims that Graham rescued William of Orange in the battle of Seneffe in 1674 when the prince's horse was killed, thereby earning his gratitude. Graham came home in 1675, when his mother died, but returned to William's army in the following year and on 24 November was promoted to *Ritmeester*, a captain of horse.

The second Indulgence of September 1672, when promulgated, showed a novel tactic, of allocating about 80 of the outed ministers to 58 parishes in the south-west and Argyll, in pairs or with the current incumbent, sharing the stipend and the pastoral activities, but not allowed to leave the parish without licence from the bishop. No conscience-straining oath was demanded. After stormy discussion, the majority of ministers named accepted the terms, and 'presbyterians, who before this had been very much of a piece, did now divide'[15] – a rift opened between the Indulged and those who still resisted, and the reproachings from Holland became intense. The indulged ministers were by no means conformist, and many refused to acknowledge the May 29 holiday, or to take any sort of note of their bishops, and some were re-deprived in the course of 1673. Robert Leighton, saddened at the failure of his own policy, and despondent for the future, resigned his archbishopric in 1674 and withdrew to lead a contemplative life in the south of England.[16] Alexander Burnet, with zeal unabated by four years on the sidelines, was restored to his old see. Leighton's retreat marked the end of the interval of moderation, and coincided with new alignments in parliament and government.

Lauderdale's administration was beginning to come apart at the seams. Insufficient success of the Indulgence policy, harm to trade caused by war with Holland, the inevitable jealousies and rivalries within an aristocratic regime in which too many grandees competed for a modest range of posts and privileges, all contributed. There was a falling-out with Tweeddale in 1671 when the collection of customs revenue was taken from the earl, who had been efficient, and given to Lauderdale's corrupt brother Charles Maitland, Lord Hatton, who was already embezzling funds from the Mint. But observers then and since also regarded Lauderdale's new wife, Elizabeth Murray, Countess of Dysart in her own right, as a schemer and interferer, with her own motives, including a supposed penchant for presybterianism, and a long list of old scores to be paid off. At the time of the marriage, in 1671, a pasquil-writer enumerated a series of her lovers including Cromwell (which was not the case) and ends:

'... O rusty, musty tub –
At last in Hell thou'llt cuckold Belzebub.'[17]

How much of this crude denigration can be attributed to the masculine chauvinism of a society in which men considered themselves to be the natural and only leaders? An intelligent and strong-minded woman might easily feel that she could manage the state's affairs as well as, or better than, the men who formed the Government. Denied any chance of formal involvement, 'meddling' was the only possibility; and the Countess had seen what power could be wielded, in London, by the King's mistresses.

A glimpse into how private disputes affected public life is seen in a pamphlet published by Tweeddale in 1683 but going back to events 12 years earlier, when Lauderdale effectively disinherited his daughter Mary (of his first marriage) in favour of his new wife. Mary was married to Lord Yester, Tweeddale's heir, and in the Parliament of November 1673 Tweeddale had moved to open opposition to Lauderdale.[18] Following his marriage, other former allies drifted away from Lauderdale, or were dropped, including Kincardine, who by spring 1676 joined with Tweeddale in opposition; and Sir Robert Moray, who had abandoned politics some time before his death in 1673. But Lauderdale's credit with the King survived, and he was raised to the rank of duke in May 1672. He also found new allies, including Sir James Dalrymple and Sir George Mackenzie.

These new friends did not share the same motives. Sir James's emergence

The Duke and Duchess of Lauderdale
Reproduced from Kirkton's *History*

into the political arena – he was elected as shire commissioner for Ayrshire and in the parliamentary session of 1672 was appointed to the Committee of the Articles – seems to have been impelled by pressure, or his own desire, to lend some support to the Presbyterians in their travails. In 1669 Mackenzie, in opposing most of Lauderdale's legislation, had been identified with the loose opposition grouping headed by the Duke of Hamilton, which had links to Lord Shaftesbury's opposition faction in England, and was known as 'The Party', the first time such a term had been applied in Scottish politics. Hamilton had been born William Douglas, a younger son of the Earl of Selkirk, and the title of the senior non-royal duke had been given him for life when he married his wife, who as the only child of the second duke was, under Scots law, duchess in her own right; but his pride and pretensions were quite as great as if he had inherited it. 'The Party' was his support group, and he showed skill in holding a motley collection of burgh, factional and personal interests together for almost a decade. But Mackenzie was not Hamilton's creature, and by 1673 his concern for social and political stability was inclining him towards support for Lauderdale. Andrew Lang saw his change of sides as driven mainly by a growing sense that with dissension mounting in England as well as Scotland, only the King and the power of the royal prerogative, in effect a regal dictatorship, could hold things together.[19]

Lauderdale was a deeply suspect figure to the English House of Commons, and the Duke made no bones to the King about the fact that he could raise an army for him in Scotland, should difficulties with the Commons come to a head. In Edinburgh, Hamilton and his associates wanted to abolish the Committee of the Articles, an action which would remove Lauderdale's ability to control proceedings in Parliament. The political temperature was hotting up, but Mackenzie, still earning his bread from the law, did not let his changing views stop him from drafting a petition on behalf of the Convention of Royal Burghs in 1674, asking for a new Parliament to be called, at a time felt by Lauderdale to be most inopportune. The provosts responsible were fined heavily but no action was taken against Mackenzie.[20]

In the autumn of 1674 the authorities in London arrested a suspect person, who had been under surveillance for some time in his comings and goings between Britain and Holland. This was William Carstares, by now ordained in Holland as a Presbyterian minister. He would have been a welcome recruit in the eyes of McWard and Brown, but also in 1669, through a letter of introduction to the court physician[21] he had met that man of destiny, only a year younger than himself, William, Prince of Orange. A lifelong association began, and Carstares became a confidential courier and reporter, moving between plotters in London, the Scottish dissidents in Holland, and the immensely discreet William, who wanted to know everything and be committed to nothing. William Carstares, no less discreet, was the perfect go-between. Letters to his sister Sarah from this time are mostly pious platitudes, but one of 17 April 1674 shows a glimmer of self-regard and ambition: 'It may be at last in providence I may have some door opened, whereby I may be in a capacity to do some little service in my generation and not always be insignificant in my station.'[22]

Ciphers, of a more or less cryptic nature, were in very frequent use, for reasons of basic privacy as well as essential secrecy. At their simplest they were bland and referential, expressing apparent generalities; at the next level, false names, or numbers were used for people, places and institutions. 'White ink', which could be made legible by the careful application of sulphate of copper, was often used. Letters sent through the postal system were liable to be opened and read, and couriers or agents were preferred when hot messages were being passed. Under the name of William Williams, Carstares had been coming and going between Rotterdam and London at least since 1672, carrying coded or 'white ink' letters which referred to him as 'Mr Red'. In London he was questioned by Lauderdale personally, but in a letter smuggled out to McWard, he wrote of his captured papers: 'There were produced some few Instructions from one Moulin to me... I was pressed to give an explication of those which at that time I refused to do and answered all their questions with silence, saying only that there was nothing there that prejudiced his Majesty's interest... Lauderd. told me my shins would pay for all... I hear also that I might have favour if I would but tell names, but tho' I know no ill of my friends, yet I hope through grace never to do that which may have the show of wronging of them.'[23] This no doubt gave assurance to the plotters in Holland that their secrets were safe. Reference to Carstares's shins introduces the 'Boot', an instrument of torture legal in Scotland but not in England, the fear or actual employment of which was used by the Council to gain information from reticent prisoners. Carstares may have been involved in highly secret discussions with the Duke of Hamilton,[24] but the only thing that could be proved against him was his own admission that he had organised the printing of a Presbyterian pamphlet from the busy pen of James Stewart, *The Accompt of Scotland's Grievances by reason of the D. of Lauderdale's Ministrie, humbly tendered to his Sacred Majesty*, and he was sent by sea to Edinburgh in February 1675, where he would remain a prisoner, without trial, in the Castle until 1679.

If Carstares had to be locked up, he was perhaps fortunate to be in the castle, with members of his family able to supply his needs. At this time, numerous Presbyterian prisoners were confined on the wind-blown Bass Rock, a sea-girt crag rising from the heaving waters off North Berwick. He was also well treated by his chief warder, John Drummond of Lundin, when appointed Lieutenant-Depute of the castle in 1679[25] – a fact worth mentioning since Drummond appeared much better at making enemies than friends.

Whilst the incarcerated Carstares may not have appreciated it, his country at that time should be considered a land of diversifying commerce, and growing prosperity rather than one groaning under politico-religious oppression – the standard of living, for most, was still rising. Lauderdale's business-minded associates' period of government had coincided propitiously with an era of commercial expansion. British neutrality in the continuing warfare of Europe provided opportunities for international trading and transport which benefited Scotland as well as England. Despite the loss of trading privileges in France, and the adverse effects of the English parliament's Navigation Acts, imports and exports both increased. Although one of Lauderdale's numerous sources of income was a substantial retainer from the Convention of Royal Burghs, his Parliament of 1672 ended their long monopoly of overseas trade, reserving to them only wine, wax, silks, spices and dyestuffs (all highly valuable commodities). The duke's retainer was indignantly withdrawn, but he more than recouped its loss by the increase of trade through the harbour of Musselburgh, which he controlled, at the expense of nearby Leith, the country's busiest port. Recent research has shown how effective and intensive the network of Scottish traders in the Baltic ports was. Ships went out with herring, oysters, linen, woven stockings, and other goods, and came back with iron, hemp and tar. At least one Scottish tramp vessel was carrying salt between La Rochelle and Sweden.[26] The royal appointment of 'British' consuls at one or two key points like the Sound betweeen Denmark and Sweden usefully supported the work of Scottish factors and official representatives at a string of ports from Bergen to Danzig.[27] Monopolies on certain commodities and processes were granted, or sold, and the country's first joint stock companies were formed, on a tentative and small-scale basis – it was all very new. Construction of small factories, cloth-works, fish-curing stations, tanneries, went on, though factory-based industry was as yet a modest user of work-people, and far more numerous were those who combined small-hold farming with home-based weaving or knitting. The pattern of wealth increase was patchy; in the manner of the time, certain people profited much more than others, and it was far short of a mercantile golden age. Seasonal hardship could still arise: the harsh late winter of 1673–74 was said to have killed off a third of the country's cattle.[28] Lauderdale never showed much interest in the Highlands and Islands, but his success in having English import duty on Scotch cattle lifted in 1669[29] promoted a dramatic rise in the cattle trade and the incomes of Highland proprietors.

Against this busy background, Covenanter historians continue to painstakingly record the sufferings of the unreconciled Presbyterians. Conventicling spread northwards through Fife and into the coastal farmlands of Moray and Easter Ross, while a series of Council proclamations through 1674 tried to stem the process by creating new offences and penalties. Fines were levied in a steady stream whenever evidence could be found, but the conventicles continued. Lauderdale's pressure on the Council was answered by long defensive accounts of what had been done. In August 1674 they were ordered to raise a standing force of a thousand foot and three troops of horse; the latter with the main aim of suppressing conventicles.[30]

After ten years the Council faced an entrenched phenomenon, civil disobedience in a selective form, on a wide scale, by people who were otherwise productive, law-abiding and respectable. House-meetings especially could be very difficult to detect, in communities where, despite official efforts to encourage informers, solidarity or fear of vengeance kept mouths firmly shut. In such situations, soldiers could not be of much use, unless they were so numerous as to be everywhere. Lacking both the political skills and policing resources to cope with what was happening, the authorities veered between pacification and new attempts at repression.

The litany of presbyterian endurances between 1673 and 1679 is long, but even its compilers had to admit that the degree of persecution was by contemporary standards not severe. They could have produced longer and more harrowing accounts if they had instead considered the plight of the bonded toilers, men, women, and children, in the collieries and the salt-panning works. But these people were beyond normal society, its compassion and its laws, and no-one recorded their injuries, punishments, degradations and complete lack of civic rights. For the Presbyterians, it was very largely a matter of fines: troubling enough to those caught, but not threatening to life or limb. A very large amount of money was recirculated in this way: Wodrow's reckoning of fines paid by non-conformers in only six years between 1679 and 1685 is £Sc3,174,819 18s 8d,[31] and it is an interesting question, though beyond the scope of this book, whether the effect of these redistributions was positive, negative, or neutral within the economy. The reluctant contributions of the Presbyterians paid for many examples of contemporary art and design, and helped finance cultural change, as beneficiaries remodelled their homes, had new furniture made to new patterns, extended their wardrobes, bought books and pictures, had their portraits painted and enlarged their gardens, with ever-growing interest in the latest discoveries, fashions and styles of Europe and England.

Glasgow Tolbooth
Reproduced from Anderson, *Ladies of the Covenant*

CHAPTER FOURTEEN

Experiences of an Advocate

THE PARLIAMENT SUMMONED IN 1673 was even less docile than that of 1669. Hamilton rose at the opening to propose that no supply (financial support for the government) should be discussed until the distressed state of the country was reported to the King. Lauderdale, again Commissioner, first adjourned, then dissolved the recalcitrant assembly on 17 January 1674, 'the last time ever our mighty duke durst venture upon a Scottish parliament,'[1] wrote Kirkton gleefully; but in the absence of Parliament, Lauderdale simply ruled by royal proclamations, and any chance of reasoned debate, or consensus, was lost, while he made use of the wide powers of the royal prerogative to replace hostile councillors in the royal burghs with his own chosen men. Hamilton and his associates were sidelined by their own strategy: their aim had been to obstruct Lauderdale enough for Charles to lose patience with him, throw him over, and make Hamilton, duke-in-waiting, his Secretary of State, gaining control of all the patronage currently wielded by Lauderdale, and access to the well-paid sinecures currently being pocketed by the Maitland brothers and their clique of friends and pensioners. Lauderdale had outstayed virtually every other of Charles II's ministers and had no intention of yielding his position and powers. To the King, he remained the only reliable executor of the royal policy.

James Mitchell, Sharp's would-be assassin, was recognised and 'taken at a burial'[2] in Edinburgh in early February 1674. At first he denied the charge,[3] but on being assured of his life by the Chancellor, Rothes, he confessed. Later, apparently doubtful of the promise given him, he withdrew his confession (this was possible because it was an 'informal' one, not given before a quorum of the criminal judges). His case was deferred and meanwhile he was committed to the Bass Rock.

In what he must have hoped would be seen as a substantial gesture of generosity, Lauderdale announced an Act of Grace on 4 March 1674, which pardoned those who had attended conventicles prior to then, though not preachers or persons listed as seditious. Conventicles were still banned however, and the campaign against them went on, but the consequence was that: '... from that day forward, Scotland broke loose with conventicles of all sorts... house conventicles were not noticed, the field conventicles blinded the eyes of our state so much.'[4] Leighton wrote to Lauderdale on 16 June to say the Act had not produced 'the good effects that were wished and expected from it.'[5] House meetings were mostly in the cities, because the country people 'had a sort of affection to the fields above houses,'[6] and most of those attending were women, because 'Not many gentlemen of estate durst come.'

Presbyterian women caught Archbishop Sharp himself in a hurly-burly in the Parliament Close, in Edinburgh, on 4 June, where a determined group had gathered to waylay the Chancellor, and present a petition for restitution of all the outed ministers. Sharp, also in the official party, was jostled, and attracted shouts of 'Judas.'[7] Sir James Dalrymple, who was also present, when offered a copy of the document, threw it to the ground.[8] Whilst the female demonstrators of Galloway had been termed a rabble, these were mostly ministers' widows, who 'spoke very well and handsomely' to the Chancellor, and were answered civilly by him. The leaders, including Margaret Johnston, a daughter of Johnston of Wariston, were eventually banished from the city for a time.

At some point in 1674 Sir George Mackenzie was injured, breaking his leg in an incident that remains mysterious – a pamphlet attacking him four years later claimed that the injury was 'in the service of that party or interest' from which he had just broken: this was the Hamilton 'Party', and it suggests an ugly edge to political life. Roughs and toughs in plenty were available for hire by anyone who wanted to have an adversary, or ex-friend, beaten up or frightened off. In a letter to Archbishop Sharp, in 1675, Mackenzie says his enemies 'have broken my leg, and are trying to break my reputation.'[9] The break did not heal well, and from that time, he walked with a limp, though he remained as energetic as before.

At the same time, he became embroiled in a legal-political storm which blew up, or was inflated, in 1674–75. This was the 'Appeals Affair', begun when Sir George Lockhart and his client the Earl of Callendar, disappointed in a verdict of the Court of Session, decided in May 1674 to appeal from the court to Parliament.[10] Such protestation was not supposed to be used as a backdoor form of appeal, and it became an issue between the Bar and the Bench. Mackenzie, a loyal member of the Faculty of Advocates,

Sir George Lockhart of Carnwath
Reproduced from *Cassell's Old & New Edinburgh*

and also one of Callendar's counsel, gave reluctant support to his professional colleagues.[11] The judges, headed by Lord Stair, sent a protest about this attack on their authority to Lauderdale and the King, who, feeling more confident of the judges (whom they appointed) than of Parliament, supported them. Refusing to back down, the advocates were disbarred and banished from Edinburgh. Mackenzie, confined to bed by his injured leg, was disbarred with the others, some of whom removed to Linlithgow, most to Haddington. It was a stand-off – they were unable to practise, but the courts could not function without them. A general letter or petition of the advocates, drafted by Mackenzie but, he claimed, heavily altered by Lockhart, was refused by the Privy Council as seditious and sent on to London. By 15 January 1675 a few advocates gave satisfactory assurances and were reinstated, but most stayed out. Lockhart and two leading colleagues went to London in February to to explain their case, and somehow Mackenzie got sight of a letter from Lockhart saying that they would wait in England to see how things went in Edinburgh, expecting Mackenzie to be called before the Privy Council, and, 'if he was found guilty, the malice of the pursuers would be blunted before it reached them'.[12] Feeling dangerously exposed, Mackenzie composed his own petition to the King, which was accepted on 29 June and he was restored. In the next months, the rest, including Lockhart, followed his example.

This apparently straightforward sequence of events, spread over more than a year, becomes a tight little knot in accounts of the time, painted over with prejudice and impossible to fully unpick. Andrew Lang believed that Lockhart had set up Mackenzie as fall-guy: he 'found that they were sacrificing him and his associates';[13] Stair's biographer believed that Mackenzie was 'actuated by a mean jealousy of Lockhart';[14] Mackenzie's own later account shows that he believed Lockhart to have been intriguing against Stair to engineer his removal as Lord President.[15] Certainly Stair wrote to Lauderdale around the turn of 1674–75 to say that 'Sir George Mackenzie has done himself and us all a great deal of right and is fully resolute against all such courses.'[16] The 'courses' are unspecified but clearly relate to Lockhart's actions. Caught between professional loyalty and his own sense of what was proper, Mackenzie, not for the only time in his life, would seem to have behaved rather naively. Like some clan warrior, he was liable to place himself in the front row of an attack without troubling about a means of retreat. Lockhart, the prime stirrer-up of the trouble, had more prudence, or guile.

The episode coincided with, and perhaps underlined, Mackenzie's dropping of his links with the Hamilton 'Party', in which Lockhart was prominent, for support of Lauderdale, or of the King through the Duke. The Secretary of State was glad to have him on board as a counterweight to Lockhart. In 1674 or '75 he was offered the unsalaried post of Lord

Justice General, but declined it.[17] At the end of August 1676 he was made 'understudy' to Sir John Nisbet, the King's Advocate, and in September 1677, he took over from Nisbet. This was a much more overtly political post and he assumed it at a time when political tension was again high. To James Kirkton, he was a man 'thought fit for the state's design'.[18] With conventicling seemingly established as a part of national life in most areas outside the Gaelic-speaking Highlands and the lowland North-East, Lauderdale was embarking on what he may have felt to be a last-ditch attempt at ending activities which were making his administration look ineffective and incompetent.

CHAPTER FIFTEEN

The Highland Host

IN THE WINTER OF 1675–76 a number of the wandering ministers withdrew across the border to Northumberland. John Welsh preached a sermon standing between Scotland and England, in the centre of the icebound River Tweed.[1] Welsh had been in Fife in 1675 and it was probably his skilfully plied spade that struck ore in Richard Cameron, who this year came out as a Covenanter. Or perhaps it was a long-pondered move – anyway Cameron's conversion was not well received in Falkland (though another Fife burgh, Culross, was reprimanded by the Council for allowing a 'fugitive and banished person' to be its schoolmaster), and he quit his teaching job there to become chaplain to Lady Cavers in September 1677,[2] then tutor in the family of Sir William Scott of Harden. The Scotts were sincere Presbyterians,[3] but they attended the church of an Indulged minister, and Cameron, who had acquired a particular animus against the Indulged, did not stay long, leaving to join the escort of the itinerant preachers.

Welsh and the others were glad to have such an intense new colleague, still in his early 20s, and in 1676 they gave him a licence to preach, despite his announced determination to denounce the Indulged clergy. Within the Presbyterian camp, this was a delicate issue: all Covenanters were Presbyterians but by no means all Presbyterians were ardent for the Covenant, certainly not in its political implications. Many of the ministers who had accepted Indulgence were open sympathisers with those who still refused any degree of conformity, and Welsh did not want to provoke a complete separation with his old colleagues. Cameron was sent to Annandale to preach, with Welsh recorded as saying to him, 'Go your way, Ritchie; set the fire of hell to their tail,'[4] but Welsh's eye was on episcopalians and backsliders, and he wanted the new recruit to moderate his strictures against fellow-Presbyterians. Cameron's sense of mission was too strong to be contained easily, and the restraint made him depressed and melancholy.[5]

The atmosphere of the later 1670s was a strange one. Heavy legislation against conventicles was still in place; the Covenants were illegal; unindulged ministers were still under ban. Yet conventicles were happening with almost the regularity of the official church services. The official campaign against them had by no means been given up, though it was not strongly pressed, and there were occasional skirmishes and scrimmages, when troops on disperse-and-arrest missions met armed resistance. Outed ministers walked the streets and held deep and earnest discussions with sympathisers. All issues were shrouded in uncertainty, and speculation ranged over everything. What was Lauderdale's plan? His Act of Grace had started a flood of conventicles: was this deliberate? What was Hamilton up to? A reshuffle of the Privy Council in 1676 had cleared it of his associates and left him so isolated that he rarely attended. And the bishops? Sharp was reduced to writing pathetic letters from St Andrews to the Archbishop of Canterbury, bewailing the condition of his church and the manner in which he was treated by presbyterian-minded ministers.[6]

No-one expected the situation to last, but, remarkably, things went on like this for several years. That in itself shows the relative artificiality and isolation of the confrontation, like an ugly growth within the organic system of national life, exerting a depressive and weakening effect, but with normal activities going on around it. Suspicion hung like a miasma in the air; skulduggery might lurk in any dark close. A *cause célèbre* occurred in June 1676 when the confusingly named Captain Carstairs (no relation of the still-imprisoned William) arrested James Kirkton, an outed minister, on a street in Edinburgh. Kirkton was brought to the Captain's chamber, 'an ugly dark hole' where, in a baffling exchange, Carstairs claimed to believe Kirkton was one John Wardlaw, who owed him money. Carstairs himself pretended to be Scott of Earlston, a well-known Presbyterian sympathiser. Assuming himself to be a victim of blackmail, Kirkton was about to offer some money when (by some unknown cause) his brother-in-law, the sturdy Robert Baillie of Jerviswood, with two companions, was heard at the door. The Captain drew a pistol, Kirkton grappled with him ('a feeble body'); the rescuers pushed open the unlocked door, and bore Kirkton safely away.[7] Captain Carstairs then reported to the Council that his attempt to arrest a 'fanatic minister' had been frustrated by a 'numerous tumult of the people of Edinburgh'.[8] Baillie was subsequently fined £500, even though it emerged that Carstairs had had no warrant, and, Wodrow claims, was provided with a postdated one by Archbishop Sharp, who may have been his chief patron, since later he was 'very bussie in the east end of Fyffe'.[9] It was generally believed that the episode led to the removal of Hamilton and Kincardine from the Privy Council, for seeming over-sympathetic to dissidents.[10] Sir John Lauder noted that in September 1677 Lauderdale, 'to ingratiate himself', had Jerviswood's fine remitted.[11]

Captain Carstairs was one of many who made a living out of an ideological cleavage that no-one knew how to cope with. Another spy sent in a report on a huge conventicle near Girvan, with 7,000 people in attendance, and Communion celebrated with silver cups: 'Before admission to the Sacrament the people promised never to hear Curates again, but to adhere to the glorious ends of their League and Covenant... Kennedy [the minister of Girvan] was censured for not preaching warmly enough against the wicked ways and nobles and prelates... it was enacted the people should not rise in arms until oppressed and provoked. Last week at a fair in Maybole a great many swords were sold.'[12]

In a district hardly affected by the troubles, one observer recorded a significant change in national life that had come about in his own time. Patrick Lyon, 11th Lord Glamis, who was made first Earl of Strathmore in 1677, noted in that year that the tall, narrow, fortified towers in which he and his fellow-nobles lived were obsolete: '... such houses are truly worn quite out of fashion, as feuds are... the country being generally more civilised than it was in ancient times.'[13] Nearly half a century had gone by since the last of the private wars, between Gordons and Crichtons in the North-East, but that region, like Strathmore, was outside the Highlands, where such things were still possible.

Lauderdale in 1677 still clung to the idea that if the country gentry were squeezed hard enough, they would enforce conformity further down the social scale. On 2 August a Council proclamation renewed that of 1674, which required all heritors, wadsetters (mortgagees), and life-renters to sign a bond committing themselves and their tenants and servants not to attend conventicles or to employ any outed minister for baptism, under all the penalties already provided. Protests streamed in from those who knew they could not enforce it even if they wished to; the Ayrshire gentry combined under the Earl of Loudoun to excuse themselves; the Duke of Hamilton refused it, and Lauderdale, who had made intimations at the same time about a third Indulgence for deprived ministers, found he had done nothing but increase the confidence of the armed Covenanters, the 'slashing communicants' as Sir James Turner called them.[14]

Lauderdale at this time has been called 'a statesman without a policy, and possessed of a furious temper, and a bitter memory of events long past'.[15] Something different was needed: a new *démarche*, dramatic enough to have an effect, and also to show the King, whose restlessness at the continued resistance to episcopacy might easily bring an end to Lauderdale's long spell of power, that energetic measures were being taken.

The men whose names would be most closely identified with the 'Killing Time' were moving into position. At the end of 1677 John Graham of Claverhouse was home, his Dutch service over, with a letter of recommendation from William of Orange to James, Duke of York and Albany, brother of Charles II and heir presumptive to Charles's kingdoms. Claverhouse was keen to obtain a military commission that reflected his experience, and, at first offered only a lieutenancy in His Royal Highness's Regiment of Horse, refused it.[16] After a brief return abroad, to Holland or France, in early 1678, he came back for good, and in September obtained the captaincy of one of three new troops of horse raised to improve internal security, and was assigned the district of Dumfries and Annandale. William's recommendation must have been a strong one, because Graham had no personal claim on Lauderdale's consideration. He also started on a campaign of his own, to win the hand of a lady he had probably never met. His efforts shed some light on how a marriage campaign was conducted when lands and titles were at stake: the lady, Helen Graham, was the daughter of a distant kinsman, Sir James Graham, and heiress of her cousin, the childless Earl of Menteith. She was living with her parents in Ireland. Now 30, Claverhouse had to consider the future of his family and its properties. His own estate, worth some £600 a year, was a relatively modest one[17] and he hoped to acquire the inheritance with the bride, and also to make himself eligible for the earl's title on Menteith's death. Although kidnaps and forced marriages were by no means unknown, there were more conventional procedures. Apart from the lady's father and Menteith, he had to have the support of the head of the Grahams, the Marquis of Montrose. This seemed to be granted, and Claverhouse wrote to Menteith to tell him that the Marquis was 'very well satisfied' and to underline his own suitability: 'I may say without vanity that I will do your family no dishonour, seeing there is nobody you could make choice of that has toiled so much for honour as I have done, though it has been my misfortune to attain of it but a small share.'[18] Though making fair replies, Menteith was considering other possibilities, including the sale of his title to another ambitious young man, Sir John Dalrymple.[19]

As King's Advocate, George Mackenzie was quickly plunged into controversy, with the long-delayed trial of James Mitchell, the would-be assassin of Sharp, which was held between 7–10 January 1678. Writing on 8 December 1677 to describe what must have been a preliminary hearing of the case, an English observer, Lauderdale's chaplain, Dr Hickes, was alarmed by the attitude of others in the public gallery: 'You cannot imagine how the Presbyterian party, especially the women, were concerned for him. The Court was full of disaffected villains[20]... ' Hickes was spat upon and 'they pelted me now and then with such things as bits of apple and crusts of bread'. This was not in Lanark or Ayr, but in Edinburgh, in the very building where the 'Secret Council' held its meetings. Mitchell still clung to the retraction of his original confession of guilt, but a sequence of privy councillors including Rothes, Lauderdale himself, Sharp, and Hatton appeared, to swear that no assurance of his life had been given to the prisoner in 1674 – or, in the case of the two latter, that they had not heard such an assurance being given – in order to procure a confession. The retracted confession was judged as admissible. Then the defence, led by Sir George Lockhart, produced a piece of evidence which should have destroyed the Crown's case: a copy of the Act of Council which contained the assurance whose existence had been so solemnly denied. They asked for the official register to be read. Lauderdale exhibited his famous temper, saying 'he was not there to be accused of perjury',[21] and the judges refused, on the grounds that the request should have been made before the trial began, and that in any case, any suggestion of the existence of an assurance was cancelled by the testimony of members of the Privy Council. Mackenzie, defending his case in the *Vindication* and the *Memoirs*, gives contradictory accounts, claiming quite wrongly in the former that the Registers were produced but did not contain 'the least Mark of a Promise'.[22]

Mitchell worried the governors by his insistence on the 'Call', the voice that had told him to strike down Sharp. Replying to a shrewd question – if the call were divine, why had his shot missed? – Mitchell quoted the story of Achan from the Book of Joshua, when '... the children of Israel could not stand before their enemies, but turned their backs before their enemies, because they were accursed: neither will I be with you any more, except ye destroy the accursed from among you'[23] – as he saw it, Mitchell was facing a whole bench of Achans 'who had taken of the accursed thing'. Sentenced to hang, he was executed on 18 January, but the blatant perversion of justice by the country's highest criminal court, and the leading figures of its government, was deeply embarrassing to the administration's friends and easy meat for its enemies. Even the statute under which he was condemned was an obsolete one.[24] Sir John Lauder remarked: 'And thus they hounded this poor man to death, a prey not worthy of so much pains, trouble and obloquy as they incurred by it.'[25] George Mackenzie received death threats,[26] and Lang believed it possible he was duped about the assurance given to Mitchell. This does not seem over-likely. A diligent prosecutor, Mackenzie could hardly have failed to study the Privy Council record of Mitchell's first and crucial examination; and Wodrow cites a claim by Mitchell that on his first arrest in 1674, Mackenzie was actually assigned to him as counsel.[27] In Sir George's philosophy, *raison d'état* and defence of the royal prerogative would take precedence over the matter of justice for a fanatic like Mitchell.

Ironically, in the same year Mackenzie published *Laws and Customes of Scotland in Matters Criminal*, dedicated to his new patron, Lauderdale, whom he salutes as a scholar and statesman. The criminal laws, some of them reaching back for centuries, were in great need of ordering and interpretation, and the book, intended as a working lawyer's guide, is in two parts, the first defining types of crime and the second examining jurisdictions and procedures. It was valued and used until well into the 19th century. Among his peers it confirmed him, with his philosophical writings, as a man of eminence.

The administration's big idea for 1678 was rapidly becoming reality. Few other schemes could have more clearly shown the divisions and contrasts within the country. While government's task is to contain and harmonise such divisions, a hard-pressed ruler would not shrink from exacerbating and exploiting them for his own purposes. On 8 November 1677 Lauderdale, writing about his plans to the Earl of Danby, head of the English government, said, 'this game is not to be played by halves, we must take this opportunity to crush them'.[28] In December 1677 a warrant was issued for a number of territorial lords in the southern Highlands to raise a force of their servants and vassals, in order to aid the normal forces. The 'Highland Host', as it speedily became known, some 7,000 strong, assembled on 24 January 1678 at Stirling, marched south, and, supplemented by around 2,000 Lowland militiamen, was dispersed to find 'free quarters' within the counties of Lanark, Renfrew, Ayr, and the Stewartry of Kirkcudbright. Mackenzie later wrote that 'most men paid for their quarters'[29] but there is no evidence, or likelihood, of this.

The operation was carefully planned, with the Marquis of Huntly commissioned to keep the peace in Highland districts where the withdrawal of fighting men might have tempted neighbours to make incursions; no-one of rank was allowed to leave the kingdom without permission, and all males between 16 and 60 commanded to be in readiness to join the King's army, if summoned.[30] Fife, which might have been likewise occupied, was spared when a meeting of its gentry and heritors, under Rothes's persuasions, agreed to sign a bond that made them responsible for the good behaviour of tenants and servants. If the Council was not trying to provoke a rebellion, it was certainly preparing to oppose one: and a train of field artillery was sent from Edinburgh to Glasgow. Troops and militia in Northumberland were placed at the disposal of the Scottish Council.[31] Instructions to the 'Committee of the West' included orders to gather up arms and ammunitions and all horses above £Sc50 in value. There was to be nothing haphazard about the method: commanders were to obtain 'true and perfect lists' of the heritors from the sheriffs, and summon them to appear and either sign the bond of 2 August, or be immediately subject to 'fining, confining, prisoning, banishing, or other arbitrary punishment, according to law, as you find cause'.[32]

Invited to co-operate with (but not to join) the Committee, the Duke of Hamilton pleaded indisposition. The Earl of Cassillis complained about the infliction of the Highlanders, 'differing in habit, language and manners from all mankind' who had invaded a region 'while there is not the least shadow of an insurrection'. The Council's reply was robust and dwelt on the inability of such leading men as Cassillis himself to exercise control over the people.[33] It was found that in some places, presbyterian meeting-houses had been put up, and these were ordered to to be demolished. But the vast majority of inhabitants, from Hamilton down, declined to sign the bond. On 14 February, the Council raised the stakes by putting non-signers under the sanction of 'lawborrows' – an old legal device intended to enforce peace between hostile neighbours, to obtain which the complainant had to swear that he dreaded 'bodily harm, trouble and molestation', and by which the other party was bound to provide caution and surety against committing such offences. The King was the guarantor of the status and effectiveness of lawborrows, and for them to be enacted between him and his subjects was a grotesque distortion of the law. Mackenzie was almost certainly responsible for this piece of legal ingenuity.

The overwhelming majority of presbyterian non-conformers were not hostile to the King. The concept of the king as somehow separate from his own policies was strongly held, if only because without it, there seemed no solution at all. The south-west was not in chaos: markets were held, business done, normal taxes collected, cases of civil law were followed in due process. Its inhabitants considered themselves to be loyal citizens and the attempt to invoke lawborrows against them merely increased their anger and obstinacy. Official labelling of their behaviour as 'sedition' was genuinely wounding to their minds. But to the angriest, and most extreme, it was very clear that the King's government was bent on making an end to the long rampancy of civil disobedience and would not hesitate to manipulate the law, and, if necessary, to use force of arms. For those who held to the Covenants as well as to presbytery, it was obvious that Charles II was not a king in the National Covenant's terms, and, indeed, as a renegade in their eyes, was worse than his father. Against such a king, the Covenant licensed and required action.

The Highland occupation was intended to be both a punishment and a deterrent to further disobedience, and Covenanter historians saw it as a deliberate attempt to provoke the people into revolt. Wodrow claims that in Ayrshire they 'committed the most notorious outrages, wounded and dismembered some persons without the least shadow of provocation,'[34] but he does not record a single death as directly caused by them. For a 17th-century army of occupation, this is remarkable and possibly unique, but it can also be seen as a tribute to the capacity of the south-westerners to thole their tribulations, to resist attempts at provocation, and make none. Crimes such as rape are not recorded, though that may say more about the status of women than the restraint of the occupiers. Between the mildness of the Highlanders, and the stoicism of the Lowlanders, it was a failure. On 18 February, the Council gave order for most of the Host to go home, and the men from Balquhidder, Atholl,

Stormont, and the Braes of Strathmore set off, with as much as they could carry: Bed-clothes, carpets, clothes, pots, and grid-irons were among the loot.[35] The termination of their stay is most probably explained by the lack of food stocks at that time of year, as well as a lack of incident; once they had consumed the inhabitants' supplies of food, drink, coal and firewood, they could not remain. A detailed estimate of the losses through fines and plunder in Ayrshire amounts to £137,000.[36] Small troops of militia, locally garrisoned, replaced the occupiers. The Highland Host would not be called up again.

CHAPTER SIXTEEN

Beloved Sufferers

FROM LONDON, LAUDERDALE RETURNED a cordial answer to the Council's report of its actions.

Among the opponents and victims of the policy who went to court to complain were two who had sent men with the Highland Host, but now emerged as critics of Lauderdale: James Drummond, who had succeeded his father as Earl of Perth in 1675, and John Murray, Marquis of Atholl. Perth was ambitious and keen to improve his family's wealth and status, which he described as at 'a low ebb' in an unctuous letter to Lauderdale of 6 December 1677.[1] Their drawing away from Lauderdale suggests that there were already hints abroad that the King was considering a change of Secretary of State. So many of the administration's critics were in London that in April 1678 the Council sent Sir George Mackenzie down, to make sure their point of view was represented. As part of their own manoeuvrings, the King's brother, the Duke of York, supported Lauderdale and the Council, while Charles's illegitimate son the Duke of Monmouth, with the Earl of Shaftesbury, provided a rallying-point for the opposition.

At the level of tea-house conferences and private discussions, Scottish and English politics were being drawn together. The House of Commons, still hostile to Lauderdale, continued to take what some considered an unseemly interest in Scottish affairs. Mackenzie wrote to the Duke at the end of April to complain: 'I reproved Secretary Williamson [English Secretary of State] for opposing the King's interest and meddling in points of our law which he understood not.'[2] Among the numerous Scots at court was Claverhouse, angling for a commission and clearly making himself useful to the York/Lauderdale group: a letter from Mackenzie to Lauderdale at this time notes: '... you and we all are much indebted to Claverhouse, who is our generous friend.'[3]

Meanwhile, a pamphlet war was raging over the Highland Host episode, with Mackenzie a vigorous participant. Condemning the efforts of the Kirk which in 1638 'violently grasped at all, even the civil government,' he traced the way in which, 'rent in pieces by its own viperous brood' of Remonstrants and Protesters, it had opened the way for Cromwell's Usurpation.[4] Mackenzie was very much in royal favour, and an act of the Privy Council on 26 June 1678 commended him for 'maintaining his Majesty's just and lawful prerogatives.' Hamilton and his associates achieved nothing with the King, and backed off from putting their complaints about Lauderdale into written form. Under Scottish law, this could have been interpreted as 'leasing-making', fomenting divisions between the King and the people, a capital offence; and Mackenzie, hot for the King's rights, would have jumped at the opportunity. Away from the political storm, either on this visit to London, or his next in 1679, Mackenzie met John Dryden, Poet Laureate in England, then still a stout defender of Anglicanism, and the two men discussed poetry. It was a mark of a certain cosmopolitanism and polish to have English friends outside the bounds of official contact, and Mackenzie took pride in hob-nobbing with men like Evelyn and Dryden. Dryden later noted that 'that noble wit of Scotland, Sir George Mackenzie' had given him the beneficial advice to study the style of their contemporary poets Edmond Waller and Sir John Denham.[5]

With the King's favour so obviously still behind Lauderdale, something more than mere jealousy of the Duke must be accorded to Hamilton, the Duke of Queensberry and others who by virtue of their rank had high profiles in the opposition. If they had little to gain by supporting Lauderdale, they had much to lose if their opposition could be construed as treasonous. Their status offered them a degree of protection, but in opposing the regime (which was after all implementing royal policy) they were walking on thin ice. When they could safely be damaging, they went ahead. With these men, the power of Kirk patronage could backfire on its purpose: they deliberately left pulpits empty rather than appoint an 'orthodox' man proposed by the bishop, and as local justiciars tolerated preaching and the celebration of the sacraments by outed ministers or by younger men who had not received episcopal ordination.[6]

As a result of information received, or perhaps the sheer blatancy of the event, a large conventicle was broken up at Williamwood, in Cathcart parish, in May. Around 60 men were arrested, and, most of them refusing to take the bond, were taken to Edinburgh, tried, and sentenced to banishment and lifelong penal servitude in 'his majesty's plantations in the

Indies.'[7] A London-based merchant, Ralph Williamson, contracted with the Council to ship them to the Indies, where he would sell them. But when the ship carrying them arrived at Gravesend, Williamson was not to be found, and after a few days the prisoners were simply dumped ashore in England, from where they gradually straggled back to their homes. Others arrested were not so lucky and lived out their lives as slaves, or were sold into the armies of France and other continental powers.

In June 1678 a Convention of the Estates was summoned, in order to ensure supply. All members signed 'a Declaration against the Covenant, asserting the King's prerogative.'[8] Though supposedly restricted to taxation matters, the convention provided a platform for Hamilton and the 'Party' to protest about the blatant rigging of elections in many places. Lauderdale as Commissioner, in confident mood, a 'Huffing Hector' as a contemporary satirist called him, obtained majority support for a new cess, or tax, to raise a very large sum, '£Sc eighteen hundred thousand pounds,'[9] which would be spent on raising and maintaining a new regiment of foot and three troops of horse. The cess was to eliminate the need for the soldiers to find themselves 'free quarters' in disaffected districts but it threw the Presbyterians into a new internal dispute: should they pay, or refuse? Many who still held out against signing the bonds paid the cess, on the basis that the government had a right to levy taxes. The example of Marcus Arethusius, a fourth century Arian bishop who had destroyed a pagan temple and suffered martyrdom rather than pay for its rebuilding, was much discussed. Quintin Dick of Dalmellington, a respected figure among Presbyterians, adopted their proper course, of consulting his conscience and 'pouring out my heart to God.'[10] Dick found it was proper to pay Caesar, and though some consciences returned the opposite answer, the great majority paid up on demand, with whatever protest or reservation they might have. Decision-making among the Covenanters was neither democratic nor authoritarian: it relied on inspiration, and matters were agreed 'not after a carnal manner by the plurality of votes, or authority of a single person, but according to the word of God; so that the word makes and carries the sentence.'[11] When successful, this method of spiritual guidance could produce adamantine unity, but the required unanimity of spirit was not always present, which led to hesitations, delays and divisions.

Robert McWard tossed into the debate *The Poor Man's Cup of Cold*

Water, Ministered to the Saints and Sufferers for Christ in Scotland, published in Edinburgh late that year: a long tract, self-deprecating in title but meant to be a stout bracer to the resolve of the Presbyterians, after the Highland Host, the execution of Mitchell, and the lawborrows. It came out before the cess affair but its message was clear: their resistance was making the non-conformers ever more dear to God. He did not dodge unpalatable issues – 'We still think there is a Way (because we would have it so, and often make a way where He hath made none) to shift these hard Sayings, and shun these heavy Things; and yet come at heaven: we fancy a possibility to pass through the World with the World's good will, and be religious too. But this is to be wise above that which is written: the Devil must first cease to lie' – and even, '... yet if you look within you, and lift up your Eyes above you, and consider how the Cry of your Transgressions is come up into his Ear, you will be constrained, not only to justify him, in this seeming Severity, but to confess, from Clearness and Conviction, you are *punished less than your Iniquities deserve:* and that *it is of the Lord's Mercy you are not consumed, because his Compassions fail not*'. At the same time, he stresed the ultimate rewards which the 'Beloved Sufferers' would reap, if they kept to the way, even if it should be long and hard, and the final day of reckoning long postponed.[12] McWard and the other leading preachers were always concerned to curb any sense of millennary over-enthusiasm or hysteria among their flocks; they knew this could wreck the cause, and always emphasised that the end would come in God's time, and they might not live to see it.[13] Thirty years before, David Dickson, Professor of Theology at Glasgow, had said that 'God's presence among his people will not exempt them from trouble, but from perdition in trouble: he will not exempt the bush from burning, but from being consumed;'[14] a few years later James Renwick spelled out their expendability to his own generation in a letter from Holland in early 1683: 'What is the matter though we all fall? The cause shall not fall.'[15]

Graham of Claverhouse was a zealous gatherer, at the head of his troops, of the new cess in the far south-west. In February 1679, legal powers were added to his military commission, as a sheriff-depute of Dumfries, Annandale, Wigtown, and Kirkcudbright, along with his lieutenant, Andrew Bruce of Earlshall. At the same time, the mood within 'this poor, persecuted, and now divided church'[16] began to change. Zeal and fervour were increasing; something ascribed to the young people who had been drawn in. The renewed severity of the Government tended to discredit the Indulged clergy, and encouraged the fierier spirits to preach against them. Pamphlets for and against continuing to listen to Indulged ministers were circulated. Older field preachers like Welsh, who had once been established ministers, were giving way to a new generation who had never known any state other than that of persecution, and who began to preach the people's right to violent resistance. Among the veterans, the ascetic Donald Cargill, 59 in 1678, stood out as a vocal opponent of any compromise, and became a bell-wether of the extremists. The Covenants were much discussed, and the King's abandonment of them angrily recalled; those who still advocated 'meekness and patience under affliction for Christ's sake' were less and less heeded. But the new spirit also caused dispute, and discouraged many adherents: 'By reason of these unhappy jars, many deserted us, and many more never joined us.'[17]

Numbers of those involved are difficult to gauge. The heartland of dissent, between Glasgow, the Mull of Galloway, and Annandale held perhaps a fifth of Scotland's population, around a quarter of a million people, overwhelmingly of presbyterian persuasion, though to varying degrees. By 1679, it seems likely that even here, committed Covenanters were hardly more than 10 per cent of all adults, but the number of those who sympathised, whether or not they had ever been among the faithful, is likely to have been much greater. They would not 'come out', but they might give aid or shelter, and would be unlikely to turn informer. In August 1678, Matthew Mackail, an opponent of the Covenanters, wrote to John Adams, a Scottish merchant based in Lisbon, describing how John Welsh 'with 36 other nonconformist Ministers convented 10,000 of the king's I know not whether to say Lieges or enemies, at Maybole near Ayr, celebrated the Lord's supper with great solemnity, preached up the Solemn League and Covenant, the lawfulness of defensive arms... declaring they will defend themselves if opposed by His Majesty's forces.'[18] Mackail was reporting on hearsay, but even allowing for exaggeration, it is clear that large-scale and militant conventicles were organised. In March 1679 a skirmish at Lesmahagow involved a troop of dragoons and a Covenanter force said to number 300 foot and 60 horsemen. Ordered in the King's name to disperse, their leader replied that he farted in the King's teeth, 'for we appear here for the King of Heaven'.[19]

Claverhouse, constantly on the move in policing a vast expanse of hills and moors, threaded by rivers, with any number of ravines and rocky places where groups and gangs could hide, was increasingly convinced that some kind of rebellion was imminent.[20]

At this time the violent reactions in England to the 'Popish Plot' against the King, as alleged by Titus Oates, were in full force, and Charles's Scottish Council could congratulate itself on the fact that no Scot had been implicated (in what turned out to be a tissue of fabrications). Catholics, the Pope, and the whole apparatus of the Counter-Reformation, prime demon-figures 40 years before, were nowadays hardly considered in the deliberations of the Council, and the penal laws against them rarely had to be enforced. This was chiefly because they were extremely few in number and discreet in their practices; but also, the governors of Scotland knew that harassment of Catholics would not be at all to the liking of Charles II, whose brother, Duke of York and Albany, heir-presumptive to the Scottish crown, had been an openly professed Catholic since 1672. During the furore he was in temporary exile on the continent, but while in England there was a strong movement to exclude him from the succession, there was no similar call in Scotland.

CHAPTER SEVENTEEN

Assassination, Schism, Defeat

WITH SUCH AN ENERGETIC officer as Claverhouse in the field, and the new militancy of the still-substantial Covenanting 'remnant', a collision of some kind was inevitable, but the critical act happened not in the southwest, but in Fife, where the 'submission' achieved by Rothes in 1677 had merely papered over the resentments of the Presbyterians. Conventicles were frequent, and outlawed persons passed freely, but counter-measures were being taken. On 3 May 1679 a posse of 12 Covenanter lairds, hard cases all of them, was out near Ceres looking to intercept sheriff-depute William Carmichael. An incomer from Edinburgh, he was zealous in the tracking down of conventiclers and the imposition of fines. According to the account given later by James Russell, one of their number,[1] they meant only to give Carmichael a fright and chase him off, but their intentions changed when a local woman told them that the Archbishop's coach was not far away, carrying Sharp back to St Andrews. Taking it as a Mitchellian 'call' from God to the righteous, nine of them set off in pursuit of the coach, overtook it, and forced it to a halt on the desolate expanse of Magus Muir, a little to the west of St Andrews, already within sight of the tower of St Salvator's College and the great, shattered western gable of the cathedral. Sharp was travelling with his daughter. Dragged out, he begged for mercy, but was ordered to make his peace with God, in preparation for death. They fired their pistols at him, and failing to kill him, drew their swords. '... Upon the sight of cold iron, immediately his courage failed... he made hideous and terrible shrieks.' One of them slashed at his face, 'and one of his chops fell down', then all fell on him, stabbing and slashing repeatedly.[2] Only one of the group, David Hackston of Rathillet, played no part, not because he would have spared the victim, but because he considered himself to have a grudge against the Archbishop and did not want to sully the God-inspired deed with a personal motive. When the wounded man crawled towards him, pleading for help, he backed his horse away.

Despite the pathos and the brutal circumstances of Sharp's death, there has always been ambivalence in Scotland about this crime. Sharp was detested by the presbyterians like no other; it is likely that many rejoiced at his killing, while others saw it sombrely as divine retribution on the arch-traitor to Kirk and Covenant. The killing of Cardinal Beaton, by a very similar band of Protestants, in 1546, was often referred to; and Wodrow quotes Sir David Lindsay's comment on that earlier assassination, as equally apposite in 1679:

> But of a truth, the sooth to say,
> Altho' the loon was well away,   [fellow was well rid of]
> The fact was foully done.³   [deed]

Eight years later, after the 'Killing Time', Alexander Shields would record that 'several worthy gentlemen... executed righteous judgement upon him'.⁴ To yet others, of course, it was a source of dismay, horror and outrage, an act of terrorism against an unarmed churchman, but also against a great officer of state. Philosophy temporarily laid aside, Sir George Mackenzie wrote in passion to Lauderdale: '... we will put them all to the torture. Remember that King Alexander II killed 400 for the death of one Bishop of Caithness and gelded them and what law had he for that?'⁵ It seemed possible that a campaign of assassination was begun: in another letter to Lauderdale, Mackenzie reported that while riding from Shankend into Edinburgh with two others, they had been intercepted by four armed men. They asked if Mackenzie was in the party, but retreated when Mackenzie's servants approached.⁶

Through a countryside crackling with tension, and by no means friendly, with Council agents watching ferries and river crossings, the assassins made their way west to Dunblane, then southwards, sometimes pretending to be among their own hunters, towards their only safe haven, among the Covenanters. For those who chose to see it in that way, the elimination of Sharp and the escape of his killers provided a beacon to further action in testimony 'against the iniquity of the times'. God had given the moment: they must seize it. Among the leading figures the most vocal was the 29-year old Robert Hamilton, son of the laird of Preston and Fingalton, a minor member of the extensive range of Hamilton gentry. His impassioned demands for a show of strength were not held back by Cargill or Thomas Douglas, the two senior ministers in their councils.

Carving from Archbishop Sharp's Tomb, St Andrews Parish Church
Reproduced from Kirkton's History

In order both to rally the faithful and to shake a lance at the Privy Council, they resolved to make a public demonstration in Glasgow, by burning some acts of parliament and setting out their own tenets. In the end, Glasgow was felt to be too well guarded, and the small nearby burgh of Rutherglen was selected. On 29 May, the day on which loyal citizens celebrated the King's birthday and restoration, there were bonfires burning, which the party of 80 armed Covenanters promptly put out before making one of their own to burn the copies of the acts, and fixing their Declaration to the market cross.[7] The preamble to its seven points refers to 'an evil and perfidious adversary to the Church and Kingdom of our Lord Jesus Christ in the land. Now we being pursued by the same adversary for our lives...' As a rallying-cry it left much to be desired, but its seven points summarised the Covenanters' grievances, from the Act Rescissory to the divisive Indulgences and the outlawing of the Covenants.

After the Rutherglen episode, Claverhouse made it his special concern to track down Robert Hamilton and his party.[8] On 31 May, he left Glasgow with three cavalry troops and an infantry detachment. Passing through Hamilton, his dragnet picked up a Covenanting preacher, the Rev. John King, and some of his supporters, and he also was given information of a conventicle to be addressed by Thomas Douglas, on the following day, a Sunday, at Loudonhill, a few miles west of Strathaven. He set out to disperse it and take as many prisoners as he could, but if he knew about them, they also knew about him, and around 200 armed men left the gathering and intercepted the troops at Drumclog, two miles to the eastward. Graham's training in large armies and big battles had not, perhaps, prepared him for an encounter like this. In correct style, he offered a parley, to give the non-conformers the opportunity to surrender, but this was rejected out of hand. The sense of extraordinary events at work sharpened the Covenanters' zeal; at least three of Sharp's killers were among them, though Robert Hamilton seems to have considered himself the commander. Foremost in the fighting, however, was a youth of 19, William Cleland, a recent graduate of St Andrews, said to be a son of one of the Marquis of Douglas's gamekeepers.[9] He led one attack which was driven back, then headed another. Armed mainly with pitchforks, and with few guns, the irregulars' only hope was a fight at close quarters, and the vigour of their second attempt broke right through the troops, killing some 30, and the rest fled in disorder or claimed quarter. This was given, not without angry disagreement among the victors, and Hamilton shot one prisoner dead.[10] Some 40 Covenanter horsemen pursued the fugitives. Claverhouse's horse, speared by a pitchfork, ran wild, bearing him away from the site of the battle.

The victory of Drumclog, small-scale as it was, blared as a bugle-call through the south-west. Revealing sympathies previously safe-hidden, the citizens of Strathaven had turned out to attack the retreating troops, though Claverhouse reported he 'made them run, leaving a dozen on the place'. In his despatch to the commander-in-chief, the Earl of Linlithgow, he also wrote, 'This may be counted the beginning of the rebellion.'[11] To the jubilant Covenanters, it seemed yet another sign of God's favour, and the call went out for men to join what was rapidly becoming an army. Having feared to enter Glasgow before, the Covenanters moved in on 2 June. The troops there remained behind barricades, but, according to their commander's report, '... we galed them so with our shot that at last they run for it throwing down their arms'.[12] The rebel force left to base themselves around the small town of Hamilton, where they availed themselves of the Duke's parkland, he being in London. Couriers were racing between the Council in Edinburgh and the court at Whitehall, and with rumours of thousands coming to join the rebellion, action was prompt. The army commander, Lord Linlithgow, concentrated his regular forces on Stirling, while a government army was assembled with remarkable speed, showing how much things were already on a military footing. The Duke of Monmouth was placed in command as Captain General. Monmouth, who had held this role in the Dutch war, also had a Scottish title as Duke of Buccleuch, having married the Buccleuch heiress, but his presence was a sign that London had finally stretched its long arm to deal with the people whom Edinburgh had failed to control. Substantial forces from England, 3 regiments of foot, 3 of horse, and 800 dragoons were sent to bolster the Scottish regulars and shire militias. The army of the Covenant only had to wait, and prepare, for their cause to be put to a far greater test than Drumclog.

Experienced, ruthless and determined men were not lacking among them, but there was no general. Robert Hamilton assumed this role but he had no military training and no notion of how to command a large army. In any case, he was convinced that God was on the march with them, and that so long as the Covenanting army was formed of true believers, all would be right on the day. 'Never did any fatalist more absolute than Hamilton bend to Allah or Mohammed'[13] – Hamilton himself would have preferred a comparison with Joshua or Gideon. Discipline, management and tactical planning were all lacking. The presence of a lord or two might have made the force cohere around a resonant name, but the presbyterian nobility kept well away. In this army of small lairds, farmers, craftsmen, townsmen and villagers, every man was his own master. Its numbers fluctuated between four and seven or so thousand as people came and went. Among the leaders it was generally agreed that some form of declaration should be published, to justify and advertise the rebellion. But this was the only matter agreed on.

With the arrival of John Welsh and a band of fighting men from Carrick in Ayrshire, it became plain that there were two minds among the Covenanters. Welsh was chief spokesman of a group which wanted the declaration to be as widely based as possible in order to win the support of all Presbyterians. Cargill however insisted that the declaration should condemn the Indulgences and by extension all who had accepted them, whether clergy or laity. This would shut off support from very many potential recruits, but neither Cargill nor Robert Hamilton cared about that. Rival drafts were made, argued over, and abandoned, and the whole army was drawn into the debate. The Cargillite proposal made no mention of the King. Welsh's party tried to pre-empt things by fixing their document to the Hamilton town cross on 13 June. Known as the 'Hamilton Declaration', it professed loyalty to the King as well as to the Covenants. The extremists, perhaps fewer in numbers but not yielding an inch, disowned it. Appointment or election of senior officers was impossible as each side rejected adherents of the other. Even as the royal army was approaching, the disputes raged on. Since each side claimed divine inspiration, neither could retreat. Hamilton and his supporters walked out of a meeting set up on the 21st to promote harmony, when battle was plainly imminent. The two armies faced each other from positions on each side of the River Clyde, with the stone hump of Bothwell bridge between them. On 22 June, with shots already being exchanged, both factions agreed to ask Monmouth for a parley. Carried over by two of the 'moderates', their paper laid out demands for freedom of worship, a free Church assembly, a free parliament, and an indemnity. The Duke was courteous, even sympathetic, but refused any sort of dealing until the Covenanters laid down their weapons and trusted to his mercy.[14] Even if the moderates had been willing to agree to this, the extremists rejected it out of hand. 'And hang next' was Hamilton's comment.[15] No answer was returned, and Monmouth scarcely waited for one before opening his attack.

After a short artillery barrage, a detachment of dragoons went forward and stormed the bridge, whose defenders, led by David Hackston, very quickly ran out of ammunition. With no prepared positions, and not having properly barricaded the bridge itself, or tried to mine its piers, they fell back, leaving the way open. Once the royal army had gained the bridge, the infantry began to cross, forcing the Covenanters back; then the cavalry, including Claverhouse and his troop, came over, and the battle proceeded to its inevitable conclusion. Disorganised, confused, battered by cannonade, increasingly dismayed, the Covenanters' resistance dissolved into rout. Robert Hamilton fled from the scene of his incompetence. 'Never was a good cause and a gallant army... worse managed,'[16] wrote Wodrow. Around 400 were killed, and 1,200 taken prisoner; apart from a few killed in storming the bridge, the government losses were negligible. Vigorous pursuit of the fleeing rebels[17] was virtually the only task the cavalry had to perform, though Monmouth is credited with ordering his men not to kill the prisoners and fugitives. The wandering minister Alexander Peden, who was not at the battle, and to whom various prophetic utterances are credited, is said to have cried out, 'Our friends

The Battle of Bothwell Bridge, 22 June 1679
Reproduced from Wodrow's *History*, Vol. III

are fallen and fled before the enemy at Hamilton; and they are hagging and hashing them down.'[18]

Again, an unplanned, uncoordinated and ill-equipped rising had collapsed in the face of state power, but this one, even before military defeat, had virtually imploded through its own disunity. Never again would anything like a mass of the people rally in nominal support of the Covenants; from Bothwell Bridge onwards, the cause would be sustained only by a Remnant, though a fiercely dedicated one. In considering later assessments of the period from 1670 to 1690, it is important to keep this in mind: all Covenanters were Presbyterians, but an ever-growing majority of Presbyterians were no longer Covenanters.

In the immediate aftermath of the battle the Privy Council expressed its eagerness to hang the ringleaders, but the official mood that prevailed, both in London and with Monmouth, was relatively lenient. Some of the leaders had escaped; also it was not easy in this army of individuals to identify real leaders. Many of the prisoners were held within the walls of the Greyfriars Churchyard in Edinburgh, for several months. The only two clergymen to be captured, John King (who had escaped at Drumclog) and John Kid, were hanged as 'incendiary preachers' in Edinburgh in August, and later five men were hanged at Magus Muir, victims of a grisly ceremony offering retributive balance to the murder of James Sharp.

Circuit courts were set up to try local heritors who had participated in the rising, but a third Indulgence was also proclaimed on 29 June, which, exempting Sharp's assassins and those who helped them, offered remission to almost everyone else. Its tone was placatory, showing the King as 'desirous to reclaim all... such as have been misled by ignorance, or blind zeal (the pretexts of disorders), and to convince all indifferent persons, that too great severity is... far from our mind.' And house conventicles were allowed, apart from in Edinburgh and St Andrews, and within a mile of Glasgow University. So soon after an armed rebellion, this was remarkably moderate, and it has been ascribed to the influence of Monmouth. However, the King cannot be denied some credit, and he personally tried, without success, to get Robert Leighton to return to Scotland to help towards civil concord; but Leighton, at 67, was not willing for negotiations which he thought would be 'another drunken scuffle in the dark'.[19] The oath required of the Greyfriars prisoners, before they were released, did not require any religious commitment, merely to desist from taking up arms against the King. Even so, many refused it, and about 400 were in due course shipped into bondage across the Atlantic.

Monmouth left Scotland on 6 July, with the thanks of the Privy Council, a gold box containing the certificate of a Freeman of the City of Edinburgh,[20] and a constituency of support among moderate Presbyterians for his own aspirations. Three weeks later, Claverhouse, diverted from hunting the Bothwell fugitives, was on his way to London, in the company of the Earl of Linlithgow; Chancellor Rothes followed a little later. Scottish affairs were, for the moment, the pre-occupation of Charles II and his court. Claverhouse, as a relatively junior figure, may have been a staff officer to Linlithgow, since his own royal patron, the Duke of York, was still in exile. While in London, he had his portrait done by the industrious court artist Sir Peter Lely, as a military cavalier with lustrously rippling black wig, and a flamboyant cloak thrown over an armoured breastplate.

The period of appeasement was to be a short one, but one of those who benefited was William Carstares, released with other imprisoned ministers on 29 July 1679. No record exists of his having been tried and no engagement was required of him other than to 'live peaceably.'[21] After a visit to relatives in Ireland, he went to England in the autumn of 1680, and in 1681 was appointed as minister to a presbyterian congregation at Theobalds in Hertfordshire.

At the end of 1678 Richard Cameron had crossed to Holland and introduced himself to Robert McWard, who found him 'of a savoury gospel spirit'.[22] Finding the militancy of McWard and Brown more to his taste than Welsh's relative moderation, he stayed in that cockpit of Presbyterian politics and plots through most of 1679, and was duly ordained by them, despite protests from Scotland, where his divisiveness was feared by the more moderate element.[23] Too late for the action at Bothwell Bridge, he returned in October, sped by blessings from Rotterdam, sombre, purposeful, reinforced in principle and attitude, to link up with the Remnant. Determined, in McWard's words, to 'lift the fallen standard and display it publicly before the world',[24] Cameron found that some spines needed stiffening. On 30 October he wrote to McWard that he had consulted with two others about going to the fields and found them both opposed to it, on account of the hazard: 'This is the greatest strait and sharpest trial I ever yet met with, for their arguments do not satisfy my conscience.'[25]

Their position as ordained presbyterian ministers meant far more to Cameron, Cargill and their colleagues, than their own personal qualifications. They considered themselves to be the Church of Scotland, the only true heirs of the General Assembly of 1648. The pride of the Remnant expanded in inverse ratio to its numbers and perceived status by the rest of the country. Neither military defeat nor official clemency was going to eradicate 'phanatisme'. Cameron's message was open revolt: 'If ye would have God be for you, ye must cut off this king... If ever ye see good days in Scotland without disowning the present king, then believe me no more,'[26] and this was enough to establish him as the prime public enemy. To the annoyance of Welsh and others, outdoor conventiclers began to be indiscriminately labelled as 'Cameronians'.

An incidental victim of the rising was the Duke of Lauderdale. He was only 63 but very fat,[27] his powers were beginning to fail, his subservience to his wife had become a public joke, and his policies had led – again – to an uprising. At the very time of Drumclog and Bothwell Bridge, his enemy Hamilton, along with the Marquis of Atholl and Sir George Lockhart, was making trouble for him at court. Sir George Mackenzie of Rosehaugh was also there, to present the case for Lauderdale in what became almost like a trial before the King, with the two advocates making long statements. The complainers presented a lengthy set of grievances, including the infliction of the Highland Host, the lawborrows, and the Bond which made gentry responsible for the activities of their tenants. Even the Kirkton-Carstairs incident was included. Mackenzie continued to rest his case firmly on the defence of the King's rights to take action: the King of Scots, he claimed, derived his authority directly from God; there was no contract with his people, and the Council was there only to apply his power as instructed. Few other Scottish lawyers would have agreed with this version of the constitution (certainly not Lord President Stair, who was also present) but the news of rebellion cut across the dialectics. If Lauderdale was discomfited, Hamilton, in whose meadows and orchards the Covenanters were refreshing themselves under the indulgent eye of his wife (Duchess in her own right), did not cut a good figure either. Lockhart prudently withdrew from the debate, leaving Mackenzie triumphant.[28] Lauderdale was to be sidelined, however. He retained the title of Secretary of State until autumn 1680, but others were now to make the running with Scottish policy.

Monmouth had been a shrewd choice to lead the army that summer. His Protestant views, his supposed sympathy for Presbyterianism, his regally affable manner, and his lack of vengefulness after Bothwell Bridge made him popular. But his stay in Scotland was brief, and at the end of 1679 a royal duke of very different taste and temper arrived. James, Duke of Albany and York, had returned to England when his brother was taken suddenly and seriously ill in the early autumn. Charles had recovered, but the event heightened the political storm in England over whether a Catholic should be allowed to be heir to the throne. A sojourn in Scotland was preferable to renewed foreign exile, and the Duke took up residence in the newly extended Holyrood Palace, its interior not quite completed. Sir William Bruce the tax collector had also been Surveyor-General of the Royal Works from 1671 to 1676, and was responsible for the design of the additions to James IV's 15th-century fort-house. From 1679, Bruce would also embark on the building of his own Kinross House, the country's first complete neo-classical mansion.

With James's arrival, Scots found themselves to all intents and purposes ruled, for the first time since Queen Mary more than a century earlier, by an avowed adherent of the religion they had been taught to label as Antichrist, Babylon, the Great Whore and other offensive epithets. It fell to Sir James Dalrymple to utter a speech of welcome on behalf of the

Bar, an uncongenial task, in which he emphasised the commitment of Scotland to the Protestant religion rather more than its loyalty to the royal house.[29] Among those better pleased to see the Duke in Edinburgh was Claverhouse, who, with his patron now so close at hand, could hope for better things.

During the autumn of 1679, as the presbyterian community came to appreciate the full import of the Third Indulgence, the number of conventicles surged again, mostly in houses, as permitted; and the only field conventicles were those held by the still-outlawed but mutually hostile factions of John Welsh and his fellow veteran 'Auld Sandy' Peden; and that of Cargill, Cameron, and one or two others like Walter Smith. Smith's great theme was 'the 22 steps of defection' by which Scotland had slipped from the high place of 1638. Even the renewal of the Covenant by some in 1666 was a 'defection' because they had failed to acknowledge former breaches. For Smith, the sparing of prisoners' lives at Drumclog was a sin, 'doing the work of the Lord deceitfully, by withholding our sword from the shedding of their blood'.[30] The great increase in house-meetings, and the confidence with which the newly released ministers seemed to be setting up a parallel Church,[31] alarmed the Council. The Indulgence began to seem like a crack in the dam, that could swiftly become a wide and unfillable gap. In the autumn, the hunt for the still-uncaught assassins of the archbishop was intensified, and a proclamation was issued in November against all those who had taken part in the Bothwell Bridge rising and failed to sign the bond of peaceable behaviour required in the 'remarkable and unexpected proclamation' made after the battle. Now they were promised the full severity of the law.

CHAPTER EIGHTEEN

Blood shall be their Sign

'THE DUKE,' WROTE GILBERT BURNET, 'behaved himself upon his first going to Scotland in so obliging a manner, that the nobility and gentry, who had so long been trodden on by Duke Lauderdale and his party, found a very sensible change.'[1] Edinburgh had something like a court again, since James, for all that the tarty Nell Gwynn called him 'Dismal Jimmy', had a sense of regal style, and the Duchess was a glamorous Italian. The 'cavalier' element could put on some swagger. Members of the 'Duke's Company' of actors came up, and the teenage Princess Anne took a part in *Mithridates, King of Pontus*.[2] Milton's *Comus* was performed; there were routs and balls, and Edinburgh's first tea parties. Rothes, aged 51, was made a duke in 1681, which turned out to be the last year of his life. Although James had no formal role, he was deferred to as if he were a viceroy,[3] and immediately made a member of the Privy Council, without having to take the oath – an instruction from Charles indicated that his brother was not to be regarded in the same light as any other subject. Before long his position in the Council was a dominant one.

To the Cameronians, the Duke was 'that pimp of the Romish whore'.[4] But although the presbyterian chroniclers continue to relate the sufferings of those who were outside the terms of remission, or who transgressed the legislation that was still in force – incurring fines, imprisonment and often rough handling by government troopers, the decade of the '80s opened in a manner that was comparatively peaceful, and this was reflected in extensive building and rebuilding in both towns and country. 'There is a fund of good sense and good manners to be learnt by the study of the old Scottish burghs,' wrote George Scott-Moncrieff.[5] Edinburgh's first piped water supply was installed in 1681. Inside houses, great improvements were taking place. More people could afford a wider range of furnishings, accessories and clothing, and the businesses of craftsmen and tradesmen expanded. Commerce spread, and though some new trade may simply have been siphoned away from the old royal burghs, 246 licenses for new markets and fairs were granted in the years between 1660 and 1707: a vast increase on earlier years, indicative of the existence of surpluses that could be traded, and of imported items that could be afforded.[6] Economic improvement was driven by the continuing growth of small-scale industry and commerce. The Mint was busy: a new coinage of 'dollars' was issued from 1675 and between then and 1682 more half a million quarter-dollars were struck in addition to a large issue of copper coins.[7] Agricultural prices remained low. For many cottars and labourers, there may have been little change, but their brighter or more enterprising children had new opportunities to improve their circumstances. Many were excluded from economic or social improvement, however. The colliers and salt-panners, locked in serfdom, remained a wretched and brutalised under-class. In hardly better and often worse condition was the large body – around a tenth of the population – of beggars and vagrants, a permanent underworld of untouchables for whom the social system could find no place. An act of parliament of 1672 had enabled the Kirk Sessions of individual parishes to license people to beg locally, who otherwise would have had to be supported by the sessions' funds. Those who wandered from parish to parish were regarded as thieves and disturbers of the peace, liable to arrest, branding, whipping, and transportation to the plantations. Some of them may have been followers of the conventicles but they were more likely to be excommunicates or indifferent. The plight of blind, crippled, epileptic and otherwise disabled people who had no family to support them was bleak. To the writers of the time, they are an invisible presence.

Thomas Dalyell
Reproduced from Dalton, *The Scots Army*

General Tam Dalyell, by now almost 80 but not lacking in rancorous energy, temporarily demitted as army commander in favour of Monmouth, was reappointed and drove renewed attempts to catch the Bothwell Bridge leaders known to be still in the country. Commissioned to uplift the goods of declared rebels, Claverhouse played an active part but was frequently called away to join the Duke of York's entourage, both in Edinburgh and on his visits to London; and on one occasion to a diplomatic meeting at Dunkirk. These court interludes gave him some opportunity to pursue his courting – at a remove – of Helen Graham, and the favour of the Duke should have done him no harm in this. Whereas at first all he could offer was his honour and his prospects, he had been awarded in April 1680 the substantial forfeited estate of Freuch in Galloway, though it was not until February 1681 that he received the charter; and he was also relieved of paying taxes on his property of Glenogilvie. But Menteith was looking for ready money, and, as one commentator remarked, 'Her parents, and her mother in especial, aimed undisguisedly at disposing of her to the highest bidder.'[8] The Marquis of Montrose, not a man of comparable character to his grandfather, played a double game, for a time even considering Helen as a bride for himself, and also seeking to obtain the reversion of the Menteith earldom. Claverhouse had an unsatisfactory meeting with the Marquis in the summer of 1680, and ended up despising him. As the months went by, Helen Graham caught smallpox but recovered,[9] and the ardour of Claverhouse, who had been able to meet her in London, was not diminished, even when her inheritance was lost. In October 1681, he wrote to Menteith, who had informed Sir James and Lady Graham that they had nothing to expect from him, that: 'I need nothing to persuade me to take that young lady. I would take her in her smock.'[10] But in the spring of 1682, Miss Graham was married to a nephew of the Earl of Conway.[11]

On 14 May 1680, a considerable paring-down of the Third Indulgence was announced, to the pleasure of the Council, who wrote to the King on 17 June to say that its former latitude had led to 'insufferable disorders'.[12] The toughening of official attitudes offered its own opportunity to the ultras, who were preparing a new declaration. Helped by a group of women supporters, Cargill narrowly escaped from a scuffle with government agents at South Queensferry early in June, in which his companion Henry Hall, who had commanded one of the Covenant horse troops at

Bothwell Bridge, was killed. In Hall's pocket was found a lengthy draft setting out the Cargill-Cameron position. Although the Remnant would claim it was not a final statement, the 'Queensferry Paper' is a chilling document. At the time, repudiation of the King was its most notable feature, but it also promised punishment for witches, and that its government would rule 'principally by the civil or judicial law given by God to the people of Israel', presumably excluding its provisions for polygamy and slave-ownership. On the 22nd, Cargill and Cameron, escorted by around 20 armed men, entered the small Dumfries-shire town of Sanquhar, sang psalms, and Cameron's brother Michael read out their manifesto before it was fixed to the market cross. Claiming to come from 'the true presbyterian kirk, and covenanted nation of Scotland', it was an open declaration of war on Charles Stuart as a 'tyrant and usurper', an enemy to Christ, his cause, and his covenants. It also disowned Charles's brother, 'that professed papist'. Promising to execute righteous judgement on 'Blasphemy, Idolatry, Atheism, Bougerie, Sorcerie, Perjurie, Uncleanness, Profanation of the Lord's Day, Oppression and Malignancy', it ends defiantly: '... We hope after this, none will blame us for, or offend at our rewarding these that are against us, as they have done to us, as the Lord gives opportunity.'[13] Here was the legacy of the Covenant in all its bitter purity, offering nothing but vengeance, conceding nothing, summoning the people back to their neglected compact with God. In the eyes of the Government, Richard Cameron was the prime leader, and 5,000 merks was offered to anyone who brought him in 'dead or alive',[14] with 3,000 merks on Cargill, Michael Cameron, and Thomas Douglas. Some words from his last sermon breathe a sense of the yearning as well as the rancour which inflamed his thoughts:

> ... the Church of Scotland has been high in her time, fair as the moon, clear as the sun, and terrible as an army with banners. The day has been when Zion was stately in Scotland. The terror of the Church of Scotland once took hold of all the kings and great men that passed by... It is hard to tell where it shall first be erected, but our Lord is to set up a standard, and oh! that it may be carried to Scotland. When it is set up it shall be carried through the nations, and it shall go to Rome, and the gates of Rome shall be burned with fire... [15]

Patrick Walker quotes him as saying on the same occasion: 'Blood shall be their sign, and "No Quarter" their word.'[16]

Seven troops of horse were scouring the countryside for the party. Although they represented only a very small extremist wing of Presbyterianism, the searches, inquiries and arrests involved a much wider spectrum of non-conformers, many of whom had failed to take the post-Bothwell Bridge oath, or the previous bond, or had been delinquent in some other way, and were now punished for it. Sympathy for the ultras was further eroded. Robert Law, himself an 'outed' Presbyterian minister, condemns their 'corrupt principles and practices'[17] and makes a stark point about the heroism of Covenanter deaths: 'It is not the suffering but the cause that makes the martyr.'[18] Cameron and his associates, including David Hackston, kept on the move, sleeping rough, and on 22 July were at Airds Moss, in the parish of Auchinleck, in Ayrshire, when a military troop under Bruce of Earlshall came up on them. With 23 horsemen and 40 on foot, the Cameronians were more than doubly outnumbered, but they made a fierce fight of it. Richard Cameron and his brother were killed, with seven others, and Hackston, his horse trapped in boggy ground, was among the prisoners. He was led through Edinburgh in a grim procession, tied on to a horse and facing backwards, preceded by Cameron's decapitated head and severed hands, borne as trophies. Cameron's period of leadership was short, but his refusal to compromise, his eloquence, and his fighting exit, made him the best known leader of the Covenanters.

At last the Council had one of the group who had killed Sharp, albeit a non-participant. On 30 July, the same day on which he was condemned in a trial whose legitimacy he refused to recognise, Hackston was taken to the Cross of Edinburgh, where a huge crowd was gathered. He was not allowed to speak, and first his hands were lopped off, and with a rope round his neck he was drawn up three times to the top of the gallows by a pulley. Next he was castrated: '... the hangman cutting off his secrets and throwing them at his face'.[19] The executioner then cut open his breast, pulled out his still-beating heart, and held it up. He was disembowelled, and his heart and intestines burnt; his head was cut off, to be set with Cameron's on the Netherbow gateway of Edinburgh; and his body divided into four anonymous chunks of flesh which were sent to be displayed at Leith, Burntisland, St Andrews and Glasgow. Hackston was reported to bear the horrors with fortitude.[20] Lest Scotland seem unduly barbaric, comparable torments would have been inflicted for the same crime in every capital from Lisbon to Warsaw.

Cargill, still free, breathing fire, and attracting hearers, chose a meeting in the Tor Wood close to Stirling, in September, to make a solemn excommunication of the King, the Duke, and several others including General Dalyell and Sir George Mackenzie. Invoking his authority as an ordained minister of Christ, he placed his curse on them and their souls, for eternity. Here Robert 1 had stationed his army on the eve of Bannockburn in 1314, and they had knelt in prayer before the battle; and Cargill may have picked the place deliberately, since the Covenanters set their own claims on great events of the past. The King's Advocate was included '... for his apostacy... his constant pleading against, and persecuting to death the people of God... his pleading for sorcerors, murderers and other criminals, that before God, and by the laws of the land, ought to die'.[21] Supporters printed and pasted up copies of Cargill's sentences in Edinburgh, and the Council responded by issuing a special proclamation against him on 22 November, promoting him to the 5,000 merk reward level.

The Remnant's continuing ability to make its presence felt was a red rag to the all-too ready bull of authority, which had a tendency to treat all non-conformers as though they were covert Cameronians. As long as there was an organised group in existence that proclaimed war against the King, the Government had to try to stop it. Cargill maintained his will-o'-the-wisp existence into 1681, and the efforts to track him down, including torture of his arrested adherents, grew more heavy-handed. Women were not spared, and two, Isabel Alison and Marion Harvey, were hanged on 26 January in the Grassmarket of Edinburgh for refusing to deny the Sanquhar Declaration, and having given shelter to the outlawed preachers. At last, on 15 May, James Irvine of Bonshaw applied to the Council for his reward, having captured Donald Cargill. The preacher was kept in prison until mid-July before he was brought before the Council. On the 27th of that month he was hanged, with four other Cameronians. Those on the look-out for divine judgements noted that Rothes died on the previous day. His recent elevation to a dukedom made less noise in the country than the circumstances of his death, when he, so lately one of the scourges of the Covenanters, sent for presbyterian ministers to console him. Among them was John Carstairs, whose prayers at the Chancellor's death-bed were said to have moved almost everyone present to tears.[22]

A young man of 19, James Renwick, son of a weaver from Glencairn in Nithsdale, was in the crowd that watched the executions[23] and heard Cargill cry from the ladder that he was near the getting of the crown. He had completed his course as a Master of Arts at Edinburgh University, but refusal to take the necessary oath made it impossible for him to graduate formally. In this cause of fiery elders and ardent youth, he would emerge as the last spiritual and political leader of rebellion. That would not be until 1683, and meantime, the movement divided into cells and sections, known as the United Societies, partly for self-protection, partly to conserve its purity. At this time they were much embarrassed by the antics of a breakaway group, from the Bo'ness area in Linlithgowshire, led by a former sailor, 'Muckle John' Gib, who called themselves the 'Sweet Singers of Borrowstounness'.[24] Gib's 30 or so associates, mostly women, became a sort of ambulant harem, and some were retrieved by angry husbands. Fearing both public ridicule and the dangers of the wrong sorts of enthusiasm, the earnest-minded took due precautions. Society delegates met every quarter, the first time at Lesmahagow in December 1681.[25] By 1683, according to the testimony of Gordon of Earlston, under examination by the Council, there were 80 societies, with a total membership of around 7,000.[26]

Walter Smith, recorder of national defection, had also set out *Rules for Meetings*: 'It is the duty of private Christians to meet together for their mutual edification, by prayer and conference'[27] and his optimum number was 10 or 12 persons: any more than that, and the cell should re-divide (a precept discovered by many undercover organisations before and since). The Societies were inevitably highly politicised, secretive, and suspicious of new converts who might be informers; but there were many other presbyterian praying groups, common at least since the Third Indulgence allowed house meetings, whose purpose was as set out by Smith, but non-militant, and which tacitly ignored the demands of the Covenant. Most if not all would include the King in their prayers. This pietist, domestic aspect of presbyterian worship chimed in with a broad, developing trend across northern Europe and shows something other than the typical picture of dogma bellowed out across the grass and heather. Attenders at these meetings would have shared Smith's concern to guard against dissension and the amateur probing of specialised matters: 'Let no question be proposed anent any sublime point of divinity, in which there are great difficulties, such as the decrees of God, predestination, election.'[28]

Two matters of importance to the Government required the summoning of a Parliament, which met on 28 July 1681: one was the guarantee of 'supply'; the other was to guarantee the Duke of York's claim to succeed his brother as king. Although the 'exclusion' controversy which so preoccupied England had not spread north of the border, it was thought best to assure the matter, not least for the effect it would have on opinion in England. The Duke himself was Commissioner to this parliament. The required Acts were duly passed, with the Act of Succession confirming that the next heir by blood of a reigning monarch should succeed to the 'imperial crown of Scotland', and that no difference of religion could affect the succession. But this Parliament was not wholly biddable. A proposal for an 'act against popery and a Popish king', framed by Sir James Dalrymple, commissioner in this Parliament for Wigtownshire, was avoided by the dissolution of the committee set up to draft it. Sir James was not easily thwarted, however. Once succession and supply had been confirmed, the Government deferred to the demand for an Act to strengthen the status of the Protestant religion. The Act brought in a new oath, the Test, which was to be required of everyone holding a public office, down to the level of the village dominie, and also encompassing all those entitled to vote in parliamentary elections. Only 'the King's lawful Brothers and Sons' were formally absolved from having to swear it, so that the Catholic James did not have to denounce his religion.

It required the swearer to own and profess 'the true Protestant religion contained in the Confession of Faith received in the first Parliament of King James the Sixth' and also to renounce 'all such practices, whether Popish or Phanaticall,' contrary to and inconsistent with that religion and confession. If the genesis of the Test was concern for Protestantism, the Government could not resist incorporating themes of its own, including the affirmation that 'the King's Majesty is the only supreme governor of this realm over all persons and in all causes, as well ecclesiastical as civil'.[29] The Act also repudiated the Covenants.

The reference to the 1567 Confession of Faith had been put in at the instigation of Sir James.[30] Gilbert Burnet suggested Dalrymple was perhaps the only person who had read the old document and knew that it treated Christ as the head of the Kirk, and contained the assertion that: 'the repressing of tyranny is reckoned a duty incumbent on all good subjects'.[31] This aspect of the oath was hardly consistent with the admission of absolute royal supremacy.

'Our Sovereign lord, from his princely care for the wealth and flourishing of this his ancient kingdom' also was pleased to approve an Act of the 1681 Parliament 'for encouraging Trade and Manufactures'. James had become chairman of a Council of Trade and summoned merchants to 'advise anent the causes of the decay of trade' and suggest remedies. The drain

James Dalrymple, 1st Viscount Stair
Reproduced from Mackay, *A Memoir of Sir James Dalrymple*

of bullion to France through salt purchase, and the poor quality of Scottish coins were cited among major problems.[32] Factories and new joint-stock companies were encouraged, and the Act also noted that the importation of foreign goods 'which are superfluous or may be made within the kingdom… had exceedingly exhausted the money of the kingdom.'[33] Merchants were forbidden to import items of gold and silver and a whole range of expensive fabrics and fashionable foreign-made items of clothing. It is unlikely that this had much effect, as few workshops (silversmiths a notable exception) in the country could replicate the quality and style of European-made articles. Demand would always generate supply, and excisemen would be kept busy as a result. Favourable conditions were decreed for entrepreneurs, including the lifting of import duty on their raw materials and of export duty on their made goods, for a period of 19 years; their servants to be free of military duty, and their immigrant workers to become naturalised Scots. The Government was responding, rather belatedly, to the rampant Protectionism now enforced by almost every other country in favour of its own trade and industry. The Act of 1681 prompted the setting-up of about 50 joint-stock undertakings[34] over the next 15 years. Some, like the Royal Fishing Company, were complete failures; others, like the Linen Company, eventually became very successful. The known world was expanding and international trade increasing, with commodities like tea, tobacco, chocolate and coffee on the way to becoming essentials rather than expensive luxuries: the sense of fortunes to be made 'out there' might stimulate bright young men whose predecessors had hardly thought of being more than pedlars or mercenary soldiers.

After the proroguing of parliament in mid-September, the Duke of York may have felt reassured, as would such supporters of his as Graham of Claverhouse, and Sir George Mackenzie, for whom a straightforward succession was the key to peace and sound government. Both probably believed, or wished to believe, that James would consider his Catholicism a private matter which would not affect his reigning over a Protestant Scotland and its national Church with the hybrid amalgam of bishops and presbyteries. Episcopalians with good will to James, and not too concerned over religious niceties, could stomach the new oath. Even moderate Presbyterians saw it as a further attack, however, and anyone who took the Covenant seriously, or who believed in the independence of the Kirk, could not honestly take it. For them, the Test oath, however inconsistently phrased, was a repudiation of their personal covenant of grace, and a hazarding of their own eternal salvation. As for the Act of Succession, whatever combination of national grievances had forced the unwilling abdication of Mary I in 1566, her Catholicism was not the least; and if her great-grandsons thought a simple parliamentary majority could nullify 100 years of intense anti-Catholic feeling and indoctrination, they were about to discover their mistake: '... although it may be concluded that repression had broken the covenanting movement as such, it would be unwise to assume that "the main body of presbyterian dissent" had been similarly affected.'[35]

Sir James Dalrymple abstained in the parliamentary vote on the Test Act, and declined to take the oath. In a similar situation before, he had been called to London, and excused; now he made the trip on his own initiative and was refused an audience with the King. On his return to Edinburgh he resigned as Lord President of the Court of Session. When a man so eminent and discreet took a public stance in opposition, many others would feel equally strongly. The Duke of Hamilton temporised for six months before finally swearing. Four earls refused it and lost their heritable jurisdictions. Between 30 and 80 ministers refused and were compelled to quit their pulpits,[36] and many men in official posts, senior as well as minor, evaded it or were forced to quit. Most notable among those who baulked was Archibald Campbell, ninth Earl of Argyll. After much negotiation, he agreed to repeat the oath, but only 'as far as it was consistent with itself and the Protestant religion'.

Argyll's pursuit of fines and territory through his own justiciary courts had virtually ruined the McLean clan[37] and made him many other enemies. Two recently put in high office, Sir George Gordon of Haddo, Dalrymple's successor as Lord President, and Sir George Mackenzie of Tarbat, Lord Clerk Register, were among those suggesting to the Duke of York that for such a man as Argyll to put limitations on his loyalty was equivalent to treason.[38] The Earl was imprisoned, and though Sir George Mackenzie of Rosehaugh seems to have played no part in the machinations of his arrest, and later wrote that he never believed Argyll had treasonable intentions,[39] at the trial in December 1681 he led with great vigour for the prosecution on a charge of leasing-making, centring his argument on the premise that any fanatic could take the oath if he were allowed to make the same personal reservations as Argyll. Sir George Lockhart led for the defence, with Sir John Dalrymple as his junior – the first notable appearance of the future Earl of Stair. But this was a show trial and the verdict was inevitable. Claverhouse was among the jurors who found Argyll guilty. The Earl was sentenced to death, but, perhaps with the connivance of officials, was able to escape from Edinburgh Castle, using his small stature to dress as the page-boy of his step-daughter. He left the country and went 'underground', living first in London and later in Holland.

Argyll's trial made a focus for open criticism of the Test Act. Strong feelings were expressed, and an official *Explanation of the Sense in which the Test Act is to be interpreted* was issued in November, explaining that the reference to the Confession of Faith was to be taken as upholding Protestantism in a general sense, not in every one of its clauses. The verdict made Argyll even more of a Presbyterian hero, and even the schoolboys of Heriot's Hospital demonstrated, staging the mock trial and hanging of their official guard dog when it 'absolutely refused' to swallow the Test oath, even when smeared with butter to make it more palatable.[40] In a more radical manifestation of protest, students of Edinburgh University burned an effigy of the Pope with a copy of the oath in each hand. The Privy Council closed the university, and allowed it to reopen only if all students signed a bond of good behaviour.

York's period of government, more beneficial to the country than some historians will concede, also saw 'the only phase of conciliation in the Highlands during the Restoration era'.[41] Despite the prosecution of the presbyterian Argyll, self-interest can perhaps be too readily be seen in James's appreciation of the dynastic loyalty, and distaste for Presbyterianism, among the Gaels. A Commission for Securing the Peace of the Highlands operated between August 1682 and September 1684, formed of Highland as well as Lowland landowners. Four new justiciary courts were set up but surviving evidence suggests they found surprisingly little to do, contrary to 'the myth of endemic lawlessness'.[42]

CHAPTER NINETEEN

My Lord Advocate Does Wonders

FORCED BY HIS CONSCIENCE back into private life, Sir James Dalrymple found a congenial occupation in preparing the final version of a great work on which he had long been labouring. Begun to provide himself with his own set of basic codes and provisions of Scots law, it had gradually grown until by 1681 it could be published as *Institutions of the Law of Scotland*. Judges and lawyers, who had had to rely on incomplete and obsolescent collections of laws, and on the records of the courts themselves, now had at their disposal a comprehensive and magisterial compilation. Its quoted sources of judgements range across a wide range of legal authorities in France, Italy, Germany and Holland, and go back to Roman and Greek legists, since Scottish law, in common with the states of continental Europe, was derived ultimately from Roman Law. Sir James's great achievement was to marshal this varied and often confused tradition into a coherent national code based not simply on a conservative standpoint but on the up-to-date concept of 'natural law' taught by the influential Dutch jurist Hugo Grotius, who died in 1645 and whom Dalrymple had certainly studied, and may have met in France. An indication of how Scotland was acquiring some of the essential attributes of a modern European state, the *Institutions,* much modified and developed, remains the foundation of modern practice. The ill luck of the Dalrymples prevented Sir James from the rewards he deserved; when his work appeared, he was already identified with the 'wrong' party. Misfortune struck his household again in 1682. John Dalrymple had married an heiress, Elizabeth Dundas, in 1669, and they had two young sons. In the house at Carsecreuch a pistol lay on a table in the hall, loaded, and in playing with it the younger boy shot his brother dead.

Such a domestic tragedy might all too easily happen in a country where firearms were always at hand, but to the anti-Stair pasquil writers, it became a Biblical stain on the family:

'Off them ther sprang ane Abell and a Cain;
Would Cain his father as his brother use,
It something would the former act excuse;
Would he give his grandfather the thridd shott,   [third]
The parracide would turn a patriot[1] – '

A loaded gun in the hall was a sign that Carsecreuch might receive unwelcome visitors, inquiring after guests who might have been preachers at conventicles. Sir James was later to complain of 'hundreds of examinations and re-examinations… by way of inquisition.'[2]

The consequence of widespread resistance to the Test Act was a renewed stepping-up of the effort against dissenters and non-conformers generally, in what has been described as a policy of 'blundering violence'.[3] A party of Cameronians burned a copy of the Act in Lanark, on 12 January 1682, reiterating the manifestos of Rutherglen and Sanquhar; and the Government retaliated by making a bonfire of these declarations, along with a copy of the Solemn League and Covenant, in a gesture which only seemed to award greater significance to the Covenanters: 'Some thought it but a sorry politique, to burn the Solemn League, to revive the memory of what was long ago buried in oblivion.'[4] Claverhouse was one of the Council's 'chief instruments' according to one historian[5] though another felt his role was 'probably least intolerable'[6] among those with responsibility for arresting dissidents and levying fines.

Although there had been little public disturbance in Galloway, it was well-known that church attendance was minimal and conventicles both numerous and well-attended.[7] The Sheriff of Wigtown, Sir Andrew Agnew, had been deposed for refusing to take the Test, and the vacant sheriffdom was conferred, along with the rights of the heritable Regality of Tongland, on Claverhouse, who was also re-appointed a sheriff-depute of Dumfries, Annnandale and Kirkcudbright – a vast swathe of country, with instructions to enforce the laws throughout the region. Scotland's still-feudal political-legal structure made regalities – some 200 in total – separate legal enclaves, whose rights gave the holders responsibility for the administration of justice within their bounds, for all cases except treason, and entitlement to inflict the death penalty.[8]

Diligent as ever, Graham set his men to making lists of defaulters and conventiclers, administering the Test oath, and prosecuting refusers.

A legal dispute immediately arose with the Dalrymples. Claverhouse was a bitter pill for them – he was a 'usurper' in the Freuch estate of their friend Macdougall; he had obtained the sheriffdom of their friend Agnew; he was bringing a brusque approach to the identification of defaulters and conventiclers, and was set on inflicting the full scale of fines. Everything he did upset the *status quo* which had obtained up till now in their backyard. Perhaps misinterpreting his motive, both father and son seem to have completely failed to read Claverhouse correctly. Sir James's refusal to take the Test had deprived him of his rights as hereditary bailie of the regality of Glenluce, and these had passed to Sir John, who had taken the Test oath, and now contested Graham's right to jurisdiction in his district. He proposed to hold his own Regality Court, but Claverhouse, aware of the Dalrymples' previous laxity in enforcing the law, had already reported in his own correspondence with Queensberry that: 'The said Sir John did cabal and meet with several of the gentry and endeavour to make them combine with him to sustain his false representations... he had the impudence in their name to draw a most seditious, false and malicious representation against forces both officers and soldiers.'[9]

Queensberry's role in the dispute is interesting: after the long Lauderdale occlusion, his star was rising; he had recently been made a marquis, and was trying to put himself at the centre of affairs. To have both sides write to him as a confidential friend was a sign of his new importance. In July 1682 Sir James wrote to him that he was obliged to Claverhouse for his civility,[10] but open antagonism soon broke out. No-one attended Claverhouse's court in Glenluce except the two Dalrymples, who, he reported to the Council, 'offered to bribe the complainer [Graham] and give him a sum of money not to meddle with that regality'.[11] The sum offered, £150, might have corresponded to an estimate of Graham's share of fines, but nothing could have been more likely to antagonise Claverhouse than the suggestion that he was only interested in lining his own pockets.

Both sides took their case to the Privy Council, and meanwhile Sir John held his own court in August, imposing what Graham derided as 'mock fines, not extending to the 50th, 60th, or 100th part of what by law they ought to have been fined in'.[12] Something about Sir John stung Claverhouse out of his normal military correctness: one element in

Dalrymple's complaint was that in the hearing of other Privy Councillors, Claverhouse had threatened 'to give the complainer a box on the ear'.[13]

In Claverhouse's letters he speaks his mind, rarely carps, and never sneers, though sometimes he may indulge in a touch of irony. At this time, thanking Queensberry for precise answers, he remarks that this especially cannot be said of: '... my good friend the Advocate, who writes to me very kindly but very little in return of anything I desire of him; but I know he ordinarily loses the letters and forgets the business before he have the time to make any return.'[14] This may just be a rueful comment on Sir George's working habits, or it may imply that he was not being as helpful as he should. Mackenzie had a high regard for Sir James, and things were not going well for the Dalrymples. In September, acting on a timely hint from the King's Advocate that his arrest was imminent,[15] Sir James took passage on a ship to Holland, and settled at Leiden. Mackenzie himself was very conscious that Lauderdale's era was over and the Duke of York was assembling his own team. After Lauderdale had ceased to be Secretary of State, Mackenzie asked him for a letter from the King 'for my future security' – a testimonial to his loyalty and services, since 'the Advocate is in a singular condition because all whom he pursues turn his adversaries'.[16] But Sir George would not find the new regime quite so receptive to his ideas.

In December Claverhouse had Sir John Dalrymple brought before the Privy Council to answer charges of opposing and obstructing the commission given him by King and Council. To Sir John's claim that the people of Galloway had become orderly and regular, Graham retorted that 'there were as many elephants and crocodiles in Galloway as legal or regular persons'.[17] The Council was not swift in judgement, but unsurprisingly, it supported Claverhouse, and on 12 February, Sir John was deprived of his regality rights, fined £500, and committed to Edinburgh Castle during the Council's pleasure, which lasted two months. In the spring of 1683 his mother was called before the Council on charges of non-attendance at church and frequenting conventicles. She admitted these and 'promised to live orderly and regularly',[18] but later in the year she left the country to join Sir James, with their son David and grandson John. Sir John, who had craved pardon of the Council, appears to have kept a low profile, but was arrested in September 1684, his papers seized for examination, and questioned by the Council about his dealings with Lord Aberdeen, who had just been dropped as Chancellor. After three months' close confinement in the Edinburgh Tolbooth, with no charge against him, he was released on bail of £5000, but not given full liberty until January 1686.

Claverhouse's letters also show that he was capable of looking objectively at his own methods, and he realised that to wield the laws like a bludgeon was counter-productive: '... what effects does that produce, but more to exasperate and alienate the hearts of the whole body of the people? for it renders three desperate where it gains one, and your Lordship [Queensberry] knows that in the greatest crimes it is thought advisable to pardon the multitude and punish the ringleaders...' But he was also sensitive to the law-enforcers' problem; he knew that '... within a short time I could bring two out of three to the church. But when I have done, that is all to no purpose, for we will no sooner be gone than in comes their ministers, and all repent and fall back to their old ways.'[19] On 17 April, he comes back to this theme: 'Did the King and the Duke know what those rebellious villains, which they call ministers, put in the heads of the people, they would think it necessary to keep them out. The poor people about Minnigaff confess upon oath that they were made renew the Covenant, and believe the King was a Papist'...[20] He may have allowed more influence to the ministers than they really possessed; James Renwick was the son of a Minnigaff weaver. These were people who thought for themselves, albeit within a narrow focus. But generally, the effects of law enforcement and military harassment were enough to to create an apparent conformity. The churches were well-attended, because lists of non-attenders were passed on to the authorities; but very often the 'curate' or Indulged minister addressed an inattentive or hostile congregation, whose members talked among themselves, slept obtrusively, made no proper responses, and loitered menacingly by the door when the minister came out. To do the work of a 'curate' in such circumstances needed courage – the dragoons could not be in all places at all times.

In June 1682 William Carstares married a lady of Cornish descent, Elizabeth Kekewich, daughter of the vicar of Raynham. He had not lost the taste for that secret involvement in political affairs of which his father disapproved: the old man had said his son 'would plod and plot till he plotted his head off... Ministers of the Gospel are not called on to meddle with that work.'[21] He was still a confidential go-between, helping to co-ordinate the plans of two groups, one of Presbyterian and dissident English emigrés in Holland, and another of anti-regime schemers based in London. His sister Sarah had married their cousin, and his close friend, William Dunlop, an active but moderate presbyterian, and a rare hint of ebullient personality breaks through in a cheery letter to Dunlop of 14 June 1681, 'I know not upon what account she should have been so much in love with such a sotchell drunken-faced little fellow.'[22] Carstares asked him for a 'particular account of public affairs at the sitting of our parliament', and ends enigmatically: 'Sham plots are the great business of some, but God doth strangely detect them, though I am afraid they may some time take effect.' By the following year, plots, sham or otherwise, were everywhere, exceeded only by the rumours of plots.

The Duke of Albany and York removed from Holyroodhouse in March 1682 to rejoin the court circle in London. His wife stayed on for a time and he came back in May to collect her; in returning to England they, and the Earl of Perth, who was with them, almost lost their lives by shipwreck. Scotland had been a trying-ground for James's methods of statecraft, and he retained his influence on its government. New men occupied some of the top places. George Gordon of Haddo, now made Earl of Aberdeen, was Chancellor, James Douglas, Marquis of Queensberry, was Lord Treasurer (he had made almost as much difficulty over taking the Test oath as Argyll, but he was a firm episcopalian), James Drummond, Earl of Perth, was on the way up as Lord Justice-General. It was not a

William Carstares
Reproduced from Wodrow's *History*, Vol I

harmonious government; Queensberry was jealous of Aberdeen, whom he considered an upstart, and found an ally in Perth, though that earl and his brother John were playing their own game. Their sister Anne was married to the Earl of Errol, hereditary High Constable, whose family's Catholic sympathies had until now kept it well out of the sphere of government. Lady Errol, like the Duchess of Lauderdale, had a relish for behind-the-scenes involvement in public affairs – Graham could write to Queensberry about 'a business concerning myself, of which... my lady Errol will tell you'.[23] Drummonds had once stood high in the land: Annabella Drummond had been Robert III's queen in the 14th century, and this trio of clever, handsome and ambitious siblings were determined to play a leading part in the nation's affairs.

In August 1682 Lauderdale died at Tunbridge Wells, and was buried in Haddington in April of the following year, with florid funeral rites and effusive posthumous tributes, but the corpse of his administration was already stinking. A Commission for Trial of the Mint in 1682 had revealed his brother Hatton's criminal exploitation of his superintendency. In March 1683 Hatton, now third Earl of Lauderdale, was found guilty of malversation, and it was established that he and his subordinates had embezzled at least £Sc699,873.[24] The Mint was closed down. Hatton's repayment was reduced by the King to £Sc240,000, of which £Sc192,000 was to be paid to Lord Aberdeen, and £Sc48,000 to Claverhouse. This latter amount was to be redeemable by Hatton's hand-over to Graham of Dudhope Castle, outside Dundee, and its lands, with which went the title and privileges of Constable of Dundee. The oily earl did his best to stave off the moment, and it needed Charles II's intervention before Claverhouse finally got possession in April 1684.

Meanwhile his star continued to rise. In December 1682 he was promoted Colonel, at the head of the newly formed His Majesty's Regiment of Horse, combining his own troop with three others, and in April 1683 he went to attend at court, an experience which he did not care for, writing home to complain about the preoccupation with cockfighting and racing, which made it difficult to get any business done. Such things, said one biographer, 'offended his plain-speaking Church of Scotland soul',[25] but primarily they got in the way of his anxiety to push his claim with the Duke and the King for the Dudhope estate and title.[26] Claverhouse had become enough of a courtier for the Marquis of Queensberry to enlist his aid in his campaign to get a dukedom,[27] and Claverhouse in turn looked for the Marquis's support in the Dudhope matter; their letters at this time show how a great amount of the managers' (as Wodrow called them) time and energy was spent on the pursuit of estates and titles. They were not full-time officials, and certainly not members of any sort of salariat: they were men whose position and ambition led them to serve the state, and they were determined to get their due and desired rewards. In May 1683 Graham was appointed a Privy Councillor.

Twenty-two years had passed since the Restoration and the rise of Presbyterian dissent, and each side was experienced in combating the other. The Council – often known at this time as the Secret Council: a synonym for 'privy', though 'secret' seems to carry its own sense of *terribilità* – had never been so powerful, never known so much, never had such a network of informants: and yet nothing seemed to get rid of the spirit of dissidence. As further reports of conventicles came in, new commissions of justiciary were sent out, even to far-off Ross, where on the eastern seaboard conventicling had spread among farmers and fisherfolk.[28] An intensive circuit traversed Stirling, Glasgow, Ayr, Dumfries, Jedburgh and Edinburgh in June and July, Claverhouse in attendance with a military escort, with Mackenzie as prosecutor and Perth as senior judge. They seem to have been happy in their purpose: 'The judges go on very unanimously,' wrote Claverhouse to Queensberry on 9 June, 'and my Lord Advocate does wonders.'[29] Three men were hanged as a result, two of whom had participated in an ambush which had killed a soldier. The third, William Bogue, had been caught with a false certificate of indemnity and was hanged despite a last-minute willingness to swear the Test oath. 'It clearly appears that he would do anything to save his life; but nothing to be reconciled to the Government,' wrote Claverhouse to Lord Aberdeen,[30] asking for the Chancellor's ruling on whether the death sentence should be enforced. He was in no doubt about his own view: 'I am as sorry to see a man die, even a Whig, as any of themselves; but when one dies justly for his own faults, and may save 100 to fall in the like, I have no scruple.' The comment paraphrases one of Justus Lipsius, the Neo-Stoic thinker, which he might perhaps have got from Mackenzie in after-dinner chat '… it is better that one member be cast away, than that the whole body runne to ruyne.'[31]

CHAPTER TWENTY

The Tolbooth in Winter

TWO DECADES OF HARASSMENT and fining, of exclusion from participation in government, of feeling oppressed and victimised in their own country, were having an effect on the presbyterian gentry. Some of the most energetic and able began planning to set up a colony of their own in North America – a presbyterian statelet in Carolina. England claimed sovereignty over the territory, which was inhabited by native Americans and disputed by Spain, and it was necessary to negotiate in London to secure two counties to be administered on presbyterian lines.[1] The intention was genuine: Scottish desire for a foothold in North America was strong for commercial reasons too, as a trading partner and as a property investment. During 1684, some of Perth's and Melfort's profits were invested in land in East New Jersey; and other investors in this colony included Sir John Dalrymple and Ewen Cameron of Lochiel.[2] But some of the Carolina proposers, among them Baillie of Jerviswood, Sir John Cochrane of Ochiltree, George Campbell of Cessnock and his father Sir Hugh, were also meeting Englishmen involved in the 'Whig Plot' against the accession of the King's brother, which, since Charles II's serious illness in spring 1681, seemed possibly imminent. A central, if elusive, figure in these goings-on was Robert Ferguson, 'the Plotter', hailing originally from Aberdeen, one of the quite numerous Scots ordained in the Anglican Church, though he had been ejected from his living at the Restoration. Now under the Earl of Shaftesbury's protection as a pamphlet-writer, propagandist and would-be fixer, he was involved with at least two plots, which partially overlapped each other.

An element of the 'Whig Plot' was that the Earl of Argyll – now in Holland – should mount an invasion of the British mainland while the Duke of Monmouth raised an army of resistance in England. Sir James Stewart and William Carstares were the link-men with Argyll and his associates, who by 1683 included Sir James Dalrymple. Argyll reckoned that he needed a minimum of £30,000 from England to raise and supply the necessary forces: a huge but not unrealistic estimate, and by no means impossible for the supposedly anti-Stuart, pro-presbyterian City of London to find. But Ferguson was better at intrigue than raising funds, and even when Carstares with great reluctance got the estimate reduced to £10,000, nothing was forthcoming. 'The people of England do nothing but talk,' complained Baillie,[3] who was keen for action to start in Scotland. Carstares prevailed on him to wait, though they broke off negotiations with the English plotters until these should come up with a clear plan of action.

Carstares was startled when 'Plotter' Ferguson told him of the other scheme: to assassinate the King and his brother. Story records that he 'indignantly repudiated' the idea, as he and his associates wished no harm to the King, wanting only to obtain a free Parliament, exclusion of the Duke of York from the throne (the next in line after him, whether Monmouth or York's daughter Mary, were safely Protestant), and redress of grievances – a portmanteau sufficiently full of contentious items. In fact though Carstares recoiled from any personal involvement in an assassination plot, he did suggest, according to his own later testimony under the thumbscrews, 'That's work for our wild people in Scotland' because 'my conscience does not serve me for such things'.[4] The Cameronian leadership would certainly not have shrunk from the idea.

But Cameronian aid was not invoked, and the Scots on both sides of the North Sea were still debating among themselves whether to mount their own anti-York revolt (Robert Baillie in favour, Carstares against, Sir James Dalrymple in Holland also adding his counsel against hasty action) when on 12 June 1683 the ill-concealed and never-attempted 'Rye House Plot' was finally betrayed to the English Government. The ants' nest of conspiracy was thoroughly kicked about, many people were named, and a rapid series of arrests ensued, with Baillie among those captured. Carstares fled from London, but was arrested in late July at Tenterden in Kent. His erstwhile jailer Drummond of Lundin, now Under-Treasurer of Scotland and a close associate of the Duke of York, identified his handwriting in a letter written in code.[5]

After two weeks' confinement in Kent Carstares was sent to London and twice interrogated by members of the Privy Council. He denied any involvement in plots against the 'King and Government', which in his own terms was true; or in any other criminal matters. It was rightly presumed that he knew a great deal more than he was admitting, and a mixture of threats and offers of clemency was applied. Sir Andrew Forrester,

Under-Secretary of State for Scotland, offered 'life and favour if I would confess what I knew of the Cessnocks and others;'[6] Sir George Mackenzie, who had been summoned to London, visited the prisoner in the Gatehouse of Westminster and 'told me that the Boot in Scotland should drive out of me what he alleged I refused to confess'.[7] At this time, Mackenzie, with other members of the administration, must have been thoroughly alarmed at how actively the Scots had been conspiring and how far their plans had been developed. Compared to this, the Cameronians on whom official attention had been so obsessively focused were a mere sideshow. In September James Renwick, ordained as a minister in Groningen in April[9] (McWard and Brown had died in 1681 and 1679 respectively) returned from Holland. Ian Cowan's comment, 'the council's alarm turned to fear when James Renwick returned as an ordained minister to the Remnant'[8] is an exaggeration: Renwick, a youthful unknown, with no strategy (that was God's business), and no standing in the country, was scarcely a Lenin figure, sweeping in on the tide of mass revolt. The Council had far more reason to be concerned about the Earl of Argyll.

A warrant of 17 August ordered that Carstares should be kept a close prisoner 'for high treason in compassing the death and destruction of our sovereign Lord the King, and conspiring to levy war against His Majesty'. From a letter written to his wife more than a year later, on 8 December 1685, it seems that during this imprisonment he had gone through a religious crisis which strengthened his faith: 'God does all things well and as he is a jealous, so he is a compassionate God... I would fain think he will never forget what he did for my soul in Tenterden and the Gatehouse: he allured me then into the wilderness; and how great terror so ever I was under, yet he spake comfortably to me.'[10] He had been arrested in England, was charged with a crime in England, and Mrs Carstares applied for a writ of *habeas corpus* for him to be put on trial, or to be given bail. But he and the other Scottish prisoners were transferred by sea to Scotland: a different country and a different jurisdiction, under which, as Carstares pointed out, 'I had committed no crime... There needs no great inquiry into the reason of my being so used... it was judged that the violent tortures which the laws of England – at least the custom – does not admit of – would force to anything.'[11] But it was not merely to enable the more brutal methods of Scottish law to be used: the authorities were determined to show that Scotland was firmly under their control.

After a stormy two-week voyage, Carstares and the others were imprisoned on 14 November in the Tolbooth of Edinburgh, conveniently close to the Parliament House, which was also the seat of the Privy Council and Court of Session. The Tolbooth in winter was at its ugly worst, cold, damp, dark, dirty, and disease-ridden, and they were closely confined. It was January before Carstares's wife, mother and sister were allowed access to him.

Amid rumours of plots and invasion, with arrests, impending trials, and the thought of more to come, alarm and anticipation flickered like summer lightning. Knowledge that ramifications of the English plots extended into Scotland drove the authorities into intensive action. When men of estate went on trial for treason, forfeitures were to be expected, and friends of the King and Duke would be the beneficiaries. No-one could tell who might end up being implicated in this tenebrous affair. The Council remained disunited. Aberdeen, the Chancellor, was being undermined by Lord Treasurer Queensberry, with Drummond of Lundin as his right-hand man, peddling accusations of disloyal protectiveness towards Argyll's family and the Dalrymples.[12] Claverhouse felt that his proposed military dispositions were frustrated by Dalyell's jealousy and eccentricities, and his intimacy with Queensberry was cooling. A letter to Queensberry from Lundin at the time of Carstares's arrest refers in hostile and patronising terms to Mackenzie, who was about to make a visit to London, almost as if he were an unwitting tool: 'If once the Advocate were come, of whom we must make the cat's foot (to scrape the Chastanes out of the fire), I am confident matters will go to our mind.'[13] What the chestnut metaphor means is not clear; manoeuvring was going on at the time over the provostship of Edinburgh, and, on a grander scale, the Duke of York was setting up a Junto or 'Secret Committee' of the Council, which would concentrate power within a select group. Mackenzie was involved in this, though plainly not of the innermost circle; Drummond wrote that he was 'humoursome as the wind. But he is engaged past retreat, and just as he had done all he could for us, so he discredited himself, that I do not fear his after game.'[14] More sourly, he noted of Mackenzie: 'People here see only his best side, and that is so good, that he has more influence on men's minds... than can be imagined.'[15] Sir George's humane, literary side was getting little exposure in Scotland in this and the following years.

Like most other official secrets, the junto plans were widely leaked and anticipated: 'The affairs of the Junto is no secret here,' wrote Claverhouse to Queensberry from Edinburgh at the end of October 1683.[16] Graham had his own problem with Aberdeen, who was putting difficulties in the way of the Dudhope transfer. He was in favour of the Junto, though he was not included in the group of seven nominated by the King 'to manage all affairs'.[17]

Ensuring efficient administration was always a headache for the Privy Council, in a country of bad roads, frequent bad weather, and with a degree of civil disorder. For many local magistrates and officials the fines levied on non-conformers had become a sort of gravy trough, at which they were accustomed to sup. But by the end of 1683 it was apparent that the money reaching the government's coffers was only a fraction of what it should amount to, and in January 1684 the Earl of Moray, now Secretary of State, wrote from Whitehall to Lord Treasurer Queensberry, requiring a full accounting from all judges and magistrates of what fines had been levied since the indemnity after Bothwell Bridge, how much had been collected, and what had happened to the money. The resultant investigations showed such irregularities, and reluctance to give information, that Hugh Wallace, the king's cash-keeper in Edinburgh, asked the Council to 'ordain letters of horning' against all the magistrates who had failed to respond.[18] Claverhouse would also find himself caught in this net.

Another aspect of fines also troubled the Council: to what extent should a husband be compelled to take responsibility for his wife's actions? Often, it was known or suspected, the husband's conformity and attendance at church services was a screen for his wife to attend conventicles and to give aid to the non-conformers. But could a 'loyal' husband be forced to pay up for his wife's delinquencies? The question was referred to London, and the reply was that: 'his majesty approves of husbands being fined for their wives, but authorizes the council to dispense with the fines on loyal husbands, who do not connive at their obstinate wives' ways, and are willing to deliver them prisoners'.[19] This tactic would have called the bluff of conniving husbands, but even a loyalist might draw the line at handing his non-conforming wife over to the mercies of the Council. Several women of the gentry were in prison and many others had been harassed and fined if, like Lady Cardross, mother of the diarist John Erskine, they were widows in control of their own estates.

CHAPTER TWENTY-ONE

Torture under Law

FROM THE START, 1684 was a bad year for Sir George Mackenzie. In February he was ordered by the Council to begin proceedings against Sir Hugh Campbell of Cessnock. The charge had nothing to do with recent events but harked back to encouragement of the rebels at Bothwell Bridge. Sir Hugh denied the accusation. Inside the courtroom, the public was very much on his side, and for the first time in Scotland, a 'Protestant roar' was heard from the 'mobile' – a trick learned from the Earl of Shaftesbury's populist techniques with the Whig mob in London. Mackenzie lost his temper. Erskine of Carnock records him shouting in fury at a witness: 'I hate you, William Fletcher, I hate you. I swear I hate you, ye speak nonsense.'[1] Campbell was acquitted by the jury and promptly sent back to jail. For Mackenzie, who prided himself on not losing cases for the Crown, it was more than a personal rebuff. Political trials were supposed to bolster the government, not leave it defeated and humiliated. The same thing must not be allowed to happen in the trials to come.

On 23rd April, after prolonged negotiations and a Court of Session hearing, John Graham finally got possession of Dudhope Castle and the Constableship of Dundee, just in time to instal his bride there. If a reason were required for his exclusion from the 'Secret Seven' on the Council, other than his military juniority to Dalyell, it could have been that by the end of 1683 his colleagues all knew that the Colonel, so assiduous in his duties against the rebel Whigs, was compromising himself by courting Lady Jean Cochrane, grand-daughter of the Earl of Dundonald. The Cochranes, living in the conventual buildings of the former Paisley abbey, were a Presbyterian family, with close links to the 'fanatics'. Lady Jean's widowed mother was a daughter of the covenanting Earl of Cassillis; her uncle, Sir John Cochrane of Ochiltree, had fled to Holland after the uncovering of the Rye House plot. The lady herself was not so presbyterian as to object to the handsome colonel, and her grandfather's sense of the value of a match with a coming man on the 'other' side overruled his daughter-in-law's hostility. Claverhouse did his best to dispel any suspicion that his marriage indicated a change in sympathy or sense of duty, suggesting to Queensberry that his new family contacts would be 'not unuseful' to him in the shires of Ayr and Renfrew.[2] 'For my own part,' he added, 'I look upon myself as a cleanser. I may cure people guilty of that plague of presbytery by conversing with them, but cannot be infected.'

They were married at Paisley on 9 June, with Colin Mackenzie, his lawyer, George's younger brother, as the best man. The bride's mother stayed away and the day was interrupted by an order from Dalyell to Lord Ross (who was among the wedding guests) to go in pursuit of an armed conventicle at the Black Loch in Stirlingshire.[3] Ross commanded one of Claverhouse's troops, and his selection may show an untypical touch of delicacy on Dalyell's part, but Claverhouse, perhaps scenting a trap, left his bride to join the hunt. Jean's dowry was 40,000 merks, and the jointure settled on her was an annuity of 5,000 merks. The marriage was not destined to be a long one, and was punctuated by long absences on his part, but it was a genuine love match.

For a time, the Drummonds looked askance on Claverhouse. Many people had relatives in both camps, but he, a Privy Councillor, had deliberately chosen his Jean. Dundee's welcome to its Constable was also cold, for other reasons; he was seen as an interloper, despite his local connections. Its council protested against his appointment as its First Magistrate: 'ye towne of Dundie be a free royal burgh hes constantlie elected their owne magistrats, as they doe to this dy, and are noewayes

Jean Cochrane, Viscountess Dundee
Reproduced by courtesy of Dundee Art Gallery

subject to the Constables jurisdiction.'⁴ Claverhouse's friendship with Queensberry ended with his marriage, though military jealousies were also involved. The Marquis's son, Lord Drumlanrig, was made second-in-command of Claverhouse's regiment in July 1684,⁵ and the Marquis's brother James Douglas, also a colonel, had always been a rival. Though he too made descents on the Whiggamores and had his share in the 'Killing Time', Douglas was more of a parade-ground officer than the campaign-hardened Graham – the Galloway 'curates' when in need of protection were in no doubt that 'Claverhouse's name was more formidable'.⁶ Both men had a hopeful eye on the supreme command, still held by the octogenarian Dalyell, but the Douglases had far more 'interest' than Graham.

Pushed on by the seven men at the heart of the Council, with York's hand behind them, the wave of action against dissidents steadily rose through 1684, with frequent executions, including (according to John Erskine) the hanging of one man for protesting at the rough handling of three men hanged on 15 August, on the same afternoon as they had been condemned: one of whom had been 'interrupted when at prayer, and abruptly thrown over'.⁷ In many towns the small tolbooth jails were overcrowded with what Wodrow calls 'the meaner sort' of non-conformers, and magistrates were encouraged to arrange for deportation of such prisoners as appeared penitent, without requiring them to take any oath. The Glasgow merchants and shipowners Walter and James Gibson provided the transport, and when Carstares's brother-in-law William Dunlop sailed with other emigrants to Carolina in July that year from Gourock on the *Carolina Merchant*, 35 involuntary fellow-passengers were imprisoned below deck.⁸ On 5 May the Council published a list of almost 2,000 named fugitives, giving them until the first of August to take the oath of loyalty or face 'condign punishment' on arrest.

The eminent self-exiles in Holland were not included in the list, but their position was not, or did not always feel, secure. Protests streamed from London against the Dutch Government's hospitality to the refugees. Campvere was still Scotland's official 'staple' port, run by Government appointees who angrily protested when presbyterian traders tried to slip their goods through Rotterdam. Fear and mistrust permeated the community; spies spying on one another and double agents trading lies with triple agents. In a mysterious incident this year Sir James Dalrymple eluded the attentions of some 'Russians' with apparent designs on his life by leaving Leiden for a time.[9] In December, Sir George Mackenzie was instructed to raise a process of forfeiture against Sir James, Sir John Cochrane, the Earl of Melville, and some other conspicuous fugitives. Forfeiture, for the Perth administration, had become something of a family business. The laird of Monkland had been deprived of his estates in July 1683, for dealings with the rebels, and after some infighting with the Duke of Hamilton, Lundin secured the estate for himself.[10] Monkland was one of the many people who had lent money to the late Marquis of Argyll, and a bond held by him, for 10,000 merks, was now acquired by Lundin.

Resistance by the 'Remnant' sharpened in the face of intensified military and legal action, and in July a troop was ambushed while escorting 16 prisoners through the desolate Enterkin Pass between Thornhill and Sanquhar; 14 escaped and a soldier was killed. That month Aberdeen was dismissed as Chancellor and Perth was appointed in his stead. It had taken a long campaign of undermining and an alleged bribe of £27,000 for Perth and Queensberry to achieve the fall of Aberdeen. Paid to Charles II's mistress, the Duchess of Portsmouth, it came from the Scottish Treasury, described as payments for 'intelligence and casual expenses'.[11]

At last, after much time, intrigue and patience, James Drummond was at the head of affairs, with the opportunity to do his best for what he had called, at the time of the 'Highland Host', 'my poor despised family'.[12] With his appointment came a royal instruction to put the laws 'vigorously in execution against the fanatics',[13] and Claverhouse was appointed to a fortified Committee of Public Affairs specifically charged to direct 'the execution of the laws

James Drummond, 4th Earl of Perth
Reproduced by courtesy of Fitzwilliam Museum, Cambridge

against fanatical and disorderly persons'.[14] Renwick and his party, about 50 strong, moving about the south-west, were the prime cause of official fury, and a proclamation of 22 July denounced the sheriffs for lack of diligence in tracking them and taking action against those who harboured them. As a reminder that the Council was perpetually dealing with other business too, it requested the Secretary to intercede with the King for the linen industry, which was said to employ 12,000 people (seasonally and part-time but a prime source of cash earnings), whose prime market was England, where Scottish linen-sellers were currently being impeded, arrested, even whipped as criminals. The council also did its best to help at home by enacting that all corpses should be buried in plain linen, made and spun within Scotland. Poor tenants and cottars were excused.[15]

One of the prisoners in the Edinburgh Tolbooth was a presbyterian minister named Spence, an associate of Argyll's and compiler of the ciphers used in his correspondence. In the hope that his testimony would implicate Carstares and Baillie, Spence was brought before the Council on 26 July 1684, and tortured.

In later, more sophisticated times, interrogation under torture has become a matter for specialists, whose reports are sent to their superiors. Often its existence is officially denied. In the judicial torture of 17th-century Scotland the only professional was the Edinburgh hangman, or his assistant, who merely attended to the instruments, and the questioning was done by members of the Privy Council. The traditional instrument, the 'Boot', was a metal frame fitted round the prisoner's leg between knee and ankle. Once the boot was secured, wooden wedges were hammered down between it and the leg until the constriction was so great that the shin-bones cracked or burst. Rarely used in the 17th century before 1660, the fear of conspiracy among dissident presbyterians brought it back. As an instrument of law, its use was subject to regulation, and its purpose was not to force admissions of guilt, but to obtain or verify information, especially in cases of conspiracy, from a prisoner who was recalcitrant or whose word was suspect. Despite the torture of the Boot, Mr Spence at first refused to say anything, and was sent to the Canongate Tolbooth, where General Dalyell took personal charge of a sleep-deprivation regime; and on 7 August he was subjected to the thumbscrews, 'till the broken bone was appearing through the skin'.[16] Also known as the 'pilliwinks', adopted by the Privy Council only on 23 July 1684,[17] this device was already well-known to the bonded colliery workers whose overseers used it to maintain discipline.

Violence was an almost daily sight or experience for most people. Husbands beat their wives, parents beat their children, work overseers wielded sticks, and street brawls and fist-fights were common. In 1676 Sir John Lauder noted a case of lynching in Abernethy: a fletcher 'nicked' another man in an alehouse argument, and some 'gentlemen in the next room' dragged him out to the regality gallows and summarily hanged him.[18] On an official level, whippings were regular punishments for minor offences, and malefactors might have an ear nailed to a board, or have a hand cut off. The hangman had much to do apart from executing people. Most other countries had similar punishments, but Scotland was certainly not a leader in moderating the pattern of social and engrained violence. Indeed, in a country where the doctrine of Original Sin was strongly taught, beating it out of children and adult offenders might even be considered therapeutic. But these were all punishments for crimes or alleged misdemeanours. Torture under the law, of people who had not been found guilty of any crime, was something different. Here again Scotland had its own ways of doing things. Even in the 21st century, many Scots take some pride in the much-diluted atavistic traditions that still survive in their land; their forefathers took a similar, proud-rueful pleasure in the blend of modern and medieval that then typified national life far more. When in 1680 two distinguished English churchmen cast doubt upon the fabulous genealogy of the Scottish kings, Sir George Mackenzie not only wrote a *Defence of the Royal Line of Scotland*, but dropped some heavy hints on what fatal penalties he could arrange to inflict to these sceptics if they should cross the border.[19]

Fear of the Boot and thumbscrews was employed more often than the devices themselves. After his leg had been crushed, Mr Spence, still bravely silent, was again subjected to the 'pilliwinks', and at last admitted to having known of a plot, and deciphered some of Argyll's coded letters for the council to read, identifying Carstares under the code-name of 'Mr Rid' [Red] and showing him to be a trusted counsellor. Spence's example was meant to have its effect on William Carstares. At 35 he was a stoutish, grave, respectable-looking person, a gentleman and a cleric. In family background, education, and in the comparative moderacy of his

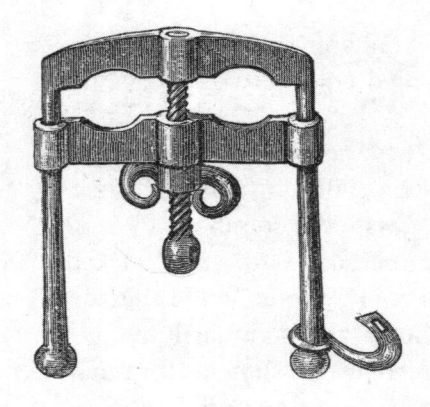

A set of Thumbikins
Reproduced from *Cassell's Old and New Edinburgh*

presbyterian views, he was for most of the Councillors very much one of their own kind. Not a fanatic, he had no commitment to the Covenants, was not a man of violence. It cannot have been unknown that he was close to the inner circle of William, Prince of Orange, son-in-law to the Duke of York. The Dutch Government had had no involvement in the Rye House plot. But maybe the Privy Council, secure and supreme in the Parliament House of Edinburgh, did not concern itself with the wider sweep of European affairs. No-one in the chamber would have expected William to be King of Scots in less than five years, and to them Carstares, however inoffensive-looking, was also 'Mr Red', deeply implicated in treasonable designs against the integrity of the state, a conspiracy whose ramifications were wide and not fully clear.

At times Carstares was in close confinement, at others he was allowed contact with the outside world. From April he was allowed to receive money[20] and clothing, and to send out letters to his family. At least two members of the Council came to urge him to confess without making recourse to torture necessary. Sir George Mackenzie told the prisoner he had begged leave of the Council to come, 'having a kindness for me, and therefore obtested me to be ingenuous [urged me to come clean, in modern parlance] as I loved myself'. Carstares replied that he knew nothing, and did not know what he might say under torture; and that 'I could not swear in anything criminal in itself, whatever it might be made to me; and did, as I had reason, and so it became an honest man, clear myself of all plots whatsoever.' He committed himself to God: 'Himself be my strength, for I have none of my own.'[21] There is no obvious reason why Mackenzie should have felt personal concern for Carstares, and his previous visit to Carstares's prison in London does not read like that of a well-wisher; the Edinburgh conversation seems a rather clumsy effort to encourage a confession. Another visitor was John Drummond of Lundin, whom the prisoner had more reason to consider as a friend, and who several times urged Carstares to tell everything he knew. But Carstares had resolved 'through divine assistance, to adventure upon the torture'.[22] From 8 August he was put in irons, part of a softening-up process. His wife was allowed to share his cell from 27 August, and on 6 September, around mid-day, he was brought before the Council.

In the old Parliament House, the interior gives little indication of its arrangements in 1684. Story refers to 'that long, low-browed chamber in the Parliament House, where the Privy Council held its sittings and tortured its victims'.[23] Twenty-seven councillors were present when Carstares was brought in, with the Chancellor, the Earl of Perth, presiding. Among the others were Sir William Paterson, the Council's Clerk, who had been Carstares's regent at Edinburgh University, the Duke of Hamilton, Queensberry (also a duke as of 1684), Drummond of Lundin, Mackenzie of Rosehaugh, the grimacing, long-bearded General Dalyell, and the composed figure of Graham of Claverhouse. Statements from two captured London conspirators, Shephard and Holms, both implicating him, were read out, but he refused to accept them as evidence against him, and further refused to answer, on oath, any questions that should be put to him. He was then sent back to the Tolbooth, and a messenger followed with a list of questions which he was required to answer, on oath, that same evening, or be tortured.

Evening and night were the preferred time for these sessions. By September the days were growing shorter, and the evening light was fading into the deep dark of a city devoid of street lights. The doors were closed, and the outside world, with its normal courtesies and decencies, shut out. Candles were lit, spreading light and shadow across the faces of those who sat surveying the prisoner. Edinburgh did not go to such an extreme as the lightless interrogations conducted by the Council of Ten within the Doge's Palace at Venice, where the victim, strung from a beam to an agonising poise on the tips of his toes, never saw his questioners – but the atmosphere was intense and ominous. The Councillors were at a long table, the prisoner sat facing them. Carstares maintained his refusal to answer questions under oath, and was asked if he had any reason to offer against being put to the torture. By his own later account, he replied that the order by which he had been committed to Scotland was that he should be tried for crimes committed against the government in that kingdom; and asked if the Lord Advocate had anything of that nature to charge him with. Mackenzie answered that: 'he had not, but that I was now in Scotland, and if I had been guilty of contriving against his Majesty's government at Constantinople, I might be tried for it'.[24] Carstares pointed out that his alleged crimes were said to be committed in England, where the King's laws were in force, which was not the case at Constantinople. But the attempt to have his case referred back to England was overruled. He then claimed that for torture to be legally inflicted, there had to be *semiplena probatio*, that is, a partial proof of guilt, with only one witness, and that this was lacking in his case. The reply was that presumption of guilt was sufficient to warrant torture.

A brand-new set of double thumbikins was brought in by the city hangman, accompanied by an Edinburgh bailie who knew how to work them; they were 'of an improved construction, by which much greater force could be applied to the screws'.[25] Carstares's hands were drawn behind his back,[26] his thumbs were placed inside, and the screws were gradually tightened. Hamilton, known to be opposed to the use of torture, left the room. As the prisoner began to sweat with pain, but refused to give any answers, Queensberry too walked out, saying, 'I see he will rather die than confess.' Perth ordered a further turn of the screws, at which Carstares burst out with: 'The bones are squeezed to pieces!' 'If you continue obstinate,' said Perth, 'I hope to see every bone of your body squeezed to pieces.' In his own grotesque and sinister manner, Dalyell left his seat to approach Carstares and promise to roast him alive next day, if he did not confess. Carstares remained obdurate, and the order was given for the Boot to be brought in. The city hangman, very new to the job (his predecessor had been jailed for a violent assault), failed to fix the implement properly around Carstares's leg, and eventually the boot was laid aside and they reverted to the thumbscrews, having them tightened until the prisoner was plainly on the verge of fainting. The Council record shows the torture as lasting for an hour – understandably Carstares recalled it as longer – before it was called off. The screws were now so tight that the official blacksmith, who had been kept on hand, had to be called in to undo them. Informed that the Boot would be used properly on him at nine o' clock next morning, Carstares was returned to the Tolbooth.[27]

A doctor, obtained by his family, examined him that night, found him feverish, and asked for a delay of further torture for a few days, but this was refused. Next morning Carstares was first brought into a side-room of Parliament House, where Drummond of Lundin spoke to him. Acting as Mr Nice to his brother's Mr Nasty, Drummond had a deal to offer. If Carstares would answer a few questions, it would be guaranteed that he should not be asked to appear as a witness against anyone else. This was not enough for Carstares, even with the Boot waiting: 'I absolutely refused to say anything, till I obtained that my depositions should not be made use of at the bar of any judicature against any person whatsoever, which the Lord Melfort [Drummond's title from 1685], after going twice or thrice from me to know the mind of the Council, did at last yield to.'[28] Mindful of the Council's perfidy in the case of James Mitchell, Carstares asked what assurance he had of being honestly dealt with, but Drummond's answer, agreeing 'that that was a d–d perjury, and the stain of the government' satisfied him, perhaps surprisingly, but he still thought of Drummond as a friend.[29] A document was drawn up, agreeing that Carstares would answer questions, on oath, up to the first day of October, under six specific conditions, assured, for the council's part, on the word of honour of the Lord Thesaurer Depute, John Drummond. Andrew Lang described Drummond as 'jobbing, unscrupulous, cruel, greedy and treacherous',[30] and few historians, even those writing from the Jacobite standpoint, have been much kinder. The copy of the agreed text given by Drummond to Carstares and preserved in his papers provides in clause three that 'he shall never be brought as witness, *directly nor indirectly*, against any person whatsoever'.[31] In the Council's copy the italicised phrase is omitted.

Now a 'free prisoner', Carstares was transferred to Edinburgh Castle, and received further medical attention. Here he was questioned twice by a committee of the Council and gave answers on oath, admitting involvement in plans for Argyll's invasion and naming others, including Baillie of Jerviswood. To his consternation, an edited version of his 'deposition' was speedily published by the Council and openly sold as 'Mr Carstares's Confession'. Totally excluding the 'just extenuations' and explanations he had given, it read as if he had betrayed his associates in return for his own life, and he would spend time over many years in assembling a rebuttal of the implication, which he never seems to have published.[32] Around 19 September Carstares was moved again, to Dumbarton Castle,[33] and was still there in December when the trial of Robert Baillie of Jerviswood plunged him into angry despair.

Obsessed by actual and possible plots, the Government was now far more concerned about treason than non-conformity, though the latter was generally taken to imply the former. No-one knew how far conspiracy had spread among the presbyterians, who themselves often suspected provocation by disbanded soldiers hoping for new levies to be made.[34] In the course of the year around 20 prisoners were hanged for refusing to accept the royal supremacy, or to acknowledge Bothwell Bridge as a rebellion. A new series of circuit courts went through the south-west and the eastern borders, exacting another round of punitive fines. Resetting (harbouring) and conversing with rebels was now an act of high treason. When John Porterfield of Duchal was asked by Sir John Cochrane to give £50 towards the cause of the Earl of Argyll, even though he refused, he was found guilty of treason for not reporting the conversation to the authorities, and sentenced to death. 'This was a time when stretches of obsolete laws, knights of the post, half or no probation, malicious informers, scandalous rogues, and miscreants, were the Government's tools to ruin men of estates, honour, and principle.'[35] But the authorities, deeply alarmed about Argyll's intentions, were obsessed by the thought of being taken by surprise, and every scrap of evidence was magnified, both in the interest of defence and, if necessary, later self-justification.

To the United Societies, trials, hangings, fines, stopping and searching of travellers, interrogations, banishments, all gave a degree of grim satisfaction. The Remnant preferred to see its Adversary clad in armour, claws unsheathed, roaring hate and breathing fire – behaving as it should, and so justifying their own stance. In James Renwick they had a leader of Cameron's steeliness, of Cargill's mystical vision, of a deeper vatic note than Peden, and with a reckless idealism equal to theirs. His response was to issue *The Apologetical Declaration and Admonitory Vindication*, on 28 October 1684. 'Informers and intelligencers' were its prime targets: those who would deliver up the faithful for money. It affirmed that the Society People had declared war against 'Charles Stuart and his accomplices, such as lay themselves out to promove his wicked and hellish designs' and promised punishment for all who showed themselves 'enemies to God and the covenanted work of reformation', looking forward to a day when Covenanter courts, civil and ecclesiastical, would give judgement against 'the offences of such persons as at this time our power cannot reach'. It also contained the emphatic assertion that although, 'we do hereby jointly and unaninmously testify and declare, that as we utterly detest and abhor that hellish principle of killing all who differ in judgment and persuasion from us, it having no bottom on the word of God, or right reason', they will nevertheless defend their own lives when attacked.[36]

Alexander Shields, Renwick's later companion and biographer, claimed that Renwick did not wish to make an inflammatory statement, and was pushed by some of his followers into a more extreme position than he wanted. But Renwick was their minister and their leader; they were already far past any thought of compromise, and he had nowhere to take them but closer to the brink. It may even be that he felt the *Apologetical Declaration* to be a relatively moderate document. As on previous occasions, the verbal violence of those who had nothing left to lose made things worse for the less extreme Presbyterians.

CHAPTER TWENTY-TWO

The Killing Time

THE MIGHTY PIKE ROSE terribly to the tiny stickleback's taunt. In Edinburgh on 22 November 1684, the King's Privy Council came to an affirmative (that is, not unanimous) decision regarding the *Apologetical Declaration*: '... any person who owns or will not disown the late treasonable declaration upon oath, whether they have arms, or not, to be immediately put to death; this being always done in the presence of two witnesses, and the person or persons having commission from the council for that effect.'[1] Thus the Killing Time, as the Covenanters called it, began. For the first time since the rule of law was established, the forces of government were licensed to kill civilians without evidence, arrest or trial. The Societies' declaration of war on the King had offered the reason, and though there was no war, or general uprising, they fired the first shots of the campaign.

On 20 November, two soldiers of the Life Guards were shot dead coming out of an inn at Swineabbey, in Linlithgowshire. The killers were never identified. On 29 November the entire town of Edinburgh was searched, at less than 12 hours' notice; beginning at four in the morning. The town was divided into 16 zones and every occupant of every house was checked against the roll of householders' names. Late on the evening of 11 December, a party of armed men confronted Peter Peirson, parish minister of Carsphairn, in Galloway. A 'curate', he was among the most active in denouncing non-conformers to the laird of Lagg. The aim may have been only to scare and silence him, but Peirson was not a man to be easily cowed, and he was shot dead. The killing was disowned by the presbyterians, but it gave some justification to the Council's policy. Five days later, over 100 men stormed the tolbooth of Kirkcudbright, set all prisoners free, and removed stocks of arms and ammunition. On the 18th, Graham of Claverhouse met a body of them at Bridge of Dee, about two miles south of Castle Douglas, in the district of Tongland where he was justiciar. The Cameronians fled, but five were killed and three captured; among those dead was James McMichael, one of

Peirson's killers. Two prisoners were tried, condemned and hanged at Kirkcudbright.

In the midst of these grim events, which may have seemed more like incipient civil war at the time than they do in retrospect, the trial of Robert Baillie began. His active and impatient nature had suffered imprisonment more hardly than Carstares's God-given fatalism. Ill and weak, with swollen legs,[2] it seemed likely he would die in the Tolbooth, if kept there through another winter. But he had been sent up to Scotland for trial, and to be made an example. The Council had chosen to accuse him of complicity in the Rye House plot, despite the lack of any evidence. Like Carstares he had refused to testify on oath, and for this had been fined £6,000, an amount equivalent to his whole property. In Scottish law, that would normally have ended the process, but having accused him of planning regicide, the Council was unwilling to let him die a 'natural' death, and hasty preparations for a trial were made, with the prisoner brought to court 'in his nightgown' on 22 December[3] to be indicted for treason.

Having mentioned Baillie in his deposition, Carstares was 'earnestly desired' to appear and make a statement at the trial about Baillie's involvement with plots in London, but replied that 'I had rather die a thousand deaths than be a witness against any that had trusted me.'[4] Possible ways of implicating Baillie were put to him, which would not involve his facing his friend in open court, but Carstares reminded them of his agreement with the Council. On the 22nd, he was required to sign a statement that his depositions (the originals are not preserved) were truly his, and next day Mackenzie produced them in court as part of the prosecution's case. He brought them forward not as hard evidence but as an 'adminicle', normally a supplementary and non-essential proof offered as part of a strong body of evidence. Carstares was aghast to learn of this, but Mackenzie was using the version of his agreement given to the Council. To this extent at least Mackenzie was acting in good faith. But here there was no solid evidence against Baillie, and Mackenzie glossed over this by conflating the Rye House plot with those of Argyll and Monmouth and suggesting that Baillie was at the centre, with 'Ferguson the contriver... and Carstares the chaplain of the conspiracy'. Seizing upon Carstares's reluctance to testify on oath as a reluctance to incriminate his friend Baillie, he said, quite falsely, that: 'Mr Carstares likewise knew... that his deposition was to be used against Jerviswood', going on to add: '... And albeit the King's servants were forced to engage that Carstares himself should not be made use of as a witness against Jerviswood, yet I think this kind of scrupulosity in Carstares for Jerviswood should convince you more than 20 suspect, nay, than even indifferent [neutral] witnesses.'[5]

Short on fact, long on insinuation, his tirade might have been ludicrous if a man's life had not been at stake. It was after midnight when the trial adjourned, and in the morning of the 23rd, the jury's expected guilty verdict was announced. After the inevitable death sentence had been passed, Mackenzie was reminded, in a crucial exchange, that he himself, the King's Advocate, had recently told Jerviswood that he believed him to be innocent. Mackenzie's reply, noted on the day by an observer,[6] was an admission: 'I said I thought you was indeed innocent of any design against the King.' Wodrow's later account makes a famous flourish:

'"Jerviswood," was the answer, "I own what you say. My thoughts were then as a private man, but what I say here is by special direction of the Privy Council. He" (pointing to the Clerk) "knows my orders."

"Well," said Jerviswood, "if your Lordship has one conscience for yourself, and another for the Council, I pray God forgive you. I do. My Lords, I trouble your Lordships no further."'

However there is no contemporary record of this dramatic exchange.[7] Baillie was sentenced to be hanged, drawn and quartered, with the execution to take place in the afternoon of that same day.

'My Lords,' he said, 'the time is short, the sentence is sharp; but I thank my God who hath made me as fit to die as ye are to live.'[8] In the afternoon, the drums rolled again to drown out a valediction that would have troubled the authorities.

That year, Mackenzie had published his *Institutions of the Law of Scotland*, a 'pocket Stair' for lawyers,[9] summarising the status of the law in general; personal rights and holdings; obligations; and actions and sentences. It was to be useful for more than a century, but it appeared in the year that marked the moral nadir of its author's career as advocate and politician. Mackenzie had watched Carstares pay in sweat and tears to retain his moral integrity; while his own character was left in shreds by Baillie. Eight years earlier, in his book on the criminal law, he had written that: '... where the King's Advocate pursues, he is not obliged to swear the Verity of the Dittay, because he pursues only *ratione officii*.'[10] As things turned out, he was doing the regime a disservice: the hugger-mugger trial and execution of a sick man was a scandal to many people of moderate views, and a number of similar trials left the Government's already grubby reputation thoroughly befouled. Events and actions had attached Mackenzie to a party whose direction he did not like and which he could not influence; he was too sensitive not to be aware that the Drummond brothers, who saw the future James VII as the rising sun, were laughing at him behind his back. He was not one of them – he was more liberal in his thoughts, more reliable as a friend, less opportunistic and self-seeking – but he was hopelessly linked to them, their policies, and their practices. The epithet of the dissident Presbyterians, 'Bluidy Mackenzie', probably troubled him much less than the sly smiles and the pats on the back from those whose work he was so effectively doing. On 6 November Drummond of Lundin was promoted from Deputy-Treasurer to joint Secretary of State with the Earl of Moray.

William Carstares made approaches to various members of the Privy Council, including Perth himself, about the misuse of his testimony, but got no satisfaction. Perth agreed there had been a breach of the conditions, but merely said it would not be repeated.[11] Early in 1685 Carstares was released. Refusing to petition for, or accept, any financial recompense from the Government, he obtained permission to travel with his wife to London. There he saw Lundin, who suggested – jocosely perhaps – that he should seek an audience with the new king, but Carstares dryly said that he might 'say certain things' and Lundin agreed it was 'more advisable to dispense with that ceremony'.[12] He arranged for Carstares to obtain a passport to Holland: Mrs Carstares, who was unwell, remained in England.

A proclamation on 30 December made it necessary for every person over 16 to obtain a 'testificate' of their loyalty and good principles before making any journey, 'and all such as adventure to travel without a testificate in manner aforesaid... shall be holden and used as concurrers with the aforesaid execrable rebels.'[13] Any innkeeper or boatman neglecting to check this document was himself liable to arrest. The Council's aim was to force every adult in the suspect districts to take the oath of allegiance, and abjure the declarations of the Covenanters; and to arrest all who refused, and in some places this policy was followed rigorously. Sir Robert Grierson, laird of Lagg in Galloway, was notorious for his zeal in holding courts and interrogations. People who took the oath under compulsion were required to show their good faith by informing on others who, whether they had sworn or not, were still active presbyterian sympathisers. Militias as well as regular troopers were active, and the Earl of Home, with his men from the Merse of Tweed, hunting non-conformers around Newton Stewart, had two brothers, Gilbert and William Milroy, tortured with lighted matches between their fingers, to give information against their neighbours.[14] Solid tenant-farmers, William had already reluctantly taken the test oath in 1683 and Gilbert had bribed the sheriff-depute to remove his name from the official register. Taken to Edinburgh, with others they were sentenced to ten years' banishment and to have their ears cut off. Cropping the ears of arrested non-conformers was a new practice at this time, which became 'pretty ordinary' as a treatment of presbyterian prisoners.[15] Gilbert was so weak that the surgeon employed for the purpose, expecting him to die, refused to slice off his ears. With 188 others they were conveyed to a ship at Leith, shackled two-and-two under the deck, and transported to Jamaica, the voyage lasting three months during which 32 prisoners died. In Port-Royal the survivors were sold by one Sir Philip Howard, who had been gifted them by the King. Gilbert at first got in trouble with his master by refusing to work on Sundays, but before long he was appointed overseer of the black slaves, a job he did so effectively that 'they made various attempts to murder him'. He survived to return to his native Galloway after 1688, but many other prisoners lived on and died in Jamaica, making their contribution to that island's rich inheritance of races and cultures.

The effect of cracking down hard in the south-west was probably counter-productive, helping to motivate hard-core resisters and intensifying the general sense of angry resentment. More success was had in the north, where resistance was not so deep-seated. In January 1685 a judicial commission was sent up to Moray, with a request to the Bishop to get his clergy to provide a list of all those guilty of 'church disorders, or suspect of disaffection to the present established government in church and state' and its remit was extended to the shires of Inverness, Ross, Cromarty and Sutherland. In March the commissioners, the Earls of Errol and Kintore, and Sir George Munro of Culcairn, reported that they had cleansed the area of vagrant preachers, dealt with all disorderly persons, and procured from the heritors and burghs declarations of loyalty and 'voluntary offer of three months supply to his majesty', as well as levying £Sc120,000-worth of fines, chiefly among the Nairnshire and Moray lairds.[16] Summoned by them to Elgin, Alexander Brodie 'had no favour with the Lords; found them look stern and squint to me'.[17] They fined him £Sc24,000.

Just because a war is going on does not mean that senior military officers behave with obedience, grace, or a sense of their own deficiencies; more likely they will ditch all three and squabble among themselves, and so it fell out between Claverhouse and Colonel Douglas. The ostensible cause was that Douglas had used funds intended for soldiers' pay arrears to refund his own costs of new uniforms for his men. Like the later Frederick the Great, he wanted uniformity of height, dress, and appearance in the troop he personally commanded. Claverhouse was more concerned with his men's fighting qualities, and he backed a complaint made to the Privy Council by some of Douglas's men on 11 December 1684.[18] This resulted in a shouting match in Council between him and Queensberry, and neither wasted any time in relaying his version of events to the Duke of York. But Queensberry was a duke and the head of a great family, while Graham was a mere heritor and had recently allied himself by marriage to a family of dissidents and traitors, and York did not back him. George Drummond, Perth's cousin, and Douglas were assigned to service in the south-west, Claverhouse's particular district, while Queensberry took action to recover from him the 'superplus' of fines he had collected and not paid in to the Treasury. While agreeing the system to be vicious and uneconomical, Professor Terry noted that Claverhouse had had to use fines to pay his own and his men's expenses, but that: '… there is not a shred of evidence to prove that Claverhouse had put into his own pocket more than his office entitled him to by way of stipend, namely the balance of funds applied by him to the public service.'[19] Lundin, with a sure instinct for knowing who was up and who was down, wrote to Queensberry on 10 January 1685 to say: 'I am sure the Duke [York] does not at all approve his carriage [behaviour].'[20] In the rudimentary system of checks and balances that characterised the public service, it was always easy to seize on misuse of funds in order to discredit an official who had fallen from grace; and it is unlikely that Graham, when on active service, kept close accounts. In the end, under heavy pressure, he paid £596 to the Treasury.

Charles II died, after a sudden, short illness, on 6 February 1685, and James VII acceded to his brother's triple crown at the age of 52 without compromising his Catholicism. In accordance with the provisions of the Act of Succession, he was proclaimed at Edinburgh, with no mention of the Covenant. For the occasion a 'theatre' was erected at the Cross, with heralds, the Privy Council, the Lords of Session, and the Town Council all in attendance, and 'the Chancellor, weeping, proclaimed James Duke of Albany the only undoubted and lawful King of this realm, under the name of James the seventh'.[21] In all but name, he had already been King of Scotland for three years: ever since his stay in Edinburgh it was to James that the Scottish leaders had looked for position, instruction, approval, and support. With his Scottish ministry already in place, there was no interruption to ongoing business, including the putting in his place of Claverhouse. He was anxious to see the new king and put his side of the case, especially as Drumlanrig was at court, but leave to go to London was refused him.[22] To Queensberry, who was threatening heavy legal action to recover the fines, Lundin wrote on 18 February that: 'I am confident that it will not be in his power to disturb the King's servants' peace in anything; nor I hope will he have the impudence to design it.'[23] Graham remained at Dudhope, completely sidelined. His name was not listed among the Privy Councillors of the new reign[24] and his sheriffdom, which had expired with Charles II, was given to Colonel James Douglas. He attended the Council until the last sitting for which he was admissible, on 3 April, but it was a gesture of pride: nothing was asked of him, though his commission as a colonel was renewed on 30 March. Moray, the joint Secretary of State, characterised him as being of 'a high, proud and peremptory humour'[25] and though an apology to Queensberry would have righted matters as far as the King was concerned, he would not budge until a further request to see James had been denied; then in late April he made an apology so minimal that Moray thought it worse than none at all. Nevertheless it was enough for James, who liked him and who could perhaps appreciate the positive value of his fixity of character better than the courtiers. On 11 May the King ordered his reinstatement on the Privy Council. Already Claverhouse was back in active service – with fresh troubles in the south-west, and Argyll's invasion under way, he was badly needed. That month he and Douglas were promoted to brigadiers; Douglas receiving his commission two days earlier after a spat between the joint Secretaries. Moray had objected that Graham, as a cavalry commander, would be senior to

Douglas as a brigadier of foot; John Drummond had supported Graham (by now again in the King's favour) but Moray won the argument and the Duke's brother was given precedence.²⁶

CHAPTER TWENTY-THREE

A Carnival of Blood?

ON THE OTHER SIDE of the North Sea, with an understandable need for physical and mental recovery, perhaps pleased to be away from political intrigue, and a free man again, William Carstares travelled on his own for almost three months through Holland and the Rhineland in the spring of 1685, stopping in quaint old towns, driving through Ruïsdael and Hobbema landscapes, keeping a diary, noting places, people, and his daily expenditures, while momentous events went on in Great Britain. With a man of such iron discretion it is impossible to say he was just an innocent tourist enjoying a much-needed break, but his diary, not intended for others to see, has nothing to suggest that he was involved in intrigues or even took much of an interest in what was going on. His biographer Story wondered where his funds came from: some may have been from William of Orange's treasurer but a few months later Carstares made a note of receiving a sterling bill for £335 8s from a Mr Parsons on 24 August, which suggests a source in Great Britain. The traveller was able to do himself quite well. At Spa, he wrote: '...the best in town is at the sign of the Spinet, where I staid, and paid for my chambers and dyet twice a day a rix dollar a day.' At The Hague, 'I this day dined at an ordinary with some gentlemen, some of whom carried themselves very indiscreetlie, endeavouring to bring me to speake of publick affairs in England; but they came short of their design, I not concerning myself in their discourse.'[1]

Certainly there was nothing in public affairs to give him any cheer. The Killing Time had plunged Scotland's government to its most dismal level. The much-planned, long-anticipated attempts to promote risings against James VII in Scotland and England fizzled out in disastrous military adventures by Argyll, whose attempt in May to rouse western Scotland was a wretched failure, and Monmouth, whose hopes were crushed at Sedgemoor on 6 July.

Government, in the 17th century, was supposed to be conducted in order to maintain the stability of the realm, from its standing among other nations down to the peacefulness and good order of village and parish. The central machinery of Scottish government, Privy Council and Court of Session, capable of handling matters that could be seen, measured, proved and regulated, was baffled in dealing with an ideology that had taken root strongly in people's minds. Symptomatic of this was an exchange between Sir George Mackenzie and the Covenanting preacher Alexander Shields, during the latter's interrogation by the Privy Council in April 1685 – under threat of a death sentence, Shields protested that 'thought is free and diverse of men have diverse sentiments about government', to which the King's Advocate responded that 'such a freedom would destroy human societies', and the Council pronounced its view that 'the Laws and Acts of Parliament did reach men's thoughts'.[2] This pre-Orwellian spectre of controlling and policing people's thoughts reveals the almost-hysterical condition of some of the Privy Council. While only a minority of the total population, in certain districts, participated in activities named as illegal – and 'supporters of a moderate episcopal settlement may have been in the majority'[3] – sympathy with

Presbyterian Sufferings: frontispiece from Alexander Shields's *A Hind Let Loose*

the anti-episcopalian view (as distinct from the pro-Covenant view) was widespread among those who conformed. The assertion that Christ was the direct Head of their Church has been criticised even by Protestant historians as an attempt to tell God what His job was, and by others as impious, but in their own terms it was perfectly logical.

Now in February 1685 there was a new king who exercised the same claim to regulate the Kirk as his predecessor. But he, the legitimate Stuart heir, was a Roman Catholic. To a nation long taught to regard the Pope as Anti-Christ, it was a profoundly confusing turn of events. Hardly any public protest or resistance was made, and the machinery of state operated smoothly. An indemnity was announced on 2 March, relating to all who had committed illegal acts, apart from some specifically named exceptions and Sharp's assassins, if they would either take an oath of allegiance within 20 days, or transport themselves peaceably and permanently out of the king's domains. This latter option was clearly aimed at preachers and people of status, who might have contacts in Holland or the German states: most of the non-conformers could not have afforded or even imagined such a move. It drew a very modest response, and further commissions were given to the military to scour through the south-western shires. Society-members were the main quarry, and by the summer several score were condemned in batches, to be sent to the colonies and sold as slaves; the most intractable, if men, also had an ear cut off; if women, their hand branded.

During these months the commissions for killing out of hand remained in force.

> 'Owning the Work of God was all their Crime,
> The Eighty-five was a Saint-Killing Time'

– so ran the legend on a gravestone in Mauchline churchyard, and for many the topic still remains an emotive one. Killing one's fellow-citizens for their beliefs is detestable and abhorrent, to quote James Renwick, though if he had become a Scottish Savonarola, he would certainly have shaped the laws to do the same thing in the name of his own severe creed.

But though death, harsh, ugly and final, was inflicted in many places, there were no swathes of bodies, no killing fields, massacres, corpses toppled by the hundred into pits, no hidden deposits of nameless bones. Wodrow claims that the soldiers did not keep a close account, and that 'good numbers were massacred, of whom no accounts can be given',[4] but the soldiers were not the only ones counting, and meticulous study of the records, by later historians sympathetic to the Covenanters and with no reason to minimise the number of victims, has come up with the total of 78 persons summarily shot. Each of these deaths was a brutal act and a shameful stain upon the Council which legitimised them. But, as Professor Terry pointed out in 1905, there was no 'Carnival of Blood'.[5] General Drummond, Colonel Douglas, Sir Robert Grierson, and numerous junior officers all ordered or carried out summary shootings and hangings on the strength of the Privy Council's commission. Grierson's ragings were widely reported, but might be queried as hostile propaganda against a hate-figure: he was an episcopalian-loyalist with authority over presbyterian dissenters. Viscount Kenmure openly challenged him about his cruelties at Kirkcudbright and only the presence of Claverhouse prevented a fight.[6] But the reason for the confrontation was that Grierson had shot dead Kenmure's stepson, John Bell of Whiteside, a short time before, and Graham, it may be noted, was a restraining influence. He did not cease to be the efficient, correct soldier, yet his name is linked more strongly to the atrocities of the Killing Time than that of any other. In part this is a back-handed tribute to his previous record of speed and promptitude in such episodes as the Bridge of Dee: of the Covenanters' pursuers, he was the most assiduous.

Martyr's Head Carving
Reproduced from Hewison, *The Covenanters*, Vol. 2

But the real reason for his pre-eminence has nothing to do with his conduct in the 'Killing Time' or before. After 1689 all the other military persecutors of the Covenanters aligned themselves with the new, Presbyterian, regime. Only Claverhouse would maintain the loyalty that all of them had sworn, and on him was heaped the abuse and spleen of later generations of writers and propagandists who needed a villain's long shadow to help bring the fallen Saints into the bright light of presbyterian hagiography, and who preferred that villain to be not of their own persuasion.[7] Long before Sir Walter Scott's sinister, almost diabolesque portrayal of 'Bluidy Clavers' in 'Wandering Willie's Tale' from *Redgauntlet*, he had been established as arch-enemy.

Wodrow records the 'horrid murder of that excellent person John Brown of Priestfield'[8] by Claverhouse on the first of May. Brown is described as a man of exemplary piety and Christian life, whose only offence was to refuse to attend the services of episcopal ministers: 'I do not find they were at much trouble with him in interrogatories and questions, neither do any of my informations bear that the abjuration oath was offered to him.' Too honest to make an outright claim that Brown was not given a chance to take the oath, Wodrow still leaves the imputation; he also notes that: 'with some difficulty, he was allowed to pray.' In Claverhouse's terse account:

> John Broun refused it [the oath], nor would he swear not to rise in arms against the King, but said he knew no King: upon which, and their being found bullets and match in his house and treasonable papers, I caused shoot him dead.[9]

Brown's nephew, arrested and questioned at the same time, was sent to General Drummond, who had a justiciary commission, because Claverhouse did not have sufficient evidence for summary execution. Brown himself was plainly involved in armed resistance. The episode shows Graham's obedience to indefensible orders. An officer might reasonably pause to consider whether such orders could be carried out by a man of honour. But Graham undoubtedly supported the policy. He had criticised the lawborrows, in a letter to Queensberry in late 1684: 'I think it a thing not to be desired, that I should be forfeited and hanged if my tenant's wife, 20 mile from me, in the midst of hills and woods, give meat or shelter a fugitive,'[10] but he accepted the killing orders without demur.

A few days later, Claverhouse is recorded as trying to prevent the shooting of a young presbyterian prisoner, Andrew Hislop, by Sir James Johnston of Westerhall, at Craighaugh in Eskdalemuir. Johnston insisted on summary execution, and Graham eventually acquiesced, apparently Pilate-like, with the words: 'The blood of this poor man be on you, Westerraw; I am free of it.'[11] But Westerhall had a judicial commission and Graham did not; he had caught Hislop and handed him over to legal authority.

At Mauchline, on 6 May, five men were hanged and their corpses buried in a single grave; one of them, named as John Binnen or Brounen,[12] was probably the nephew of John Brown. Although Graham (under the name of Dundee) is noted on their subsequent gravestone, they were hanged by authority of General William Drummond and Graham played no part in the action. Even his most creative critics could not link him directly to what was perhaps the most notorious of all executions of the 'Killing Time', on the 11th of that month of May 1685. It was not a summary action but came after a form of trial in the previous month. Margaret Mclauchlan, a widow of 63, Margaret Wilson, a girl of 18, and her sister Agnes, only 13, faced a court formed by Lagg, Claverhouse's brother David Graham who had been made Sheriff of Wigtown, Provost Coltrane of that town, and two army officers, one of them Major Windram. The charges were rebellion, attending conventicles, and failure to take the abjuration oath. All three were sentenced to death by drowning. Agnes's father procured her freedom for a bond of £100, but the other two were tied to stakes below the tideline on the shore of the Solway Firth, the elder woman deliberately set ahead of the younger. Despite exhortations to take the oath, both refused, and were drowned by the advancing tide. Much of the evidence for this event is circumstantial and it has been elaborated in many imaginary descriptions; there is no official record of the executions and some writers have doubted whether they really happened. There is no doubt about the trial and sentences, but Wodrow discovered that the Privy Council had made an order on 30 April postponing the executions; the copy he found had a blank for the date to which the sentence was put off, and the paper requests the Secretaries of State to issue a reprieve. No other contemporary documents relating to the executions have been found. The fate of the two Margarets became a major item in Covenanter folk-memory and writings.

Of the 78 victims of the 'Killing Time' orders, Claverhouse can be held responsible for two: one of them John Brown, the other Matthew McIlwraith of whom no more is known than that his gravestone at Colmonell, in the Ayrshire district of Carrick, was recorded by Terry to include in its epitaph: 'By bloody Claverhouse I fell, Who did command that I should die, For owning Covenanted Presbytery.'[13] Drummond,

Grierson, Douglas, Johnston and others all showed much greater zeal. Compared to the thousands who died for the Covenant between 1640 and 1650, the 'Killing Time' had few victims. Sir George Mackenzie, in his *Vindication*, defends but tries to minimise its intention: 'it was thought necessary by some... to terrifie them out of this Extravagancy, by allowing the Soldiers to use them as in a War', and also claims that secret orders were given 'that this should not last above a Fortnight'.[15] In the unending grim annals of human atrocity it stands for a shameful government decision rather than a carnival of death.

CHAPTER TWENTY-FOUR

Argyll's Adventure

A PARLIAMENT OPENED, for the first time since 1682, on 28 April 1685, with the Duke of Queensberry as the King's Commissioner. Touching on the troubles, he expressed the hope that effectual means would be found of dealing with rebels and fanatics, and their supporters, for, 'however inconsiderable soever they appear, assure yourselves they ought not absolutely to be contemned [ignored] for if they had not support and correspondence not yet discovered, it is not to be supposed they could have so long escaped the care and vigilance of the government.'[1] An act was passed to affirm that the King ratified and confirmed 'the security, liberty and freedom of the true church of God, and the protestant religion presently professed within this kingdom'.[2] People who took an interest in the framing of official documents would brood over the significance of the comma fencing off the true church from the protestant religion. This parliament also passed a renewal of the Test Act, and another stating that all preachers at fanatical house and field conventicles, and all hearers at field conventicles, should be punishable by death and the confiscation of their property. The National Covenant was referred to as 'an accursed document' and to sign it or swear to it was made a treasonable crime. No mention was made of a coronation, or of the administration of a coronation oath.

On May 1 the long-anticipated invasion got under way. Argyll, who had once rejected the idea unless a capital sum of £30,000 was raised, and 1,000 cavalry put at his disposal, now had to pledge his own resources against a much more modest budget, though Gilbert Burnet says 'a rich widow in Amsterdam' contributed £10,000 to his war-chest.[3] Dissension was clear from the beginning. Having nerved himself for the effort, Argyll was in peremptory mood, and '... now fancied Scotland was his own, and was very insolent in all his discourses with the other gentlemen, who really thought his brain turned'.[4] He left Holland with only three ships, at most 300 men, and a disputatious committee of exiled lairds, to raise insurrection in a country bristling with hostile preparedness.

Regular and militia troops were ready for action, and the Council had ordered all fencible men in the counties from Aberdeen and Inverness north to Caithness to be ready for call-up. The Marquis of Atholl was made lord lieutenant of the shires of Argyll and Tarbert, which might be supposed to rise in support of *MacCailein Mór*, their hereditary chieftain. With a substantial force of regulars and Highlanders, perhaps as many as 5,000, Atholl avenged the unforgotten ravaging of his own father's earldom by Argyll's father in 1640, when he himself was a boy of five or so. On its way, the little convoy first touched at Kirkwall in Orkney, where there were skirmishes with the Bishop's retainers, before sailing round to the western coast. But the Earl's landings at Tobermory and Campbeltown brought few to join him.

Archibald Campbell, 9th Earl of Argyll
Reproduced from Hewison, *The Covenanters*, Vol. 1

At Campbeltown a wordy declaration was issued, much of it a recitation of past presbyterian grievances and government misdeeds, from the execution of Argyll's father to the torture of Carstares and procedures against the civil population 'no less barbarous than what was practised by the Spaniards in christianizing the wild Indians'. James VII was proclaimed an apostate and rebel, unfit to hold the meanest office in the kingdom, and all good men were called on to join in the defence of 'true, reformed protestant religion, in its power and purity'. No mention is made of the National Covenant, however. An odder feature of the declaration is the absence of anything about who or what might replace James and his regime, other than 'righteous laws and methods of government, as may be meet for securing of liberty and property, with the greatest ease and equality'.[5] Argyll had a reputation for being anti-monarchic and in favour of a 'Free State like the Estates of Holland'.[6] All in all, it was a less than stirring call to arms. Atholl was occupying the Campbell headquarters at

Inveraray, and the sub-chiefs of Clan Diarmaid, and the chiefs of its traditional allies, mostly muttered their excuses or made vague promises of support. It was widely believed that Argyll's personal reasons for keeping James off the throne were what really mattered to him. Under James, the Earl's estates were likely to be forfeited, and the long-built up Campbell power broken. Already there was a strong token of what might happen when in early 1685 John Drummond of Lundin was given the title of Viscount Melfort, a place well within the Campbell lands. To counter this, Argyll published a personal statement denying private motives, promising to pay all debts owed by himself and his father, and requiring all his vassals 'within my several jurisdictions' to raise their fighting men on his behalf.[7]

By mid-May some 1,500 men had been mustered at Tarbert, in Kintyre, but Argyll's plans were disrupted by the most vocal of his committee-men, Sir John Cochrane of Ochiltree, Jean Graham's uncle, who demanded the opening of a second invasion front in his own county of Ayrshire, where he was sure of finding strong support. This was to come from the 'Society People', but Cochrane's confidence, backed by an over-optimistic report from the minister George Barclay, sent as an emissary, was wildly misplaced. The region was heavily policed by government troops, and despite hints in John Erskine's journal that William Cleland at least was keen for action,[8] most Cameronians were not convinced. Argyll wanted to get rid of King James, but beyond that, his policy was unclear. Their own cause could not be more clear: re-establishment of the Covenant, and purification of the nation under the rule of a purged and de-bishoped Kirk. If Argyll was not openly for this, they were not for him. For them the removal of James VII was a mere detail, and though Renwick encouraged them 'to put themselves in some Posture for Action, waiting until their Call should be cleared',[9] clearance never came, and they stayed aloof.

Government warships, and militia patrols on the coast, put paid to the notion of a landing south of the Clyde, except for a skirmish on the shore at Greenock on 3 June,[10] and for a few days, the rebel force's attentions returned to the lands of Argyll. The Earl's instinct was to get control of his family domains and consolidate his power-base, but his wish to attack Atholl at Inveraray was frustrated by his associates, Lowland gentry dominated by the over-sanguine Cochrane and the excitable Sir Patrick Hume of Polwarth, who felt ill at ease in a Gaelic milieu and still

Dumbarton Castle
Reproduced from Hewison, *The Covenanters*, Vol. 1

hankered after action on their home ground. Leaving the mountains and lochs of Cowal, having set up a depot of boats, arms and gunpowder at the castle of Eilean Dearg on Loch Riddon, the army made its way south towards Dumbarton, with the aim of capturing Glasgow. Hardly any Lowland sympathisers joined, and a few who did asked to make it look as if they had been forced, to avoid reprisals.[11]

The senior professional officer, an Englishman, Colonel Rumbold, was no more able than the Earl to master the arguments and dismiss the hesitations of the amateur commanders. Disputes on tactics prevented any direct confrontation with a militia force headed by George Douglas, Earl of Dumbarton, appointed commander-in-chief. Abandonment of Eilean Dearg by its garrison and its capture by government troops cut off any hope of return to the Argyll heartland. Trying to bypass the militia by night, the army became dispersed, and the march on Glasgow finished as a disorderly retreat, with some, led by Cochrane and Polwarth, on the west bank of the Clyde, and some remaining with the Earl on the Dumbarton side. By now it was evident that the cause was hopelessly lost. With a small party, Argyll crossed the Clyde, but militia troops were everywhere, and he was captured, dressed as a countryman, while fording a stream near Inchinnan. Already under sentence of death, he was interrogated by the Council, and threatened with torture, to make him disclose information about his associates and intentions: the Councillors too were curious about his views on a successor to James VII. Hill Burton[12] passes on a suggestion that Sir George Mackenzie deliberately did not propose a new trial, out of consideration for the future of the house of Argyll. The death sentence relating to the Test oath was palpably unjust and could be posthumously annulled, while a sentence for high treason, with automatic forfeiture, would be more difficult to undo. But a letter from Melfort to the Council[13] makes it clear that this was official policy. Urged on from London, the Council confirmed the old death sentence and on 30 June Argyll was executed at the Market Cross of Edinburgh, on the same 'Maiden' which had beheaded his father.

Yet again, the thunderclouds of presbyterian rebellion had evaporated without a storm. James's position seemed wholly secure, and the exiled Scots still in Holland[14] could only mourn their failure, and continue to conspire. Before his execution, Argyll wrote that certain friends had been his greatest enemies, and that ignorance, cowardice and faction were the cause of his downfall.[15] He might have added his own inability to organise or give commanding leadership to the venture. The lesson of Argyll's and Monmouth's disasters would not be lost on William of Orange, who in 1688 made very sure of his support base and funding, and also brought a large and well-equipped army.

Rumbold suffered the horrors of a traitor's execution, and some others were hanged; Atholl supervised his own court at Inveraray where more supporters of the invasion were hanged, imprisoned or fined. If Scotland did not experience a course of bloody retributive judgment like that which Judge Jeffreys would conduct in England after Monmouth's defeat, it was partly because so many had been executed or imprisoned already. Polwarth survived in hiding; Cochrane bought himself off by bribes and giving evidence of the conspiracy; in the words of one letter-writer, he 'played the good bairn'.[16] Old fortresses like Blackness Castle on the Firth of Forth had sometimes been used to confine prisoners, but, at the time of the invasion, the Council decided to transfer a large number of presbyterian prisoners from town jails to the ancient stronghold of Dunottar

Castle on its rock above the North Sea. Around 170 people were sent there on a seven-day forced march from Edinburgh, under military escort, but in the course of a two-day halt, packed into the cramped space of Burntisland's tolbooth, forty accepted the oath of allegiance and even (the greater sticking-point) the royal supremacy over Kirk as well as state, and were released. Herded northwards, around 100 people were for a time crammed in inhuman conditions in a damp and foul vault beneath the castle. Alexander Peden sent them a message of encouragement from his own haunts among the southern peat-haggs: 'God is giving the Saints a little trial... O how sweet will it be to see Christ marching up in a full body, with all the trumpets sounding the triumph of the Lamb's victory, when his sword shall be made red with the blood of his enemies...'[17] At the end of July this short early effort at 'concentration' was ended, and the prisoners, according to whether they would swear allegiance, or the supremacy, or refuse both, were liberated, removed to regular jails, or condemned to banishment and colonial servitude.

Renwick was still active, and Shields remarked of him, 'I doubt if ever one Minister since the Apostles' days baptised so many as he did.'[18] But even though the core group of Cameronians had not been caught, and even though all the laws, enactments and requirements for oaths remained in force, through the second half of 1685 and into 1686 there was a distinct relaxation of the more extreme severities against the non-conforming Presbyterians. Just why this should be is not clear: there were no official announcements, and there is no record of orders given to desist from rigorous application of the killing commission. But in 1686, only one Cameronian death at government hands is recorded.[19] By its own standards, the Council's drastic policy had been successful: the frequency of conventicles was now much less, and fewer people attended them. Argyll's failure, and the disappearance with him of any credible national opposition leader, also contributed, discouraging many Presbyterians as well as easing official anxieties. Perhaps a degree of fatigue had set in on both sides. But also, the Cameronians were by now isolated within the Presbyterian community. Shields reported that Renwick's greatest difficulties came from 'professed Presbyterians', and these opponents represented him as '... a poor, unlearned, empty, blown-up, proud Thing', with only 'about a Hundred silly, poor daft Bodies, that were running through with him, and robbing the Country'. He was castigated for breaking up families – a tricky point for Renwick, who thought it right that professed Covenanters should desert families who did not take the same strict line, though he felt that they should be 'tender of offering in their withdrawing'.[20] Less influential than its Government pursuers assumed, the Remnant trod its own narrow path. By August 1685, the 'Killing Time', without being revoked, was at an end. In that month, General Dalyell died, and the supreme command went to neither Douglas nor Claverhouse but to William Drummond, cousin to the Chancellor. Like his predecessor, he was an ex-'Muscovite'. But the new King welcomed John Graham when that officer was finally allowed to come to London and attend at court in December 1685, and Queensberry was directed to repay the £596 so reluctantly paid over earlier in the year.

CHAPTER TWENTY-FIVE

Dancing at Holyrood

IN A SCOTLAND MORE securely at peace with itself during the 17th century, cultural life might have diversified in interesting ways. Just across the North Sea, in Holland, painters of genius were depicting the visible and inner lives of their countryfolk, working in and developing a well-established artistic tradition. Scotland might have assembled the necessary elements of demand, ability, and taste, had it kept a court or been able to build on its trading links. The Kirk, with its iconoclastic urges and its Old Testament aversion to 'images', has often been blamed for the country's artistic deficiency, but Dutch Reformed church interiors were just as stark and bare as Scottish ones. A country of tough, intelligent people with a necessary sense of austerity, developing a mercantile economy, might have evolved a distinctive form of art. As it was, a derivative artistic tradition was just getting under way, started by the industrious Aberdonian George Jameson (died 1644) who visited the homes of the the wealthy to paint their portraits. In *Caelia's Country House and Closet*, George Mackenzie devotes a verse to the London portraitist Sir Peter Lely, 'Lillie who has no Rival but his Glass', and also describes paintings of shipwreck and church interiors.[1] We cannot see back into the 17th-century Scottish town, harbour, or domestic interior as we can for Holland and Flanders, nor interpret the people through contemporary eyes. No painter in Scotland was capable of recording the festal solemnity of the Presbyterians' open-air, all-day communions, or the Riding of the Parliament, with the representatives of the Estates making procession in their finery behind the nation's Regalia, while the crowd lined the sides and leaned from the many-windowed tenements along the High Street of Edinburgh.

A richer subsoil was available for musicians, though none of great distinction emerged. To an extent hardly imaginable today, people sang, as they worked, or walked, or to entertain one another. Apart from the burgh song schools, every small-town or village teacher was expected to teach singing. Musical instruments were made, imported, and used: lutes, viols, trumpets, harps, horns, even spinets. And with music went dance: public display dances of the morris kind, but also jigs and reels and French dances. If a Puritan element in Kirk and society frowned, and did not indulge, very many presbyterians, and even more episcopalians, were not out-and-out Puritans, or not Puritans at all, and the music could not be stopped even though after 1650 it was barred from the Kirk. Wealthy and cultured royalist families, like the Maules of Panmure in Angus, kept their own music collections, in the old courtly style as well as the popular one. When Forbes published his *Songs and Fancies* in 1662, he wrote that the Aberdeen town council comprised 'as many musicians as magistrates' and even allowing for flattery, they were clearly willing to be complimented in this fashion. During the reign of James VII, there was music and dancing in Holyrood Palace, where Lady Errol had a suite of rooms (she, incidentally, remained a Protestant despite her brother James's prayers 'that you who see so far in all things else may at last see the unreasonableness of being a Protestant');[2] John Macky recorded that her brother Melfort, as well as being very handsome, was a fine dancer.[3] But there was very little in the way of musical innovation or new composition, except in the hermetic Highlands and especially on Skye, where the great piper Patrick Mòr MacCrimmon, until his death in 1670, refined the tradition of the classical pibroch begun by his father Donald Mòr. Hereditary pipers to the chief of the MacLeods, the MacCrimmons kept a famous piping school. But though every Scottish town had its piper and drummer, the *piobaireachd* was an art form unknown beyond the Highland line.

Literature was among the casualties of the age. George Mackenzie never got around to *Aretina* Part Two, though an opponent suggested that the title would suit his pamphlet defending the 'Highland Host' in 1678.[4] The national way with words, which previous centuries had shown capable of expressing humour, tenderness, insight, and deep emotion as well as sarcasm, irony and inventive insult, was sidetracked into pamphlets, broadsheets and polemic works, and sermons uncountable. A tradition of popular verse was kept up by the laird of Beltrees in Renfrewshire, Francis Sempill, though some of the poems attributed to him, like the immensely popular 'Wedding of Maggie and Jock' may have been reworkings of traditional songs. None were published in his lifetime, though they may have been printed on penny broadsheets. Sempill was a stout anti-Whig, but another poet of the time was William Cleland, the doughty teenager on the Covenanter side at Drumclog, who as an 18-year-old student added eight verses to the otherwise anonymous *Hallow, My Fancy*,[5] beginning with:

> In conceit like Phaeton
> I'll mount Phoebus' chair,
> Having ne'er a hat on,
> All my hair a-burning
> In my journeying;
> Hurrying through the the air.
> Fain would I hear his fiery horses neighing
> And see how they on foamy bits are playing,
> All the stars and planets I will be surveying –
> *Hallow my fancy, whither wilt tho go?*

– light-hearted, engaging verses by a clever youth, they seem to come from a different world to the fulminations, recriminations and solemn ecstasies of the field preachers with whom he associated. Cleland also wrote a satirical poem, *Hudibras*-style, on the plaid-clad Highland Host of 1678:

> Their head, their neck, their legs, and thighs
> Are influenced by the skies;
> Without a clout to interrupt them,
> They need not strip them when they whip them;
> Nor loose their doublet when they're hanged[6]

– the theme of mockery of the Highlander was already hoary. Far more significant was the unrecorded, unconsidered, slowly accumulating body of anonymous work, sifted and enriched through many retellings, with no 'absolute' version of any of its songs and poems – ballads that were remembered, made and sung about past and present events, all over the country. Here was a traditional art form that the 17th century not only preserved but extended. Striking with the haphazardness of lightning it found its themes sometimes in the most unlikely places. John Kennedy, sixth Earl of Cassillis, a deep-dyed Presbyterian, had married Lady Jean Hamilton, daughter of a newly ennobled lawyer, the Earl of Haddington. Cassillis was one of the observers sent to the Assembly of Divines in 1643 and out of his lengthy absence a strange legend came; that his lady had loved another man before her marriage, Sir John Faa of Dunbar, who came to her, disguised as a gypsy, with a gypsy retinue, during the Earl's absence. But Cassillis, already on the return journey, and forewarned, came hastening home, caught Sir John and his men, and hanged them all from a tree in front of her bower window. It was the stuff of a tragic ballad, and such it became:[7]

> There cam' seven Egyptians on a day,
> And, wow, but they sang bonny.
> And they sang sae sweet, and sae very complete,
> Down cam' Earl Cassilis' lady
>
> She cam' tripping down the stair,
> And all her maids before her;
> As soon as they saw her weel-faured face,   [lovely]
> They cast the glamourie owre her.   [the charm]

– but there is no truth in it, as far as the Cassillis pair were concerned. Lady Jean died in 1642 and the Earl remarried in 1644. Its origins may relate to some older tragedy, or to a source outside Scotland. Like the stories arising around the Dalrymple family, it comes from those same south-western country people typified as stern, catechising Covenanters, obsessed by the Old Testament.

Accumulating and altering generation by generation, the folk tradition was deep, complex and enduring, and emerges in another aspect in the researches and personal experiences of the Rev. Robert Kirk of Aberfoyle, who died in 1692, aged about 50. A son of the manse, he was a serious and dedicated pastor, bilingual in Gaelic and English as any minister north of the Highland Line had to be, episcopalian though not militantly so, responsible for the publication of a Gaelic book of psalms and a Gaelic New Testament. But he also was a studious recorder of the world of fairies, as reported to him (he was at pains to make clear) by parishioners and others with first-hand experience. His short book, *The Secret Commonwealth of Elves, Faunes and Fairies*, is one of the few European texts of the time that claim to give an objective view of a parallel world of beings, unseen by the great majority:

> 'The usual method for a curious person to get a transient sight of this otherwise invisible crew of Subterraneans, if impotently and over-rashly sought, is to put his foot on the Seer's foot, and the Seer's hand is put on the inquirer's head, who is [then] to look over the wizard's right shoulder...

> 'Then will he see a multitude of wights like furious hardy men flocking to him hastily from all Quarters, as thick as atoms in the air. These are not nonentities or phantasms, creatures proceeding from an affrighted apprehension [or] confused or crazed sense, but realities appearing to a stable man in his wakening senses and enduring [undergoing] a rational trial of their being. These [beings], through fear, strike him breathless and speechless, but the seer or wizard, defending the lawfulness of his skill, forbids such horror, and comforts his novice by telling of Zacharias being struck speechless at seeing of apparitions [Luke 1:20].'

Kirk's personal papers show that he followed Church affairs closely,[8] but he was probably typical of many other ministers who avoided current controversies, preferring scholarly or antiquarian interests; others may have simply preferred to farm their glebes. Often seen as a pioneer work of anthropology, his bizarre little book is the most widely read work by any Scots minister of his time. Use of Biblical references to shore up or gloss his descriptions and analyses shows how different sets of beliefs could be syncretised by a community which accepted the one without wishing to reject the other. What was true of Kirk's parishioners on the Highland fringe was equally true of their fellow-citizens to north and South. On Hallowe'en 1684, John Erskine saw many bonfires and noticed people dip their sleeves in 'a south-running well', near his home at Cardross: if they then went to bed without speaking to anyone, they would dream of the person they were to marry. As a good Presbyterian, he was shocked by this, 'in a nation professing Christianity'.[9] Abundant evidence from this century and the next[10] shows continuing belief, particularly in the countryside, in nature spirits, harvest demons, brownies, ghosts and bogles, who had to be placated and avoided. It had always been easier to harmonise these pre-Christian beliefs with the religion of the saints and the cult of the Virgin, than with the unmediative doctrine of Calvinism. Consumers of more up-to-date knowledge were sought by another episcopal minister, James Cockburn, founder of *Bibliotheca Universalis* in 1688. Intended to be a monthly digest of 'What is doing Abroad, by the Learned World' it was closed down after a single issue, for anti-Catholic sentiments.[11]

At a more elevated social level, as Duke of Albany, and then King, James VII gave some encouragement to the arts and sciences in Scotland, though he is also credited with introducing cock-fighting.[12] James regarded his family's 'ancient kingdom' more favourably than had Charles, and was much more willing to give time to Scottish affairs. The Dutch painter Jacob DeWitt was brought over in 1684 to paint, largely from his imagination, the series of Scottish kings that still hangs in Holyrood Palace, for a payment of £250. James also backed the fourth and finally successful effort to establish a Royal College of Physicians in Edinburgh, in 1681, against the opposition of the guild of surgeon-apothecaries. By September 1685 Edinburgh University also had three professors of medicine. As King, James sponsored the reinvention of the knightly Order of the Thistle,[13] in an attempt to reach back to the supposed chivalric tradition of early Stewart Scotland, and to affirm the aristocratic principle (this would have appealed to Sir George Mackenzie, author of *The Science* [Knowledge] *of Heraldry*). The gesture underlines the fact that James VII had no interest in a pan-British union, and saw Scotland, including the Highlands, as a useful separate political unit which might be a counter-weight to the parties hostile to him in England. The Thistle processions also provided a new occasion of festive flummery in a country whose almost universal clothing shade, outside the Highlands, was 'hodden [homespun] grey', and whose vernacular language had a range, hardly to be paralleled in Europe, of words for stockings without feet and gloves without fingers.

James VII felt no need to revisit Scotland, and was confident enough to summon a second parliament in April 1686. The Commissioner this time was the Earl of Moray, who was correctly rumoured to be on the verge of becoming a Catholic. These conversions have generally been seen as opportunistic, perhaps unfairly. Everywhere in the country, to a far greater extent than today, lofty walls, broken traceries of stone, grass-grown naves and truncated pillars marked the presence of former abbey churches. With neglect, simony, pluralism, royal bastards made juvenile abbots, and all the other old faults by now a historical memory, these grey and red sandstone ruins might strike some as relics of a lost splendour. In the North-East, within the powerful network of Gordon families, Catholicism had been preserved, and also among many of the clans of the western Highlands and the Hebrides. Elsewhere, to be a practising Catholic was far more dangerous and difficult, but many families which accepted Protestant episcopacy might have felt privately drawn to the Church which remained so strong in much of Europe. For the inquiring mind, Calvinism was not the only satisfying religious answer, and the Church of Rome had an aesthetic dimension which that of Scotland altogether lacked. James and John Drummond's mother, Lady Anne Gordon, was a Catholic,[14] and her sons had a cultivated interest in art and music. Having converted, the brothers remained faithful Catholics for the rest of their lives. James VII himself was Catholic by conviction. A letter of 1687 to his daughter the Princess of Orange[15] relates how from having been brought up in the doctrines of the Church of England, he had come to decide that the Reformation was not divinely inspired and had let great disorders loose in the world. No doubt James would have approved of the vigour of the Counter-Reformation which in France, with the revocation of the Edict of Nantes in 1685, launched persecution of the Huguenots on a scale that vastly outweighed the repression in Scotland. Temperament and circumstances made him impatient: 'The King was every day saying that he was king, and he would be obeyed, and would make those who opposed him feel that he was their king.'[16] Victory over Argyll and Monmouth encouraged him to promote his own religion, and understandably, he wanted men about him who shared his vision and would work with him through commitment as well as obedience or for profit.

Perth's conversion trumped his former ally Queensberry, a staunch episcopalian who had been deeply uneasy about the Catholic toleration. For a time, he led what would now be called a 'charm offensive' focused on eminent people who might follow his example. The difficulties of Sir Robert Sibbald show the pressures and problems. A polymath even in a time of diverse learning, he had been both Geographer Royal and Royal Physician since 1680, with the Earl of Perth as his friend and patron. Under Perth's persuasion he converted to Catholicism in 1686. To his surprise and terror, a Protestant mob staged a riot outside his house and he escaped to the sanctuary of Holyrood Palace, then fled to London, where, after deep soul-searching, he renounced his new faith. Returning to Scotland and episcopal Protestantism, he made a public recantation which was widely read and quoted. His namesake the Rev. Patrick Sibbald of Aberdeen commented that the episode 'may prove very edifying and a media to stablish many in these dangerous and slippery times'.[17]

Queensberry, still Lord Treasurer, was now of no value to the

John Drummond, 1st Earl of Melfort
Reproduced by courtesy of Scottish National Portrait Gallery

Drummond brothers who not only dropped him but bad-mouthed him behind his back; James VII showed more sense than they did when he ordered them – as Melfort with remarkable candour told the Duke of Hamilton in a letter of December 1685 – to keep on proper terms with him: '... though I told his Majesty that Duke Queensberry was an atheist in religion, a villain in friendship, a knave in business, and a traitor in his carriage [behaviour] to him.'[18] On 23 February 1686 James finally dismissed Queensberry as Lord Treasurer and instead formed a commission to manage the Treasury, whose board included Claverhouse. The Duke was made Lord President of the Council, but it was evident that his days of power were gone.

The parliament of 1685 had been oleaginous in its proclamations of devotion and loyalty to the King, and that of 1686, with very much the same set of members, might be expected to be dutiful. Well before the opening, it was known that James wished the penal laws against Catholics to be repealed or modified. Knowing that the policy was controversial, the administration left nothing to chance. Three influential Protestant members of Council and Parliament, the Duke of Hamilton, Sir George Lockhart, and General William Drummond, commander of the army, were called to London in the hope that they would form the kernel of a loyalist group. Their reluctance to support any kind of relaxation of anti-Catholic laws without equivalent concessions to the Presbyterians had an effect on the reluctant King. The royal message to Parliament was carefully phrased, with an early mention of something long desired by the Scots, free trade with England, in which he was 'proceeding with all imaginable application' and hoped for considerable advances. He offered a full indemnity to presbyterian rebels for all crimes committed against the royal person and authority, and also commended to the parliament's care 'our innocent subjects, those of the Roman Catholic religion, who have, with the hazard of the lives and fortune, always been assistant to the crown... though they lay under discouragements hardly to be named.'[19] It asked Parliament to give them the protection and security of the law. Moray's address also emphasised the Government's efforts on behalf of Scottish trade both with France and Holland, and in other mercantile grievances, 'the abuses in importing Irish cattle and victual, the want of an open mint, and all the oppressions of commissary courts'.[20]

The anti-Catholic statutes were stringent: a third conviction for hearing a mass carried the death sentence. But it was more than a quarter of a century since they had been invoked against anyone. The Catholics had given no trouble, and the Government could be represented as offering religious toleration, civil peace, and economic benefits. Nevertheless, it became obvious that the King's wishes would not get an easy assent, and intense argument and lobbying went on inside and outside Parliament House, with lengthy pamphlets arguing the different points of view. Both sides were kept well informed about parallel events in England, where the King was striving to control anti-Catholic activists in the London streets, and the defenders of Anglicanism were mounting an intellectual barrage of pamphlets and sermons against his policy. The Committee of the Articles had the task of framing a bill that would be acceptable. It proved impossible. Even the Bishops were disunited.[21] The most the Committee could bring itself to propose was that Roman Catholics should be allowed to practise their religion in private houses, but without removal of the 'laws or acts of parliament made against popery', or of the Test Act. No good Catholic could swear the Test oath, and since the king's aim, as everyone knew, was to clear the way to place Catholics in official positions and allow them public worship, the proposed bill was of no use to him. On 6 May Parliament, while assuring James of its loyalty and fidelity, invoked that abstract Scottish organ most irritating to the Stuart monarchs, its conscience: with regard to his wishes for the Catholics, they would go 'as great lengths therein as our conscience will allow, not doubting that your majesty will be careful to secure the protestant religion, established by law'.[22] But the 'wee bitt actie' as the commissioner for the burgh of Cullen termed it[23] was not passed, and by royal command Parliament was prorogued indefinitely.

Parliament's stand was popular in the country, but a brusque reshuffle of the Privy Council followed, with five Protestant members removed and replaced by Catholics. At the same time, Sir George Mackenzie's long tenure as King's Advocate was terminated, and his old rival Sir George Lockhart appointed in his place. Despite his belief in the sanctity of the royal prerogative, Mackenzie can only have been queasy about the King's intentions. For him, the prerogative was to be used for stability and good management, and James's policy had already stirred up Protestant roars such as had not been heard in the streets of the capital since 1650. Whether to ask for his job back or to ensure that the King had no malice towards him, in July he went to London, but James refused to see him. Back in Edinburgh, he resumed private practice, and 'Bluidy Mackenzie' successfully defended 22 out of 23 persons who had been accused of resetting rebels after the battle of Bothwell Bridge. The prosecutor was Sir John Dalrymple, who, by contrast, was managing to make himself increasingly well-regarded by the Government.

A letter from the King on 21 August notified the Council that he was allowing his Catholic subjects the freedoms which Parliament had refused them, and that the Chapel Royal at Holyrood had been reconsecrated as a Catholic church with its own chaplaincy. Melfort ordered special guards for the chapel but a mob broke in during a mass, and, wrote Burnet: 'If the Earl of Perth had not been conveyed away in disguise, he had very probably fallen a victim to popular rage.'[24] Mutual hostility intensified among the governors, with Queensberry and others being suspected of promoting or encouraging the riots.

The awakening of a Protestant, if not necessarily Presbyterian conscience, among the nation's parliamentarians, might have seemed a positive sign to the Cameronians, but they were in no mood to make overtures to anyone. As suffering standard-bearers of the true Kirk, they required a suppliant nation to approach them on bended knees, bewailing its lapses from grace. But the non-conformers were increasingly disunited. 'Wandering ministers' like Peden, who did not agree with the Cameronians' extreme political views, were angry at their refusal to help Argyll's revolt. If they kept in contact with the extremists, they also maintained good terms with some of the indulged ministers who scarcely troubled to conceal their non-conformity. These resented their condemnation by Renwick and were angered by the Cameronians' letters to other Calvinist Churches, proclaiming themselves the true and only Church of Scotland. News came to Holland of a meeting on 28 January 1686 between Renwick and delegates from the Societies, where there had been disagreement on which ministers should be heard, and many had withdrawn their support for him, and moved to less extreme presbyterian groups.[25] As the atmosphere hardened, Renwick was coming more and more under attack from the increasingly confident 'mainstream' body of presbyterian ministers and their supporters.

CHAPTER TWENTY-SIX

... before the Delivery come

FOR THE FIRST TIME since the Whiggamore-dominated Government of 1648, the country was being ruled by a minority group, this time with even less support across the broad base of the population. The various administrations of Lauderdale had many shortcomings and official crimes, but the popular sense had always been that even at his blundering, self-interested worst he did not wholly ignore the country's interests. Yet the re-introduction of bishops had brought 25 years of civil disobedience and put a heavy drag on social and economic progress. With a far more ambitious aim, the Perth-Melfort Government's agenda set the sectarian interest of a tiny minority[1] before that of the wider nation. Few people engaged with politics believed that the King's intentions would stop at lifting the penal laws against Catholicism, and it needed little mental effort to foresee a day when the same laws would be turned on Protestants, and Catholic bishops and Catholic church courts enforce obedience. But this kind of thinking was confined to those who were politically committed. Most people were inclined to take the government's actions piece by piece, and so far, these actions did not threaten them in any direct way – on the contrary, they could be seen as promoting civil peace. For most people, that was enough. The atmosphere was very different to that of 1637. This king had promised to maintain the Kirk and had done nothing to interfere with its doctrine or mode of worship. But if the Government felt safe in its power, it was an illusory sense of security. Its roots of support did not spread among the community of the realm, and every new appointment of a Catholic or 'fellow-travelling' provost, militia officer, or sheriff, detached it further from the majority. If a hostile wind should blow, its instability would be speedily exposed.

Edinburgh, still by a long way the most populous town, seems to have been the focus of the new Protestant fervour. The presence of the Privy Council, the Parliament, the Court of Session, and the Palace (now with its Romanised chapel, Jesuit school, and printing press) all helped to increase the pressure. Students at the university, as well as townspeople, participated in protests, despite stern warnings from the Council and the Town Council, which controlled the university, and they were compelled to sign a bond of good behaviour.[2] After the break-in at Holyrood, trials were held, a leading rioter was executed, and things quietened down. James VII and his government did not shorten sail to this Protestant wind. However sanguine courtiers might be, or represent themselves, in pursuing a policy on behalf of their monarch, it must have been apparent to James's officers of government that a kind of race was going on. The king was 53 in 1686, and healthier than his brother had been, but he too might die relatively young, and, like Mary I of England, leave the ambition of a counter-Reformation unaccomplished, to be destroyed by a Protestant successor. For the regime, it was a matter of retaining control and installing Catholics, or loyal Protestants – with Claverhouse a prime but not the only example – in positions of power and command. In Claverhouse's case it was his Constableship of Dundee, which, during these years, he exercised firmly. In September 1686 he was also promoted to Major-General. The silence during 1686–88 of certain magnates, including the dukes of Queensberry and Hamilton, carried its own implied threat to the Government, but Perth and Melfort (advanced to an earldom in 1686) felt themselves to be in firm control of the machinery of the state.

During these dangerous and slippery times, at least two protagonists remained calm and semi-detached from events. Sir James Dalrymple had not been a member of Argyll's war council, and during 1685 he was putting the finishing touches to a book. Like Sir George Mackenzie, Sir James was one of the few men in public life concerned to encourage interest in wider intellectual issues. He aspired to the contemporary ideal of the *virtuoso*, a man possessing the totality of humane knowledge. His *Physiologia Nova Experimentalis,* an ambitious and wide-ranging survey, was published in Leyden at the beginning of 1686. Though dedicated to the Royal Society of London, it was an old-fashioned work, ignoring or attempting to disprove recent discoveries made on a basis of experiment and close observation. For Sir James, the Earth remained at the centre of the universe. But the fortunes of his family were rising from the dire days of 1684. Although he had been cited before the Privy Council as a rebel and candidate for forfeiture, his case had been suspended. His son John, in the course of 1686, effected a remarkable transformation from his status as a cautioned dissident. In December he travelled to London, and returned in February 1687 with his £500 fine of 1682 repaid from royal funds, plus £700 for his expenses,³ and in the post of King's Advocate. Exactly how the son of the exiled Presbyterian became a member of James VII's Privy Council is not known, but the appointment did not lessen the Stair family reputation for diabolical alliances. By the end of March, the Government's case against Sir James was closed, and a remission was issued in his favour, and another to the boy who had shot his brother.

Though now free to return home, Sir James elected to remain in Holland. Some others were returning, or making plans to do so, prompted by reports of toleration, and also of the breaking-away of many of the Society People from Renwick, and their need for (somewhat) more moderate ministers. Since McWard's death religious militancy had cooled. Erskine of Carnock noted on 8 September that: 'The country was now fit to be wrought upon, in order to their receiving a right impression of religion.'⁴ After years of grinding attrition, the mainstream Presbyterians were, cautiously, coming out of their trenches. William Carstares too had kept back from over-close involvement with Argyll's invasion and for a time enjoyed an uncontroversial, peaceful time of ministry, study, and meetings with friends. He had first settled in the duchy of Cleves in 1685, and there drawn up his own 'Rules of Conduct', allocating time to scripture study, French, philosophy and theology but also: 'I would spend two hours a day upon what I design for a just vindication of myself, principles and friends, from the aspersions cast upon them in the narrative of the plot printed in England...'⁵ In 1686 he and his wife moved to Leiden in Holland where he was back among the conspirators, appointed an honorary chaplain to the Prince of Orange; who also arranged in 1688 for him to become Second Minister of the Scots Church in the city. The focus of the exiles' interest was no longer on home-bred leaders of revolt, but on William of Orange himself.

James VII was not a man of magnanimity or foresight. If Scotland was not going to give him what he wanted, it need not expect consideration from him. Its Parliament was not to be summoned again. No more was heard of furthering free trade between Scotland and England, or of promoting Scottish manufactures and exports. The Mint, which had remained closed after the Hatton scandal in 1682, partially reopened in 1686, but there was no general issue of coinage during James's reign, and only a few silver coins were produced.⁶ A national shortage of coin had a restrictive effect on business. Among those who were prepared to swallow a lot as long as the Government seemed to be encouraging commerce and trade, acceptance of the regime could melt away quickly.

The Government's own toleration policy was pressed ahead, and a new proclamation of indulgence was sent down to Edinburgh and published there on 18 February 1687, allowing 'moderate presbyterians' to meet in private houses to hear indulged ministers; likewise Quakers. Freedom of worship 'in houses or chapels' was allowed to Catholics, all crown appointments were opened to them, and all oaths and tests were dispensed with, to be replaced by a single oath of loyalty to the King, which made reference to him only as 'supreme governor of these realms', with nothing about authority over the Church, though the latter was something James both claimed and exercised, having dismissed two bishops for their failure to give him adequate support in the 1686 Parliament. All these things were granted under 'our sovereign authority, prerogative royal, and absolute power, which all our subjects are to obey without reserve'.[7] Conventicles and field meetings remained subject to all sanctions already in place. A royal letter to the Council on 31 March amplified the statement of toleration by lifting the neeed for presbyterian ministers to take the oath of loyalty, if the Council were otherwise satisfied with their attitude.

The Scottish reaction was satisfactory enough for James to make his declaration of liberty of conscience in England, on 4 April, and a further proclamation relating to Scotland was published in Edinburgh on 5 July, to align policy in both kingdoms. Now, invoking the same 'absolute power' as before, he conferred on his subjects 'leave to meet and serve God after their own way and manner, be it in private houses, chapels or places purposely hired or built for that use' so long as nothing be taught or preached to alienate the people from the King and his Government, and that all meetings be free and public. Field meetings remained under ban and penalty.

Reaction from the Cameronians was as might be expected: '... such a Liberty, as overturns our Rights, our Privileges, our Laws, our Religion, and *Tolerates* it only under the Notion of a *Crime*, and indemnifies it under the notion of a *Fault* to be Pardoned... cannot be accepted by any to whom the reproach thereof is a burden,' wrote Alexander Shields in *A Hind Let Loose*[8] published that year in Holland, under the rubric of 'A Lover of True Liberty'. On the other side, the thoughts of the archbishops of St Andrews and Glasgow must have echoed those of their predecessor Spottiswood when he lamented the breaking of the tub in 1638. The July proclamation had promised to protect 'our archbishops and bishops, and all our subjects of the protestant religion, in the free exercise of their protestant religion, as it is by law established', but the King and his advisers completely failed to appreciate the residual vigour and determination of Presbyterianism. Ministers who had left the country, or been banished, returned, ready to resume where they had left off. On 20 July a substantial number convened in Edinburgh and, having sent a message of thanks and loyalty to James VII (with prayers for his 'divine illumination') proceeded to set up the presbyterian structure of what was effectively a church within the church, though they were careful not to make any such claim for it.[9]

All over the country, in parish churches or in meeting rooms, presbyterian ministers were exercising their new-found freedom. Where supervision was closest, they landed in trouble, for not having got the Council's permission to officiate, or for making incautious criticisms of the 'King's religion' – as Burnet sardonically noted, this was the euphemism of those in public posts who could scarcely bring themselves to believe they were acting in support of Catholicism. By 20 August, the Synod of Glasgow and Ayr was able to hold a meeting, elect its own Moderator, and plan for the training of new presbyterian clergy. But the spirit was generally temperate, with the tone set by Andrew Morton, Moderator of the Edinburgh meeting, who in a widely circulated letter urged 'laying aside all heats and animosities, mutual jealousies and suspicions'.[10] For the 'curates' '... the auditories of the episcopal clergy turned very thin, yea, in many places in the south and west, they had nobody to hear them but their own families',[11] but there is no evidence of 'rabbling' them at this time, and where an episcopal incumbent was in charge, the Presbyterians either gathered in houses or built their own meeting-place. Only the Cameronians spurned the opportunity, darkly certain that: 'The very design of that Popish toleration was, to lull all asleep, that they might get their bloody designs effectuate in a massacre.'[12] Renwick, with nothing to expect from the Council but the noose, continued to preach in the open. Shields, who was with him at this time, claimed that Renwick was successfully gaining recruits to his own group,[13] but also mourns their isolation: 'We are at a greater loss than any suffering people, in that among other bitter ingredients we have this Gall also in our Cup, that they that suffer most among us have not the comfort and benefit of the sympathy of others, that sufferers use to have from good people.'[14]

In those years of religious toleration, not everyone could live at peace; the laws and penalties against rebels were still in place, and individuals were still being investigated, arrested, tried and punished for their presence at Bothwell Bridge or in Argyll's force. Avidity for fines and forfeitures drove the process at least as much as zeal against Presbyterianism and the Covenant. In October 1684, Drummond of Lundin wrote to Queensberry that the south-west 'lies at the king's mercy, and I assure your lordship he may take from them what he pleases, and the ruin of the obstinate heritors is absolutely necessary'.[15] The Government was not popular in the towns, partly because of the pro-Catholic policy which was imposing new people in civic and legal posts, with consequent interference in the undemocratic but traditional process of local elections. Elections were suspended in 1686–87, and even after that, candidates were often imposed in the more important towns. In March 1688 Graham of Claverhouse, a safe man for the Government, was appointed Provost of Dundee, to unavailing protests from the town council. With him as Provost and Constable, Dundee was not a place in which to overstep the mark, and several visiting preachers were expelled from the town. Compared to earlier severities, these were minor things, and the most ardent recorder of persecution could find little reason for serious complaint.

A degree of disaffection was also aroused by the Government's snooping and repressive style, typical of an administration which feels unsure of itself. It was particularly sensitive to political criticism, and a string of presbyterian works was banned. Royal proclamations of tolerance had required the authorities to take special care that no affronts were made to Catholics, and many people were disgruntled to find themselves informed on, arraigned and fined or jailed for remarks about Papism which, not long before, would have been considered evidence of their own worthiness and right thinking. Archbishop Alexander Cairncross of Glasgow was deposed in January 1687 for supporting James Canaries, minister of Selkirk – himself for a short time a Catholic convert – who had been arrested and fined for preaching an anti-Catholic sermon. Canaries was a seasoned self-publicist and his sermon was well advertised, but in very many less public cases, informers were involved. Delating others had long been an unattractive feature of Scottish society,[16] encouraged by successive Councils which found it a useful adjunct to their management. Sir John Lauder of Fountainhall suspended his diary of events and opinions in April 1686 after threats that his papers would be searched in case 'they contained anything offensive to the party then prevailing'.[17] But life was far from intolerable, and protest ran at a relatively low level. Troops were still spread in small garrisons through the south-west, but conventicles had largely ceased, and the inhabitants saw a return to an almost-forgotten normality, perhaps dull by comparison.

The growing surge of opposition in England that would shake James II off his throne had no equivalent in Scotland. It had been generally presumed in both countries that James would be succeeded by his elder daughter Mary, whose Protestant convictions were well known and who furthermore was married to the champion of the Protestant cause in Europe, William of Orange. Taking the long view, James's religion and his efforts on its behalf could be considered an aberration which time would cure. The news, in January 1688, of the queen's pregnancy, brought an element of uncertainty into the matter. If the child was a boy, he would take precedence over Mary, as Heir Apparent, and the prospect of a Catholic dynasty would be extended indefinitely.

At the beginning of February 1688 James Renwick was caught, not out on the moors, but in the centre of Edinburgh. He had been there more than once, visiting sympathisers, and arranging for the printing and distribution of Cameronian proclamations. In a sense, the Government's failure to secure free trade between Scotland and England was his undoing. His host in Edinburgh, a known adherent of the Cameronian cause, was an importer of English cloth and other goods, and under surveillance by excise officers. One of these, Thomas Justice, tipped off about a strange visitor, and made suspicious by some extra bustle and activity, staged an early-morning raid supposedly in search of contraband goods. In the scuffle, Renwick fired his pistol without effect, then got away but was arrested after a chase through the streets.

Most of Renwick's interrogation went on in the chamber of the other George Mackenzie, the Lord Clerk Register, made Viscount Tarbat in 1685, but Sir John Dalrymple led the prosecution. Like many others, Renwick was more afraid of torture than of the prospect of execution. Two notebooks were found in his pockets, and he willingly gave the names of persons indicated by initials, 'knowing they were as obnoxious already as anything he could say would make them', except for one, a Mrs Miller of Glasgow, whose name he did not reveal until it was promised that no action would be taken against her.[18] He continued to deny the King's authority, and the people's duty to pay tax, and affirmed their right to bear arms against a government which oppressed them. Claverhouse, leader of many vain attempts to catch him, was among the prosecution witnesses. The guilty verdict was inevitable, and the death sentence for treason prescribed by the law, but the Council was not bent on killing him. Execution was put off until 17 February and a succession of official visitors, including John Paterson, Archbishop of Glasgow, and Sir George Mackenzie, tried to persuade him to at least acknowledge the King, and so save his own life. Mackenzie advanced a reason of peculiar subtlety – rumours had long been spread that Renwick was a Jesuit agent, sent by Rome to provoke dissension among the Presbyterians; now the Papists, outraged that one of their faith should deny the King's authority, were pressing for his death. The import was that Renwick could disoblige and confound his Catholic enemies by accepting the King.[19] Probably some members of the Council appreciated that a living Renwick, discredited among the Society People by a recantation, would be far more valuable to the Government than a Renwick glorified by martyrdom on the gallows. But the prisoner was resolute, and two days after his 26th birthday, he 'went very cheerfully to the place of execution, where there was a vast number of spectators. Executions had not been frequent for some time, and his circumstances were very singular.'[20] Continuous drum rolls drowned out most of his final address, but a lengthy speech affirming his beliefs is given *verbatim* in Wodrow,[21] with a last indication of the oracular vision and power of the Covenanter preachers, and one of their favourite images:

> Ye that are the people of God, do not weary in maintaining the testimony of the day, in your stations and places; and whatever you do, make sure an interest in Christ, for there is a storm coming, which will try your foundations. Scotland must be rid of Scotland before the delivery come.

Ordered up the ladder at last, he committed the Remnant, and himself, to God, and the hangman thrust him off. Renwick's was the last in the long toll of executions which had begun with that of James Guthrie in 1662. The Remnant did not disappear and Alexander Shields continued to preach to the remaining faithful, but he was a minister, not a leader. With Renwick the threat, or possibility, which had obsessed the authorities for so long, finally disappeared – that the minister-politicians would inspire so many people to rise up in the causes of Presbytery and Covenant as to sweep away the government, constitution, and institutions of the country. In latter years at least, the danger had always been exaggerated, through genuine fear or deliberate policy: Renwick, and Cargill and Cameron before him, had been turned into bogey-men whose shadow was made to lie across the face of the land. Until now, the presbyterian-covenanting movement had been hydra-like: each time a leader was hanged, another appeared. But among the crowd that packed the Grassmarket to watch James Renwick's last agonies, there was none to pick up his torch.

Renwick's final words point up a sharp contrast in perceptions. In the letters exchanged among the governors, references to their own country are typically to 'poor old Scotland', 'poor distracted Scotland'; engaging in a kind of rueful, not unaffectionate commiseration about the nation whose affairs they managed. Familiar with England, especially London, with its vast wealth, immensely varied pattern of activity and weight of international involvement, they saw Scotland as a modest and homely place by comparison. Pragmatic, automatically fitting self-interest into the national picture, they were caught up in trying to maintain some kind of balance in what was akin to a three-legged race, with Scotland attached to the long shank of a swift-stepping giant, and which frequently strained their own energies and capacities. But the leaders of the Covenant saw Scotland with a passion. Caring nothing for themselves – with the exception, for some, of their egos – wealth, circumstance and earthly show were things to be despised and shaken off. For them, Scotland was anything but a poor relation: it was a dream of splendour, a new Israel, a beacon to other nations, a set of shining possibilities – if only its people could be made to share the vision and shoulder the glorious burden. Implementation of the ideal would have brought its own grisly realities, but the preachers taught a feeling for non-material values, and fostered a spirit, almost a sense of destiny, which the magnates could not grasp. Having to be special remained part of the national sense of self long after the Covenants were forgotten.

Between Renwick's trial and execution, Sir John Dalrymple was relieved of the post of King's Advocate, and Sir George Mackenzie was reinstated, an exchange which shows either the lack of talent among other members of the Faculty of Advocates, or their political unsuitability. It would seem that the Drummond brothers had not found Sir John wholly satisfactory – the Dalrymple annalist notes that he was considered a conspicuously lenient prosecutor compared with Mackenzie[22] – but he had the support of the Earl of Sunderland, James's chief secular adviser in England, and was given the post of Lord Justice Clerk. Sunderland, anxious to stabilise James's position in both England and Scotland, had hoped to bring some kind of understanding between the Catholic and Presbyterian interests, but Sir John must have given some very solid assurances before Perth and Melfort admitted him to such confidential posts. In July 1688 Sir John removed from the ill-fated house of Carsecreuch when he bought the nearby estate and house of Castle Kennedy. His was not the only surprising appointment of this time; even more remarkably Sir James Stewart, impassioned author of *Naphtali* and *Ius Populi Vindicatum*, reappeared from Holland, via London, as a close aide of the Earl of Melfort, although he had been sentenced to death, *in absentia*, as recently as December 1685. The middleman was William Penn, Quaker and unlikely friend of the King, who had made several missions to Holland to recruit support among the exiles (and from the Prince) for the toleration policy. Stewart's *volte-face* has never been satisfactorily explained, and his later actions do not suggest that toleration had much appeal for him. One student of his life believes he was acting as a double agent,[23] though there is no evidence for this; and it seems more probable he made a career misjudgement.[24] He tried hard but vainly to convince his former colleague Carstares of the King's sincerity, and seemed surprised to be cold-shouldered by the presbyterians. If the account of Lord Balcarres[25] can be trusted, he very soon adapted to the climate of Drummond government, in which corruption was blatant. Balcarres noted the unofficial 'remissions' required by Melfort from those who accepted public office or its renewal, without taking the Test oath: £8 was payable, £7 to Melfort, and £1 to Sir James Stewart, until protests to the King put a stop to the practice.

On a more positive note, Perth established a new Council of Trade in May 1688, with Claverhouse as one of its members, 'for considering and regulating all matters and things relating to the improvement and advancement of the Trade and Commerce' of Scotland.[26] But there was little it could do, before it was overtaken by political events.

Loyal celebrations were ordered by the Council on the news that a boy had been born to the Queen on 14 June 1688. Mary of Modena had been married to James for 15 years; her previous babies had died soon after birth, and she had borne none for several years. The news of an heir-apparent was received with considerable scepticism by those already hostile to the king, and in England set the latent revolutionary movement into active motion. There was much talk of the baby being smuggled into the birthing-chamber in a warming-pan, and some presbyterian ministers refused to pray for the infant Prince of Wales.

CHAPTER TWENTY-SEVEN
Interregnum

BENEATH A SUPERFICIAL STABILITY, deep forces were gathering. Unofficial but confident presbyterianism and official but apprehensive episcopalianism could not be partners in the Kirk, and both camps feared and resented the growth of Catholic influence. Exclusion from official posts drove up anger and anxiety among the Protestant nobility and gentry. It was obvious that the King meant to continue ruling by decreee and had no intention of calling a Parliament. At some point these pressures would have become critical, but even to a somewhat jittery government, now hunting evidence of anti-Catholicism as well as Cameronian-type sedition – the Council ordered another of its occasional house-by-house searches in Edinburgh that summer – the country in 1688 was far from being in revolutionary mode. Events in Holland and England were to set the frame for, and precipitate, what happened in Scotland.

In England, the King was floundering in a largely self-made crisis, facing a disaffected army, the public opposition of the Archbishop of Canterbury and six other bishops, and a nobility for the most part alienated. Among the general public, opinion was hostile or indifferent to him. In July, seven Englishmen of influence had made strong representations to William of Orange to replace James, and the Prince, seeing an opportunity that might not recur, decided to take action. By late summer it was apparent that William was making diplomatic, military and naval preparations for an invasion of Great Britain. Unlike the days when Robert Baillie and his friends schemed in London with English plotters, no Scots were involved with the invitation to William, and there was no grouping in Scotland ready to pave the way there for a change of king, though the exiles in Holland, including William Carstares, Sir James Dalrymple, and Gilbert Burnet (who had removed himself from court hostility in England) were strongly in support.

Remembering how easily Argyll and Monmouth had been defeated, many people doubted whether William of Orange would fare any better.[1] But as the scale of William's expedition became clear, the Government took greater precautions than before, with a proclamation on 18 September calling out the various militia forces, and arranging for the setting up of coastal and hill beacons between St Abbs Head and Fife, though giving no reason for the action. As the King's situation deteriorated in England, his Scottish Council pledged him their lives and fortunes in a message of 3 October.[2] A proclamation on the same day made reference to 'the vast preparations of the states of Holland' and summoned all 'heritors, liferenters and wadsetters' between Nithsdale and Caithness to convene with arms and horses and report to local leaders on specific days. Most of the kingdom was to be mobilised, excepting Argyll and the Northern and Western Isles, and the detail with which this order names men, places, assembly dates, sometimes specifying numbers and the days' provisions required, shows how far the Government's information and control now extended. The regular forces, about 3,700 strong, were assembled in early October at Moffat, with Claverhouse and Douglas commanding the cavalry and infantry respectively. At the King's order, they proceeded south into England, with the cavalry directed first of all to York. Soon after, William of Orange's declaration was issued and widely if stealthily circulated. Styling him as 'protector of the protestant religion, and defender of the liberties of England', it describes Charles II's death as murder and the infant prince as an impostor. No mention is made of Scotland or Ireland, but then it was England which had summoned him. It disclaims any pretension to the crown by himself and the Princess 'at present' and promises to deal with various English issues. For many Scots, its pledge to Protestantism was a positive sign, but their country was being prepared to repel William's invasion.

On 3 November, 12 of the 14 Scots bishops sent a joint letter to the King, remarkable even in that era of royal adulation for its fulsome tone, declaring their loyalty and wishing him 'the hearts of your subjects, and the necks of your enemies'.[3] A week later, a Council declaration forbade people to read or pass on any public messages from the Prince of Orange. By then, a further declaration from William had made it clear that his intention involved Scotland as well. Its authorship is unknown, though Gilbert Burnet 'corrected it it in several places, chiefly in that which related to the church: for the Scots at the Hague, who were all presbyterians, had drawn it so, that by many passages in it, the Prince by an implication declared in favour of presbytery. He did not see what the consequences of these were till I explained them; so he ordered them to be altered.'⁴ Long-winded, but shrewdly worded, its main premise is that Scotland's laws, liberties and customs have been grossly transgressed and annulled, especially with regard to the maintenance of the protestant religion, by the King and his counsellors. The people have been deprived of their 'civil rights' and the King has set himself up as 'an absolute monarch, to whom obedience ought to be given in all things without reserve', bringing the kingdom to a deplorable state. Considering these miseries, 'the giving such a remedy to them as may be proper, and may answer the expectation of all good men and true Protestants, is the great thing we propose to ourselves in this undertaking'. A list of abuses of power follows, from interference with burgh elections, to the killing commissions: some of them predating James VII's reign. It repeats the claim that 'the pretended Prince of Wales was not borne by the Queen'. Acknowledging the interest of William and his wife in the succession to the throne, it declares their intention for 'the freeing of that kingdom from all hazard of popery and arbitrary power for the future, and the delivering it from what at the present doth expose it to both... the settling of it by parliament, on such a solid basis as to its religious and civil concerns, as may most effectually redress all the above-mentioned grievances.'⁵

The omissions would not go unnoticed: nothing was said about the fate or future of King James VII, there was much about Protestantism but nothing about Presbyterianism, and, for those who still cared, nothing about the Covenant either. As a manifesto it was vague and unspecific, and relied chiefly on the assumption of popular grievance about past wrongs, the preferential Catholic policy, and the King's assertion of absolute power. Very soon, though, the challenge was more than merely verbal. By the end of the first week of November, everybody knew that William of Orange and a large army were landed at Torbay. Part of his force was made up by three Scottish regiments, from the service of the States General, under the command of Hugh Mackay of Scourie. Among the Prince's immediate entourage were Sir James Dalrymple, William Carstares, and Gilbert Burnet.

As in the winter of 1659–60, there ensued a limbo-esque period of several weeks, with the country in a state of high tension and excitement, hungry for news, feeding on rumours, speculating endlessly and fruitlessly on what might happen. The militias remained on alert – for what? This time, Scotland potentially had a hand in things: the army was in England, summoned by the King, but would it fight? William also had Scottish troops. What should a right-thinking Scot do – support a Stuart king, or accept that the country's situation was so dire that a foreign potentate should intervene in its domestic affairs? Could the Dutch invasion be used to correct the King's behaviour, and would William of Orange just go home again? Most men of power and influence, national or local, spared themselves the necessity of making a public decision, until they had a better idea of how things would fall out between the rival power-centres in England.

Among those who pondered the question of kingship, there was a greater sophistication now than in 1637, when the status of King Charles I had scarcely been questioned and loyalty to him was expressed even as limitations to his power were asserted. But the fate of Charles I, and the behaviour of Charles II, had inspired a continuing, and wider, debate. The English had already shown they could chop off the head of an unsatisfactory king. For most Scots this was still scarcely thinkable. But the thought gained strength that it was the kings who had changed the order of things, not the people. Sir George Mackenzie might exalt the notion of the King's right to rule, but the work of George Buchanan from the previous century, insisting on the historical limitations of Scottish kingship and the separation of the monarch from the lawmaking process, was republished, banned, burned, but widely re-read. Thomas Hobbes's *Leviathan* was also much discussed, in its many aspects.[6] Even though that work set no limits on a sovereign's rights, it also allowed that a man had no duty to a sovereign who could not protect him.

If some were confused by these mutually contradictory claims, John Graham saw his loyalty in straightforward terms. He had sworn himself to the service of James VII. By early November he had moved his cavalry to Salisbury, and from there he was summoned to London where, on the 12th, the King presented him with a charter ennobling him as Viscount of Dundee and Lord Graham of Claverhouse. His 'many good and eminent Services' were cited, 'Together with his constant Loyalty and firm adherence (upon all occasions) to the true interests of the Crown.'[7] From now on, he was no longer Claverhouse, but Dundee.

King James was becoming increasingly isolated, with daily reports of noblemen, towns and army commanders declaring for William and Mary.

John Graham of Claverhouse, Viscount Dundee
Reproduced from Dalton, *The Scots Army*

Between the 17th and the 25th, during his time at Salisbury, where his reluctant and disaffected army was blocking William's way to London, James's hopes finally collapsed. Following the example of senior English officers, the Scottish infantry, under James Douglas, transferred their allegiance to William, and Drumlanrig, Dundee's lieutenant-colonel, deserted his chief to join them. Dundee, supported by the Catholic Earl of Dumbarton, was now the supreme commander of what was left of James's Scottish army, and he withdrew with his cavalry to Reading. The two Douglases are most unlikely to have taken this action without the acquiescence of some members of the Privy Council. Perth was still Chancellor, but Sir John Dalrymple, Sir George Lockhart, Lord Tarbat, the Marquis of Atholl, and the Earl of Breadalbane were having private discussions. Overstating matters somewhat, one historian wrote: 'Scotland, managed by Sir John Dalrymple and well-chosen agents of his father's, was ready for revolt.'[8] James had formed a new 'Secret Council' at the time of the invasion, headed by Perth, with Atholl, Tarbat, Archbishop Paterson of Glasgow, Colin Lindsay, third Earl of Balcarres, and Sir George Lockhart. On 4 December, having heard nothing from the court for some time, this group sent Balcarres, a firm loyalist, to London, 'to attend his sacred majesty and receive his royal commands at this juncture'. Melfort had already left for France on the third, well-stocked with cash but leaving behind his collection of 150 paintings[9].

All the news from England was encouraging Protestant demonstrations in Edinburgh and Glasgow. At first these were restrained, arrests were made, and people punished; one man, allegedly uninvolved, was hanged after a riot in Edinburgh. But Perth, becoming as isolated in Edinburgh as the King in London, found that the apparatus of government was ceasing to respond to him. In normal times, the official machine not only follows the instructions, but senses and interprets the will of the administration; now, in this highly abnormal interlude, the machine was detaching itself from him, in anticipation of an imminent change of regime. Demonstrations in Glasgow were no longer opposed, and effigies of the Pope and the two archbishops were burned, but more serious things happened in Edinburgh on 10 December. Riots on the previous day had already forced Perth to leave the capital for his own safety, and in the evening, a band of apprentices, students and others marched by torchlight to Holyrood Palace, and demanded access. Captain Wallace, commanding the palace guard, refused, and a battle began. The town council declined to act,[10] but some people went to the Marquis of Atholl, who with other privy councillors signed a warrant requiring Wallace to surrender the palace. Wallace defied it, and fighting continued until the palace was stormed from the rear by members of the city guard, and the surviving defenders fled. Control was impossible: the chapel royal, the new Jesuit-run school, the printing-press, the library, the Chancellor's lodging – all were wrecked. A huge bonfire consumed ripped-out woodwork, fittings, statues, vestments, and books. Tombs of bygone kings and queens were opened by hopeful looters. For years afterwards the despoiled chapel, which it was nobody's business to clear up, remained a sort of charnel-house for ghoulishly inclined visitors to poke about in.[11]

On the 11th, the houses of Catholics were attacked and any objects suggestive of papist practices taken out and burned. No action was taken against the assailants, and on the 14th, the Council, in the process of performing an unacknowledged *volte-face*, ordered that the houses of papists be searched for arms and ammunition, though officers of the law were also instructed to protect 'the persons and houses of the said papists'. On the 24th, its turn-around complete, the Council ordered the militia (stood down on Perth's order) back into service, but now against 'papists being in arms... for security of the protestant religion, and securing their own lives, liberties, and properties'.[12] Nimbly, the leaders of the nation had adjusted to regime change before there was even a regime to change to.[13] Having done nothing to bring the Revolution about, the Privy Council snatched at it in a way that was only possible because firstly, James's Government had detached itself from the general commitment and loyalty which the community might be expected to give to a king and his nominated governors; and secondly, William presented an apparently viable as well as more attractive alternative. Riots as wild as the Holyrood incident had been contained before, but the will to do so was absent in Edinburgh in 1688 as it would be in the collapsing Soviet Union 300 years later.

In England, Balcarres found Dundee at Watford, to the north of London. James had already ordered his forces to disband, on 7 December, without arranging for their payment; and on the 10th he left the capital, intending to make for France, where his queen had already gone with the baby prince. Dundee and Balcarres, trying to rally others who might be of the 'episcopal party', had an unsatisfactory meeting on the 13th with the Duke of Hamilton, whom they suspected, rightly, of inclining to join William. Three days later, having been identified and arrested at Faversham in Kent, James returned to London, and briefly resumed his royal role as if he had never fled. But William was now in the western suburbs. On the 17th, walking in the Mall with Balcarres and Dundee,

James asked 'how they came to be with him, when all the world had forsaken him', and told them he was going to France because, 'as you know, there is but small distance between the prisons and the graves of Kings'.[14] On the 18th, when James left London for Rochester, Dundee saw him for the last time, and on the 23rd, with William and his advisers established in Whitehall, he learned that James VII had left the country. Dundee was undoubtedly deeply affected. Among the King's advisors, he had spoken up for resistance, and at one point,[15] he had suggested that James should remove to Scotland, which would certainly have created an interesting situation, but James had no intention of putting himself in such hazard. Dundee's loyalty to the King was not simply that of a dutiful man towards his royal patron. It had a personal quality. Like Montrose, he was unlucky in the master to whom he gave his devotion.

His Majesty's Privy Council was still the ruling body in Scotland, but what was its authority, when the King had abandoned his throne? His Lord High Chancellor was under arrest. With a glee reserved for overproud Catholic politicians getting their just come-uppance, Macaulay gives a picturesque account of Perth's furtive journey from Castle Drummond 'by unfrequented paths over the Ochil mountains, which were then deep in snow', to Burntisland on the Fife coast, where, just as his ship was getting away, it was overhauled by a boat captained by 'an old buccaneer' and he was dragged out of its hold, disguised in women's clothes, 'stripped, hustled and plundered'.[16] This conflicts with Perth's own account[17] – he was not disguised as a woman and had his wife with him; she, though pregnant, was disguised as a man. He spent some time in the Kirkcaldy tolbooth before being transferred to Stirling Castle, where he would be kept prisoner for three years, and 'hectors such as do not still term him Lord Chancellor of Scotland';[18] with a further year under house arrest at Stobhall before he left the country under a bond of £5,000 never to return.

So the Drummond brothers exit from dominance of a stage on to which they had come sidling, in their wide-brimmed hats, tight-fitting hose and folded-down boots, so much like a pair of melodrama villains, fleering and sneering, oozing unction, eyes darting about for the main chance, that one is prompted to look for evidence of probity and statesmanship simply on the basis that they cannot be so bad as historians, mostly with a Protestant bias, have painted them. But if they performed acts of generosity and selflessness, these are unremembered, apart from Melfort's kindly behaviour to Carstares on his first imprisonment. Other 17th-century politicians intrigued their way into power, and, once there, used it for their own enrichment, though few with such naked eagerness as Melfort. Since their ship, with hindsight, was heading for an iceberg, their political navigation has not been closely examined by historians. The toleration policy has never been seen as anything other than a preliminary to a new religious authoritarianism; and the effort to bring in the Highlands, and the economic policy have also, perhaps rightly, been seen as self-interested. They were using methods no different to Lauderdale's, but did not have his broad base of support. In the end, even the Jacobites would not want Melfort back in office. Yet one guesses that their dances and routs at Holyrood, with their sister adding her own touch of glamour and behind-the-scenes intrigue, were more fun – laced with an edge of danger and a slightly sinister *frisson* – than most social events in the grey capital. Rare birds on the Scottish political tree, they were cavaliers – aesthetes trying to be politicians and falling into ugly ways which more professional operators might have avoided. When freed, Perth went to Rome and was James VII's ambassador there in 1695–6, before joining the Jacobite court at St Germain, where he became 'governor' of the Prince of Wales, moved in elevated Church society, and was the friend of Bossuet. In 1695 he was raised to the rank of duke in the Jacobite peerage. He died in 1716, the longest-lived of that group born in 1648–9 whose lives coil around one another's through these pages in baroque spirals. Melfort was also made a duke, in 1692. Having exercised a disastrous influence on early Jacobite politics, and later fallen foul of Louis XIV, he is best remembered in France as a connoisseur of art, one of the first to allow the public to see his (new) collection of paintings.

The bishops' authority had evaporated: their letter to James, which had been published in London, attached them irrevocably to his cause. Only his abdication could release them, and he had no intention of abdicating. Kings of England had made strategic withdrawals from the realm before, and returned to triumph, but James was no Edward IV. Among the remaining members of the Council, one or two were committed to him, including the Duke of Gordon, Lieutenant of Edinburgh Castle, who was holding that fortress in his name. Others, including Sir George Mackenzie and Lord Tarbat, had gone to London. For all, the moment of decision could not be put off much longer, and the trend of their thoughts was indicated by the anti-Catholic proclamation of 24 December. A vacuum of power at the very source of national authority, always a cause of alarm to government agencies, was developing. James VII was in no position to send instructions, and William forbore from doing so, or was more preoccupied with immediate matters in England. Among leading figures, so far only General Douglas and Lord Drumlanrig had declared openly for William.

By the last days of 1688, public business was in complete abeyance, not merely because of traditional Yuletide festivities or even political uncertainties, but because so many Scotsmen of rank and influence had betaken themselves to London, either to claim their rewards or make their excuses at the court of Whitehall. The diarist John Evelyn noted on 15 January 1689 that he had dined at the Archbishop of Canterbury's with Bishop Rose of Edinburgh and Sir George Mackenzie, Lord Advocate.[19] Rose had set off to London to reiterate the bishops' loyalty to James, and was now staying on to see what might transpire. He does not seem to have been included in the committee of some 30 peers and around 80 gentlemen – lairds, burgesses, knights of the shires – then gathered in London, formed at William's invitation on 7 January, which elected the Duke of Hamilton as its chairman. Its brief was to recommend what should now be done. While some of their number were inclined towards James, or uncommitted, the initiative was held by William's supporters, and its members were almost entirely from the centre and south of the country, with Highland representation restricted to the Earls of Argyll and Sutherland, both strongly pro-William, and the equivocal Earl of Breadalbane.[20]

Following the example of a similar English committee, this group agreed on 14 January that William should assume the administration of Scotland as an interim measure, until a Convention of the Estates could be called to settle matters. Dundee did not attempt to join them, but disbanded his regiment and sent them homewards, keeping 50 men to escort himself and Balcarres through an increasingly hostile England, not to mention southern Scotland, where armed bands of Cameronians were considering their own next moves. He had sent a message to William, via Gilbert Burnet, his relative by marriage, asking to know 'what security he might expect if he should go and live in Scotland without owning the Government', to which the reply had been positive, 'if he should live peaceably and at home'.[21] Once home, he continued to exercise the office of Provost of Dundee, presiding over town council meetings on 24 and 27 February, procuring an oath of loyalty to King James, with only one dissenter. Following that the municipal record is blank until 20 April, when with Provost Fletcher in the chair, and Claverhouse proclaimed a traitor, the council recorded its loyal support for William and Mary.[22]

CHAPTER TWENTY-EIGHT

The Revolution Settlement

A HISTORIAN OF ENGLAND writes that 'the glory of the Revolution settlement was that it drove people with incompatible views towards each other despite the passion of beliefs and the heat of the moment'.[1] This was emphatically not the case in Scotland. William's proclamation to the Scots had promised the settling of the country's freedoms by parliament, and, as proposed by the 'committee' in London, a convention of estates was summoned in due form for 16 March.

In the course of the century, Parliament had confronted some momentous issues; now it had the solemnising task of deciding whether to acknowledge the right of James VII to continue as king, or to make some other dispensation. Elections were held in burghs and shires, and though the Test Act was still in force, the provisional administration accepted the London committee's recommendation that it should not be applied either to candidates or electors. In the burghs, where the previous regime had in many cases installed its own men as provosts and officials, the widest franchise yet was authorised: instead of the town council making the choice, every Protestant burgess was allowed to participate.[2] Shire elections were conducted on the old basis, and more proto-Jacobites were elected in the counties than in the towns. To strict Jamesian loyalists, not only the new electoral arrangements, but the parliament itself, were illegal, but already they were being outmanoeuvred: they had to participate or let their cause go by default. A third possibility, to opt for immediate civil war, was unrealistic as long as it remained conceivable that James would be restored by peaceful means. Lord Tarbat famously observed that the Presbyterians were the more zealous and hotter, but the others more numerous and powerful; the others however did not come out in protest. The last to hold all three 'estates', this parliament was attended by 35 burgh members, 44 from the shires, 36 peers, and 9 of the 14 bishops. Some members were known to be committed to William, some to James, many kept their own counsel. The parliament of England had offered that nation's crown to William and Mary on 13 February. Once that was accomplished, no legislator could ignore the fact that to maintain James must mean war with England, sooner or later.

But there were other reasons to choose William. He was, after all, offering an alternative to the present difficulties and future uncertainties caused by James's religion and his autocratic style: a Protestant kingship that respected civil rights. That was not the only issue, however. Many Scots felt strongly about the country's economic relegation and inability to develop foreign relations under the regal union. For some of these, total separation and therefore a different king seemed desirable, while for others the solution was to reopen the question of complete union with England. And there were those who considered it their, and the country's, duty to support the legitimate King of Scots, whatever the English might do – while this group included all Catholics, it was far from being a 'Catholic' party in a narrow religious sense, and its adherents got the name of 'Tories' already familiar in England as a label for religiously conservative royalists.

Parliamentarians, and the nation, were confronted not only by the need to end uncertainty with an early decision, but also to justify that decision as constitutional and legally secure. To maintain James was not a problem in this sense, but to depose and replace him most certainly was.[3] Offering guidance through uncharted waters, a range of pamphlets on the nature of kingship in general and Scottish kingship in particular, speedily appeared. A vocal and influential group outside Parliament but wholly for William was the body of presbyterian ministers, who had met in Edinburgh in January to petition him for the abolition of episcopacy. To support the same cause, large numbers of presbyterians trekked to the capital from the south-west, some of them in the personal retinue of Hamilton and other notables, others as an organised body of Cameronians, come to defend the Convention against any attempt by Malignants to stage a *coup*. Although armed and intimidating, peering into faces to detect a Jacobite countenance, they failed to match the dominance achieved by the 'Whiggamores' Raid' 40 years before. But their noisy presence in the streets and outside Parliament House, while Gordon held the castle in the name of King James, helped to heighten the sense of crisis. For the historically minded, there seemed a correspondence between events now and those of the early 1570s, when supporters of rival royalties, 'King's Men' and 'Queen's Men', had ended up fighting in open war.

The first task of the convention was to elect a president to control its proceedings. Hamilton, who had assumed leadership in London, was proposed, but so was the Marquis of Atholl. Though both kept their affiliations somewhat veiled, Hamilton was the candidate of the pro-William members, and Atholl was backed by the Tories. Hamilton's election confirmed that the Williamites had a majority, but the Jacobites formed a substantial minority, and no matter of substance had yet been voted on. Only once more, in its final sessions, would Scotland's old Parliament meet like this, facing a stark choice, with two passionately opposed policies, and in between, the equivocal expressions and uneasy shiftings of those who knew that, very soon, they would have to declare themselves. Outside, steel-breasted pikemen held back the surging, shouting, gesticulating mob. Dundee and his friends were in touch with the shaky Duke of Gordon, who had already indicated his readiness to surrender on suitable terms, and they sent a message on 14 March, 'to put him in mind of his engagements to us'.[4] On the 16th a formal party of heralds, pursuivants and trumpeters was sent to the gate to demand that he quit the castle or be named a traitor. Gordon now allowed those of his garrison who wanted to leave, to do so, and about 80 came out. Soon it was being said that the castle's gunpowder was damp, and the food stocks low. But the Duke still held on, and it was also known now that James VII had landed in Ireland to head a loyalist army raised by the Earl of Tyrconnel – his cause seemed far from hopeless.

Both William and James sent messages to the Convention. In case James's should be an order to dissolve the assembly, a vote was taken to ensure that any such instruction would be disregarded; then the letters were read out, William's first. Respectful in tone, it restated the proclamation already made and asked for advice and support. James VII, with a group of counsellors who included the Earl of Melfort, had had time to consider his position and strategy, but his letter dismayed his supporters. Dundee had sent him a draft, which was ignored, and instead from Melfort's pen[5] came an imperious claim on the nation's loyalty, promising nothing other than that James would pardon 'all such as return to their duty before the last day of this month'.[6] Balcarres's memoir to James said that his supporters had not supposed 'any about you could have produced a letter so prejudicial to your affairs.'[7] James's letter pushed the uncommitted members towards William, whose ultimate majority was probably never in doubt. Dundee planned to call a rival Convention at Stirling, in the name of King James, but as James had already acknowledged the Convention by writing to it, even if he complained of its 'Usurped Authority', the notion was a desperate one. Intense negotiations went on as the Jacobite leaders claimed and probed the loyalties of possible allies. Sir George Mackenzie, as a loyalist (elected as a commissioner for Forfarshire) was in the thick of these. From the Whig side, death threats were directed against Mackenzie and Dundee, and on 17 March, Mackenzie put forward a motion asking for security for members of the Convention. In the tumult that followed, Dundee informed the Convention that it was an illegal assembly, and that he had the King's commission to call a legitimate convention at Stirling. Then he left the chamber, followed by members of the 'loyal party'.

The moment of decision had come, and very soon, Mackenzie found that ostensible supporters, from Atholl down, were backing away from direct action. So few would commit themselves to the rival Convention that the idea had to be dropped. Dundee, who would have accepted the verdict of a 'packed' Jacobite assembly, would not go along with the votes of a Williamite majority. Genuine democratic politics were not in anybody's repertoire. Quite likely at least half of the nation shared his view, if not his determination. On the morning of the 18th, with a troop of 30 horsemen waiting, he climbed the Castle rock for a final parley with the Duke of Gordon, who refused to make any commitment to active effort for James. This is the moment when Dundee, asked what he was going to do, is supposed to have replied: 'I go wheresoever the shade of Montrose will direct me.'[8] One of his anticipated allies, the Earl of Mar, Governor of Stirling Castle, had at the last minute declared for William, and Dundee rode through Stirling and on to Dunblane, where he met Alexander Drummond of Balhaldie, whose lands were nearby. Though he lived on the Lowland fringe, Balhaldie had intimate links with the Highlands; his real name was MacGregor (a name whose use had been forbidden by the Privy Council in 1603) and he was son-in-law of Sir Ewen Cameron of Lochiel, chief of Clan Cameron. He confirmed that Lochiel was actively mustering support for an uprising in favour of James. After a dismal day, this was better news for the King's General. Knowing the possibility of making war to be at his disposal, Dundee went to his home at Dudhope Castle to rejoin his wife (who was about to give birth), make plans, and recruit support for the Jacobite cause. In

Stirling Castle
Reproduced from Hewison, *The Covenanters*, Vol. 1

his own case, it seems to have been axiomatic that as a loyal servant of King James, ennobled by him, bound by oaths of fealty, he should defend the King's rights by whatever means he could raise. How far he was motivated by hostility to the 'Westland rabble' once again arrogant in the streets of Edinburgh, and who had already chased out many of the 'curates' whom he had long protected and defended, is hard to say, but in his own way Dundee was a purist: he also had a vision of Scotland as it ought to be.

The interim administration began to move against him. On 20 March, Dundee was proclaimed an outlaw, and on the 26th, the day after Hugh Mackay reached Edinburgh with his three Scots regiments,[9] heralds were sent to Dudhope to repeat the message. He wrote in answer that he was merely living peacefully at home. His son James was born on the 30th and two weeks later, learning that a force was on its way to arrest him, he moved his family to Glenogilvie. There was talk of English militias being despatched, which aroused the scorn of that erstwhile campaigner Sir James Dalrymple: '... new raised English from their soft beds, will never be proper in Scotland, nor to fit anywhere as our hard-bred people', he wrote to Lord Melville on 23 March.[10]

The Convention was still in session, with only a handful of Jacobite loyalists remaining. On 4 April, Sir John Dalrymple, commissioner for his local burgh of Stranraer, as smoothly as if he had never held high office under James VII, moved a resolution that James had 'forefaulted' his right to the crown, on 15 separate counts. No Scottish Parliament had ever deposed a king and no precedent existed for this effective, if unstated, assertion of its right to do so. Only 12 votes opposed the motion. One was Sir George Mackenzie's. Perhaps gratefully, the Convention seized on the fact that James VII 'did assume the Regal power, and acted as King, without ever taking the oath required by law' – if his kingship could be shown to be invalid anyway, that made things much easier, quite apart from the fact that he 'by the advice of of evil and wicked counsellors, invaded the fundamental constitution of the Kingdom, and altered it from a legal Limited Monarchy, to an arbitrary despotic Power'.[11] On the 11th, a Claim of Right was passed, confirming the deposition of James and the offer of the crown to William and Mary as joint sovereigns, with 'an entire confidence, that his said Majesty, the king of England, will perfect the deliverance so far advanced by him'.[12] Two days later the Articles of Grievance were passed, listing 13 prime complaints, beginning with the existence of the Committee of Articles, and ending with the maintenance of a standing army in time of peace without parliament's consent.[13]

The Marquis of Atholl had removed himself to Bath, and Sir George Mackenzie was preparing to retire permanently from public office. At 53, with a new precipice in the ups and downs of public life opening before him, the Neo-Stoic had had enough of the fray; it was time to move to the sidelines, if not completely out of the arena. He had seen one of his ambitions completed, when as the moving spirit among the founders of the Advocates' Library in Edinburgh, he gave a Latin oration at its formal inauguration on 1 March 1689 (it had actually been in existence since 1682). The Library, kernel of the present National Library, was also intended for use by members of the public. Sir George, who had presented his own law books to the Library, celebrated the glory of law and learning in his speech, and made no reference at all to current events.

Musing perhaps a little melodramatically on his fate, he wrote from Dunfermline on 15 April to Lord Yester: 'The President being gone [Lockhart had been shot dead by a deranged litigant] I remain the only man of our old stock of Lawyers and therefore it may seem reasonable to suffer me to live, for in conscience all the Lawyers now alive in Scotland put together, know not how to resolve one difficult case by a sure rule... if I cannot be allowed to live peaceably I will go to Hamburg or go to England which last shews I will live peaceably and with great satisfaction under the new elected King, for tho' I was not clear to make a King yet I love not civil wars nor disorders and we owe much to him.'[14] The reference to lawyers was a dig at the Dalrymples, and by June, Mackenzie, feeling more confident, wrote to Lord Melville, the Secretary of State, renewing his request to be a judicial advisor: 'I seek no public employment, and so am rival to no man; but the liberty of informing judges (who, to my great regret, need it).'[15] Unsurprisingly, Sir James and Sir John felt no need for Sir George's advice.

On 8 April, an Irish messenger bearing James VII's formal commission to Dundee as Lieutenant-General was arrested and his papers seized, but five days later, the Viscount unfurled the royal standard on the Law Hill above Dundee town and opened his campaign for James's restoration. His standard-bearer, James Philip of Almerieclose, would live to set down his exploits in a Latin epic, the *Grameid*. Most of his supporters were men of his own district, and on the 19th they rode northwards into the Highlands to recruit wider support.

Dundee was entering what was in most respects *terra incognita*. In the years following Argyll's adventure, disorder had increased. The last of the clan battles had been fought only a year before, at Mulroy in Lochaber, between the Macdonalds of Keppoch and the MacIntoshes of Badenoch (who came off worst despite the aid of an Independent Company of militia).[16] Yet the trend towards commercialisation and the erosion of the Gaelic patriarchal tradition were accelerating. In the Lowlands, the mainspring of opposition had been among ordinary people, acting whether lairds and lords concurred or not; in the Highlands, the opposite was true. Everything depended on the will of a small number of proud and more or less aristocratic persons: territorial lords and clan chiefs. How those Highland magnates would react to the new dispensation was a cause of concern and speculation to the Government. Lord Tarbat, now a firm adherent to William, believed that all the potentially dangerous leaders could be bought off for an outlay of £5,000. He himself visited numerous leading men in the north to put the case for backing the Government, but Dundee was also finding support[17] or at least promises.

By the 21st he was at Keith, in country dominated by the Gordons; his ally Alexander Seton, fourth Earl of Dunfermline, was at Gordon Castle.

General Mackay, appointed Commander-in-Chief, was struggling to put together an army he could trust, knowing that among the regular forces there was considerable support for Dundee. His campaign would be hindered by suspicions, and actual cases, of dealings with the enemy and intended defections. On 29 April he set off from Dundee in pursuit of the Viscount and former Provost of that town. In the first of a series of almost-encounters, his force and Dundee's came close near Fettercairn, in Kincardineshire – Dundee had come south again in the hope of adding Lieutenant-Colonel William Livingstone's dragoons to his own force: Livingstone had signified his willingness. But Dundee only had a small troop on horseback, and Mackay's advance, even with a modest force of some 400 men, made him swing back into the mountains. On the first of May he was in Inverness, arriving at a critical moment. The town, its citadel empty of troops, was under threat of burning by one of the last of the Highland warlords, Macdonald of Keppoch, 'Coll of the Cows' as he was known, victor of Mulroy, who was encamped outside it. Keppoch was demanding a ransom and various privileges for his clansmen in the town. With a force of some 700 fighting men, he might have played the part of Alastair MacColla to a new Montrose, but though Dundee resolved the dispute, compelling the burgesses to pay £Sc2,700 against a bond they had little hope of redeeming, his verbal dressing-down of Keppoch, telling him that his actions were against the King's interest and those of a common robber and enemy of mankind,[18] had an unfortunate result. Unaccustomed to such home truths, the affronted bandit chief led his booty-encumbered followers away on 2 May, the day Mackay and his men reached Elgin. On the 8th, Mackay marched on Inverness, and Dundee withdrew southwards.

He had made a rendezvous with the chiefs for 18 May, and badly needed to show them evidence of success. Still with an eye on the Dundee-based dragoons, he passed through Atholl, surprised a tax-collecting party at Dunkeld and took their moneys, and, on the night of 10 May, showed his teeth more sharply in a night attack on Perth, capturing the local militia leaders in their beds, taking 40 horses, and a stock of arms, ammunition and cash, as well as prisoners, who were sent to one of the Treshnish isles. On the 13th he marshalled his troop outside Dundee town, but the garrison stayed inside the walls, and Livingstone could not prevail on his men to break out and join the small band hopefully waiting for them. Next day Dundee began a gruelling Montrose-style cross-country dash through the mountains and the Moor of Rannoch, arriving in Glen Roy on the 16th, in good time for the meeting of the 18th at Dalmucomir in Lochaber.

The day after the Perth raid, three eminent Scots were in London, ambassadors sent by the Convention to convey its offer of the crown to William and Mary: the Earl of Argyll, Sir James Montgomery, and Sir John Dalrymple, elected to represent the nobility, the gentry, and the burghs respectively. They had brought the Sword of State, but the crown itself remained in Edinburgh. At the Banqueting House in Whitehall, raising their right hands 'according to the Scottish mode of affirmation',[19] the joint monarchs repeated the coronation oath. Perhaps William, notoriously careless about scanning documents which meant little to him, had not read the text, but he baulked at the penultimate sentence: 'And we shall be careful to root out all heretics and enemies to the true worship of God that shall be convicted by the true Kirk of Scotland of the foresaid crimes, out of our lands and empire of Scotland.'[20] 'I will not lay myself under any obligation to be a persecutor,' he said. One of the ambassadors replied that neither the wording of the oath nor the laws of Scotland required that of him and, 'In that sense, then, I swear,' said William. The business was concluded: Parliament had shown that it could unmake, and make, a king. Unfortunately, like chopping down a tall tree in the heart of a dense forest, the exercise could not be achieved without destructive and harmful side-effects.

Having accepted the kingship, William set about forming a permanent government. Scotland was not of much concern to him, and he devolved responsibility on one of his closest associates, Hans Willem Bentinck, newly made Earl of Portland. The Secretary of State was the Earl of Melville, a former Presbyterian exile, dull but conscientious. Sir James Dalrymple had been busy for William's cause in London, and Sir John equally so in Scotland, and both were given office, Sir James once again Lord President, Sir John, in a last box-and-cox with Mackenzie, as Lord Advocate. Carstares was appointed Scottish chaplain to the King and Queen, and lived at court. Portland knew little about Scottish affairs, but Carstares was there with advice and background knowledge, and soon it became apparent that he was the only man in whom William had real trust and reliance for Scottish matters, and his advice or support was widely sought, though he had no official position other than his chaplaincy. When honours were bestowed, with Sir James Dalrymple made Viscount Stair in 1690, and Sir Patrick Hume the Earl of Polwarth, he remained plain Mr Carstares, and this was undoubtedly how he preferred it. After all, he was a presbyterian minister – not a man for titles or baubles.

Having been legitimised as a royally confirmed Parliament, the Convention proceeded to other business. The Claim of Right – focused wholly on past wrongs rather than on future rights – had contained a gratuitous clause (bishops could hardly be blamed on James VII) that prelacy was 'a great and insupportable grievance and trouble' and 'ought to be abolished'.[21] Mackenzie and Tarbat had used some of their time in London to compose a defence of Scottish episcopacy in the hope of persuading the Prince of Orange, but Carstares was convinced that the Presbyterians were William's best supporters and he vigorously argued the case for re-establishing the Kirk on presbyterian lines.[22] Gilbert Burnet, newly appointed Bishop of Salisbury, hovered officiously but also anxiously at court to present the alternative point of view; although he detested the Scottish bishops as a group, he did not want to see the episcopalian bathwater thrown out with the unwanted babies.

The Revolution Settlement has generally been taken to mark the triumph of presbyterianism, but at the time, it was more the collapse of episcopacy. There was no inevitable reason for this to happen. The hapless bishops of 1688 have been badly treated by later writers; Robert Story wrote that they 'were not the men to quarrel with his [William's] policy, if its result should be to keep them in safe possession of their sees'.[23] The sneer is contradicted in his own account of how Bishop Alexander Rose of Edinburgh, still in London in January 1689, was given a 'strong hint' that if he and his colleagues would support William, the King in turn would support them. Though a presbyterian himself, William was well aware that episcopacy was favoured by most of the Scottish nobility and accepted by a large proportion – perhaps a majority – of the population. Rose was summoned to a meeting with William, who said, 'I hope you will be kind to me, and follow the example of England.' But Rose would not say more than, 'I will serve you as far as law, reason, or conscience shall allow me' – in other words, 'No'.[24] It was a principled, if also fatal, reply, and shows that the Presbyterians had no monopoly on conscience. From then on, especially with Carstares drumming the loyal virtues of the Presbyterians, the Episcopalians had little chance of influencing the debate, either in London or in Edinburgh. On 22 July an act was passed to 'abolish prelacy, and all superiority of any office in the church of this kingdom above presbyters', and stating that 'the form of church government most agreeable to the inclinations of the people' would be settled by law.[25] For the time being, that form was left undefined. But all ministers were required to pray publicly for the new King and Queen, and any who did not were to be ejected. In the course of the year, about 300, who continued to pray for James VII, were ousted from their churches, and hardly any were admitted to the re-established Kirk.

Tolerance, in religion at least, was William's belief and policy, but it was not a congenial concept to most Scots (its one-time lone apostle Robert Leighton died in 1684), and though the Government refused to accept an Act attempting to reimpose the Act of Classes,[26] there were many local instances of old scores settled, harassment of Catholics, and 'rabbling' of episcopal-minded ministers. Dundee's campaign afforded an excuse:[27] Jacobite rebellion was balanced by a presbyterian revanchism and the Government had to struggle to control the latter while putting down the former. The process of restitution of Presbyterians' forfeited estates caused its own disruptions, disputes and bad feelings among the landowning families and their tenants. Restoration of his family's estates to the 10th Earl of Argyll, an ambitious magnate busily making up for the lost years, increased the willingness of neighbouring clan chiefs to give active support to Dundee.

CHAPTER TWENTY-NINE

Dark John of the Battles

AT DALMUCOMIR, WITH THE Great Glen stretching away to the north-east, the Lochaber braes to one side, and the vast haunch of as-yet unclimbed Ben Nevis rising on the other, a spectacle unique in Europe was mounted for the General and his few Lowland friends – the muster and parade of some 2,000 fighting Highlanders, with many more as spectators and hangers-on. The whole tenor of the event, the demeanour of the people, the presence of bards[1] and pipers, the warriors in saffron shirts and long plaids, the language, costume and music, owed nothing to the custom and fashion of elsewhere. Picturesque, anachronistic, but formidable both in intention and potential effect, Gaeldom was girding itself to step out and confront the workaday world of early capitalism, as much in its own defence as to promote the cause of *Seumas Righ*, King James. Behind their chiefs and war captains came the various divisions of Clan Donald, including Keppoch and his men; the Camerons, the MacLeans, the MacNeils, Stewarts of Appin, as well as smaller groups from clans less united in the Jacobite cause.

Dundee at last had his army, but he yearned for an element of regular troops and above all for more arms and ammunition, which were in desperately short supply. Hugh Mackay was still occupying Inverness, and sooner or later there would have to be a battle. For all the brave flamboyance, among the clansmen and their leaders the mood was volatile and uneasy. Breadalbane and Tarbat, influential in the southern and northern Highlands, were urging support for the Government, or at least neutrality. Mackay, with a more distinguished military record than Dundee, had the resources of the state to draw on (it did not feel like that to Mackay, who felt that the new government was doing very little to help his efforts).[2] Tarbat was also protesting to Melville about the sweeping powers given to Mackay to take action against those who did not oppose the rebels. Pointing out what a small proportion of the Highlanders actually were in arms against the Government, he feared that official over-reaction would make matters much worse.[3] Religion among the Highlanders ranged from Catholic to Covenanter, with between these extremes many who might incline politically either way. Careful diplomacy by both generals was needed. Mackay disliked everything about his native region. Two elder brothers had been killed in a clan battle with the Caithness Sinclairs, and though he had inherited the Scourie estate in 1668, he never returned there. He had a Dutch wife, and much preferred Holland[4] to Scotland.

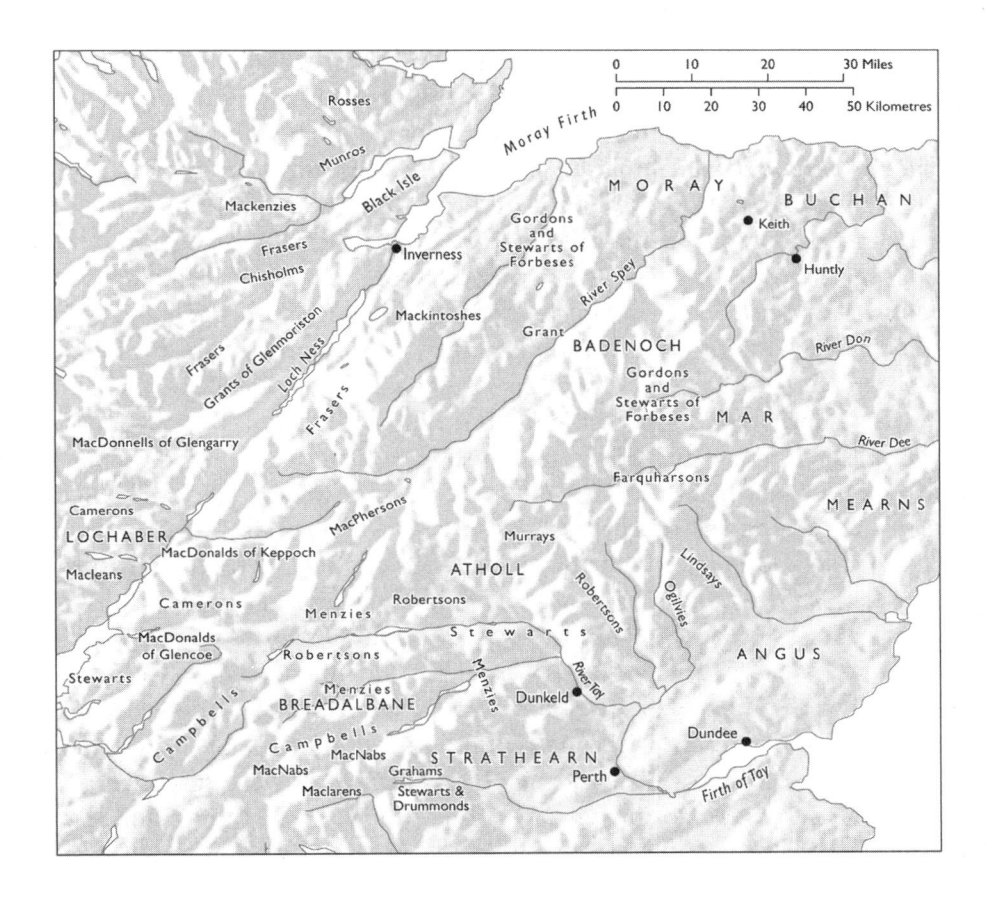

Years of conducting operations as a military law-enforcer had made John Graham familiar with guerrilla-type tactics, but he was a Lieutenant-General who had never directed a real battle, and whose troops had until now been on the Government payroll. In the course of the summer of 1689 he showed an adaptation to circumstances, and qualities of leadership, that transcended his former record. The confrontation with Keppoch taught him about Highland susceptibilities, but he was not deterred from demanding discipline. A general of irregulars had to make every man under his command feel personally acquainted with him, and Dundee proved adept at this. His men watched him with fascinated interest; Drummond noted that he was strictly observant of religion: '... he retired to his closet at certain hours, and employed himself in that duty.'[5] Hardly surprisingly, his manner became somewhat warm on occasions, but they never saw him lose his temper, and though he was reputed to be careful with money, he never incurred the Highlanders' ready contempt for meanness: 'He was in his private life, rather parsimonious than profuse; and observed an exact economy in his family. But in the King's service he was liberal and generous to everyone but himself'.[6]

Dundee led his army out of Lochaber on 26 May, the same day that Mackay's force left Inverness. The next few weeks saw a fraught stalemate of manoeuvrings and skirmishes across the central Highlands. In Badenoch, the irrepressible Keppoch took the chance to repay old scores against the MacIntoshes, alienating a powerful clan whom Dundee had hoped to enlist, or keep neutral. On 30–31 May, the two armies almost met in Strathspey, close to present-day Aviemore. Expecting reinforcements led by Colonel Ramsay, which failed to arrive, Mackay ordered a retreat eastwards, pursued by Dundee. Livingstone's dragoons, now part of Mackay's force, passed information to the Jacobites until they were discovered, and five officers were court-martialled on 8 June. At this time Dundee was ill with 'the flux', the usual term for severe diarrhoea or dysentery – an ever-prevalent affliction in those times. Mackay was strengthened by reinforcements of around 1,000 men, and Colonel Ramsay had finally managed to get to Inverness, while many of the Highlanders, having collected cows and other plunder on the march, were returning home. Dundee had to retreat to Lochaber, where he arrived on 11 June. Two days later, the Duke of Gordon surrendered Edinburgh Castle to the Government. Dundee remained sanguine, knowing that the Highland army could be rapidly re-formed, and having gained valuable knowledge of the terrain and the fighting style of the men.

Still relying on the arrival of aid from King James, he needed forbearance in dealing with Melfort, who was still James's Scottish Secretary, and if James were restored, would undoubtedly be the master of Scotland – a thought which in itself was enough to deter men like Lord John Murray, son of Atholl, from joining the cause. In Dundee's letters to Melfort, always courteous, frustration shows through his efforts to be tactful. On 27 June, he wrote from Moy in Lochaber, 'I thought, in prudence, for your own sake as well as the King's, you might have thought it best to seem to be out of business for a time, that the King's business might go on the smoother.'[7] He complains about lack of contact: 'I wonder above all things that in three months I never heard from you.' His letters report on various people: 'The Advocate [Mackenzie] is gone to England, a very honest man, firm beyond belief'; Tarbat by contrast is 'a great villain... gone up to secure his faction, which is melting, the two Dalrymples and others.' Proposing a landing at Inverlochy in Lochaber, Dundee hopes for 'a good party, about 5,000 or 6,000' plus 6 or 800 horse to land there, while he lays a false trail to the south-west. Next day he writes to say he is down to under 20lb of powder: 'I wonder you send no ammunition.' He dares not go down into the Lowlands, for want of horse and because the Highlanders will plunder and make enemies. Again he returns to Melfort's personal role and almost begs him to stand down: 'I do really think it were hard for the King to do it, but glorious for you, if once you be convinced that the necessity of the King's affairs requires it, to do it of yourself...' Melfort saw no such need. The Jacobite court's attention was still obsessively focused on Ireland, where the King was, and where the siege of Derry was in progress. Good news from there should mean the release of men and supplies to help Dundee, who in July was reduced to falsely assuring Lord John Murray that Melfort was willing to stand down, 'if he sees that his presence is in any way prejudicial'.[8] Dundee hoped to win over Lord John, who was besieging the ancestral home, Blair Castle, for the Government; it was being held against him by Patrick Stewart of Ballechin, his father's chamberlain.

Military campaigns in the Highlands, though their progress was followed with intense concern, did not disrupt life in the rest of the country. As long as Mackay could keep Dundee and his army bottled up among the mountains, people were not seriously alarmed, and normal activities went on. Civil peace was more widely disturbed by the unsettled disposition of the Church. Over 200 ministers of the Episcopalian-Jacobite persuasion, rabbled out by parishioners or forced out by the Privy Council, were a potent propaganda force, and many others who prayed formally for William and Mary were Jacobite sympathisers. And the Kirk was a formless body, awaiting re-structuring. No General Assembly was called in

1689, for 'the vote of the majority would undoubtedly have declared for Episcopacy',[9] and so its new dispensation was imposed by Parliament. The necessary bills, drafted by Sir James Stewart – who had become part of the new establishment with remarkable speed: perhaps he managed to make it seem he had been on William's side all the time – were sent to London and closely studied by Carstares, who toned down some of the language, removed contentious assertions, but naturally approved the substance. His involvement may have been crucial, for, in the words of an American historian, William found that: 'No-one had ever driven a harder bargain than the Scots.'[10] The bill was moved by Sir John Dalrymple. Supremacy of the King in ecclesiastical causes, enacted in 1669, was annulled – but there was no suggestion of the Kirk's involvement in civil matters. The Church of Scotland was re-established on the basis of the Confession of Faith, and the Presbyterian structure as set out in the Act of 1592. The laws against conventicles were repealed, the surviving outed presbyterian ministers were reinstated, and the Kirk was given powers – tempered by the King's adviser – 'to try and purge out all insufficient, negligent, scandalous and erroneous ministers'.[11] A motion put by Sir James Montgomery, to re-obtain recognition of the National Covenant, was defeated, and earlier Acts condemning the Covenants were left in force.

The Act passed on 7 June created a church system shorn of the grandiose political claims and ambitions that had excited the nation in 1638 and 1643, and it fixed 'the government of the church in this kingdom established by law', not by divine providence. It was established, ratified and confirmed by 'Their Majesties, with advice and consent of the said three estates'. The Church's independence was acquired only by the abandoning of any pretension to ultimate supremacy over the state. William Carstares was in Edinburgh to see the triumph of his policy, and, back in London in September, he wrote a little peevishly to Dunlop to say that it might be nice to get a letter of appreciation from 'the Ministry' for his pains and achievements on their behalf.[12]

Instead of 5,000 men and enough ammunition to mount a war, Colonel Alexander Cannon, a Lowland Scot, was landed at Duart on Mull, on 12 July, with about 250 men and 35 barrels of ammunition. They had survived a sea fight two days before in which three French frigates had defeated the *Jannet* and *Pelican*, Glasgow vessels hired by the Government for coastal protection, sinking the former and capturing the latter, along with 143 Scottish seamen.[13] Balhaldie dismissed the newcomers as 'new-raised, naked, undisciplined Irishmen' and said their arrival had a discouraging effect.[14] Dundee had put in hand a re-muster of his Highland army, but did not wait for the full complement to assemble before he set out on the 22nd. The prime reason for his urgency was the siege of Blair Castle, though the Earl of Argyll was also mustering his forces under government commission. If Atholl fell to Williamite forces, it would be much harder to break out of the Highlands. By the 25th, he also knew that Mackay's army was at Perth, preparing to march north. At the Highlanders' approach, Lord John Murray broke off his rather half-hearted siege and withdrew, leaving a detachment to guard the narrow Pass of Killiecrankie, three miles to the south, through which the track to Perth passed; and on the morning of 27 July, Dundee and his chiefs held a war council in Blair Castle. The question was whether, tired, under strength and ill-supplied as they were, they should fight or retreat. Their numbers were about 2,500, with 40 horsemen.[15] Ewen Cameron of Lochiel, the grizzled veteran, his grey moustaches 'like curling tongs' – celebrated for a feat in one of the Highland skirmishes of the Cromwellian campaign, when, wrestling with an English officer, he had torn out his adversary's throat with his teeth – who knew and shared the temperament of his followers, was for battle, and Dundee agreed.

As bright summer morning wore on, both armies converged on the mile-long cleft at Killiecrankie, where the dark River Garry races between steep wooded slopes. Mackay's 4,000 men, with 2 cavalry troops, having marched up from Dunkeld, safely traversed the narrowest part and emerged on the broad eastern shoulder where the Pass widens. With no sign of the Highlanders, they formed a line of battle facing up the valley towards Blair Atholl. The sight of a small body of clansmen seemed to confirm the correctness of their disposition, but it was a feint. Dundee's main force took a high-level route on the east side of the valley and in the early afternoon Mackay saw them form up on the slopes above him. He swung his lines round to face them, but his position was weakened, with the river below and behind, and rising ground in front. Marshalled in their regiments and battalions, and clan groups, the two armies stood for nerve-straining hours confronting each other. Dundee commanded the delay: facing west, his men were looking straight into the sun. Mackay's men, three-deep, were strung out in a longer line than the Highlanders.

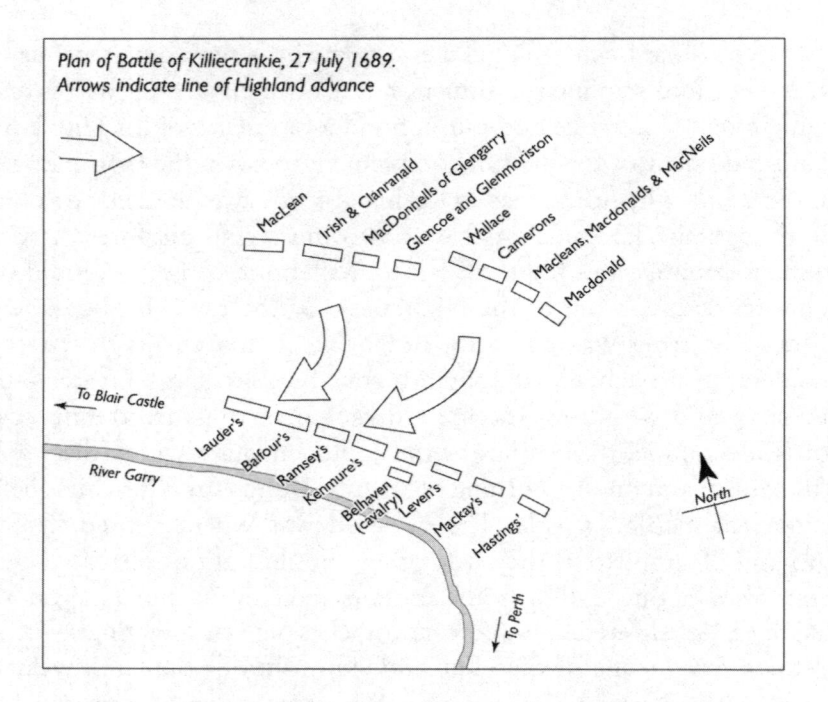

Plan of Battle of Killiecrankie, 27 July 1689.
Arrows indicate line of Highland advance

- MacLean
- Irish & Clanranald
- MacDonnells of Glengarry
- Glencoe and Glenmoriston
- Wallace
- Camerons
- Macleans, Macdonalds & MacNeils
- Macdonald

- Lauder's
- Balfour's
- Ramsey's
- Kenmure's
- Belhaven (cavalry)
- Leven's
- Mackay's
- Hastings'

To Blair Castle ←
River Garry
To Perth ↓
North ↑

They had three lightweight field guns, and fired these, to minimal effect. Otherwise they could only wait, and it was eight in the evening before Dundee gave the order to charge. Into a volley of musket-fire, to the sound of pipes and war-cries, the Highland front swept down the hill. The contour of the slope swung their line into a scimitar curve, and Dundee's right came round to crash into Mackay's line between the centre and the left, those with guns holding fire until they were almost upon the opposing lines. Too soon for the troopers, before they could fix their bayonets, the broadswords and pistols were among them, and in the space of a few minutes, the regiments on the left wing broke and fled. With the line on his right largely unscathed, Mackay struggled to rally his men, but it was hopeless. Swift to turn and maintain their advantage, the Highlanders engulfed the triple line. Only two of Mackay's regiments, Hastings's and the Earl of Leven's, were able to conduct an orderly withdrawal, and with around half his army dead or wounded, fled into the hills, or taken prisoner, he assembled what men he could, forded the river and retreated southwards to Dunkeld, preserved from further pursuit by the gathering dark and the Highlanders' delighted discovery of his 1,200 baggage horses.

He did not know yet that Dundee was dead, shot in the side by a musket ball as he turned to encourage his men to attack the troops on Mackay's right. Lochiel had tried to make him promise to stay back from the fight, but he had refused, begging leave to give 'one shear darg' [day's harvest work] to the King.[16] *Iain Dubh nan Cath*, 'Dark John of the Battles' as the Highlanders liked to call him, had proved his generalship beyond all doubt, and his loss was a demoralising blow to them. Leaving some 900 dead on the field, the Highland army fell back on Blair Atholl, with their general wrapped in plaids, and Dundee was buried in the old church there.

He had stirred up 'a war no-one wanted'.[17] But public opinion follows a winner. Probably he could never have assembled enough men and resources to get control of the kingdom, though Colonel Hastings reckoned that had Dundee survived, 'there had been 20,000 of the best men in Scotland against us before this'.[18] The men running the state were dour professionals who had access to professional military reinforcements and knew how to exercise power, but mainly, perhaps, had a better understanding of what the majority of Scots wanted. In those months they were able to represent themselves as the upholders of stability, tradition, and national sentiment. For all his denunciations of their illegitimacy, Dundee was the one seen as disruptor, and the many who felt uncommitted to either side chose to opt for peace, and whatever benefits the Revolution might bring.

Rumours and assumptions abounded in the capital. Defeat was known before the details, and Dundee's name, Dundee's plans, Dundee's wild Highlanders, dominated all conversation. Disbelief, followed by incredulous delight, was the response among the governors to the news of his death, which was not assured until the 30th. But there was still a victorious and vengeful Highland army within a day's march of Perth. More clansmen turned up at Blair Atholl in the immediately ensuing days than had fought in the battle, easily replenishing the losses. Mackay, still Commander-in-Chief, had no time to brood on his misfortune. His army had to be reconstituted, quickly, and he set to, helped by the knowledge of reinforcements ordered from a suddenly concerned court in London. Command of the Jacobite army devolved upon Cannon, who pulled back into the hills. He lacked the rank and moral authority to hold the chiefs' respect, and Lochiel and Macdonald of Sleat both went home, though they instructed their men to remain. Then, information that a new and somewhat unorthodox regiment, the Earl of Angus's, had been sent to

Dunkeld in order to secure Blair and Finlarig Castles for the Government, encouraged Cannon and his officers to come back down by Killiecrankie to storm Dunkeld and chase them away.

The young Earl of Angus had lent his name to a fighting unit better known as the Cameronians. After their 'guarding' the Convention of 1689, many aligned themselves with the new government, 'having good Designs; thinking thereby to be in a better Capacity to drive away the prelatical Curates'.[19] Eight hundred men formed it initially, a startling indication of the movement's continuing 'grass roots' support. But these hundreds joined up to do a government job for government pay – and a congenial one, to strike a blow at the ideological enemy. If they had been summoned in the name of revolt, very many would have stayed at home. Not all the Society folk approved of the new regiment: 'The main body of the grim religionists, thus reduced in aggressive strength, and no longer stimulated by persecution, watched in sullen acquiescence the progress of events.'[20] Hugh Mackay did not want them and they had been sent to Dunkeld by the Privy Council's order, not his.[21] Their commander was William Cleland, a Lieutenant-Colonel at 28. Dunkeld was a tiny town, a tight ganglion of lanes around its cathedral and the big houses of the Bishop and the Marquis of Atholl, beside the River Tay. The Bishop, still in residence in May, when he gave Dundee dinner, was gone before the Cameronians, 1,200 strong, arrived. At seven o' clock in the morning of 21 August, the Highland army attacked. Five thousand men were estimated to be in Cannon's force, but the Cameronians held them off doggedly, house by house, gradually retreating in towards the cathedral, burning the thatched cottages as they went. Running out of bullets, they ripped lead from the cathedral roof and cut it up. Surrender was never considered – it was not a matter of castles: they were battling the old spiritual foe against whom their leaders had so often declaimed. Although the Covenant was a dead letter, it was the Covenant's last fight, and a victory. Before noon, the Highlanders drew back, leaving the surviving defenders to sing a hymn to the God of Battles.[22] But early in the day, Cleland was killed. In a sense, his zestful, ardent young spirit, with all its energy and dedication, had been lost long before he was struck down: half a century of unproductive strife had devoured much that was positive and promising.

The shade of the Covenant might be allowed its day, since its fighting men were enrolled for an un-Covenanted King. Thirty years of struggle had not availed: Principal Story of Edinburgh University rang its knell: '... it faded hopelessly away, impotent and gloomy, like one of Ossian's ghosts. From that day to this it has had no authority in Scotland, and no living relation to the Church.'[23] But the evidence clearly shows that long before 'that day', the combination of Covenanters and strict Presbyterians variously labelled 'Cameronians' and 'Society People' was almost completely peripheral to the events which brought about the change of monarchy and the new constitution of church and state. In November 1684 John Erskine of Carnock, from the Presbyterian community in Holland, wrote: '... there was not one Presbyterian minister in Scotland who owned them, but on the contrary, disowned both their principles and practices... '[24] It was the equally heartfelt and determined, but more moderate and tempered views of men like Sir James Dalrymple and William Carstares, at the heart of events, which ensured the restoration of the Kirk in presbyterian form. In its terms and spirit, the revolution of 1688–89 rejected not only the Covenanters' immoderate and repressive attitudes, but also the very keystone of their conviction and programme: the supremacy of the God-inspired, conscience-led Kirk over every secular institution.

What did the Covenant achieve? In 1638, it consolidated opinion and helped to make organised resistance possible. In the following years, for the last time in its history, Scotland stood for itself. For better or worse – whatever decisions were taken, they were taken in Scotland, in the context of a debate which drew in the whole nation. At some moments they even seemed to reflect a national policy aligned on a national purpose. A vision of government, as a seamless garment extending from the general ideal down to individuals' personal conduct, seemed real and possible to many. That first period, the glory days of the Covenant, especially between 1638 and 1645, created a fervour, a feeling of unity, a sense of strength and purpose, whose residual glow drew wonder and envy from later generations. In the second period, the years of struggle, the Covenant became a distraction for all but the ever-dwindling numbers of the fully committed. Among those who now felt it to be irrelevant, admiration for the preachers' ascetic wilderness existence and truculent courage gradually changed to exasperation. Like all ideal systems, the dream proved unattainable, and its perfection and purity, remoter than the sky, yet so near in some minds, shone cold as the aurora borealis over snow-fields. None of the purgings so relentlessly demanded took them one inch closer to it. Through the centuries, small persecuted groups, from the early Christians onwards, have nourished ideals that later became part of a generally accepted way of life for the majority. No such claim can be made for the Covenanters, who had no new perceptions or fresh visions of life. Some of Scotland's old tribulations could be blamed on external forces – this was not possible with the Covenant. For 50 years it consumed lives and hopes, distracting a small but diverse and vibrant polity from a potential course of progress, cultural and material, that in various ways was being tentatively felt for. The Scots had made their own monster.

As political developments moved on in the 18th century, two interest-groups found still-live ammunition in the Covenanters' old propaganda chest. A faction of presbyterian ministers still captivated by the old militant ideals found in it a weapon against the episcopalians and Kirk 'moderates'; and Whig historians, of whom Macaulay is the best-known, used it against the Tories, though neither reached Alexander Shields's own hyperbolic height when he wrote in 1687 of the Government's intentions towards the Remnant as 'ambition to outdo all the Nero's, Domitians, Diocletians, Duke d'Alvas or Lewis le Grands'.[25] The notion dies hard that in some way, through bad, hard times, the Remnant guarded the soul of the Presbyterian Kirk. A 20th-century Church historian of conscientiously balanced views could write: '... we must hold in high regard what, by the spirited devotion which produced at last the Revolution Settlement, the Covenanters permanently achieved'[26] – even now, there are those who tiptoe round the dragon, leaving soporific tributes as they go, in case it is not dead but sleeping.

CHAPTER THIRTY

A Mirror-Scotland

FROM 1638, SCOTTISH GOVERNMENT veered between two mutually contradictory direction marks – the Covenants, and adherence to the rule of a dynastically established king. Both were seen as possessing divine authority. By 1690 both lay shattered. Between the fragments of these toppled, baroque columns, a group of cautious, un-gaudy, pragmatic, and mostly secular-minded men pushed Mother Scotland's old cart, with no sign to guide them, and no great or even clear vision of where they were heading.

Perhaps it is not surprising that the new regime, which promised so much in 1688, achieved so little. Fourteen years later, profound and apparently irreconcilable divisions still split the nation, economic development was patchy and slow, and a large-scale effort to improve the country's international trade had collapsed in disastrous failure. Oaths of loyalty were being demanded, under penalty, and the administration, quite literally, got away with murder. Food prices were high, hunger was common, poverty and beggary had increased, and it was felt that the King simply did not care: the welfare of Scotland was so low on his list of priorities as to be invisible. Far more than any of his four Stuart predecessors, William embittered and angered the Scots by making their nation appear an insignificant appendage to England. Visits were once or twice proposed, but he never came to the country, found its problems and complaints merely tiresome, and made it clear that he did not like to be bothered with Scottish business.

William's indifference to Scotland only partly explains the country's difficulties. The men entrusted with administration and governance in his first years rarely looked beyond their own personal or factional interests. The Earl of Crawford, President of the Parliament, bombarded the Secretary of State with letters about his hereditary rights to the income of half a dozen of the now abandoned bishoprics,[1] while the Secretary himself was finding ways to profit from his position. Prominent in the new power-group, the 'Court Party', was Sir John Dalrymple, whose title from May

1690 was Master of Stair. Almost any former Williamite who felt neglected in the sharing-out of offices, sinecures and honours, like Sir James Montgomery, who had been one of the ambassadors sent to offer the crown, would assume an 'opposition' role in Parliament, and from these frustrated self-interests a loose grouping emerged, known to itself as the 'Country Party' and to its opponents as 'the Club', its policy to be at odds with the 'Court Party'.

The off-stage presence of James VII and the support given him by France put a whiff of gunpowder into parliamentary opposition: anyone who felt aggrieved could start suggestive discussions with Jacobite friends, or even communicate directly with the court at St Germain. A good deal of Jacobitism, at this level, was mere posturing, in efforts to pressurise the Government, which like all governments, reacted nervously to anything smelling of treason. Plots, or suspicions of them, were endemic. Among the wider population, those with a sense of commitment to either side showed little interest in the spirit of compromise and moderation that the King hoped for. The bad old days were too recent, and ingrained patterns of hate and contempt impossible to wipe quickly away. With remarkable speed, conditions previous to 1689 seemed to be re-created in mirror image. Now the disaffected clergy were episcopalians; Saint-Germain replaced Holland, the threat of a French fleet took over from that of a Dutch one, and dissidence arose in the Highlands rather than in the south-west. New oaths of loyalty were invoked that negated those of two years before. There were differences, of course – ousted Episcopalians had no taste for sermonising on the windswept moors, and conventicles became a memory, part of a tradition that was already being worked into a mythology. More importantly, there was a regime-in-waiting, at Saint-Germain, with Melfort as its Secretary of State, in correspondence with supporters and possible adherents.

King William found that his proclaimed tenderness for parliamentary government had inconveniences. In the 1689 session, the 'Club' achieved a majority in five bills, none of which the Duke of Hamilton, as King's Commissioner, would touch with the sceptre. One of these Acts declared that the judges of the Court of Session should be approved by Parliament and that they should elect their President. This was aimed at Sir James Dalrymple, appointed Lord President by the King; and the Government's refusal to accept it was followed up by an anonymous[2] pamphlet attacking Sir James in ferocious and highly personal terms as a willing agent first of Cromwell and then of Charles II, asserting that there was no-one 'more stained and dyed with the bloody measures of the times than the Lord Stair'. Failing to find a champion to reply, Sir James himself undertook the distasteful task, in *An Apology for Sir James Dalrymple of Stair, President of the Session, by Himself.* 'Apology' meant 'Defence', and it is a detailed refutation of all the claims against him and a reminder of his own contributions both to codification of the law and reform of its procedures: 'I was also the first author and prime promoter of that order of bringing in processes [trials] for every person, without exception, as they were ready, that the greatest man of the nation could not have preference before the meanest.'[3] In May 1690 he was made Viscount Stair: 'Stair had now reached the summit of his prosperity... The friend of the King, he himself held the highest judicial, and his eldest son the highest political, office in his native country.'[4] One of the things that most united the 'Club' was their jealous detestation of the Dalrymples, both of whom were applying their considerable abilities to getting the King's business done. Sir James had arranged the appointment of judges of Session to his own satisfaction, and Sir John, unsupported, argued forcefully in Parliament for the court's aims.[5] According to a hostile witness, George Lockhart, he privately boasted that in working for James VII, he had deliberately given that King advice that would 'procure the nation's hatred and provoke his ruin'.[6]

In the parliamentary session of 1690 continuing 'Club' pressure forced the abolition of the 'Lords of the Articles', enabling the whole assembly to consider the content of bills; a change which the King had reluctantly to accept before an Act for Supply was passed. To raise the agreed sum of £162,000 for the joint monarchs, new commissioners of supply were appointed in every shire. Provision was made for election of an additional 26 shire members.[7] Among William's instructions to Melville for this parliament was one to limit torture to cases in which there was only one witness against the accused person (a modest reform prompted by Sir James Dalrymple). Some disgruntled noblemen and gentry, led by Sir James Montgomery, began to plot a *coup d'état* in collusion with the Jacobite court. A letter from Montgomery to the Earl of Annandale shows the quality of the conspirators: '... seeing there was no hope of doing anything with the King [William], we ought to apply ourselves to

King James, who was our lawful prince, and who would no doubt give us what preferments and employments we pleased.'[8] From Paris came an eager response, even with a list of potential office-holders which, interestingly, proposed Sir James Stewart as Lord Advocate, though Sir John Dalrymple was to be excluded from any indemnity. Leaks, loss of nerve and dispute over the spoils led to the plot's exposure. Montgomery fled to France, Annandale confessed everything; all were let off lightly, except for an English Catholic associate, Neville Payne, who was subjected to the thumbscrews to get information, and spent ten years in prison. William Carstares, whose thumbs might have twitched in sympathy, mentions Payne's case coolly and uncritically *en passant* in a letter to Dunlop[9].

The Presbyterian colonists in Carolina had been driven out by the Spanish at the end of 1686, and Dunlop returned to Scotland with his doughty wife, who had gone out to join him. His brother-in-law's recommendation procured him the post of Principal of Glasgow University in November 1690, and over the next years he would be a valuable source of information and a kind of coadjutor to Carstares. It was Dunlop who, having been told of it by Lord Ross, one of the participants, gave the news of the 'Montgomery Plot' to the Government.

After a stay at the Yorkshire spas, Sir George Mackenzie arrived in Oxford with his wife and their young son to set up home in September 1690. Nothing that was happening in Scotland was congenial to him. Although only in his mid-50s, his health was declining, but he spent pleasant hours in the Bodleian Library and renewed literary friendships in London, where he rented rooms in St James Street. His last works, which he did not live to see published, were *The Moral History of Frugality*, *Vindication of the Government of Charles II*, which was also his vindication of the actions of that king's Lord Advocate, and the incomplete *Memoirs of the Affairs of Scotland*. He died in London on 9 May 1691, and his body was brought back to Edinburgh and interred in a fine baroque tomb in the Greyfriars' Churchyard. Mackenzie was always something of an outsider, attaching himself to men and groups whose methods and actions he often deplored, and who laughed at his scruples. Driven by principles which they did not share, he hurled himself into attack on their behalf. He saw lesser men than himself gain greater rewards, because they were venal and needed to be bought, or just because they had no qualms about working the system. For all his efforts at self-justification, the Covenanters' epithet stuck to his reputation, and, almost 200 years later, Robert Louis Stevenson would see urchins knock on the door of his mausoleum and shout: 'Bluidy Mackenzie, come oot if ye daur!'

The first General Assembly of the Kirk since the abortive one of 1653 was convened in October 1690 – a strange gathering, formed only of 60 former Protesters who had been ejected in the 1660s, along with a few grizzled veterans of the 1650s, and 120 elders. A letter from the King counselled moderation and peace. The Cameronians' three ministers, including Alexander Shields, were formally accepted back. Most of their followers would also rejoin mainstream congregations, but a remnant of the Remnant would cling, unpersecuted, to the purity of their beliefs. The Assembly was decorous but purposeful, seeing a solemn duty ahead. Two commissions were set up, one for the north and one for the south, to examine parish ministers' behaviour and principles, and decide on their suitability to remain in office. With a zeal and thoroughness that old Archbishop Burnet could not have rivalled when he was hazing the presbyterians, these commissions set forth to purge the Kirk. Ministers who failed the inquisition were forced out, and their kirk sessions reforrmed. Seeing the commissioners just as quick as the bishops had been to call in the troops when their orders to quit were resisted, Tarbat protested, 'The reforming of the Church by the Cameronian regiment can do no good,'[10] and the Government intervened to protect some victims. To have episcopalian views was not an offence, if the minister had subscribed to the Confession of Faith. In some parishes, a converse of the planting of 'curates' took place, but the supply of qualified presbyterian ministers was far too small to do this on any scale, and

Tomb of Sir George Mackenzie, Greyfriars' Churchyard, Edinburgh
Reproduced from Lang, *Sir George Mackenzie*

some churches remained without a minister for several years. For the Presbyterians, it seemed the only way to effect the will of Parliament and their own policy, but the intolerance of the 'hot commissions' caused new anger and re-opened old wounds. Anyone of strong episcopalian conviction might well look favourably on the Jacobites.

Carstares, though not formally a member, was in constant attendance at the Assembly.[11] The Presbyterian ascendancy had been his achievement, and he was diligent in encouraging the moderate strain among the clergy and elders. This was a constituency over which the Secretaries of State had no control. Among his other concerns were the universities, which had lost some of their best teachers through refusal to take the oath of allegiance. To the annoyance – no doubt – of Lord Crawford, a modest part of the former bishops' rentals, £1,200 a year, was directed to the universities. As an 'honest broker' for the King, Carstares had persuaded the Duke of Hamilton, a dithering but prestigious figure, to assist the Government by accepting the post of Lord High Commissioner. Perpetually engaged in preventing friction between the volatile and voluble extremes of opinion, always reinforcing the centre, he accepted that this often meant brickbats: 'I have never concerned myself in the public, with an eye to thanks from those in Scotland, for whose interest I have been, and will be, sincerely concerned; but if I had not more of honesty and principle than some have of charity, it is like some affairs might have gone otherwise.'[12]

Early in 1691, the Master of Stair was appointed Secretary of State, at first jointly with Lord Melville, then with James Johnston, son of Wariston. The King hoped that his abilities would succeed in curbing the 'hot' Presbyterians whose purging of the Kirk was endangering public peace in some places.[13] Stair took a somewhat indulgent line, writing about them that:

> ... those people are neither tractable nor grateful, but yet they have something that one would not do well to destroy them, though he can neither manage nor oblige them... I shall never be accessory either to subvert their constitution or to bring them to scaffolds, though really they do some things so intolerable that they must be used as mad bodies and put up in a bedlam, if they continue their rabbling or protestation.[14]

In other words, they might be troublemakers, but they were his troublemakers. His attitude to non-presbyterian Highlanders was very different. Most of his activity was routine though not uncontroversial, with opposing interests scheming for every official post and perquisite. An indication of his persuasive powers is given in a letter from the Earl of Crawford to Carstares, of 16 June 1691, describing how Stair set about getting a majority in the Council for calling out the militia at a time of Jacobite unrest,[15] picking off the recalcitrant members one by one and offering them reasons to concur with his policy.

Among many Lowland Scots, there was a feeling that union with England, on suitable terms, would be a good thing, because of the likely economic benefits.[16] In the Highlands, there was no such view. Union would assuredly bring destruction of a way of life already deeply eroded; of traditions already heavily diluted. Livelihood, community, the security of cherished custom – all would be swept away. Jacobite propaganda played up strongly to this fear: James VII's agents and adherents employed well-tried techniques to promote a spirit of rebellion, talking up the chances of success, emphasising the Government's alien nature, insisting that the point of no return was already passed, devising oaths of loyalty, getting signatures to bonds of association.[17] On chiefs who had 'an almost mandarinical obsession with face',[18] it was not hard to exert pressures. Highland Jacobitism was not a calm, confident, spontaneous movement, but an uncertain, neurotic, sometimes panicky set of attitudes among people who felt isolated, threatened, imprisoned by their past and profoundly unsure of their future.

After Dunkeld, the Jacobite Highlanders, lacking a leader, torn by old enmities and personal rivalries, by internecine divisions relating to land claims, angry and apprehensive at the manner in which Argyll was restoring his family hegemony with the full support of the Government, were restive but disunited. In April 1690 Major-General Thomas Buchan was sent by James VII to mount a spring offensive, but his small force of 800 was routed at Cromdale in the Banffshire hills by Sir Thomas Livingstone, Mackay's successor as commander-in-chief, on 1 May. By 18 July, the old government fort of 1654 had been reinstated at Inverlochy, at the south end of the Great Glen, and named Fort William, and strong points had been established at another eight locations. Communications with the court in exile, promises, the award of

'Jacobite' titles and honours, above all the endlessly discussed prospect of a full-scale French-backed invasion to restore James VII, combined to keep up an atmosphere of anticipation and excitement among the Jacobite clans, and through the autumn of 1691, Buchan and Cannon remained among them, ready for a signal. A prudent government might well take pains to remove or minimise the danger, and in the Master of Stair, William had a prudent servant. From a king who considered Scotland to be an irritating complication in his life, the Highlands, a distraction within a distraction, were not going to receive either sympathy or attention, especially when the loyalty of so many there was either ambiguous or openly Jacobite. He wanted no trouble from that quarter, and Stair's policy was not so much punitive as repressive: it was to set the price of mere opposition so high that rebellion would be unthinkable. It was also economical, intended to assure quiescence without the need to employ armies or large garrisons: Highlanders could be found to police the Highlands.

CHAPTER THIRTY-ONE

The Interest of the State

STAIR INHERITED HIS PRINCIPAL agent from his predecessor in office. John Campbell of Glen Orchy, first Earl of Breadalbane, aged 57, was an opportunistic and practised survivor of events, described by John Macky as 'cunning as a Fox, wise as a Serpent, but slippery as an Eel'.[1] He had been commissioned in April 1690 to make an accommodation with the potential rebels. The Government badly needed a middleman, and though Breadalbane was known by both sides to be devious, their joint mistrust made him acceptable. All chiefs whose territories came near the Highland fringe had to have a double aspect, presenting a Scottish face towards the Government, and a Highland one towards the community of kinsmen, tenants and retainers who acknowledged their traditional authority. This did not have to mean double dealing, but it very often did. Lord Tarbat's belief that the loyalty of the chiefs could be bought was reinvoked, and Breadalbane was entrusted with a fund of 10 or 12,000 pounds sterling for disbursement. Some at least of this money was to be used to purchase land titles taken over by Argyll, and release them to other clan chiefs,[2] but was never spent in this way, and Breadalbane never accounted for it. On 30 June 1691 he managed to achieve a truce with the Jacobite leaders, in what was known as the Treaty of Achallader, but Stair wanted evidence of submission, and all clan chiefs were required by the Privy Council to swear an oath of allegiance to William, before a sheriff or sheriff-depute, by the end of 1691, or face treatment 'of the utmost rigour' as traitors.[3] Military preparations were put in hand on a sufficient scale to convince the chiefs that they should co-operate, though many waited to receive James's dispensation before signing.

In anticipation of the Lochaber chiefs' refusal, Stair had written to Sir Thomas Livingstone that: 'Your troops will destroy entirely the country of Lochaber, Lochiel's lands, Keppoch's, Glengarry's and Glencoe's. Your power shall be large enough. I hope the soldiers will not trouble the Government with prisoners.'[4] In the event, only Glencoe failed, on a technicality. Having waited until the last possible moment, its chief,

MacIan, found that the Colonel at Fort William was not eligible to take his oath, and had to travel on to Inveraray, where he swore it, five days late. His signed oath, forwarded to the Privy Council with an explanation, was refused, and by the 11th, John Dalrymple knew that a single, small clan group had failed to act on time. As it happened, the MacIans of Glen Coe, a sept of Clan Donald, only around 140 people in all, were enemies of Breadalbane, frequent raiders on his territory; and quite recently had burned his house at Achallader. Stair did not tell the King that MacIan had signed, and on 16 January William authorised retribution specifically on Glen Coe: 'If McIan of Glencoe and that tribe can be well separated from the rest, it will be proper vindication of the public justice to extirpate that set of thieves.'[5] From Secretary of State to Commander of the Forces, from him to Lieutenant-Colonel Hamilton at Fort William, from him to Major Duncanson, and so to Captain Robert Campbell of Glenlyon, the order was passed on. Duncanson's letter said: 'This is by the King's special commands, for the good and safety of the country, that these miscreants be cut off root and branch.'[6] Campbell and his troop of 120 from Argyll's Regiment, announcing themselves as on a tax-collecting mission, were hospitably received by the Glen Coe people on 1 February. On the 12th, Duncanson sent the order for action – that night all under the age of 70 were to be killed. Campbell accounted for his men's preparations by saying they were going on a mission against the MacDonnells of Glengarry. At five o'clock in the morning the troops, dispersed through the scattered settlements, started up, and the shooting began. In the dark and confusion, many got away on to the snow-covered mountainsides, and the hunt for victims continued as dark gave way to winter daylight. Thirty-eight people, men, women and children, were shot dead.

No-one had been intended to escape, but the plan to have the exits from the glen watched and blocked was disrupted by the snowfall. Stair was angered at this failure. Writing to Colonel Hill, commander at Fort William, on 5 March, to acknowledge his report, he said: 'There is much talk of it here [London] that they are murdered in their beds after they had taken the allegiance; *for the last, I know nothing of it*,'[7] and adds, 'All I regret is that any of the sect got away.' Stair's claim of ignorance is false. On 30 April he wrote to the same officer, 'When you do right, you need fear nobody.'[8] Stair never uttered a syllable of remorse or regret on this subject. His motivation has been wondered at by many. Macaulay's

John Dalrymple, 1st Earl of Stair
Reproduced by courtesy of the National Trust for Scotland

explanation of the kind of bureaucratic zeal which has also lain behind more recent and vaster crimes may well hold some truth:

> The most probable conjecture is that he was actuated by an inordinate, an unscrupulous, a remorseless zeal for what seemed to him to be the interest of the state. This explanation may startle those who have not considered how large a proportion of the blackest crimes recorded in history is to be ascribed to ill regulated public spirit. We daily see men do for their party, for their sect, for their country, for their favourite schemes of political and social reform, what they would not do to enrich or to avenge themselves.[9]

But the tone of some of Stair's letters suggests that he was carried away by his sense of his own power. It was in his hand to destroy a whole tribe, and he welcomed the opportunity too eagerly. The chilly superiority of his father was leavened by moral and religious values, and not least, by respect for the rule of law. In the son, the only checks were supplied by his sense of what his authority and abilities enabled him to do; a defective morality shown not only in the action but in his behaviour afterwards. But he was not alone: Breadalbane encouraged him, and a chain of military officers combined to execute orders that even Sir James Turner, in the bad old days, might have baulked at. Treachery, and the murder of women and children, were by no means unknown among the clans, but this was the action of a government that had proclaimed commitment to civil rights. If Stair considered himself to be acting in the interest of the state, the effect was the opposite of what he intended. Though official reaction came slowly, the public shock-wave was immediate. Bitterness, mistrust and fear of further attacks wrecked the chance of achieving pacification in the Highlands. Through Jacobite channels the news was published in Paris on 7 April, and the event became a central plank in their propaganda. Meanwhile, though blame was speedily passed back up the line, all those involved continued to hold their posts and the Government stayed tight-lipped. Only the most oblique of references to the Glen Coe atrocity can be found in Carstares's correspondence, although in January 1692, he was almost certainly working with Stair[10] on the King's message to the next General Assembly. In early 1693 he wrote from Holland to Dunlop to refute 'a story with you that I concerted matters with the Master of Stair at Rotterdam... it is a notorious forgery'.[11] Both were in Holland with the King, and this seems to refer to the general assumption that an official 'cover-up' was being organised to prevent embarrassment to the King and the Government. Since it is unlikely that Carstares knew of the Glen Coe plan or had any involvement with it, his avoidance of the topic looks like another case of his inflexible discretion: the issue was not only hotly controversial but profoundly distasteful for any admirer of, or apologist for, King William II of Scotland.

CHAPTER THIRTY-TWO

The Perils of Atheism

IN 1692, LADY STAIR DIED, a respected matriarch within her large family, pursued beyond the grave by offensive rumours and allegations; the disreputable verses of pasquil-writers made even more venomous by the post-Glen Coe hostility to her son John:

'Open your doors, ye devils, and prepare
A room that's warm for honest Lady Stair.'[1]

For three years, the Master of Stair continued to exercise his office, as if there were no bloody trail behind him. From March 1692 there was a new Chancellor, the Earl of Tweeddale, now 67, once a member of Lauderdale's administration, still an enthusiast for union with England, who could be expected to support, rather than subvert, royal policy. His experience and independent standing were needed. None of the four great magnates, lurking just beyond the confines of government like dingoes at a campfire: Argyll, Atholl, Hamilton and Queensberry, could be given the job without provoking the other three into oppositional wrecking tactics.

Relations between the King and the parliament, on one side, and the Kirk on the other, had hit a low point, caused by the continuing unwillingness of the dominant presbyterians to retain or accept ministers of episcopalian sympathies. Yet another oath was brought in by the 1693 parliament, to be sworn by all clergy, the so-called Oath of Assurance, requiring acceptance of William as king not only *de facto*, but *de jure* – and while many episcopalians accepted the fact, they could not swallow the legal right of his kingship. With it came the quaintly titled 'Act for Settling the Quiet and Peace of the Church', which declared that all episcopal ministers who took the oaths of allegiance and assurance, and acknowledged the presbyterian government of the church, should be admitted to the Kirk and allowed to exercise their ministry. The act also called for the summoning of a General Assembly of the Church. Uproar ensued: the episcopalians outraged by the new oath, the presbyterians because the Government was telling the Church what to do. An Assembly was called by the King for 27 March, and it was made clear that ministers must sign up to the Assurance before they took their places, or the Assembly would be dissolved. Many ministers were minded to refuse, and it seemed a 'High Noon' confontation was inevitable. How Carstares could have let such a stand-off come about is unclear, though it may be another instance of Stair making policy on his own, with William's unconsidered assent.

Carstares sometimes needed intrepidity in dealing with the King, as well as with his critics. On this occasion it appears he, with the support of James Johnston, took the dangerous and unprecedented step of intercepting a royal despatch instructing the Commissioner to dissolve the Assembly, and pleaded with William to back down and dispense with putting the Assurance oath to the ministers. The King yielded and new instructions were sent, arriving just in time to prevent a possible repetition of the Assembly which had refused to let itself be dissolved in 1638.[2] From Carstares's first biographer, Joseph McCormick, comes a picturesque tale of Carstares pulling aside the King's bed-curtains and waking him. Controverting William was not something to be done lightly (Gilbert Burnet makes a rueful note[3] that 'he did not love to be found fault with'); his sense of the royal prerogative, limited or not, was every bit as keen as Charles II's. Even if Carstares was drawing on a deep credit account, it was risky, but it paid off handsomely. Ministers on both sides of the divide felt themselves receiving the King's favour.

Factional rivalries and personal animosities played far more part than sympathy for the murdered Macdonalds in the continuing pursuit of the Master of Stair – in the Glen Coe affair, his opponents felt they had a weapon to destrroy him. The Parliament of 1693 was prevented from openly accusing him, but through 1694, when there was no parliament called and no public forum, the demand for an inquiry did not abate, and in the Parliament of 1695, Tweeddale, as King's Commissioner, found that it could not be contained. A newly formed Committee for the Security of the Kingdom demanded an inquiry, and this was headed off by the formation of a royally appointed Commisssion of 10, whose report was laid before Parliament (not the King, as had been intended) on 24 June 1695. Story describes the commission's efforts as 'directed to whitewash the King, and incriminate the Master of Stair'.[4] What ensued showed both the independence of the Parliament and its impotency. The

Edinburgh in 1693
Reproduced from *Cassell's Old & New Edinburgh*

Commission declared it 'a great wrong' that the Privy Council had not been informed that MacIan had signed; it observed that Stair knew he had signed, that there was 'Nothing in the King's instructions to warrant the committing of the foreseaid slaughter', and that Secretary Stair's letters 'quite exceeded the King's foresaid instructions'.[5] Parliament labelled the action as murder and asked for the officers responsible, then on service in Flanders, to be recalled for trial. Its Address to the King of 10 July 1695 states that because Stair's excess in his letters against the Glen Coe men 'has been the original cause of this unhappy business... we do therefore beg that your majesty will give such orders about him for vindication of your government as you in your royal wisdom shall see fit'.[6] The King saw no need for action, but Stair, his position no longer tenable, resigned, and William reluctantly replaced him as Secretary of State with Lord John Murray. No-one was prosecuted, and Campbell of Glenlyon was later promoted to a colonelcy.[7] King William issued a remission to Stair, freeing him from all consequences rising from the Glen Coe massacre, on the basis that he had 'no knowledge of nor accession to the method of that execution'.

Policing and protection of the long coastline was always a problem, and Scottish shipping suffered from not only from raids by French privateers but from the officiousness of England's Royal Navy. On 27 May 1695, following a report from its Committee for the Security of the Kingdom, Parliament voted £Sc300,000 'for providing and maintaining cruizers and convoys for the defence of the coast and trade'. In Orkney, HMS *Woolwich* seized the *Kathrine*, of Dysart, loaded with wine, and the Privy Council complained of 'frequent insults of this kind'.[8] Trade and commerce were still primarily across the North Sea, but as individuals or groups, Scots had been investing in colonial property and trade for some decades. Now, at a much more grandiose level, on 26 June 1695 the High Commissioner touched with the sceptre the Act enabling the Company Trading to Africa and the Indies. This body was also empowered to trade with America, to plant colonies and make treaties, and up to half its shares could be held by persons resident outside Scotland. Its moving spirit was William Paterson, born in Tynwald, Dumfries-shire, in 1658, a brilliant ideas man but not much of an entrepreneur, who had proposed the scheme for founding the Bank of England in 1691. While Parliament was meeting in his name, King William was engaged in the siege of Namur, in Flanders. When he read the Act, his cold rage was aroused by its scope, since Tweeddale's remit had only been for an act to acquire and establish plantations, and he felt he had been 'ill-served'.

A small book, *Vindication of the Divine Perfections*, published in London in 1695, and advertised only as written by 'a Person of Honour', was the last of Viscount Stair's published writings. An intellectual rather than a spiritually devotional work, it is formed of meditations on 16 aspects of the nature of God, and, like his *Physiologia*, it is old-fashioned for its time. But it does contain a tribute to the pleasure and progress of ideas, citing as one proof of God's goodness 'that the Discovery of the Natures of the Creatures and all the Experimental Knowledge hath proceded from the beginning, and shall to the end increase, that there might never be wanting a suitable Exercise, Diversion, and Delight to the more ingenious and inquiring men'. Stair died on 25 November 1695, aged 77, and was buried in the High Kirk of St Giles. He is remembered as a great legist rather than as the all-round virtuoso he sought to be. His son John inherited the title, but waited for some years to take up the seat in Parliament to which he was now entitled.

Carstares, the only fixed figure in the swirling shoals of Scottish politics, was not really a politician, in the sense of someone who has a set of ideas which he wants to see put into practice. He had no policy, merely wanting to see the country at peace under King William, and the Kirk behaving with moderation and goodwill. Episcopal-presbyterian hostility shook almost every parish outside the Highlands, and over 650 incumbents were forced out in the early 1690s. In parliamentary confrontations each label was used so promiscuously that the episcopalian Duke of Queensberry, when it suited him, could appear the defender of the Presbyterians, and the presbyterian (if anything) Sir John Dalrymple the protector of the Episcopalians. The manoeuvrings, demands, presumptions and posturings of the Scottish governing class show the consuming self-interest of men of largely second- or third-rate abilities, intent on exploiting positions they would never have gained by personal merit.[9] Writing to Carstares in March 1696, the Earl of Argyll refers contemptuously to 'those noble drunken patriots' including the Earl of Annandale, trying to promote a blue-ribbon wearing movement in support of Whiggery: 'a means to make divisions, and not heal them'.[10] Beset by demands for jobs for younger sons and worthy retainers, bombarded by the complaints of one magnate against another, Carstares, who had grown up in a time of religious idealism, laboured patiently with them, though sometimes he betrayed irritation. The principal achievement of King William's managers in Scotland – not managed without bitter controversy – was to keep comparative peace. Against dangerous and threatening events elsewhere: war with France, Queen Mary's death in 1694, an English Jacobite assassination plot against the King in early 1696, no serious threat to the Government emerged, and men who might have been dangerous, like the new Duke of Hamilton, were carefully neutralised. One result of this was that the Scots could work to build up their economy, and the focus on trade and commerce would create its own problems by the turn of the century.

Carstares's role was very much that of the King's fixer and in this he never lost William's trust. 'I am, in a manner, his Majesty's domestic servant,' he had written to Dunlop early in 1690.[11] John Macky, a professionally sharp and possibly jealous observer, noted of Carstares that: 'few Scotsmen had access to the King but by him, so that he was properly Viceroy of that kingdom, and was called at Court Cardinal Carstares'.[12]

Macky disliked Carstares, calling him 'the cunningest subtle dissembler in the world, with an air of sincerity – a dangerous enemy, because always hid'.[13] The politicians of the 'Club' were very much aware of Carstares's importance, sometimes bitterly so, though he often made efforts to court their leading figures. New men were emerging in what was becoming known as the 'nobility of the first rank'. The Duke of Hamilton died in 1694 and his eldest son, the Jacobite-inclined Earl of Arran, was made fourth duke in 1698, and Lord Drumlanrig inherited the Queensberry dukedom in 1695. Both were soon demanding official posts, and the new Queensberry, though financially grasping, had backbone and a sense of authority. In 1696, there was a reshuffle of posts, but the problem remained, of too many dukes and earls with not enough to do. Sir John Dalrymple, not impressed by their general quality, had written in January 1693: 'in this age... there are so few eminent men for the public',[14] which helps to explain how, in the ponderous game of musical chairs, his correspondent, a relatively junior lawyer from the Banffshire backwoods, Sir James Ogilvie, 30-year-old second son of the Earl of Findlater, a fellow-member of the 'clever and efficient' school, became Solicitor General that year. In 1696 he was appointed joint Secretary of State with Lord John Murray, who was made Earl of Tullibardine in the same year.

In what was to be his last sermon, on 3 September 1699, the veteran James Kirkton rebuked his Edinburgh congregation: '... ye are not sad enough; now I never saw so much wantonness and lightness among the people of Scotland as there is just now; woe is my heart therefor... There are too many dancing-schools, too much dancing, too much fineness of apparel, alas for it: is not this true? What will God say, when you come before him?' Of this time, W. H. Lecky wrote that: 'While England... was advancing with gigantic strides along the paths of knowledge, Scotland still cowered in helpless subjection before her clergy. Never was a mental servitude more complete, and never was a tyranny maintained with more inexorable barbarity.'[15] To a 19th-century historian of the Kirk, 'The year 1697 presents nothing demanding attention, as far as the Church is concerned... Steady and persevering care for the promotion of religion in the passing of acts against profaneness and immorality... '[16] There is more truth in Lecky's overblown rhetoric than in such bland refusal to see the blood on the carpet, but neither gets below the surface appearance, as they saw it. In fact the ministers' confidence was often shaky. If Scotland was again a fortress of Presbyterianism, its guardians were perpetually anxious about weak foundations, secret entries, laxness on the part of the sentinels, and the dangerous foolishness of the King's tolerance towards enemy creeds. Nor had they any illusions about the citizens, whose impulses towards heretical or irreligious behaviour had to be perpetually resisted.

A shiver went through the Kirk in 1698, when the King, after long deliberation, allowed the Pope's nominated Vicar Apostolic for Scotland a passport to enter the country. He was Thomas Nicolson, born in Kemnay, a former professor at Glasgow, who had been converted in 1682.[17] In 1698 10 Jesuit, 4 Benedictine, and 23 secular Catholic priests were at work, but civil and ecclesiastical authorities united to make their task almost impossible. For all the Kirk's fears, the Catholic activists had already lost the battle. They had virtually no schools, and from 1709 the Society for the Propagation of Christian Knowledge would begin to spread Protestant education through the *Gaidhealtachd*.

But there were other enemies within the walls. By the 1690s, much had changed in university teaching since George Mackenzie and his coevals had been students. The Copernican, even the Newtonian, universe was accepted, and doctoral theses from around 1670 took account of Descartes.[18] Natural Philosophy was spreading its wings, and though it remained subservient to Revealed Religion and had not entirely shaken off magic, it offered new trajectories of thought whose destinations were unclear. When one set of received ideas was discredited by modern techniques and bold thought, others might also be questioned. Under a reign whose watchword was Toleration, some teachers felt free to discuss topics that strayed alluringly from the century-old Confession of Faith which they had affirmed on accepting their posts. Seeing the dangers, the Kirk's commission for the universities ordained in 1695 that only locally produced and approved textbooks should be used: 'For Cartesius... and others of his gang, besides what may be said against their doctrine, they all labour under this inconvenience – that they give not any sufficient account of the other hypotheses, and the old philosophy, which must not be ejected.' Each university was allocated topics. Edinburgh and St Andrews managed a brief *Introduction to Metaphysics* and *Introduction to Logic* respectively, by 1701, but no more was heard of the idea after that.[19] Nothing relating to contemporary philosophy was published in Scotland before 1700, and textbooks continued to be imported, and students continued to discuss imported ideas. In places like Peter Butter's public house in Errol's Gate, Edinburgh, university students, highbrows and academics of the less strait-laced sort, declaimed such lyrics as this:

> *Cogito (ergo sum)*
> That Thirst doth us Harm,
> Sit still upon your Bum
> 'Till the Divert stop the Lum,   [amusement block the chimney]
> Drink o'er the left Arm.
>
> If you expect Degrees,
> Drink off your Cup and fill;
> We're not for what you please,
> Our absolute Decrees
> Admit of no Free-will.[20]

The tavern was dignified as *Collegium Butterensis*, Butter's College, and the learned jesters drew up a library catalogue for it, whose first entry was 'Maximilian Maltkist, *De Principiis Liquidi*', and awarded their own degrees in drinking. Such frolics may have been seen as harmless, but more serious topics were also discussed. Gnostic and Rosicrucian mysteries may have been explored in secret societies. From his studies at both Glasgow and Edinburgh between 1687 and 1690 the young Irishman John Toland emerged with a set of ideas that resulted in his first book *Christianity Not Mysterious*, in 1696 (bought by Edinburgh University Library), and further works which developed the notion of pantheism, a term he himself coined, and which held God and the Universe to be one and the same thing. Scotland was no longer intellectually behind the times. Toland left the country in 1690, but deistic ideas did not. In January 1696 a complaint was heard at the General Assembly 'that there were those who, under the name of Deists, in fact taught atheism'.[21] In November 1697 Sir James Stewart, as Lord Advocate, launched a blasphemy charge, combined with 'notorious adultery', against one Patrick Kininmonth, and demanded the death sentence: but a vigorous defence was put up, and all charges were dropped.[22]

The multi-faced Stewart, who had evidently not forgotten the sentiments of his *Ius Populi Vindicatum*, was more successful in December, when an 18-year-old student, Thomas Aikenhead, orphan son of an Edinburgh chirurgeon, was charged in the Court of Session as being guilty 'airt and pairt of horrid blasphemy'.[23] The old tradition of the informer was still alive, for remarks made over the course of a year were held against him, including calling the Old Testament 'Ezra's Fables', and describing theology as 'a rhapsody of feigned and ill-invented nonsense'. He was said to have claimed that by 1800, Christianity would be extirpated. Blasphemy was a capital crime. On Christmas Eve, 1697, he was found guilty and sentenced to death. Confronted with the long drop, Aikenhead recanted, pleading his 'young and tender years' and being misled by books lent by a friend, Mungo Craig, who was also the chief witness against him. But he was hanged at the Gallowlee on 8 January 1698, after two requests for reprieve had been refused. This, to adapt what Voltaire would say of another judicial killing, was *pour décourager les autres*, and shows how, like an ageing, decrepit crocodile deprived of nimbler prey, the combination of Kirk and Court of Session could still snatch an unwary victim. The General Assembly was meeting at the time, and one minister wrote: 'I think G[od] was glorified by such an awful and exemplary punishment.'[24] Though two ministers, George Meldrum and William Lorimer, are said to have interceded for a pardon or reprieve, 'The city clergy cannot be held innocent of his death' write two modern church historians;[25] and the hustled execution of this innocuous youth makes a striking contrast to the efforts made to save James Renwick from the rope a few years before. Later that year, the Privy Council ordered a search and inquisition of booksellers, against books deemed atheistical, erroneous, profane, or vicious.

As often with repressive, would-be totalitarian systems, the greatest severities preceded, perhaps helped to bring about, a liberalising tendency so generalised and unspecific that its fertilising spores passed through every preventive mesh. It was not top-led, but spread in universities, clubs, and meeting-places, in conversation and debate among people newly aware that they lived giddily on a revolving planet that moved through space, and who wondered what else might be revealed with the tools of scientific experiment and mathematical calculation. Accompanying this secular spirit, even more insidious, was the desire most people had – without relapsing from Protestant and Presbyterian principles – for pleasures less rarefied than spiritual exercises: tea, tobacco, free and easy conversation, music, song, dancing.

CHAPTER THIRTY-THREE

The Silence of Darien

HAVING GOT ITS ACT, the Company of Scotland for Africa, with Paterson in the driving seat, began to raise funds in London. In nine days from opening the subscription in November 1695, the full £300,000 available was spoken for, with £75,000 paid up.¹ Paterson was anxious to play down this success, but on 13 December the blow fell: at the representations of merchant interests, both Houses of the English Parliament condemned the scheme as fatal to English commerce, the books of the Company were seized at the order of the House of Commons, and English backing melted away. This was not pure dog-in-the-manger behaviour: the privileges accorded the Company in its Act had been part of the attraction, and there was some reason to fear that, although Scotland had only a small merchant fleet, English shipping would be drawn to Scotland, and England's navy called on to protect the Scottish trade (though it was all right for Scottish troops to fight for the King of England's interests in Flanders). In Scotland, this dropping of the boom was greeted with fury, and the 'heroic and fatal decision was taken to raise £400,000 sterling in Scotland'.² Contemporaries supposed this to be as much as half the country's capital, though it may be noted that in 1695, Scots had already invested two-thirds of the newly established Bank of Scotland Company's initial capital of £100,000.³ They had also found the £162,000 for the royal levy, and between 1696 and 1702, 12 new joint stock companies had been founded.⁴

Almost all the Africa Company sum was subscribed between 26 February and 31 May 1696. There was wealth, if far from evenly distributed, in the nation, and its owners had cottoned on to capitalism's ability to expand it. But efforts to raise £200,000 on the Continent were blocked by the Dutch East India Company in Amsterdam, and, even more frustratingly, by the English Resident in Hamburg, in the name of King William. The Scots would have to go it alone. Although one ship did make a voyage to the Gold Coast, came back well-loaded and made a handsome profit,⁵ the focus of the enterprise shifted westwards to the isthmus joining North and South America (present-day Panama), and from a conventional trading operation to a full-blown colonial enterprise. Behind this lay Paterson's obsessive notion that the short land-route between the Atlantic and Pacific Oceans was the key to world trade, and that if it were controlled by a dynamic, commercially minded nation, the rewards would be of spectacular vastness. His dream was bought by the Scots in a wholehearted way. Just as their grandfathers had rushed to pledge their spiritual wealth to the Covenant, those with money available hurried to invest in Darien. A hundred and fifty years before, Sir David Lindsay had asked, rhetorically, 'Why are we so poor, when we're so clever?'[6] – now the golden opportunity was there to be seized.

A few cooler heads, including Sir James Ogilvie, stayed aloof. The whole Panama region was deemed by Spain to be its colonial property, and King William's English government was anxious to be friends with Spain at this particular time. To the King, the Darien enterprise was a breach of his prerogative and an embarrassment to his diplomacy, and he ordered the West Indian colonial administrators to give no support. Meanwhile three ships were being built, not in Scotland, but in Hamburg and Amsterdam, and a stock of goods was being assembled for use and trade, the latter including 4,000 periwigs, bales of thick tweed cloth, and 1,500 Bibles.[7] After many delays the vessels sailed with 1,200 men 'and not one woman amongst them at all'[8] on 26 July 1698.

The King's attitude was well-known, and things went ahead in a spirit of half-guilty defiance. At the beginning of 1698, a stormy year in Scottish life and politics, the Earl of Tullibardine, joint Secretary of State, wrote of Carstares as 'a secret enemy',[9] and James Johnston, who had been replaced as the other joint Secretary by Sir James Ogilvie in February 1696, wrote on Carstares's arrival in Edinburgh in February 1698, 'Carstares is sent down to feel pulses. If he be used as he deserves, he will not stay nor have time to corrupt people or misrepresent honest men.'[10] In the flux of contending personalities, shifting loyalties and ever-incipient plots and conspiracies, Carstares's natural bent for back-room persuasions and fixes was perhaps the only tactic possible for the agent of a monarch who himself had no policy for the country. But he could do nothing to stem the surge of enthusiasm for the Darien venture.

At the start of November the colonists began to build Fort St Andrew, part of the city of New Edinburgh, in the territory of Caledonia. No provision had been made for communication home, and the nation waited tensely for news. Grandiose visions abounded in Scotland, while in the humid airs of Darien, disease, internal dissension, lack of suitable food, rumours of imminent Spanish attack, and the Governor of Jamaica's blocking of trade and supplies, were wearing down the colonists to the point when in late June 1699, they resolved to evacuate the place. Meanwhile on 12 May 2 further ships had left Leith, with 300 men on board. These arrived to find the settlement deserted. News of the abandonment reached Edinburgh on 19 September, but the Directors refused to believe it until information came of the survivors, reduced by plague and starvation to a few hundred, at New York, Boston, and Port-Royal in Jamaica. Captain Colin Campbell wrote from Port-Royal on 18 August to the Directors, that: '... an inevitable necessity, occasioned by want of provisions and a great mortality, obliged us, on the 21 June last, to leave our new Settlement in Caledonia,'[11] but a different gloss was put on it by three colonists writing from Boston on 23 September, blaming the misfortune on 'a viperous brood' of Jacobites, papists, and atheists, adding that '... the grief has broke Mr Paterson's heart and brain, and now he's a child.'[12] Before Campbell's letter arrived, a third squadron of four ships, with around 1,300 men, had been despatched. Arriving at the end of November, they found the colony still abandoned, but a few survivors of the first expedition had returned from New York in a small vessel, hoping to re-establish themselves. Fort St Andrew was partially renewed and its batteries restored. Accompanying this squadron as its minister was Alexander Shields, who had been as pleased to leave the country as some were to see him go; but the City of God was not to be erected in Darien: '... there was never a Colony in the world settled with more wicked debauchees,' he wrote on 2 February 1700.[13] The Spanish were closing in, and although a skirmish was won, their force was vastly greater. On 31 March, the colonists were allowed to leave, with full military honours and their portable property. Of four ships and two smaller vessels, only one ship and a sloop returned to Scotland; the others were wrecked or grounded and many died on the voyage. The total loss of life among the colonists was around 2,000, and £150,000 of paid-up capital had gone for nothing.

The 'court of directors', in February 1700, felt that the original settlement had been forsaken by those 'whose glory it would have been to have perished rather than to have abandoned it so shamefully';[14] and also noted in a simultaneous despatch to the embattled Council of the Colony that, 'The behaviour of our neighbour nation towards our Company and Colony makes this nation more deeply than ever engaged to stand by you and support you in all legal ways.'[15] Clearly the shambles was to be anyone's fault but theirs. But Darien had genuinely been a national venture, and in the glow of hope and anticipatory pride, the inadequacy of the preparations, the failure to give the colonists proper financing, the geopolitical realities, and the nature of the site itself, were comprehensively ignored. Later, in the chasm of humiliation and chagrin, clear analysis was too discomfiting and it was a convenience to blame England and the King for first frustrating, then helping to wreck, Scotland's great venture. It was the 'Mons Meg' story – grandiloquent failure where smaller-scale nimbleness would have been less risky and more useful. Caledonia was left, in Macaulay's words, to the sloth and the baboon,[16] but the Company itself continued, at a modest level of activity, as a trading operation to the East Indies.

Tullibardine, dismissed as a Secretary of State, made himself the leader of an opposition group in the parliament of summer 1698, focusing on the English opposition to the Africa Company, but also demanding a *habeas corpus* act for Scotland. On the King's side, Ogilvie, Argyll and Queensberry vigorously wielded the weapon of patronage and 'pensions' to ensure majorities. The Government was not averse to a *habeas corpus* law but had no intention of letting Tullibardine have the credit for introducing it.[17] In August 1698 Ogilvie, who had been raised to the peerage as Viscount Seafield two months before, wrote to Portland to say that future funds for the army and the civil list were provided for; his only concern was the army arrears, which would require a new tax, either a poll tax, or a tax on pepper.[18] To the annoyance of the hard-pressed gentry, a poll tax was levied in 1699. The Parliament of May 1700 was so stormily obsessed by the Darien scheme (the final debacle not yet known), that it was promptly prorogued, amid vehement protests, and one of Carstares's informants reported that Jacobites were talking of calling a Convention of Estates.[19] Despite overtures from government figures to burgh and shire members, the session resumed that autumn in a new furore over the final collapse of 'Caledonia', and only in February 1701 could it finally be persuaded to vote supply. However self-righteous the feelings were in England, and although William ignored the petitions and addresses sent to him from Scotland, the ferment of anger and recrimination could not be disregarded. Inevitably, William Carstares was sent up to Scotland to help calm the rage. He remained there from October 1699 to March 1700: a long time to be away from the King's side. Darien touched his own family as it did almost every household with money to invest: William Dunlop had been a director of the Africa Company and had persuaded the professors of Glasgow University to invest £500. The stress of involvement may have hastened his death, which happened soon after Carstares had gone south again. In June a friend wrote to Carstares from Edinburgh that 'Since you went from this, things are grown worse rather than better... God help us, we are ripening for destruction. It looks very like Forty-One.'[20] For ravished pride, there was no healing, for the sense of abandonment by the King, there were the beckoning Jacobites; but for lightened moneychests, there was the thought that the Act enabling the Africa Company had included a clause which engaged the King to exert his authority to obtain reparation for any damage suffered by the Company, 'and that at the public charge'.[21] Scotland's Treasury most certainly did not have such funds at its disposal.

Even as much of the country's capital[22] went gurgling down the drain of Darien, there were successive years of disastrous failure of the harvest between 1694 and 1699, a mini 'ice age'. No grain surplus was available for export, and there was not enough to feed the country. With cultivators'

James Ogilvie, 1st Earl of Seafield
Reproduced from *The Seafield Papers*

rents paid very largely in kind,[23] the required contributions could not be made, squeezing landowners' incomes and the whole marketing process. For many people, famine quickly became a reality rather than a threat, and, with nothing to eat, and no money to buy food, families in desperation took to the roads, hoping to scrape by on the charity of those more fortunate. Under the Poor Law, the burden of care fell on the Kirk Sessions, which fulfilled their obligations with widely varying energy and success. The purges after 1690 had left the Kirk in disarray in many parishes, and none had resources to meet the level of need. Ministers tended to interpret the disasters of nature as divine punishment for the people's sins and for them fasts – for those who had food – and humiliations were the ready answer. Some commissioners of supply, as in Selkirkshire, helped by raising a local stent or tax to buy grain, though the heritors did their best to evade it.[24] Import duty was taken off grain and efforts were made to fix its price, but farmers and merchants found the chance of profiteering hard to resist, and in some places the price even of oats rose ten-fold.[25] In 1696 the Government made a cash purchase of £100,000 worth of grain from England in order to improve supply and stabilise the market;[26] presumably this was recouped in sales, but it exacerbated the shortage of coin in circulation.

This was a far greater disaster than Darien, directly affecting vastly more people. Andrew Fletcher of Saltoun, whig politician and constitutional theorist, estimated that 1 person in 6, or 200,000 in total, were begging on the roads, half of them regular 'nomads', half victims of the famine. In his view, one of the reasons for establishing a colony was to export the surplus population.[27] The vagrant poor had always been there, and even if their numbers had doubled, the effect on the political nation, concerned with its 'We wuz robbed' howls about Darien, seems not to have been very strong. In August 1698, Seafield wrote to Carstares that 'this nation was never in so low a condition, for they have neither money nor bread', though in the next sentence he congratulates himself that 'we have rouped [auctioned] the excise this day for 40,000 pounds', more than enough to maintain the army.[28] In economic terms, a memorandum on the state of 'funds for the forces' drawn up under Seafield's auspices for the King in July 1700 noted that the land tax, normally worth £10,000 quarterly, would only yield £6,500 because of 'the badness of the crops and low condition of the country'.[28] Over the next few years there are reports of empty holdings in rural areas and it is very likely that overall population numbers were falling at this time.[30]

What lasting impact those catastrophic years had on the nation as a whole is perhaps impossible now to assess: Patrick Walker, one of the few articulate voices from among the people, graphically traced the effects of famine in the progress from anxiety to panic, then listlessness, anomie and death. A stout apologist for the Covenanters, he noted that the sufferers 'could think of nothing but food, and being wholly unconcerned whether they went to heaven or hell, the success of the gospel came to a stand.'[30] These were not loose, idle people, but the labouring poor, abandoned by almost everyone and every institution.

CHAPTER THIRTY-FOUR

Questions of Succession

PARLIAMENT'S FAILED ATTEMPT TO exercise a degree of sovereignty in the case of the 'Company for Africa' left resentful feelings. When on 20 June 1700 belated news came that the Darien Scots had won a skirmish against the advancing Spaniards, a jubilant Edinburgh mob (unaware as yet of the evacuation) staged a night- and day-long rampage. Any window not showing a light to celebrate the 'victory' was smashed, and Seafield's house received particular attention. Recriminations ensued with London on the mildness of punishments inflicted on such few of the demonstrators as could be identified and caught.[1] Beneath this fever, vital questions needed answering. How could Scotland develop as an independent state in a world of expanding horizons, when English policy, under a shared king, frustrated its projects? What kind of future was there, in asserting that independence? Why was it so difficult to cast off the 'poor relation' role and gain at least a modest prosperity? The notion that 'the crowns of England and Scotland are incompatible' had been raised during the Darien episode,[2] and would not go away.

From here on the 'Union discourse', at first sporadic, but increasingly intense and fraught, full of loose ends, mingling history and hot air, passionate and reasoned argument, personal positionings and factional posturings and shiftings, was a constant theme. It was also a 'separation' discourse – something too easily forgotten. Disjointed and untidy as it was, it is possible to see it in terms of actual problems, proposed solutions, available tools, and complicating factors.

Scotland's perceived problems were: a national economy stuck below even its normal (in western European terms) low level, its depression accentuated by a shortage of money in circulation; the crippling of international trade; the lack of free trade with England and its colonies; unconsulted involvement in English wars; the need to provide for a monarchy after Queen Anne; and political disunity and uncertainty created by the existence of the Jacobite court in exile.

Proposed solutions were: a treaty to regulate trade with England (with many variants as to the terms) quite separate from the succession question; a trade treaty linked with agreement on a continuing shared monarchy; a federal union preserving the Parliaments of both countries under one monarch; an 'incorporating union' merging the identities of both nations; and the retention of full – indeed enhanced – national sovereignty under a separate (Stuart or other) Scottish monarchy.

To be legitimate, new arrangements would have be made and passed by the two national Parliaments, as custodians of each nation's sovereignty, within the terms of the Revolution Settlement and of two unwritten constitutions.

Complicating factors were many and helped mightily to confuse the basic issues since they were intimately linked to shifting individual and group interests and attitudes. Among the key ones were: the substantial numbers of Scots in the English army; the high rate of 'brain drain' emigration into England and abroad; the extent to which leading Scottish figures also had land and titles in England – various threads of union already in place. Then there was war with France, which was backing the Jacobite cause; the sense of time and opportunity slipping by; national feeling on both sides, which among the Scots slipped into an anti-English animus; and the separate Church organisations, with Scottish anxieties about the survival of their Presbyterian system.

Union of course was not a new topic: it had been floated several times during the 17th century, and had been enforced between 1651 and 1660. Periodic flirtations with the idea might have gone on indefinitely if the problems had not constellated in a way that meant they had to be dealt with in one package. For England, a shared monarchy, permanent exclusion of the Catholic Stuarts, and the neutralisation of any possible Scottish-French pact were of prime importance and other things were negotiable to assure them. In Scotland, the expansion of trade and commerce was the first priority – this was the only point of general agreement – and unionist Scots were willing to make concessions on some other issues once this was satisfactorily dealt with. On both sides of the border, it was a pragmatic affair, but still only possible because of a mutual familiarity and involvement which had become much greater since 1689. The royal succession became the central issue – both countries had to resolve this, and for the Scots it was their main bargaining counter. It was also an area of sharply argued disagreement for them, spilling over into debate on what sort of monarchy was right for Scotland. Serious discussion of union thus became unavoidable.

The country was not on its uppers. Darien, though a heavy blow, had by no means bankrupted the nation, and after the 'ill years' harvests were coming back to normal. Seafield's chamberlain reported to him from Banffshire in July 1701 that food prices had fallen dramatically and there was an unsellable surplus, though 'All kind of cattle sell extraordinarily dear, and the country commodities are far beyond the former prices, but money is the only thing scarce.'[3] Linen yarn and cloth were by now the main export earner, worth some £45,000 annually, with black cattle bringing in around £22,000, and salmon £11,000.[4] Efforts were being made to regain traditional European markets like Holland and France which had been largely hedged off by protectionist trade policies, or war. In the summer of 1701 Alexander Cunningham, a Scottish trade commissioner, was negotiating with the French Government for restoration of Scotland's fish exports to France.[5] Big ideas were not lacking – Carstares's agent, 'J. Stewart', reported in September 1700 that a vast new trading scheme was in design, involving William Paterson, who had clearly bounced back from his breakdown in Caledonia; proposing to raise over £300,000 for trading, manufactories and fishing and not least 'To employ all the poor in the nation; so that, in two years time, there shall not be one beggar seen in all the kingdom, and that without any act of slavery.'[6] No more was to be heard of this marvel, but on a more mundane level, trade was gradually recovering, particularly with the Baltic countries. Daniel Defoe in 1706 reckoned the whole Scottish merchant fleet at 93 vessels, none of more than 180 tons, but up to 30 Scottish ships might assemble off Gothenburg to return home in convoy.[7] Ironically, a good deal of Scotland's capital was fuelling commerce outside Scotland, as shippers and traders co-operated, mainly in family- or locality-based networks, to operate factories and trade routes across northern Europe.[8]

Internal marketing had been disrupted by the long agricultural crisis, and some small towns had decayed into hamlets. Writing in December 1704 from the 'land of cakes' to the Duke of Hamilton in London, George Lockhart feared that in a little time, 'we shall have nothing left but cakes, for money is a great rarity' and added that the Abbey Close in Edinburgh, the bankrupts' sanctuary, was 'throng just now with broken lairds and tradesmen'.[9] One modern authority describes the economy at this time as remaining 'flat, if not stagnant',[10] and it was clearly a very mixed picture.

Jacobitism was a powerful force, its Highland, Catholic and Episcopalian core constituency perhaps enlarged by people who felt that a better deal for business would be got under a different regime. With English policy firmly pro-Hanover, no Scottish Jacobite could be a unionist at this time, though of course the Stuarts retained their claim over all three kingdoms. Anti-Jacobitism remained the majority view, across a spectrum from mild to obsessive. The Kirk knew its status to be guaranteed by William's kingship but was resolute in patrolling the boundaries of its own authority. The *Gaidhealtachd* was a receding ice-cap as Lowland speech and commercial interests spread north and west. Better-off burghers and the shire gentry were becoming very aware of the possibility of higher living standards with a wider range of domestic comforts, more varied diet and drinks, pleasant amenities, boarding schools for girls as well as boys – things that had to be paid for in cash. The nobility needed capital to modernise their houses and estates in ways which were not only now possible, but becoming imperative for reasons of economic survival and family prestige. For them, as for many of the gentry, the service of the state was the way to procure this, but they were too numerous for all to be satisfied. And the Treasury, with customs duties as an important resource, had been depleted by the low level of trade and by endemic smuggling. Salaries and payments were falling into arrears. Another cadre of society was the 'hungry graduate' group of teachers, tutors, domestic chaplains and clerks who had first come to notice as the curates of 1662 and whose importance in attitude and opinion-forming should not be underestimated. In the 1690s they had begun a 'brain-drain' into England, notably of medical men, that would gather pace through the 18th century.

The 'situation' of 1700 onwards belonged to these disparate, overlapping groups since, in their various ways, they had influence on what might happen. In turn their restless and not over-happy society was affected by ideas and attitudes of the time. Self-interest in classes and factions occluded the spirit of 'commonweal' once prized by Sir David Lindsay. The old debate between absolute power and constitutional monarchy was replaced by a new one about the limitations of kingship, maintained vigorously by Andrew Fletcher. And although Presbyterians and Episcopalians continued to attack each other in print and sometimes in person, the more secular, more materialist – what was becoming a more scientific – spirit was also shaping attitudes. Scottish enterprise and commercial ability were ready and able to exploit opportunities in an expanding, richer world; and the more dynamic operators were not waiting for the obstacles to be removed, but making their own chances. Merchants from Glasgow and Greenock moved into the transatlantic slave trade.

Parliament's injured sense of prestige was given an opportunity in July 1700 when the teenage Duke of Gloucester died. He was the last surviving child of Princess Anne, sister of William's deceased co-sovereign. Anne, aged 35, was next in line for the throne, but after her – what? The Stuarts back? England was already in process of identifying a Protestant succession through the Electress Sophia of Hanover, 70 years old, a grand-daughter of James VI and I, who had a grown-up family. Her eldest son, George, was 40, with a teenage son. Lord Seafield cannot have been the only person to hope that William would remarry and beget an heir,[11] though Jacobite propagandists had been mocking the King's alleged impotence since 1689.[12] When James VII died in 1701, his 13-year-old son immediately became a potential James VIII – and III – and Jacobite hopes were inflated by France's recognition of his royal titles.

King William died on 8 March 1702, while war against France, on a European scale, was getting under way, and Anne was proclaimed Queen, as provided in the Act of Succession. Even as she took the coronation oath in London, political controversy was erupting. Parliament was was not in session at the time of William's death, and a statute of 1696 required it to meet within 20 days, and a new Parliament to be elected within six months, of the new accession. Political uncertainty in England, knowledge of Scottish opposition to the war, and the Government's doubts about being able to manage affairs in Parliament, prompted the Queen's advisers not to summon Parliament but to formally adjourn it, thereby hoping to give it a sort of legal existence. Despite the protests of the Country Party, and a personal appeal to the new queen by the Duke of Hamilton, 26 May was set as the date for it to reconvene.

Anne's sympathy with episcopalianism was well-known, and though William Carstares retained his royal chaplaincy, his years of court influence were at an end. Viscount Stair, by contrast, was immediately appointed to the Privy Council. He had resumed a full place in public life in 1700. That the Dalrymple influence had not diminished in his years of lying low was shown by the fact that his brother Hugh became Lord President of the Court of Session in 1698, and his brother David became Solicitor-General. Dalrymple's title was raised to that of Earl of Stair in April 1703; he had always known the value of an English connection and made himself a useful informant and adviser to Sidney Godolphin, the Queen's chief minister. Scottish politicians quickly found that Godolphin's door was now the one they must sit outside. Carstares's experience, knowledge and discretion – and status as a leader of moderate Presbyterianism – maintained him as a personage of weight both in London and Edinburgh. For a year he remained in London, then on 12 May 1703 was elected by Edinburgh Town Council to be Principal of the 'Town's College', at an annual salary of 1,600 merks, increased to 2,200 when in September 1704 he was also made an additional minister to the Greyfriars Church.[13]

Among William's last words had been a recommendation to unite Scotland and England. Queen Anne, who cared no more for Scotland than her brother-in-law had, took up this advice, though opinion in her own court, England's Parliament, and the country at large, was generally hostile to the idea. In Scotland, there were mixed views and feelings. Some felt a distaste for pursuing political union, since it seemed to confer a supplicant status on the Scots. What would nowadays be called 'a level playing field' in trade would have resolved the matter for most people, without further links. Despite lukewarm enthusiasm on both sides of the border, a bill for a treaty of union was incorporated in the programme for the 1702 Parliament, to which the Duke of Queensberry, as front man of the court party, was made Commissioner. But the rug was pulled from under him when the Duke of Hamilton, front man of the country party, walked out with 74 followers as soon as the session opened, claiming it to be illegal under the statute of 1696. The remaining members duly ratified the Queen's title (no Scottish coronation was proposed), and passed acts for supply and for appointing Commissioners to negotiate union. From outside, the country party bellowed the illegality of the proceedings. All this set the tone for the next three years.

Hamilton, aged 44 in 1702, is a hard man to read. In as far as there was a leader of the opposition to Union, he was it. Articulate but indecisive, behind his vacillations and protestations, self-interest was consistent, but he lacked the will and capacity to weld the disparate anti-union elements into a purposeful bloc. Meanwhile, beneath the storm of 1702, and others to come, some more formidable men had begun working steadily and consistently for accomplishment of a political union, and they included Stair, William Carstares, and Lord Seafield, who was made Lord Chancellor in 1702. Seafield had been backed by Stair from his first official post as Sheriff of Banff in 1692. All three had links with Godolphin and Robert Harley, England's Secretary of State from 1704. Their motives and views of ways and means were not necessarily identical, and their opinions on other matters might diverge widely. From Stair's surviving comments, he seems to have believed that, in an embattled and apportioned world, Scotland was too weak to survive and the only way for its people to be provided with the accoutrements of a modern state was by full union. Carstares was concerned for the Presbyterian Church. Seafield had always been a court politician – in 1695 he had written to Carstares that he was prepared to be ordered by the King 'as to the method of serving him as is my duty',[14] but his work for union was consistent and whole-hearted. Queensberry, despite occasional bucking and prancing, was also focused on union, and others too, including Lord Tarbat and William Paterson, were active union campaigners. Beneath the arguments and shifting party groups, these men, not always acting in concert or sharing one another's confidence, made a significant driving force.

With the prospect of union suddenly imminent, the debate came to dominate all other public issues. Pamphlets ensured that the arguments on all sides were not confined to the political class; everyone who cared could keep in touch with the debate. Members of Parliament for shires and burghs had to explain things, and listen to, influential locals, not least the parish ministers. Overhanging the discussions was the shadow of England, the potential partner, the actual obstacle – to some, the enemy. What England wanted, what England would tolerate, could not be left out of the account. English determination to preserve the shared monarchy, under the House of Hanover, was already clear, if unstated in plain terms. Ancient claims of supremacy were asserted by a few pamphleteers, but Godolphin was wise enough not to exacerbate an already dangerous situation. In Scotland, the intellectual and historical case for separation, with a monarchy of limited powers, was put vigorously, in and out of Parliament, by Andrew Fletcher, and by George Ridpath's *Historical Account of the Ancient Rights and Power of the Parliament of Scotland* and other pamphlets.[15]

On 10 November 1702, the commissioners for union met at Westminster. Though the original impetus had come from the court, a Tory majority in the House of Commons was unenthusiastic both about union with a Presbyterian state and the Scots' interest in recovering their Darien losses. Apathy on the part of the English commissioners let the meetings drift to a stop on 3 February 1703 and never resume.

CHAPTER THIRTY-FIVE

An Unruly Parliament

BUT THE 'SITUATION' HAD not gone away. The dubious proceedings of the 1702 Parliament did nothing for the reputation of Queensberry as a political manager or for the status of the court party. But, after its grand gesture, the country party, composed as it was of magnates with conflicting personal interests, proceeded to fall apart. That autumn, one of its leading members, John Hay, second Marquis of Tweeddale, who had inherited his title in 1697, went to London to open up his own dialogue with the Government. Inconclusive then, it would have significant results later. Unsuccessful efforts had been made in the May 1702 Parliament to impose an 'oath of abjuration' against the claims of James VIII, which all office-holders would have had to swear. Consequently, Jacobite sympathisers were able to contest the election of autumn 1702 which, after 14 years, produced a new Parliament, though it did not meet until May of the following year.

This was the last Parliament to ride in procession to the Parliament House,[1] and in it three main groupings appeared, the court interest, the country party, and a new set of faces, the cavalier party, about 70- strong, loyal to the Queen but strongly Jacobite in their views on the succession. Between them, cavaliers and country party outnumbered the court party,[2] a tricky situation for Queensberry, who was again Commissioner. The cavaliers were on the side of the struggling episcopalians, while the court party, needing an alliance with the cavaliers to dish the country party, tried to balance the presbyterian commitment of some its members with nods and winks to the episcopalians. But the presbyterian element of the court party, led by the first Duke of Argyll (the 10th earl had been promoted in 1701) and the now reformed Annandale (rewarded by a marquisate in 1701), both alarmed by the rise in Jacobite and episcopalian influence, refused to support Lord Chancellor Seafield and Queensberry in this tight-rope walking exercise. The session disintegrated into noisy separate interest groups.

With the question of union in partial eclipse, the royal succession

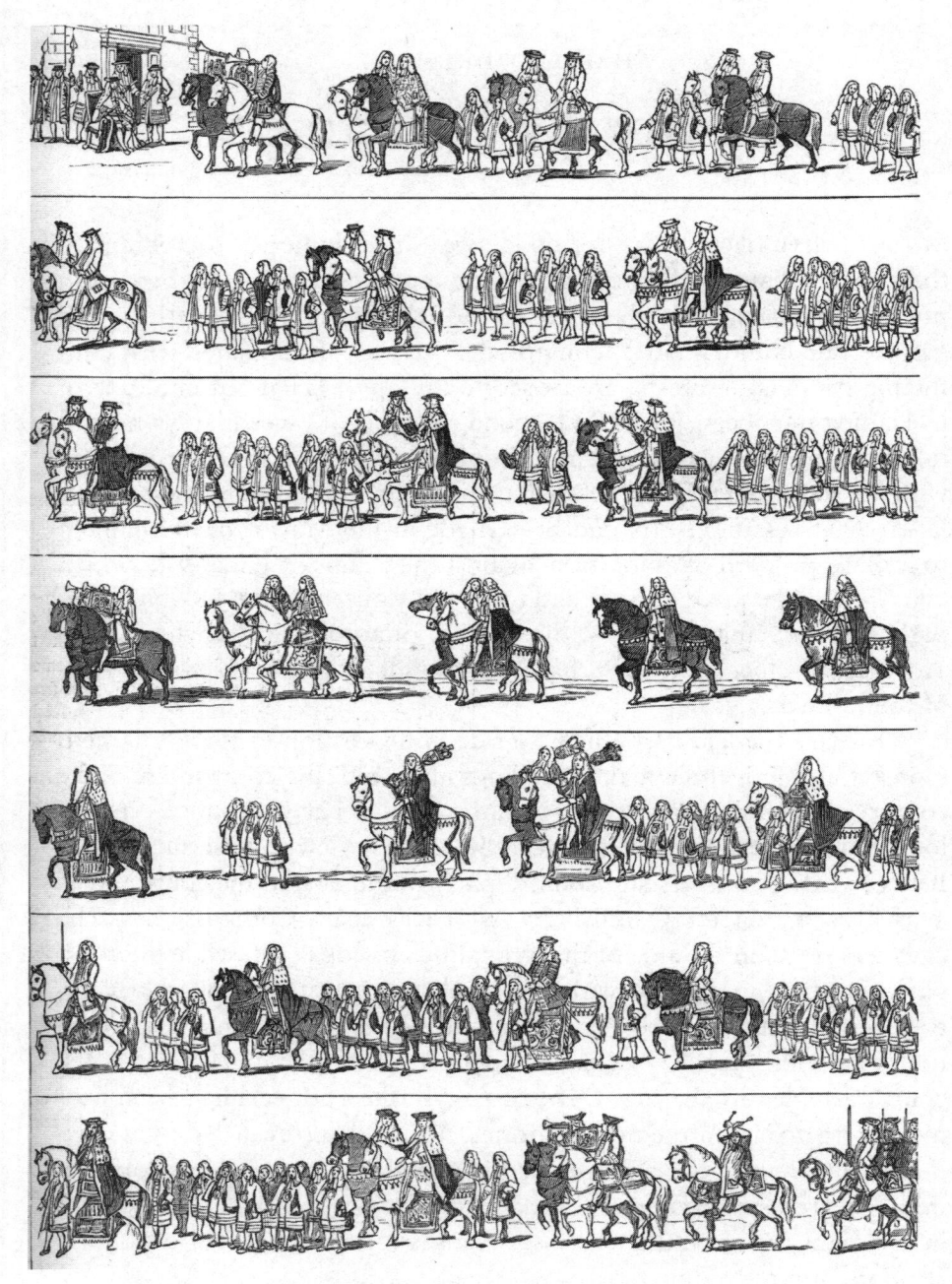

The Riding of the Parliament
Reproduced from *Cassell's Old & New Edinburgh*

was the prime issue. To the acute discomfiture of the court party, no vote for supply was passed, and instead there emerged two Acts certain to arouse anger in England. The Act Anent Peace and War provided that Scotland should not enter any war without the approval of its Parliament. The Act of Security set out the conditions for selecting a royal successor, including a clause which provided for the separation of the English and Scottish monarchies on the death of Queen Anne, unless by that time the Scots had full freedom of trade with England and England's colonies. A further clause provided for the arming and regular military drill of 'fencible men who are Protestants'.[3] Although justified as pre-emptive action against a Jacobite rising, the measure was seen as preparation against any English invasion. These days of debate were the most passionate the Parliament was ever to know, with great issues at stake and a majority in vociferous opposition to the Queen's Commissioner and the court party. From the country party, John Ker, 23-year-old fifth Earl of Roxburghe, shouted that if no vote was allowed on the Act Anent Peace and War, they would enforce it with their swords.[4] On 17 September, following a stormy debate resounding with cries of 'Liberty, no subsidy!' Queensberry prorogued the Parliament without having gained a vote of supply. It was a triumph for the combined opposition groups, and Queensberry claimed from evidence given to him by Simon Fraser, the future Lord Lovat, that all who had opposed him were part of a Jacobite conspiracy.[5]

For the promoters of union, it was a heavy setback. The Queen was affronted and her English ministers annoyed. Harley, while professing himself 'a well-wisher and a servant to the nation' asked in a long letter to Carstares whether the Scots really expected England 'to be bound by a collateral act of another nation... Are men in earnest? Does any single person believe this is the way to procure what they really desire?'[6] Harley added a very pertinent question – 'Whether, under a King of their own, the power of the nobles must not be increased, and the liberty of all the rest of the people proportionally diminished?' – which was also exercising Andrew Fletcher of Saltoun. Although the 'Jacobite Conspiracy' was eventually exposed as a fabrication of Fraser's, leaving Queensberry in deep discredit in London, the investigations uncovered enough of the actual Jacobite ant-hill to fuel English alarm about the general situation in Scotland. A well-developed Jacobite communication system existed, abetted by Scotland's senior naval officer, Captain Thomas Gordon, who 'was not averse, under the influence of the Countess of Errol, from putting his telescope to his blind eye when a French ship brought over Jacobite political agents to Scotland. Fourteen signals were agreed on between Captain Gordon and and the captain of the French frigate *Audace*... whereby they could recognise and avoid each other.'[7]

For the unionists, to see Queensberry lose a second Parliament must have been galling, but he remained their major asset. His prestige and that of the court party were closely linked, he considered himself to be the country's premier nobleman, and he had a substantial personal following, bound to him by kinship, past favours, and future expectations. But for the moment, he was stranded, and other big fish must be tried as leaders, even if they were less reliable in what were, admittedly, murky waters. Stair, it seems, had given up any hope in the Parliament at all, and was widely rumoured to have proposed that no further Parliament should be called until after the Queen's death, and that in the meantime, English funds should pay for a standing army in Scotland.[8] At this time around 3,000 regular troops were stationed in the country.[9]

The possibility of English *force majeure* helped some of the country party to remember that there was more at stake than saying 'Boo!' to the Duke of Queensberry. Seafield, by dint of much diplomacy, got Tweeddale to come out as the leader of a 'New Party' which, it was hoped, would bring a large element of the country party together with those of the court party. His aide in this was James Johnston, who returned to Edinburgh as Lord Clerk Register; Stair and Carstares appear to have kept their faith in Queensberry, still on the sidelines. Their judgement was correct: the session which opened on 6 July 1704 with Tweeddale as commissioner, was no more helpful to the cause of union than the previous ones. Even the reduced Government aims, of getting the Hanoverian succession agreed, and a vote of supply passed, were not achieved. Opposition votes ensured that supply was linked to the Act of Security from 1703, which (unlike the Act Anent Peace and War) had not been given the royal assent, and left the court to decide if it would swallow the pill to get the medicine. Godolphin reluctantly sent the Queen's agreement and the acts of supply and security were both touched with the sceptre on 5 August 1704. Efforts to nominate commissioners to treat with the English Parliament collapsed amid recriminations about the Jacobite affiliations of some potential members of the delegation, and the session ended acrimoniously on 28 August with a protest to the Queen about meddling in Scottish affairs by the House of Lords, which had been conducting its own enquiry into the 'Jacobite Plot'.

For unionists, the prospects did not look good and were to get worse. But the commitment of the small but powerful pressure-group with Seafield, Stair and Carstares at its core was intensified by the political disarray revealed in the 1704 session. They knew that the intentions of the majority were mixed. Many were not against political union, but simply wanted to get the best deal, as they saw it. Others opposed simply because they belonged to the by-passed Queensberry faction. James Johnston lost his post and returned with relief from the tumults of Edinburgh to his garden in Twickenham, but continued to be an ally of the unionists. Seafield's next choice, abetted by Carstares's persuasions, to manage the Parliament was the 25-year-old John Campbell, second Duke of Argyll, whose father had died in 1703.

In the early spring of 1705 the state of public feeling became clear. An English ship, *Worcester*, having anchored off Leith to make repairs, was seized in a tit-for-tat action after a Scottish Company ship, *Annandale*, bound for the East Indies, had been held in the Downs.[10] Soon it was being claimed, on dubious evidence, that *Worcester* and its captain, Thomas Green, had attacked the Africa Company's vessel *Speedy Return*, which had disappeared on a voyage to the East Indies. Green and his crew were arrested on piracy charges and in March 1705 he and 14 others were found guilty and sentenced to hang. A row that had been simmering for months now exploded, with angry protests in England, and equally loud demands from the Edinburgh mob for prompt execution. Two messages went from the Queen to the Privy Council requesting stay of execution until further evidence could be considered. At this time, Anne also accepted the English Parliament's 'Act for the effectual securing the Kingdom of England from the apparent dangers that may arise from several acts lately passed in the Parliament of Scotland'. Known as the 'Aliens Act', it was partly a response to the Act of Security and laid down that if the Scots did not settle the question of succession by 25 December 1705, they would be declared aliens in England, and the importing of Scottish coal, cattle and linen would be banned. Though the Scots had started this particular game, it was seen 'a gross provocation',[11] but suddenly the stakes were raised far beyond their power to reply, except, perhaps, by going to war. Since the Scottish regiments were with Marlborough in Europe, hammering the French, this was only a fantasy option.[12]

On 10 April, Seafield convened a Council meeting to discuss what to do about the *Worcester* sentences, but around half the Councillors excused themselves, and of the 14 who attended, 7 refused to vote. Wanting to get a reprieve, the Chancellor could only get seven others to put their names to the document, and nine signatures were needed. Demonstrators, avid to see Englishmen swing, attacked Seafield's coach as he left the meeting. The first three sentences had to be carried out, and Green and two of his crew were hanged. After that, the mob's rage quickly abated, and the other condemned men were eventually reprieved on 15 September. From this deeply unsavoury episode, only Seafield emerges with any credit, but the calibre of his Council colleagues is all too clearly shown. '... had these persons been never so innocent, the council could not have saved them with endangering their [councillors'] lives', wrote George Baillie of Jerviswood (one of those who refused to vote) to the Earl of Roxburghe on the following day.[13] Afterwards, each party blamed the other for allowing it to happen.

The determination of the populace to make a violent and assertive gesture at England shows a deep sense of frustration. Lived experience, as well as percolation of theories of political structures, had made the Scots, whether voters or not, into a more sophisticated but also more disoriented political body in 1705 than they had been 20 years earlier. All around them, the horizon was misty, except for one known quantity – England. By its actions, by its very existence, England had been instrumental in creating the unappealing situation in which the Scots had been floundering for 3 – or 103 – years. It was hardly to be expected that their attitude would be anything other than hostile. One lesson of the *Worcester* incident was surely not lost on Seafield, Stair and Carstares: while delaying or derailing tactics were being used in Parliament by people keen to slow down or kill the idea of union, there was a risk of government by the mob. Civil disorder might be useful to a Hamilton, but not to the court politicians. Union had to become the top priority. But they had to drive it through Parliament, using every means at their disposal.

Whoever might take the credit, by mid-1705, the debate had taken an important step forward. The Parliament of 1704 had foundered in attempts to resolve the situation without a union. Now, the idea that the succession and trade questions could be resolved without some form of political union, was pushed aside. The middle ground was made untenable, as the architects of union successfully brought matters to the point where the form of union was being discussed rather than whether union was necessary.[14]

Reassembling on 28 June 1705, with Argyll, arrogant, nervous, but determined to make his mark, as Commissioner, Parliament was again loosely divided into three groups, the court party, the cavaliers, and what still called itself the New Party but was by now more generally labelled the 'Squadrone Volante', with Tweeddale as its leading figure – the 'flying squad', at best unattached, at worst ready to take off in any direction at any time. The term began inauspiciously for the unionists, with dispute resuming on the old pattern: the court party trying to get an Act to confirm the royal succession and the others demanding first to discuss currency and trade. Parliament took time to listen to, and reject, proposals for a 'paper currency' from John Law, later to gain notoriety in France. A motion from Hamilton, proposing that no royal successor should be nominated until a commercial treaty had been made with England, and certain constitutional questions settled, was passed, helped through by Queensberry's friends in the absence of the Duke. He arrived from London almost a month after the session had begun, with an air of consequence about him. He had been made Lord Privy Seal and on his arrival, his supporters were placed on the side of the Government, and his suavity helped smooth out the debate.

On 31 July the Act for a treaty of union was 'put aside' by only three votes. Godolphin became impatient enough to hint to Seafield on 9 August that England might make the kind of military 'visits' that Scotland used to make into England.[15] Seafield is unlikely to have shown this to many people: such a threat, and the impending effect of England's Aliens Act could not be ignored, but the temper of the Parliament was not likely to let it be strong-armed into union. After further intense discussion, persuasions, promises and hesitations, the treaty act got a first reading on 24 August; on the 31st a clause maintaining 'the fundamental laws, rights, and privileges of the nation' was not carried, and on 1 September a clause insisting on no negotiations until England repealed the Aliens Act was also defeated. Instead it was agreed that an Address to the Crown, containing this request, should be presented. A head-on collision between Queen Anne's Scottish and English Parliaments was dexterously avoided. Opponents could console themselves with the thought that the negotiations might collapse as all previous efforts had done. But now, to the dismay of his own country party followers, Hamilton made that failure much less likely. Of his own accord he introduced a motion, which the unionists gladly accepted, that the Scottish commissioners to negotiate a treaty should be nominated by the Queen, not by Parliament. 'The Duke no doubt hoped in this way to secure his own nomination'[16] – if so, it was in vain. His own explanation was that it would be easier to criticise the work of externally chosen delegates. But, like a channel in pack-ice, the way to successful negotiation was now open.

Stair and Carstares now helped to get Queensberry back into the driving seat; and Argyll went off to renew a distinguished military career with Marlborough. Two hurdles remained for the unionists, to get a satisfactory draft treaty, and to see it through both Parliaments. They were helped by the timely repeal of the Aliens Act in England. The 31 commissioners, with the sole exception of the Jacobite George Lockhart of Carnwath, who was somewhat baffled by his inclusion,[17] were men who were not expected to balk if incorporating union were insisted on by the other side. This ruled out Squadrone members, despite their previous support: they were federalists.[18] Led by Seafield and Queensberry and strongly supported by Stair, who with his brothers Hugh and David was also included, the commissioners, Lockhart apart, were determined that after the failures and false starts of the past, there should be a positive conclusion. The alternative to success was very likely to be a breakdown of society into warring factions or even invasion from England. One of many reminders of continuing tension came from Captain Gordon, Jacobite-friendly commander of the *Royal Mary*, one of the country's handful of warships. In June 1706, on his way from England with 'valuable goods of the nobility and commissioners of union', he wrote from Tynemouth to compain to the Earl of Wemyss, newly appointed as Lord High Admiral, that an English navy ship had fired a warning shot at him for displaying a commodore's broad pendant, and reports that he has heard that English ships have Admiralty orders 'to make our frigates strike and salute... I am firmly resolved not to yield one jot, while I have the honour to command.'[19]

Led by Seafield, the commissioners, Stair included, had come to propose a form of federal union confirming only free trade and the Hanoverian succession, as the solution most acceptable to most Scots, though some were already willing to go further. 'I do firmly believe an incorporating union is best for both nations,' Stair wrote to the Earl of Mar, a fellow-commissioner, in January 1706, 'but that may require more time than the present circumstances do allow.'[20]

The English commissioners represented a wider spread of national opinion than their Scottish counterparts, but they too were fully in earnest this time, and their chief negotiator, Lord Somers, a leading Whig and firm constitutionalist, was well chosen as a diplomatist. Beginning work in London on 16 April 1706, the commission got speedily down to business, and immediately it was made clear that the English side would consider only a full incorporating union. Despite deep misgivings about the acceptability of this to their Parliament and nation, the crucial point was accepted by the Scots on 25 April, on condition that free trade was also agreed.

No Scottish ministers were named as commissioners, but naturally, a prime concern in the great Union debate was the security and status of the Presbyterian Kirk, as guaranteed by Parliament 16 years before. It was agreed that the two established Churches would not be provided for in the Articles of Union, but that the continuing post-Union status of each would be confirmed by the two national Parliaments. During the framing stage and then the parliamentary discussion of the Union Treaty, the Kirk's General Assembly had its own commission in force, in order both to represent church views, to react to any developments that affected the Kirk's status, and to keep some check on the ministers. William Carstares was its Moderator,[21] and was in frequent touch with the treaty commissioners. The Church was no more united on the matter than the rest of the nation. Many ministers were hotly anti-Union, and the Covenants were often invoked against what some considered a 'hellish backsliding'.[22]

Carstares wrote to presbyteries to recommend 'they do discountenance and discourage all irregularities and tumults'.[23] Prayer for a right decision was the Church's job, not agitation. To his ally Principal Stirling of Glasgow University he wrote in April 1706 that there was need for 'Great circumspection in our management'[24] – a quality he himself was eminently able to supply. In various ways Presbyterian sensitivities were grated on. English bishops in the House of Lords would have a say in Scottish affairs in the debate at Westminster, the Archbishop of Canterbury had said that though he believed the Church of Scotland was as true a Protestant Church as the Church of England, 'he could not say it was so perfect'.[25] Not the least of Carstares's achievements was to keep the Kirk fairly quiescent at a time of high emotion and contentious debate, and A. I. Dunlop considered that: 'Had the Church thrown its weight and influence against the Union it is exceedingly unlikely that it ever would have passed. At this point, Carstares probably played a decisive part in persuading the ministers not to take action.'[26] In October he wrote to Harley that, '... the desire I have to see our Church secured makes me in love with the Union as the most probable means to preserve it.'[27] As things turned out, this assumption was debatable at the least, but Carstares was preoccupied by what might follow on from the Jacobite restoration which he feared would come if there were no Union.

CHAPTER THIRTY-SIX

Forever After

BY 22 JULY 1706 THE BASIS and elements of Union were set out, in 25 Articles. The Preamble established that the 'Protestant Religion and Presbyterian Church Government' within Scotland was a fundamental and essential condition. Though opponents would claim it was 'putting the oxen behind the plough', Article One was the basis of all that followed: 'That the two Kingdoms of England and Scotland shall upon the first day of May next ensuing the date hereof and forever after be United into One Kingdom by the name of Great Britain'. Article Two laid down the Hanoverian succession, Article Three provided for a single Parliament, and so it went on, to Article Twenty-Five, which pronounced all laws in either Kingdom which failed to conform with the Articles to be null and void. Everything was intended to be secret until laid before the two Parliaments, but the Scots commissioners deliberately let slip that freedom of trade had been agreed, in the hope that this would damp down opposition to the incorporating union.

The historical import was breathtaking. In 1705, everyone accepted Archbishop Ussher's calculation of the world's creation year as 4004BC, and the sense of a long history had always been one of the mainstays of Scottish identity, with pride in being one of the first kingdoms to emerge in Europe – some claimed the first. To write *finis* to more than 1,000 years of nationhood was a momentous action. But the perceived needs were intensely pressing.

Parliament assembled on 3 October, with Queensberry as Lord High Commissioner. The Articles were immediately published, and the session was adjourned for a week for members to ponder them. There had been no new election, so apart from new members brought in through by-elections or aristocratic succession, the membership was very much that which had supported, or opposed, the treaty motion in 1705. Again there were three broad groups, the court party with Queensberry, Seafield and Stair, the cavaliers, and the 'Squadrone'. Titular head of the cavaliers was the Duke of Hamilton, who had had long discussions with a French emissary in the summer of 1705 – in a darkened room, so that he might not be said to have 'seen' him[1] – and was suspected of having his own ambition to become a Protestant King of Scots. More committed Jacobites, though ineffective either as parliamentarians or plotters, were the Earls of Errol and Home. The impossibility of arguing their real cause, without being immediately impeached for high treason, severely limited their strategy. The 'Squadrone' was under pressure from both sides. Tweeddale and his friends had wanted the succession settled, and the limitations of the monarchy agreed and fixed, before union should be agreed, but even before the Articles had been compiled, on 15 December 1705, Roxburghe had written to George Baillie that 'the more I think of union, the more I like it', and Baillie responded rather grudgingly that 'wise men will be forced to drink the potion to prevent greater evils'.[2] Seafield had patronage to dispense: Baillie became a depute treasurer, and another prominent flyer, the Marquis of Montrose, who had flirted with, and jilted, the Jacobites, was made Lord President. As far as anyone could feel confident of undeclared intentions and shifty characters, the unionists knew that with the Squadrone's support, they had a majority.

Into the winter, the debates went on, between different versions of unionism, and separatists. In the war of print, the honours were evenly shared, since respectable arguments could be mustered by all sides, though by no means all the pamphlets reflected this. Daniel Defoe, surely the most un-secret spy in history, wrote an estimated 40 tracts on the Union.[3] Much of the pro-Union literature contained unpalatable truths, such as that for over half a century, Scottish independence, undeniable in law as it might be, had been hardly more than a name. They urged the fact that there would be a new kingdom, with a new flag and new coat of arms to show the honourable union of two countries. For a country with a navy of some four ships, no diplomats, no colonies, mentioned in no treaties, utterly devoid of international standing, was it not greatly preferable to join in wielding the mighty weapons and powerful diplomacy, and exploiting the growing wealth and empire, of a United Kingdom? Though the overall effect of pamphlets on modifying public opinion is unmeasurable, some were influential, like James Hodges's *The rights and interests of the two British monarchies* (1707), a lengthy anti-incorporation tract of which the pro-incorporation Earl of Mar said 'really it has done harm'.[4] Several ministers published anti-union tracts, but the Act of Security, guaranteeing the post-Union status of the Kirk, on 12 November, helped to reduce all but the most extreme Presbyterian opposition to something like neutrality.[5]

Unionist campaigners were startled by the extent and volume of public protest against the treaty. At a meeting of burghs, two-thirds of the delegates rejected the idea of union, but they were said to represent the smaller towns. As in the anxious days of 1637, people from all over the country pressed to Edinburgh, to make representations or merely to feel close to the intensity of the moment. Outside Parliament House, the mob milled about in the icy wind and torch-flared dark to scream abuse at the pro-unionists. Queensberry's coach was regularly mobbed, and once his hand was injured by a flying stone. Demonstrations in Glasgow became riots;[6] Stirling's town guard burned copies of the articles of union on 4 December,[7] and in Dumfries they were publicly burned by a crowd of strict Presbyterians: indeed, for a short time, an unholy alliance of Jacobites and unreconciled Cameronians seemed to threaten an armed rising in the south-west. Public disorder was so tumultuous that Cromartie, after riots in Edinburgh on 18 November, asked for an adjournment of Parliament: Stair spoke up against the alarm of 'fearful friends', and Queensberry pressed on. Inside the House the shouting was rarely as loud as it was outside. Petitions and remonstrances were streaming in, almost all hostile to union; seeing them pile up on the table, the Duke of Argyll, back from his command of the Scottish Brigade, suggested making kites of them.[8]

Despite the impassioned opposition of Fletcher and others who remained convinced that the country could, and should, stand alone; and that of the committed Jacobites, and the more ambiguous behaviour of the Duke of Hamilton, who at one point seems to have almost backed an armed rising and at another pleaded toothache for absenting himself when he was supposed to lead his supporters in a walk-out from Parliament,[9] the key to success or failure, from whichever perspective, was held by the two dozen members of the 'Squadrone', who had kept quiet, in public at least, about their intentions. In the vote on Article One, the government had 93 votes, the opposition 85: had the Squadrone opposed, it would have been lost by some 15 votes. Consequently, Lord Belhaven's famous speech of 2 November was not a last plangent call to the unconverted but a lament for 'our Ancient Mother Caledonia', assassinated by her own children. For almost everyone except perhaps Stair, there was an emotional barrier that had to be passed through, the knowledge that previous generations had shed their blood to keep Scotland independent from England; and also a fear, that if the union went badly wrong, they would be held responsible. 'Patriotism' was often invoked, and any suggestion that the arguers for union were not patriots would have had swords out. Sovereignty, in their view, was not being lost but merged, and implicit in their attitude was an imaginative leap, which lodged their Scottish national feeling within a wider sense of sharing in an entity which as yet did not exist, the 'United Kingdom'.

For the unpersuaded, or uncertain, there was also this consideration – Parliament was not being offered, as in 1689, an 'either-or'. There was only one coherent, viable, well-supported proposition, and to reject it would lead to chaos. Theories of and proposals for a different sort of Scottish kingdom, produced especially by Andrew Fletcher, were too unusual for general approval. Rejection of the treaty articles would leave Scotland with all its divisions exposed and inflamed. Incorporating union was the only show in town.

Belhaven's speech made passing, dismissive references to the 'Equivalents'. As part of the negotiations, teams of mathematicians on both sides, including William Paterson, worked with available records and statistics to reach an equitable formula for merging the economies. England had a national debt, for which the Scots denied liability; and Scotland, though it had nothing as formalised, owed substantial amounts in unpaid salaries and grants, mostly to members of the magnate class for their offices or sinecures. Also, the acceptance of government responsibility for the Africa Company losses had not been forgotten by the investors: only union would see that commitment honoured. It was agreed that the sum of £398,085 should be transferred from England to Scotland, as an 'Equivalent' to compensate for new customs duties and tax levels. The Africa Company was to be dissolved and its capital stock purchased by the Government, ensuring at least partial reimbursement for investors. George Lockhart, a lone critical voice, complained that: 'Scotsmen by this means purchased their own company themselves and made a present of it to the English, since the fund from which this sum had its rise did flow from Scotland.'[10] Arrears of grants and salaries were also to be paid from it, and some was supposed to go in support of new manufactories. Although it was almost four times the Scottish state's annual revenue,[11] the Equivalent melted away with great rapidity, and since the claims of unionists received priority, accusations of bribery very soon arose.

In an age when corruption was institutionalised, deliberate bribery in connection with the union is hard to prove. When all nobles were venal, Scottish nobles were known not so much for that, as for being cheap. A famous letter from Argyll to the Earl of Mar, Secretary of State, on 18 July 1706, often taken as a demand for a bribe, may be only a demand for payment for doing the Government's work: '... when I have justice done me here and am told what to expect for going to Scotland, I shall be ready to obey my lord treasurer's commands.'[12] The Lord Treasurer was Godolphin: Argyll as soldier and politician was already operating in a union nexus. In August, Queensberry, still in London, 'railed at the lord treasurer; said he was not for the Union, &c., but at last a sum of money quieted him'.[13] A loan of £20,000 was guaranteed from England to cover immediate expenses of the Government in Scotland, of which £12,325 was promptly absorbed by Queensberry against his own claimed arrears of payments, and most of the rest appears to have gone to peers with some genuine outstanding claims. There is no doubt that the payments were intended to reinforce their loyalty. But even if the £20,000 is considered to be Queensberry's 'slush fund', most of those who benefited would have voted for the union anyway, and some recipients, like the Duke of Atholl, voted against.[14] The fiery Gaelic bard Iain Lòm Macdonald, who died that year, attacked those said to have been swayed by English gold:

> Earl of Seaforth... If I had my way, truly I would melt gold for you, and inject it into the shell of your skull until it would reach your boots.[15]

– and the 'bribes' became a consistent element in later Jacobite propaganda.

Just as Stair had stood up eloquently for William of Orange's government in 1690 and after, so he did now for Union. Though his speeches have not survived, he was accounted the most formidable defender of the 25 articles as they were debated, voted on, and passed with occasional amendments, one by one. No respecter of the Scottish Parliament, which he considered, with considerable justification, to be 'feudal' (he had been rebuked in 1701 for suggesting that its Acts were worth no more than the decrees of some local baron court),[16] now all his powers were focused on helping it towards its abolition. On 7 January 1707, in the debate on Article 22, representation of Scotland in a British Parliament, he made what the admiring Daniel Defoe described as 'an extraordinary speech', then returned to his house and wrote to his friend Robert Harley in London to say that everything should be concluded within a week. Like Queensberry, he had received death threats, but that night he died in his bed, of a stroke. In death as in life, John Dalrymple had his revilers; to the Jacobite George Lockhart, he was 'at the bottom of the Union' and so 'the Judas of his country';[17] though he conceded that Stair was 'extremely facetious and diverting' in private life,[18] an opinion shared by Macky, who rather surprisingly added: 'He made a better companion than statesman, being naturally very indolent.'[19] The Glen Coe massacre has overshadowed the importance he had in political life throughout a 20-year period. Robert Chambers excluded him (and the Drummond brothers) from his *Scottish Biographical Dictionary* of 1832, though it is not short of badhats.

When the final vote was counted, on 16 January 1707, there were 109 in favour of ratification of the Articles of Union, plus Seafield the Chancellor, whose vote could not be counted, but who insisted on showing where his sympathy lay; and 69 against. To many it seemed, then and later, that Parliament had decided against the will of the people. Perhaps a Parliament elected in 1706 rather than 1702 might have come to a different decision, but, more probably, it would have been 'fixed' to provide a pro-union majority, with the cavalier element excluded, causing far more contention. Although some burghs instructed their commissioners to vote against union, the question of a member's accountability was wide open. When Sir John Dalrymple represented Stranraer, no-one would have supposed that he was there to speak for the views of the town council, and yet he would certainly be expected to watch for the welfare of the burgh. In that final Parliament, the political nation, narrow-based as it was, debated the future of the country as a whole. In as far as they were not overtly Jacobite, the agitation and anger of the Edinburgh crowds, and the demonstrations in other places, reflected Belhaven's sense of dismay that things had somehow come to this: 'I think, I see a Free and Independent Kingdom delivering up That... Power to manage their own Affairs by themselves, without the Assistance and Counsel of any other,' but – like him – they had no clear focus on an alternative way out of the imbroglio. It would be wrong and presumptuous to say that the disturbances were no more than a token howl against the end of sovereignty, a sort of rite of passage. They had lost something obscurely precious, meaningful in a deeply personal way, and were being offered instead citizenship of a hastily invented state with an uncertain future. The union was of Parliaments, not of peoples, and any idea that either nation would abandon its sense of self – Cromartie enthusiastically hoped that both would assume the identity of 'Britich'[20] – was mistaken.

No public acclaim greeted the achievement of Union. Queensberry got most of the credit, or blame, for the result (and the dukedom of Dover, with a pension of £3,000 a year) but the real responsibility lay with the disparate group whose work to achieve union had been tireless and, in some cases at least, without self-interest. Without the pressure, influence and advice of Stair, Carstares, and Seafield (who also received a substantial pension afterwards), Queensberry, for all his own political gifts and personal following, would not have succeeded. He was more than a figurehead, but less than a leader. Indeed, in all the years and travails since 1637, the people of Scotland never produced a man with the combination of personality, policy, conviction and moral stature that could dominate the nation's affairs. But Bruces (or, as Carlyle noted, Cromwells) are rare creatures. Ratification by the English Parliament went through both Houses with vastly greater ease, the smoothness of the proceedings showing how little difference the union was expected to make to the tenor of their ways. Royal assent was given to the Act on 4 March, and the English ratification was read to Parliament on the 19th, when Seafield, having signed the exemplification of the Act, made his famous and presumably rehearsed remark, as he handed it to the Lord Clerk Register, 'Now, there's ane end of an auld sang.'[21] Parliament held its final session on 28 April, and Queensberry set off from a subdued and depressed Edinburgh for London, enjoying such triumphal receptions on his way through England as no Scotsman had received since James VI in 1603. On the first of May 1707 the day came as James Renwick had prophesied, when Scotland did get rid of Scotland, though not in the sense that he had anticipated; and the deliverance that resulted would be very different to what both supporters and opponents of union had imagined.

The 70 years centred on the 'Killing Time' were inaugurated by one significant document and closed by another. Some people, like the great survivor Cromartie, who died in 1714 aged 84, could recall, for the post-Union children of the 18th century, the excitement of the Covenant years. Of the group born in 1648–9 whose lives helped form that era, and were themselves shaped by it, none attained the Biblical span of years. Melfort and Perth both died in exile, in 1714 and 1716 respectively. Carstares lived in Edinburgh, a much respected Principal of the University, whose continuing modernisation and expansion he oversaw. He remained the senior statesman of the Church of Scotland, of whose General Assembly he was four times elected as Moderator. In July 1707, aged 59, he went to London to renew some old acquaintanceships, and to savour the new structure in whose foundations he had laboured. Still a royal chaplain, he was kindly received by Queen Anne, who presented him with a silver medal struck to commemorate the Union. Although Carstares was childless, like a good family man of his time he helped various nephews and and other connections into gainful employment and official sinecures, but for himself, this medal is the only reward he is known to have received apart from official salaries and payments for services rendered. He returned to Edinburgh with eight busy years of life and work ahead of him, before his death in 1715. One would like to know, through a sympathetic interest, whether his hands were permanently damaged. Nobody tells of Principal Carstares's thumbs – perhaps he kept them hidden – and maybe it did not seem quite nice to touch on the subject. Judicial torture was abolished in Scotland in 1710. From the agony in the council chamber, only an apocryphal story remained, of how King William once asked his chaplain to show him the thumbikins. They were produced, the King fitted in his thumbs, and the screws were turned a little – that was enough.

For Carstares's students born around 1700, the times of Lauderdale and Perth must have appeared already dim and remote – a Scotland wilder and stranger than the one they knew, narrower and more intense, where ideas and beliefs were tested in battle and declaimed from the scaffold; and words had been deployed to inflame minds and bind them to a cause that defied strict rationality. In their reasoned, post-Cartesian, Newtonian world, these young citizens of a United Kingdom could feel the constraints loosening about them, with new discoveries, new questions, new opportunities – the heavy elements of the previous century were breaking down into lighter, varied, compoundable forms. In a scarcely noticed adjustment to Europe's unstable political map, an obscure north-western kingdom had disappeared. Scottish identity, sealed in its alembic of slow, subtle transmutation, was given such a terrific jolt as it had not had in 400 years, but the vessel was not broken. The Scotland that confronted the world from 1 May 1707, self-aware, ambitious, rather angry, would enlarge and invigorate western thought in various ways through the decades to come. But it still bore the old lineaments, scars, and disunities. And with these survived the obdurate, proud and apparently inextinguishable sense of a single, if fractured, human community, perpetually emerging from its inescapable, haunted, but not unmalleable past.

Select Glossary of Names and Terms

APOLOGETICAL DECLARATION
Cameronian manifesto of 1684, ascribed to James Renwick.

ARGYLL
Archibald Campbell, 8th Earl and 1st Marquis (1607–61). Executed.

ARGYLL
Archibald Campbell, 9th Earl (1629–85). Executed.

ARGYLL
Archibald Campbell, 10th Earl and 1st Duke (d. 1703).

ARGYLL
John Campbell, 2nd Duke (1680–1743).

ARTICLES, COMMITTEE OR LORDS OF THE
A committee of Parliament, drawn from all three estates, responsible for preparing bills for the full house.

ATHOLL
John Murray, Earl and 1st Marquis (c.1635–1703).

ATHOLL
John Murray, 2nd Marquis and 1st Duke (1659–1724). Earl of Tullibardine to 1703.

BAILLIE, ROBERT (1606–62)
Minister, and reporter of Westminster Assembly.

BAILLIE, ROBERT, OF JERVISWOOD (c.1634–84)
Prominent Presbyterian. Executed.

BISHOPS' WARS
First May–June 1639, ended in Pacification of Berwick. Second, 1640–41, ended with Treaty of Ripon.

CAMERON, EWEN, OF LOCHIEL
Clan Chief and leading Jacobite.

CAMERON, RICHARD (1648–80)
Leader of the Covenanters, whose name was applied to all religious dissidents. Killed in fight at Airds Moss.

CESS
A tax.

COMMITTEE OF ESTATES
An executive body set up by Parliament but including non-members, with powers to act while Parliament was not sitting, and often when it was. Functioned 1640–51; 1660–1 and 1688–9.

CONVENTICLE
A gathering for an illegal form of worship, whether indoors or outside.

CONVENTION OF ESTATES
A Parliament assembled without a royal summons.

COUNCIL
Privy or Secret Council, an executive body to govern the country, its members appointed by the King. Its head was the Chancellor.

COURT OF SESSION
The highest court for civil and criminal cases.

DRUMLANRIG
See Queensberry.

ENGAGERS
Supporters of the agreement of 1647 by which the Scottish government agreed to switch support from England's Parliament to Charles I.

ESTATES
The three social groupings forming Parliament: Nobility, Gentry and Burgesses.

HAMILTON
James Hamilton, 3rd Marquis and 1st Duke (1606–49). Executed after the Battle of Preston.

HAMILTON
William Hamilton, 2nd Duke, previously Lord Lanark (1616–51). Killed in Battle of Worcester.

HAMILTON
William Douglas, 3rd Duke (1635–94), title given for life when he married the heiress of the 1st Duke.

HAMILTON
James Douglas, 4th Duke (1658–1712). Earl of Arran until 1698.

HIGHLAND HOST
An occupying force, mainly of Highlanders, installed in Covenanting districts for a time in early 1678.

INDULGENCE
An official guarantee of freedom from prosecution for certain illegal actions, under specific conditions.

LESLIE
Alexander, 1st Earl of Leven (c.1580–1661). General.

LESLIE
David, Lord Newark from 1661. General, a relative of Rothes (see below).

LESLIE
John, 7th Earl and 1st Duke of Rothes (1630–81).

LOCKHART
Sir George, of Carnwath (c.1630–89). Leading advocate. Murdered.

LOCKHART
George, of Carnwath (1673–1731): son of the above. The sole Jacobite among the Union Commissioners.

MORAY
Sir Robert (c.1600–73). Royalist politician and pioneer of science.

MORAY
Alexander Stewart, 5th Earl (1634–1701). Secretary of State 1680–8.

NORTHERN BAND
An armed royalist group in the Highlands, in 1650.

POPISH PLOT
A supposed Catholic conspiracy of 1678, to assassinate Charles II and put his brother James on the throne.

PROTESTERS
Covenanters who formed a vocal minority in the 1650 and 1651 General Assemblies.

QUEENSBERRY
William Douglas (1637–95), 3rd Earl, 1st Marquis (1682) and 1st Duke (1685).

QUEENSBERRY
James Douglas (1662–1711), second Duke; Lord Drumlanrig until 1695.

REMONSTRANTS
Signatories or approvers of the 'Western Remonstrance' (October 1650).

RESOLUTIONERS
Supporters of the General Assembly's resolution to have the Act of Classes repealed (1650–1).

RYE HOUSE PLOT
An English conspiracy to assassinate Charles II and his brother James, in early 1683.

TOLBOOTH
Civic prison.

TORIES
Royalists of Catholic or Episcopalian persuasion.

WESTMINSTER ASSEMBLY
A body set up by the English Parliament in 1643 to discuss the introduction of a Presbyterian system of church government.

WHIG PLOT
The conspiracy against the accession of James VII and II, 1683–5.

WHIGGAMORES
Strong Presbyterians, almost synonymous with Covenanters after 1660.

WODROW, REV. ROBERT
Minister and Presbyterian historian (1679–1734).

Timeline of Main Events, 1637–1707

1637	King Charles I imposes a new Prayer Book on the Church of Scotland.
	The 'Tables' are set up as a forum of protest.
1638	National Covenant is drawn up. Bishops abandon their sees. General Assembly sits in defiance of royal authority.
1639	First Bishops' War. Pacification of Berwick.
1640	Second Bishops' War. Scots occupy north-east England.
1641	Charles I visits Edinburgh. Scottish army sent to oppose Irish uprising. Treaty of Ripon.
1643	Solemn League and Covenant made with the English Parliament. Observers are sent to Westminster Assembly of Divines.
1644	Committee of Both Kingdoms formed. Scottish army enters England in support of the Parliament. Battle of Marston Moor.
	Montrose is named King's Lieutenant. Battle of Tippermuir (1 September).
1645	Battles at Inverlochy (2 February), Auldearn (9 May), Alford (2 July), Kilsyth (15 August) won by Montrose. He is defeated at Philiphaugh (13 September).
1646	Charles I surrenders himself to the Scottish army at Newark on Trent. Scots army defeated at Benburb in Ireland (June).
1647	Scottish Government hands Charles I over to the English Parliamentarians. The Engagement marks a change in Scottish policy.
1648	Scots defeated by Cromwell at Preston (17 August). Collapse of the 'Engagement' policy. 'Whiggamore Raid' on Edinburgh. Cromwell enters Scotland.
1649	Execution of Charles I; Charles II proclaimed king. Parliament passes the Act of Classes.

1650	Capture and execution of Montrose. Charles II lands in Scotland. Scots defeated by Cromwell at Dunbar (2 September). 'The Start' (October). Act of Indemnity and the 'Western Remonstrance'. Emergence of 'Resolutioners' and 'Remonstrants'. Whiggamores defeated by Lambert.
1651	Coronation of Charles II. Highland force defeated by Cromwell's army at Inverkeithing (2 July). Act of Classes repealed; emergence of the 'Protesters'. Scottish army enters England: defeated by Cromwell at Worcester (3 September).
1652	Protectorate Parliament formed. Guerrilla warfare in the Highlands.
1652–4	English-Dutch war disrupts Scottish trade.
1654	Scotland formally unified with England and Ireland under the Commonwealth. Monck's victory over Middleton at Dalnaspidal (17 July).
1655	Forts established to pacify the Great Glen. Scottish Council established.
1656	General Monck put in charge of Scottish affairs.
1660	Restoration of the monarchy under Charles II. Committee of Estates reconvened. Earl of Lauderdale made Secretary of State. Mackenzie's *Aretina* is published.
1661	Royalist Parliament sits. Privy Council re-formed. Bishops are restored to the Church of Scotland. Execution of the Marquis of Argyll. Council of Trade set up.
1662	Anti-witchcraft campaign. Act of Conformity reimposes Book of Common Prayer. The 'Billetting Affair'.
1663	Non-conforming ministers are expelled; conventicles become frequent.
1664	Court of High Commission established.
1665	John Brown's *Apologeticall Relation* published.
1665–7	English-Dutch war again disrupts trade.
1666	Disorder in the south-west leads to the battle at Rullion Green (28 November).

1667	Construction of Port Glasgow begins. 'Independent Companies' introduced to police the Highlands. *Naphtali* is published.
1669	Leighton's attempt at 'Comprehension'; the first Letter of Indulgence.
1670	An attempt at Scottish-English union is broken off by Charles II.
1672	Second Letter of Indulgence.
1674–5	The 'Appeals Affair'.
1676	The Physic Garden established in Edinburgh.
1678	Execution of James Mitchell. The 'Highland Host' and introduction of the 'Lawborrows'. *The Poor Man's Cup of Cold Water* is published.
1679	Assassination of Archbishop Sharp (May). Fight at Drumclog (1 June) and battle of Bothwell Bridge (22 June). Arrival of Duke of York.
1680	Cameronians issue the Sanquhar declaration; are defeated at Airds Moss (22 July).
1681	Parliament passes the Test Act. Sir James Dalrymple publishes *Institutions of the Law in Scotland*. Royal College of Physicians founded. Trial of the Earl of Argyll.
1682	Advocates' Library founded. Death of Lauderdale. Duke of York returns to London. The Mint is closed due to corrupt management.
1683	The 'Rye House Plot', in England, is uncovered. The 'Junto' is set up in Edinburgh.
1684	Earl of Perth is appointed Chancellor. Renwick's *Apologetical Declaration* is issued. A Council resolution inaugurates the 'Killing Time'.
1685	Death of Charles II (February) and accession of James VII. Failure of Argyll's invasion; his execution.
1686	James VII issues a first Letter of Indulgence.
1687	James VII issues a second Letter of Indulgence. Freedom of worship is confirmed.

1688	Capture and execution of James Renwick. An heir is born to James VII. William of Orange lands in England. Flight of James VII to France.
1689	Parliament deposes James VII and accords joint sovereignty to William II and Mary II. Viscount Dundee leads a Jacobite resistance, defeats Government army at Killiecrankie (27 July) but is killed. Cameronians hold Dunkeld against Highlanders (21 August).
1690	Jacobite force defeated at Cromdale (1 May). Presbyterianism confirmed as form of Church of Scotland.
1692	Massacre of Glen Coe (13 February). *The Scotch Presbyterian Eloquence Displayed* is published in England.
1693	The Oath of Assurance is announced, and withdrawn.
1694	First of successive harvest failures leads to widespread famine.
1695	Parliament asks for action against those responsible for the Glen Coe massacre. Company Trading to Africa and the Indies established. Bank of Scotland founded.
1698	Execution of Thomas Aikenhead for blasphemy. Darien expedition sets off.
1699	Darien evacuated.
1700	Collapse of the Darien venture.
1702	Death of William II. Acession of Anne. Commissioners for Union meet at Westminster.
1703	Union negotiations are dropped. Act of Security passed.
1705	The *Worcester* affair. Parliament agrees to Union negotiations.
1706	Treaty of Union debated.
1707	Parliament votes for Union, 16 January. Inauguration of the United Kingdom, 1 May.

Notes and References

Chapter One:
Signing Up To Revolution

1. See Hume Brown, *Early Travellers in Scotland*. Numerous Acts of Parliament and Privy Council against beggars were passed from 1579 to 1688.
2. Watt, *Recalling the Scottish Covenants*, 8.
3. Macinnes points out (*Charles I*, 19), that the Kirk had 'no clear or unequivocal standard of worship': most parishes used either the *Second Prayer Book* of Edward VI of England, or the Genevan *Book of Common Order*.
4. Spalding, *Memorials i*, 82.
5. Guthry, *Memoirs*, 28.
6. See Kirkton, *The Secret and True History of the Church of Scotland*, 35n. Rutherford's writings were perhaps most influential in creating the spirit and reinforcing the ideas of those who opposed government interference with the Kirk.
7. Watt, *op.cit.*, 9. 'Signing' the Covenant may suggest a greater extent of literacy than was the case. In 1643 the minister of Grange parish in Moray reported that 33 members of his congregation signed the Solemn League and Covenant with their own hands, and around 200 were guided by the hand of the session clerk (Henderson, *Religious Life in Seventeenth Century Scotland*, 5).
8. Johnston, *Memento Quamdiu Vivas*, 331.
9. Quoted in Watt, *op.cit.*, 14. Bishops were introduced to the Kirk in 1606.
10. Donaldson, *Scottish Church History*, 211. Four reverted to become parish ministers.

Chapter Two:
The Glory Of The Covenant

1. In an aristocratic society, certain functions could only be performed by men of noble rank: in 17th-century Scotland, any post higher than that of King's Advocate had to be filled by a lord. A certain quota of earls was needed, to ensure that there would be a stock sufficiently intelligent to occupy state posts. Even so, new earls sometimes had to be created.
2. Burnet, *History of His Own Time, i*, 47.
3. Parker, *Thirty Years' War*, 193f. An estimated 25,000 Scots participated in the Thirty Years' War between 1618 and 1648. Between 1625–42, the Privy Council authorised the raising

of 47,110 men for foreign mercenary service (Keith M. Brown, 'From Scottish Lords to British Officers', in Macdougall, *Scotland and War*, 141).

4   E. M. Furgol, 'Scotland Turned Sweden' in Morrill, *The Scottish National Covenant in its British Context*, 134ff.

5   A pamphlet of 1638, *The Intentions of the Army of the Kingdom of Scotland*, promised the English that they would not 'take from their brethren from a thread even to a shoe-latchet, they coming amongst them as their friends' (see Hewison, *The Covenanters*, i, 348).

6   J. J. Scally, 'The Rise and Fall of the Covenanter Parliaments', in Brown & Mann, *History of the Scottish Parliament, ii*, 142.

7   Some signatories to the Covenant made an express reservation in favour of keeping episcopacy (Dickinson & Donaldson, *A Source Book of Scottish History, iii*, 104).

8   *A.P.S., v*, 270, 272, quoted in Dickinson & Donaldson, *op.cit.*, 117.

9   Henderson, *op.cit*, 170.

10 Mathew, *Scotland Under Charles I*, 304.

11 Analyses of the Covenanters' revenue-raising are found in Stevenson, *Union, Revolution and Religion*, VI and VII.

12 Macinnes, *Clanship, Commerce and the House of Stuart*, 88. Stevenson, *Revolution and Counter-Revolution in Scotland*, notes an Act in favour of enclosing parks and plantations, 1641, and the first Act for protection of industry, in 1645. An Act to promote flax-growing was passed in 1641 (Symon, *Scottish Farming*, 99).

13 Scally, *op.cit.*, 138ff.

14 Stevenson, *op.cit.*, vii, 31.

15 *A.P.S. v*, 351, quoted in Dickinson & Donaldson, *op.cit.*, 119. The North-East was most affected (Spalding, *History of the Troubles, i*, 234–5; ii, 57).

16 Hill Burton, *History of Scotland, vii*, 201.

17 Henderson, *op.cit.*, 96.

18 Six hundred died in the little town of Brechin, as a Latin inscription records:
Luna quarter crescens
Sex centros peste peremptos
Disce mori.! Vidit
Pulvis et umbra sumus.
(With the moon in its fourth quarter
Six hundred folk the plague did slaughter,
Learn to die! You see
Shades and dust are we).

19 Lenman, *Jacobite Clans*, 8.

20 Gordon, *Britane's Distemper* 160; also Guthry, *Memoirs*, 162. See also Buchan, *Montrose*, 254.

21. Scally, *op.cit.*, 152. See also Stevenson, *Revolution and Counter-Revolution*, 80f.
22. Woolrych, *Britain in Revolution*, 385.
23. Young, *The Scottish Parliament*, 206.
24. Furgol, *op.cit.*, 140.
25. Hamilton had an English peerage as well as his Scottish dukedom and this enabled an English court to try him. Keith M. Brown, 'Courtiers and Cavaliers', in Morrill, *op.cit.*, 155ff, shows the extent of 'Anglo-Scottishness' already extant among the nobility and gentry of the 17th century. These were mostly, though not all, supporters of the King and hostile to the Covenant.
26. Carlyle, *Cromwell, ii*, 153.
27. Around 4,000 were sent south by the Earl of Seaforth (Mitchell, *History of the Highlands*, 510); see also Stevenson, *Revolution and Counter-Revolution*, 115ff.

Chapter Three:
The Generation Of '48

1. Figures worked out with some care for 1693 England (Laslett, *The World we have lost*, 93) suggest that a child at birth had an average life expectancy of 32 years; survival to 10 gave an expectancy of another 40.25 years; at 30, the expectancy was another 27.64 years. The position in Scotland is unlikely to have been better.
2. Buchan, *op.cit.*, 161. James was first son of his father's second marriage; no children of his first marriage outlived the third Earl.
3. Davidson, *Discovering the Scottish Revolution*, 23.
4. Brown, *Kingdom or Province?* 115.
5. Scally, *op.cit.*, 157.
6. Jamieson, *Scots Dialect Dictionary*.
7. Young, *op.cit.*, 217. Or as Stevenson says in *Revolution and Counter-Revolution* (130) it shows 'how weak support for the kirk party was among the nobility'.
8. Noted in Stevenson, *op.cit.*, 139. Export of eggs had been banned by Parliament in 1641, in the hope that 'poore laboureing people' might then afford them (Symon, *op.cit.*, 99).

Chapter Four:
The Covenant: Vainglory And Disaster

1. Burnet, *i*, 75f.
2. *Kerr Correspondence, ii*, letter to Lord Lothian, 31 August 1649, 251. Scottish collectors also imported pictures from Holland, see Williams, *Dutch Art and Scotland*, 15f.
3. Nicoll, *Diary*, 6.
4. Nicoll records that some 40,000 men assembled at Leith Links, of

whom half were rejected, 'to the discontentment of much people, and of gentlemen volunteers who had freely come in to fight for the defence of the kingdom' (*op.cit.*, 20).

5 Royle, *Civil War*, 578–9.
6 *Kerr Correspondence, ii*, 5 September 1650, 297–8.
7 Quoted in Henderson, *op.cit.*, 173.
8 *Kerr Correspondence, ii*, letter from Lord Loudon, 306–7.
9 Stevenson, *op.cit.*, 185.
10 Hill-Burton, *op.cit.*, vi, 285. Douglas published it, with an account of the ceremony, in Aberdeen in 1651.
11 Burnet, *i*, 106.
12 Mackenzie, *John Maitland*, 186.
13 Royle, *op.cit.*, 595.
14 Stevenson, *op.cit.*, 206.
15 Burnet, *i*, 99.
16 Furgol, *op.cit.*, 142.

Chapter Five:
The Usurpation

1 Dow, *Cromwellian Scotland*, 31.
2 Drummond, *Memoirs of Sir Ewen Cameron of Lochiel*, 97.
3 Dickinson and Donaldson, *op.cit.*, 463.
4 Hay, *Diary*, 160.
5 Turner, *Memoirs*, 109–110.
6 Lochiel's treaty with Monck put his clan at peace with the Commonwealth without having to acknowledge Cromwell or swear any oath. When the judges came on circuit to Inverness in September 1655, Monck instructed them that neither Lochiel nor any of his party should be questioned for anything done during 'the late wars', and that no suits against Lochiel's people should be heard (Drummond, *Lochiel*, 145ff).
7 Trevelyan, *History of England*, 424.
8 Woolrych, *Britain in Revolution*, 665.
9 Dow, *op.cit.*, 216.
10 Dickinson and Donaldson, *op.cit.*, 249ff.
11 Quoted in Hill, *God's Englishman*, 125.
12 *Kerr Correspondence, ii*, 400. Letter to Lady Lothian, 30 January 1651.
13 Burnet, *i*, 112–13
14 Woolrych, *op.cit.*, 666.
15 Brown, *Kingdom or Province?* 137.
16 Donaldson, *op.cit.*, 357.
17 Johnston, *Diary, iii*, ix.
18 Richard Franck, quoted in Hume Brown, *Early Travellers*, 192.
19 Quoted in Dow, *op.cit.*, 228.
20 Law, *Memorialls*, 7.

Chapter Six:
A Nation Of Theopoliticians

1. See Hill, *The World Turned Upside Down*, 214. There were some: Andrew Hay (*Diary*, 181) noted in 1659 that the mother of the Laird of Gradoun was 'ane anabaptist and a great interteiner of quakers, and is lik to be a snare to the young folk'.
2. Henderson, *op.cit.*, 107.
3. *Ibid.*, 117.
4. Masson, *Life of John Milton, v*, 92ff. The judges, Smith and Lawrence, were English officials, and he was said to have 'contravened the tenor of the laws and acts of Parliament' – the London one, which passed a Blasphemy Act on 9 August 1650 – but the jury which found him guilty was local. Agnew, also known as 'Jock of Broad Scotland', is referred to in Sinclair's *Satan's Invisible World Discovered*, in relation to what reads like a case of poltergeist activity in a weaver's house in Glenluce. The troubles began after he had threatened 'hurt to the family, because he had not gotten such an alms as he required' (Sinclair, 50). As Agnew was one of the few men in the country not to believe in evil spirits, it seems to be a classic case of 'give a dog a bad name'.
5. Johnston, *Diary*, 259f.
6. Brodie, *Diary*, 179.
7. Buckle, *History of Civilisation in England, iii*, 237f.
8. The Rev. Thomas Hogg, a presbyterian minister in Ross-shire, when told by a colleague that he had never seen the Devil in corporeal form, replied: 'I assure you, that you can never be happy till you see him in that manner; that is, until you have a personal converse and combat with him.' Quoted by Buckle (*op.cit., iii*, 235) who found it in *Scotch Presbyterian Eloquence Displayed*. Patrick Walker noted that Alexander Peden, while alone in a cave, had a tussle with the Devil, saying afterwards: 'I have sent him off in haste, we'll be no more troubled with him this night. (Walker, *Six Saints of the Covenant, i*, 78f).
9. Wodrow, *Analecta, i*, 246.
10. Mackenzie, 'Vindication of the Government of Charles II, in *Works, ii*, 343.
11. Tawney, *Religion and the Rise of Capitalism*, 202.
12. On the Scottish Puritan frame of mind, and its typical emphasis on sexual misconduct, C. K. Sharpe, Kirkton's editor, quotes some extracts from the contemporary Journal of the Laird of Pollock: 2 Sept 1655: Matter of sad humiliation. There being before the congregations for such gross

sins, one adulteress, one quadrilapse fornicatrix, three trilapse fornicatrix.
Close of the Weeke, Oct. 1655: Praise. Much tentation prevented. Some lusts restrained. Himself commended. Knowledge communicated.
Providences. J. D. enemies made to bow before me.
Sins. Passion. Carnall laughter. Experience. Passion while boiling restrained by prayer.
(Kirkton, *op.cit.*, 169n).
T. C. Smout doubts if Puritanism ran very deep in Scottish society except in the strongly Covenanting areas and among individual pious families, but 'The rest of the population were at least made conscious that they ought to feel guilty if they were not puritan in their hearts' (Smout, *History of the Scottish People*, 86f).

13 Graham, *Social Life*, 53n.
14 Macinnes, *Clanship*, 22.
15 Lenman, *Economic History*, 17.

Chapter Seven: Boys Growing Up

1 Brodie, *op.cit.*, 173.
2 Story, *William Carstares*, 13.
3 Aldis, *List of Books Published in Scotland Before 1700*, 44.
4 Terry, *Claverhouse*, 4.
5 Murray, *Rob Roy*, 171.
6 Scott, *Bonnie Dundee*, 8.
7 Terry, *op.cit.*, 12n.
8 Smout, *op.cit.*, 115.
9 Burnet, *i*, 61.
10 Scott, *The Bride of Lammermoor*, Introduction.
11 Lang, *Sir George Mackenzie*, 24.
12 Morer, *A Short Account*, 95. Sharp was made archbishop only in 1661, the year young Graham graduated.
13 Stewart, *Covenanters of Teviotdale*, 252.
14 Story, *op.cit.*, 13.
15 Aberdeen was the university most open to new ideas, and moderate Episcopalians like Henry Scougall, son of the local Bishop, and Professor of Theology there, who died aged 28 in 1678, found Descartes exciting rather than troubling, and liked the fact that his Method released students from a disputing humour. Scougall's book *The Life of God in the Soul of Man* is one of the few non-polemic works of the time.
16 Cant, *The University of St Andrews*, 90.
17 Henderson, *op.cit.*, 120ff.
18 George Mackenzie's poem *Caelia's Country House and Closet* (1668) has a verse on Galileo, but as inventor of the telescope rather than as cosmologist.

19 Stemming from the minister of Drumoak, Aberdeenshire, the Gregorys produced distinguished mathematicians and physicians for five generations. They kept an episcopalian-Jacobite tinge though without taking any active part in politics. Like very many others, they got on with 'their own thing' and kept out of the troubles.
20 Brodie, *op.cit.*, 330.
21 *Ibid.*, 365.
22 Leighton, *Works, ii*, 633.
23 Lang, *op.cit.*, 25.

**Chapter Eight:
Philosophers And Witches**

1 Brodie, *op.cit.*, 194.
2 Quoted in Riley, *The Union of England and Scotland*, 5.
3 Mathieson, *Politics & Religion ii*, 210.
4 Mackenzie, *John Maitland*, 216.
5 Noted in Graham, *Stair Annals*, *i*, 52.
6 Hill Burton, *op.cit., vii*, 416.
7 Burnet, *i*, 191f.
8 Gillian H. MacIntosh, 'Arise King John', in Brown & Mann, *op.cit.*, 164ff.
9 Dalrymple, *Apology*, 7.
10 Quoted in Wodrow, *History, i*, 21.
11 Aldis, *op.cit.*, 44.
12 Mackenzie, 'What Eloquence is fit for the Bar', in *Works, i*: 'Treatises on the Laws', 17.
13 Mackenzie, *Aretina*, 216–343.
14 Lang, *op.cit.*, 26ff.
15 Allan, *Philosophy and Politics in Later Stuart Scotland*, 191.
16 See Mackenzie, *Works, i*. 'Moral Essays', 39ff. The essay was reprinted eight times in Charles II's reign.
17 Mackenzie, *Laws and Customs*, 80ff.
18 Macdonald, *The Witches of Fife*, 7.
19 Sinclair, *Satan's Invisible World Discovered*, 136. This work is subtitled: 'A Choice Collection of Modern Relations proving evidently, against the atheists of this present age, that there are Devils, Spirits, Witches and Apparitions, from authentic records and attestations of witnesses of undoubted veracity'. In its author's view it was a thoroughly modern work, offering examples of actual experience rather than suppositions.
20 The penalty for these was also burning: In a case in May 1650 a man was burned to death for sexual congress with a cow, and the animal too was burned, which seems unnecessarily vindictive (Nicoll, *op.cit.*, 15).

Chapter Nine:
Owls, Satyrs, And Bangster Amazons

1. Wodrow, *Analecta*, iii, 52.
2. Kirkton, *op.cit.*, 109; Burnet, *i*, 227.
3. Guthrie, *Two Speeches*.
4. Wodrow, *History*, *i*, 192. As a warning on Wodrow's technique, the same episode in his private notes (*Analecta*, ii, 138) has Guthrie say: 'Give me a piece cheese, for it will not be my death now. 'In his book, it is a little more polished, and the explanation of the 'gravel' is introduced. Other examples could be quoted.
5. Burnet, *i*, 229.
6. *Ibid.*, 236.
7. *Ibid.*
8. McWard's last sermon in Glasgow was an attack on government policy and the people's backsliding: 'Is this the land that joined in covenant with the Lord?' His text was '… I will punish you for all your iniquities.' Arrested for seditious preaching, at his trial he drew a distinction between a 'ministerial protestation' and a 'legal impugnation' against acts of government; and, as Guthrie had done, submitted his person but not his conscience to the court. He expected the same fate as Guthrie but was sentenced to banishment, with six months' grace, only one of which to be spent in Glasgow, and to receive a year's stipend on departure (Wodrow, *History*, *i*, 206ff).
9. Burnet, *i*, 240.
10. Wodrow, *History*, *i*, 246.
11. Jackson, *Restoration Scotland*, 17.
12. Aldis, *op.cit.*, 47.
13. Kirkton, *op.cit.*, 115n.
14. Brodie, *op.cit.*, 246.
15. Macinnes, *Charles I*, 156.
16. The regalia were concealed first at Dunottar Castle, then Kinneff church, during the Occupation.
17. Brodie, *op.cit.*, 223.
18. *Ibid.*, 254f
19. Henderson, *op.cit.*, 73.
20. Burnet, *i*, 246.
21. Wodrow, *History*, *i*, 238.
22. Quoted in Mathieson, *Politics & Religion*, ii, 230.
23. *Lauderdale Papers*, ii, 215.
24. Lang, *op.cit.*, 85.
25. Kirkton, *op.cit.*, 160.
26. Burnet, *i*, 278.
27. Mackenzie, *Memoirs of the Affairs of Scotland*, 77f.
28. Kirkton, *op.cit* 162f.
29. Mathieson, *op.cit.*, *i*, 370. A different contemporary slant appears in *Lady Callendar's Epitaph*, from 1659:
Here lies the Phoenix of her sex, the ark
Where Loyalty and Honour did imbark;

The Day of our Deluge, what had she been,
Had She been He, a Soul so masculine!
Bruce, Wallace, should remounted have the Stage
Of Action, with the worthiest of that Age.
She was a Woman (I'll not shame Men much)
But had our Lords and Leaders all been such,
Our King and Country had not been sold by Knaves,
Nor should we now go supplicate like Slaves.
Watson, *op.cit.*, iii, 97.

30. Terry, *Claverhouse*, 40. In his diary for 10 May 1663, Samuel Pepys noted that at the King's Head pub the parliamentarians were talking mostly about 'the news from Scotland that the Bishop of Galloway was besieged in his house by some women and had like to have been outraged' (Pepys, *Diary, iv*, 130).
31. Anderson, *Ladies of the Covenant*, 234ff.
32. Stevenson, *Revolution and Counter-Revolution*, 188.
33. Graham, *Stair Annals, i*, 25ff.

Chapter Ten:
Improvement And Reaction

1. 'Scotland and the Puritan Revolution', in Trevor-Roper, *Religion, the Reformation and Social Change*, 396. A magisterial response is Stevenson, 'Professor Trevor-Roper and the Scottish Revolution', in *Union, Revolution and Religion*, V.
2. James Melville, *Diary*, 1592.
3. Devine, *Scotland's Empire*, 2.
4. Macinnes, *Clanship, Commerce and the House of Stuart*, 75; and Withers, *Gaelic Scotland*, 309.
5. *Seafield Correspondence*, 315ff.
6. Bateson, *Coinage in Scotland*, 143, 146, 140
7. Devine, *op.cit.*, 4. See also Murdoch, *Network North*.
8. Smout, *op.cit.*, 180ff.
9. Dickinson and Donaldson, *op.cit.*, 382.
10. Dickinson and Donaldson, *op.cit.*, 388.
11. Smout, *op.cit.*, 183.
12. A.P.S., *v*, 260, 261, quoted in Mackintosh, *History of Civilisation in Scotland, ii*, 324.
13. Macinnes, *op.cit.*, 114.
14. *Ibid.*, 131.
15. Turner, *op.cit.*, 16.
16. Burnet, *i*, 385.
17. Turner, *op.cit.*, 142.

Chapter Eleven:
I Did See The Outlaw Whigs Lye Scattered

1. Wodrow, *History, i*, 381
2. Donaldson, *Scotland*, 388.

3   Kirkton, *op.cit.*, 201.
4   Wodrow, *History*, i., 394.
5   Burnet, i, 382.
6   *Ibid.*, 535f.
7   *Ibid.*, 516.
8   Rutherford, *Lex, Rex*, Preface.
9   Letter of Rothes to Lauderdale, 14 March 1665, quoted in Jackson, *op.cit.*, 82.
10 Nicoll, *op.cit.*, 446.
11 Pepys, *Diary, vii*, 298.
12 Presbyterian propaganda did not hesitate to link the plague, and the London fire of 1666, with the burning there of the Solemn League and Covenant: 'Only I wish, that the burning of that city into ashes, where that covenant was burnt, together with that non-such plague, and war, may make them take warning, ere it be too late, who did this wickedness: for alas! all that is come, will be forgotten, when the wrath and vengeance that is yet coming shall be executed and mentioned. O England, England, I fear, I fear thy woe hasteneth! The wrath of God is upon the wing against thee, both for breach of covenant, and wiping thy mouth, as if thou hadst done nothing amiss!' McWard, *The Poor Man's Cup of Cold Water*.
13 Nicoll, *op.cit.*, 437.
14 Wodrow, *History, ii*, 9.
15 Lang, *op.cit.*, 75.
16 *Ibid.*, 75.
17 Kirkton, *op.cit.*, 246.
18 *Ibid.*, 240.
19 Wodrow, *History, ii*, 30.
20 *Ibid.*
21 Turner, *op.cit.*, 186.
22 Maidment, *op.cit.*, 232. The Covenanters were always poorly armed. Kirkton records how they used broken bits of clay 'tobacco pipes' if they had no bullets. They used to gather up fired musket balls after skirmishes. (Kirkton, *op.cit.*, 230, 432). But the alarm in London was such that on 3 December, just before news of victory arrived, Pepys records that the Duke of York was planning to go north and raise an army (Pepys, *Diary, vii*, 395).
23 Dodds, *Fifty Years' Struggle*, 173.
24 Wodrow, *History, ii*, 38.
25 *Ibid.*, 47ff, quoting from Mackenzie's *Laws and Customes in Matters Criminal*.
26 Kirkton, *op.cit.*, 248.
27 Wodrow, *History, ii*, 52.
28 Protests against Bannatyne's excesses resulted in his being called before the Privy Council, fined £200 and banished. He was said to to have tried to kill Lauderdale in London, then fled to Holland (not just Presbyterians found refuge there),

Chapter Twelve:
Naphtali and *Caelia*

1. Wodrow, *History, ii*, 100.
2. Turner, *op.cit.*, 189ff.
3. He entered Parliament as shire commissioner for Ross.
4. Mackenzie, *Works, i*, 3ff. See also Stevenson, *Origins of Freemasonry*, chapters 5 and 7.
5. Harris, *Transformations of Love*, 61. Evelyn published a rebuttal, *Public Employment* (1667) but friendship followed.
6. Tobin, *Plays by Scots*, 10; Alasdair Cameron, 'Theatre in Scotland, 1660–1680' in Hook, *History of Scottish Literature, ii*, 192.
7. Cameron, *op.cit.*, 194.
8. Terry, *Parliament*, 64ff.
9. Story, *op.cit.*, 258.
10. Young, *op.cit.*, 328.
11. Wodrow, *History, ii*, 38.
12. Graham, *Maritime History of Scotland*, 24, 20.
13. Stevenson, *Origins of Freemasonry*, 185. See also ODNB, David Allan, 'Robert Moray'.
14. Pepys, *Diary, viii*, 64. Pepys gives an insight into Lauderdale's London life when on 28 July 1666 he has dinner at the Earl's house: '… at supper there played one of their servants upon the viallin, some Scotch tunes only – several – and the best of their country, as they seemed to esteem them by their praising and admiring them… But strange to hear my Lord Lauderdale say himself, he would rather hear a Catt mew than the best musique in the world… of all instruments, he hates the Lute most, and next to that, the Baggpipe' (*Diary, vii*, 224f).
15. Mathieson, *Politics & Religion, ii*, 232.
16. Donaldson, *op.cit.*, 369.
17. Stewart, *The Covenanters of Teviotdale*, 255.
18. Burnet, *i*, 535ff.
19. Mathieson, *Politics & Religion, ii*, 247.
20. Stewart, *Ius Populi Vindicatum*, 376f.

Chapter Thirteen:
Old Politics And New Practitioners

1. ODNB, John R. Young, 'John Dalrymple'.
2. Lang, *op.cit.*, 97. The salt debate obscured all other issues for a time; Mackenzie recalled that prices quadrupled from 4s sterling a boll to 16s (*Memoirs*, 241).
3. Mackenzie, *Memoirs*, 137, 211. Charles's loss of interest was so abrupt that Ferguson suggests his

union project was no more than a blind to mask his secret dealings with France (*Scotland's Relations with England*, 157).
4. Mackay, *Stair*, 82ff.
5. Maidment, *op.cit.*, 174ff.
6. Mackenzie, *Memoirs of the Affairs of Scotland*, 214.
7. Sinclair, *op.cit.*, 155.
8. Quoted in McIntosh, 'Arise King John', in Brown & Mann, *op.cit.*, 178.
9. Wodrow, *History, ii*, 109.
10. *Ibid.*, 199.
11. *Ibid.*, 202.
12. Graham, *Stair Annals, i*, 59. During his two spells as Lord President, Dalrymple did much to modernise the Court of Session and reduce its reputation for corruption. He has been criticised for not doing more, but the Court's proceedings were regulated by Parliament and changes required parliamentary approval. One of the things that most riled him about the hostile pamphlet of 1692 was the suggestion that he favoured his own sons, two of whom were advocates. At the time, it was normal for judges to have 'pets' who received representations and gifts on their behalf.
13. ODNB, Edward Corp, 'John Drummond'.
14. Terry, *Claverhouse*, 15.
15. Wodrow, *History, ii*, 210.
16. Stewart's *Naphtali* gives an extremist's account of Leighton, who: '... under a jesuitical vizard of pretended holiness, humility and crucifixion to the world, hath studied to seem to creep upon the ground, but always up hill, towards promotion and more places of ease, honour and wealth' (301).
17. Maidment, *op.cit.*, 243ff.
18. See Maurice Lee Jr, *Relatione of the Wrangs Done to the Ladie Yester, 1683*, in SHS *Miscellany xiii*.
19. Lang, *op.cit.*, 106.
20. *Ibid.*, 110ff.
21. Cowan, *op.cit.*, 36.
22. Quoted in Cowan, *op.cit.*, 37.
23. Quoted in Story, *op.cit.*, 31. Peter du Moulin was an English-based Huguenot.
24. See Gardiner, *The Scottish Exile Community in the Netherlands*, 136.
25. ODNB, Edward Corp, 'John Drummond'.
26. See Murdoch, *Network North*, 160n.
27. *Ibid.*, 154ff.
28. Wodrow, *History, ii*, 263.
29. Brown, *Kingdom or Province?* 152.
30. Lenman, 'Militia, Fencible Men and Home Defence, 1660–1797', in Macdougall, *op.cit.*, 179.
31. Wodrow, preface to *History, ii*.

Chapter Fourteen:
Experiences Of An Advocate

1. Kirkton, *op.cit.*, 341.
2. Mackenzie, *Memoirs*, 327.
3. Letter from Lord Hatton to Lord Kincardine, 10 February, in Wodrow, *History*, ii, 249.
4. Kirkton, *op.cit.*, 343.
5. *Lauderdale Papers*, iii, 50.
6. Kirkton, *op.cit.*, 352.
7. Wodrow, *History*, ii, 269.
8. Kirkton, *op.cit.*, 345.
9. Lang, *op.cit.*, 116n. To enemies he was now 'Vulcan', lame buffoon of the gods.
10. *Ibid.*, 115.
11. Mackenzie, *Memoirs*, 293. There were 29 advocates.
12. Letter from Lockhart, quoted in Mackay, *Stair*, 115.
13. Lang, *op.cit.*, 120.
14. Mackay, *Stair*, 117.
15. Mackenzie, *Memoirs*, 293f.
16. Quoted in Graham, *Stair Annals*, i, 57.
17. Lang, *op.cit.*, 131.
18. Kirkton, *op.cit.*, 381.

Chapter Fifteen:
The Highland Host

1. Kirkton, *op.cit.*, 372.
2. Stewart, *Covenanters of Teviotdale*, 3.
3. In 1683 Sir William would be fined £Sc46,000 for irregular church attendance: the Privy Council reduced it on appeal to £1500. Lady Scott was known to be the driving force and Fountainhall (*Historical Observes*, ii, 495) thought it hard on Sir William, as 'Scottish law would not bind five merks of [her] debt on her husband.'
4. Walker, 'The Life and Death of Mr Richard Cameron', in *Biographia Presbyteriana*, i, 219.
5. Walker, *op.cit.*, 191ff.
6. Wodrow, *History*, ii, 301.
7. Kirkton, *op.cit.*, 367ff. Burnet, *ii*, 105f gives a rather different story, from hearsay.
8. Wodrow, *History*, ii, 328.
9. Kirkton, *op.cit.*, 380f. Mackenzie claimed that Carstairs did have a warrant but could not show it because other names were on it (*Memoirs*, 317).
10. *Ibid.*, 370; Mackenzie, *Memoirs*, 317f.
11. Lauder, *Historical Notices*, i, 136.
12. *S. P. Dom. Charles II*, vol 387, quoted Lang, 136.
13. Quoted in W. Mackay Mackenzie, 'Castles and Towers', in Scott-Moncrieff, *The Stones of Scotland*, 76.
14. Lang, *op.cit.*, 137.
15. *Ibid.*
16. Terry, *Claverhouse*, 36.

17 *Ibid.*, 46.
18 Letter in *Red Book of Menteith*, ii, 170., quoted in Terry, *Claverhouse*, 47.
19 Scott, *Bonnie Dundee*, 17.
20 Quoted Lang, *op.cit.*, 143, from Ellis, *Original Letters*, Series II, vol *iv*, 47–51.
21 Burnet, *ii*, 16f.
22 Mackenzie, 'Vindication', *Works*, ii, 348.
23 Joshua, 7; Kirkton, *op.cit.*, 366n.
24 Lang, *op.cit.*, 140f.
25 Quoted in Kirkton, *op.cit.*, 385ff.
26 Lang, *op.cit.*, 143.
27 Wodrow, *History, ii*, 472.
28 *Lauderdale Papers*, iii, 89.
29 Mackenzie, 'Vindication', *Works*, ii, 345.
30 Wodrow, *History, ii*, 380f.
31 *Lauderdale Papers*, iii, 91.
32 Quoted in Wodrow, *History, ii*, 385.
33 Lang, *op.cit.*, 155, see also Wodrow, *History, ii*, 397.
34 *Ibid.*, 410.
35 *Ibid.*, 413.
36 *Ibid.*, 429.

Chapter Sixteen: Beloved Sufferers

1 *Lauderdale Papers*, iii, 93.
2 Add. MSS, 32.095 (*Malet Papers*, f190). Quoted in Lang, *op.cit.*, 159n.
3 Undated letter, quoted in Lang, *op.cit.*, 159.
4 Quoted in Lang, *op.cit.*, 157.
5 Quoted in *ibid.*, 181.
6 Wodrow, *History, ii*, 481f.
7 *Ibid.*, 476.
8 *Lauderdale Papers*, iii, 155.
9 Kirkton, *op.cit.*, 393.
10 Wodrow, *History, ii*, 491f.
11 From the 'Queensferry Paper', Dickinson and Donaldson, *op.cit.*, 175ff.
12 This passage from *The Poor Man's Cup of Cold Water* gives an insight into McWard's thoughts: 'The reason then why the people of God are often in so much heaviness, and frequently hunted and harassed with troubles and tentations, is, that they may be hunted by the world's hatred and evil handling of them, out of the world, home to heaven; that since they see what they have to expect here, they may gird up the loins of their mind, and set their affections on things that are above, where Christ is and their treasure: and hence it is said, *When the scourge slayeth suddenly, he laugheth at the trial of the innocent*; which is not for want of affection, being afflicted in all their afflictions; but if I may say so, besides that he means them not to command a calm in

the greatest storm, and to have a concert of most sweet music in their soul, amidst all their miseries, who have an interest in him as their God, he rejoiceth to think how the happiness of his people is promoved by their pressures and persecutions; and how much their persecutors are befooled, who contrary to their purpose contribute their service to the saints, whom in their rage they intend to ruin.'
Many phrases strike a parallel with Catholic apologetics.

13 James Renwick would also reserve special emphasis for countering over-enthusiasm: 'Yet this his Zeal, though appearing forward enough, and seemingly fiery betimes, was impartial and uniform, against all Extremes and Extravagance; snd particularly fervid against blind and bastard delirious Zealots, who... fell into damnable Delusion, pretending Rapture and *Enthusiasms*, and cursing all that were not of their Way' (Shields, 'Life of Renwick', in *Biographia Presbyteriana*, ii, 19).

14 Quoted in Henderson, *op.cit.*, 24; the reference is to Psalm *xlv*.

15 Dodds, *op.cit.*, 311.

16 Wodrow, *History*, ii, 497.

17 *Ibid.*

18 Quoted in Lang, *op.cit.*, 165, from *S. P. Dom., Charles II*, vol. 405.

19 *Lauderdale Papers*, iii, 162ff.

20 Terry, *Claverhouse*, 49.

Chapter Seventeen: Assassination, Schism, Defeat

1 Kirkton, *op.cit.*, Appendix.

2 Wodrow, *History*, iii, 44.

3 *Ibid.*, 48.

4 Shields, *A Hind Let Loose*, 124.

5 Add. MSS. 32.095 (*Malet Papers*, f.190), quoted in Lang, *op.cit.*, 171f; the reference is to an event of 1222.

6 Add. MSS. 32.094, f.302, quoted in Lang, *op.cit.*, 173.

7 Wodrow, *History*, iii, 67.

8 Terry, *Claverhouse*, 51.

9 Salmond, *Veterum Laudes*, 172.

10 Lang, *op.cit.*, 175.

11 Report to Lord Linlithgow, in *Lauderdale Papers*, 165.

12 Lord Ross to Lord Linlithgow, 2 June 1670, *Lauderdale Papers*, 166.

13 Hill Burton, *op.cit.*, vii, 517.

14 Wodrow, *History*, iii, 106.

15 *Memoirs of William Veitch*, 477, quoted in Terry, *Claverhouse*, 75.

16 Wodrow, *History*, iii, 107.

17 Terry, *Claverhouse*, 81

18 Walker, *op.cit.*, i, 53.

19 ODNB, Hugh Ouston, 'Robert Leighton'.

20 Terry, *Claverhouse*, 82.

21 Instruction from Lauderdale to

the Privy Council, quoted in Wodrow, *History, iii*, 152.
22. Walker, *Six Saints, ii*, 162.
23. See Gardiner, *The Scottish Exile Community in the Netherlands*, 55f.
24. Walker, *op.cit.*, 163.
25. *Ibid.*
26. Dodds, *op.cit.*, 284.
27. Burnet, *ii*, 138.
28. Lang, *op.cit.*, 177ff.
29. Dalrymple, *An Apology*, 5.
30. Walker, *op.cit., ii*, 63ff.
31. Wodrow, *History, iii*, 153.

Chapter Eighteen:
Blood Shall Be Their Sign

1. Burnet, *ii*, 125.
2. Cameron, 'Theatre in Scotland', in Hook, *op.cit.*, 193. It was the future Queen's only visit to Scotland.
3. The question of naming James as Viceroy was seriously considered, but rejected as inappropriate for a 'free kingdom' (Lauder, *Historical Observes*, 42).
4. Shields, *op.cit.*, 131
5. Scott-Moncrieff, *The Stones of Scotland*, 100.
6. Smout, *op.cit.*, 117.
7. Bateson, *op.cit.*, 146ff.
8. 'Southern', *The Despot's Champion*, 81.
9. Terry, *Claverhouse*, 83.
10. *Ibid.*
11. *Ibid.*, 101.
12. Wodrow, *History, iii*, 186ff.
13. Shields, *op.cit.*, 133ff.
14. Privy Council proclamation of June 1680; Wodrow, *History, iii*, 216.
15. Quoted in Dodds, *op.cit.*, 288.
16. Walker, *op.cit., i*, 230.
17. Law, *Memorialls*, 153f.
18. *Ibid.*, 183.
19. Walker, *op.cit., i*, 233.
20. Burnet, *ii*, 126.
21. Wodrow, *History, iii*, 224.
22. Story, *op.cit.*, 85.
23. Dodds, *op.cit.*, 306.
24. Shields, *op.cit.*, 140ff.
25. Cowan, *op.cit.*, 110.
26. Wodrow, *History iii*, 470f.
27. Walker, *op.cit., ii*, 83ff.
28. *Ibid.*
29. A.P.S., *viii*, 243, c.6, quoted in Dickinson and Donaldson, *op.cit.*, 186ff.
30. Dalrymple, *Apology*, 4.
31. Burnet, *ii*, 132.
32. Graham, *Maritime History*, 51.
33. A.P.S., *viii*, 348–9, quoted in Dickinson and Donaldson, *op.cit.*, 329.
34. Dickinson and Donaldson, *op.cit.*, 331.
35. Donaldson, *James V to James VII*, 371. The suggestion that repression had broken the Covenanting movement is open to challenge.

NOTES AND REFERENCES

The schism revealed in the Bothwell Bridge debates shows the extent of disagreement between groups both claiming the authority of the Covenant: the movement could be said to have broken itself. But further, the phrase 'covenanting movement' suggests a sense of purpose and organisation for which there is no evidence. What undoubtedly did exist was 'the main body of presbyterian dissent', in whose range of views, the National Covenant set out the ideal form of kingship and – for some – provided the justification for direct action to secure it.

36 Cowan, *op.cit.*, 109.
37 Lang, *op.cit.*, 215ff.
38 *Ibid.*, 221.
39 See Mackenzie's *Vindication*, and Lang, 221.
40 Lauder, *Historical Observes*, 55f.
41 Macinnes, *Clanship*, 139ff.
42 *Ibid.*, 140. However, Drummond, *Lochiel* (208) notes how the Sheriff of Inverness-shire was frightened out of Lochaber in August 1682 and 'declined holding courts in that country ever after'.

**Chapter Nineteen:
My Lord Advocate Does Wonders**

1 Maidment, *op.cit.*, *Pasquil upon the Family of Stair*, 174ff.
2 Dalrymple, *Apology*, 2.
3 Mathieson, *Scotland and Union*, 302.
4 Lauder, *Historical Observes*, 58.
5 Cowan, *op.cit.*, 111.
6 Mathieson, *op.cit.*, ii, 302.
7 Letter from Queensberry to Gordon of Haddo, 2 January 1682, quoted Terry, *Claverhouse*, 103.
8 Davidson, *op.cit.*, 19ff.
9 Letter of 12 February 1682, quoted Scott, *op.cit.*, 30.
10 Mackay, *Stair*, 179.
11 Quoted in Mackay, *Stair*, 182.
12 Mackay, *Stair*, 183.
13 'Southern', *The Despot's Champion*, 122.
14 Quoted in *ibid.*, 103.
15 Dalrymple, *Apology*, 10: Mackenzie 'faithfully and friendly' advised Stair he was unsafe, 'and owned to the King that he had so advised me.' Probably there was an official wish to see Stair in exile rather than prosecute him.
16 *Lauderdale Papers*, iii, 220.
17 Lauder, *Historical Notices*, i, 389.
18 Graham, *Stair Annals*, i, 66.
19 Letter of 1 March 1682, quoted in Terry, *Claverhouse*, 107f.
20 Terry, *op.cit.*, 111. The people were more correct than Claverhouse, in this respect.

21 Quoted in Story, *op.cit.*, 86.
22 Story, *op.cit.*, 53.
23 Letter of 20 March 1683, quoted in Terry, *Claverhouse*, 125.
24 Bateson, *op.cit.*, 146ff.
25 Scott, *op.cit.*, 32.
26 Terry, *Claverhouse*, 125.
27 *Ibid.*
28 Cowan, 114.
29 Terry, *op.cit.*, 137.
30 *Ibid.*, 138.
31 Lipsius, *Politica*: trans. William Jones, 1594.

Chapter Twenty: The Tolbooth In Winter

1 Lang, *op.cit.*, 237.
2 Landsman, *Scotland and Its First American Colony*, 275. See also Devine, *Scotland's Empire*, 37. The Quaker Robert Barclay of Urie was leader of the ecumenical project and the Duke of York encouraged it. The township of Amboy was renamed Perth Amboy in Perth's honour in 1684. In 1983 a statue of him was unveiled in front of the city hall: here at least he is remembered in a positive way.
3 Story, *op.cit.*, 68f.
4 Lang, *op.cit.*, 241.
5 Story, *op.cit.*, 74.
6 Quoted in Story, *op.cit.*, 76.
7 Quoted in *ibid.*
8 Cowan, *op.cit.*, 118.
9 Gardiner, *op.cit.*, 59.
10 Dunlop, *op.cit.*, 48.
11 Story, *op.cit.*, 75.
12 Lang, *op.cit.*, 253.
13 *Ibid.*, 251, quoting *Drumlanrig Mss, ii*, 127.
14 *Ibid.*, 255f; *Drumlanrig Mss, ii*, 146,7.
15 *Ibid.*, 154.
16 HMC, *Rept., xv, pt viii*, 285, quoted Terry, *Claverhouse*, 144.
17 Terry, *Claverhouse*, 145.
18 Wodrow, *History, iii*, 3.
19 *Ibid.*, 5.

Chapter Twenty-One: Torture Under Law

1 Erskine, *Journal*, 51.
2 HMC *Rept. xv, pt viii*, 287; quoted in Terry, *Claverhouse*, 155.
3 'Southern', *The Despot's Champion*, 164
4 *Charters of Dundee*, ed A. H. Millar, 1880, 103–5, quoted Scott, *op.cit.*, 34.
5 Terry, *Claverhouse*, 180f.
6 *Ibid.*, 190.
7 Erskine, *Journal*, 77, 80.
8 *Ibid.*, 69.
9 Mackay, *Stair*, 207. 'Russians' may simply equate with 'desperadoes' in the language of the time, but both Dalyell and Drummond, his deputy,

10. had served the Tsar; and could have had genuine Russians in their pay.
11. Lang, *op.cit.*, 253ff.
12. Lauder, *Historical Notices, ii*, 745.
13. Letter to Lauderdale, 3 December 1677, in *Lauderdale Papers, iii*, 93.
14. Letter from Charles II to the Council, 13 June 1684; Wodrow, *History, iv*, 30.
15. Wodrow, *History, iv*, 31.
16. A.P.S., *ix*, 461, c.66, quoted Mackintosh, *op.cit.*, 311f.
17. Erskine, *Journal*, 78f.
18. Walker, *Six Saints, i*, xxii. 'Whereas the boots were the ordinary way to expiscate matters relating to the government, and that there is a new invention and engine, called the "thumbkins", which will be very effectual to the purpose and intent aforesaid...' (Council Act of 23 July 1684:, quoted in Wodrow, *History, iii*, 33); he notes: 'One week after Perth becomes Chancellor.'
19. Lauder, *Historical Notices, i*, 142.
20. They were Lloyd, Bishop of St Asaph's, and Stillingfleet, Dean of St Paul's. Both became friends of Mackenzie's.
21. Prisoners were expected to pay 'house dues' to the tolbooth keeper for their food and any comforts allowed; see *Privy Council, xi*, 71.

21. Letter to his wife, Story, *op.cit.*, 88.
22. Story, *op.cit.*, 89.
23. *Ibid.*, 90. The account of Carstares's torture is taken from Story, 90f, and Erskine, *Journal*, 82f.
24. *Ibid.*, 93.
25. *Ibid.*
26. Erskine, *Journal*, 82.
27. Story, *op.cit.*, 95.
28. *Ibid.*
29. *Ibid.*
30. Lang, *op.cit.*, 251.
31. Story, *op.cit.*, 97, quoting from *Graham-Dunlop* MSS.
32. An Act of Parliament in July 1690 had Carstares's testimony erased from the Privy Council record. See Lang, *op.cit.*, 267.
33. *Privy Council Register*, ix, 139; not Stirling Castle as Story says.
34. Erskine, *Journal*, 96.
35. Wodrow, *History, iv*, 49ff. The dialogue is probably invented.
36. Quoted Wodrow, *History, iv*, 140.
37. Quoted *ibid.*, 148f.

Chapter Twenty-Two: The Killing Time

1. Quoted Wodrow, *History, iv*, 195.
2. Burnet, *ii*, 204.
3. Lauder, *Historical Notices, ii*, 555.
4. Story, *op.cit.*, 96ff, 103.
5. *Ibid.*, 105, quoting from *State*

Trials, x, 686ff. The affair is discussed in Lang, *op.cit.*, 264ff, 276f.
6. Erskine, *Journal*, 100f.
7. Lang, *op.cit.*, 272ff.
8. Wodrow, *History*, iv, 106–112, though it is not in Erskine's eye-witness account.
9. *Introduction to Scottish Legal History*, 45.
10. Quoted in Lang, *op.cit.*, 323.
11. Story, *op.cit.*, 106.
12. Wodrow, *History*, iv, 100.
13. Quoted in Wodrow, *History*, iv, 161.
14. Wodrow, *History*, iv, 185ff.
15. *Ibid.*, 182.
16. *Ibid.*, 192ff.
17. Brodie, *op.cit.*, 507.
18. Terry, *Claverhouse*, 182f.
19. *Ibid.*, 155.
20. HMC, *Queensberry and Buccleuch MSS*, ii, 203, quoted Terry, *Claverhouse*, 184.
21. Lauder, *Historical Notices*, ii, 615.
22. Terry, *Claverhouse*, 188.
23. HMC, *Buccleuch and Queensberry MSS*, ii, 214. Quoted Terry, *Claverhouse*, 188–9.
24. Terry, *Claverhouse*, 190f.
25. Letter of 4 April 1685 to Queensberry, HMC, *Buccleuch and Queensberry MSS*, ii, 47; quoted in Terry, *Claverhouse*, 191.
26. Terry, *Claverhouse*, 213f.

Chapter Twenty-Three: A Carnival of Blood?

1. Story, *op.cit.*, 121, 127. Carstares's brother Alexander was a merchant in Amsterdam.
2. Jackson, *op.cit.*, 153.
3. Cowan, *op.cit.*, 136.
4. Wodrow, *History*, iv, 239.
5. Terry, *Claverhouse*, 194.
6. *Ibid.*, 212.
7. Morrill observes that the importance of the Covenant 'lies as much in its subsequent misrepresentations as in the retrievable historical reality' (*The Scottish National Covenant*, 1). Even in the 20th century, some writers of scholarly aspiration were dancing on Claverhouse's grave. He was '… a martinet, a mercenary, an insatiable clamourer for spoil, and a ruthless reveller in the blood of his countrymen,' in the judgement of J. K. Hewison (*op.cit.*) in 1908.
8. Wodrow, *History*, iv, 245.
9. Quoted in Scott, *op.cit.*, 40.
10. Terry, *Claverhouse*, 169.
11. Wodrow, *History*, iv, 250.
12. Walker, *op.cit.*, i, 297.
13. Cowan, *op.cit.*, 126.
14. Terry, *Claverhouse*, 209.
15. Mackenzie, 'Vindication', *op.cit.*, 346.

Chapter Twenty-Four:
Argyll's Adventure

1. Wodrow, *History, iv*, 261n.
2. Quoted Wodrow, *iv*, 266.
3. Burnet, *ii*, 249.
4. Burnet, *Supplement*, 186.
5. Quoted in Wodrow, *History, iv*, 286ff.
6. See Stevenson, *Revolution and Counter-Revolution*, 237, quoting a contemporary pamphlet by Clement Walker.
7. Quoted in Wodrow, *History, iv*, 290f.
8. Erskine, *Journal*, 140.
9. Shields, 'Life of Renwick' in *Biographia Presbyteriana, ii*, 86.
10. Erskine, *op.cit.*, 124.
11. *Ibid.*
12. Hill-Burton, *op.cit.*, 555.
13. Wodrow, *History, iv*, 300.
14. Their hospitality to Presbyterians did not endear the Dutch to the episcopalian Dr Archibald Pitcairn: 'Amphibious wretches sudden be your fall, May man undam you, and God damn you all.' (Maidment, *op.cit.*, 209).
15. Wodrow, *History, iv*, 302.
16. *Seafield Correspondence*, 11.
17. Walker, *op.cit., i*, 110. When Peden was dying in 1686, he sent for Renwick, who found him in his dug-out 'cave', 'lying in very low circumstances, overgrown with hair, and few to take care of him, as he never took much care of his body, seldom he unclothed himself, these years, or went to [slept in] bed.' His wish for the Cameronians to join Argyll had inflamed the old man against the younger. Peden is said to have apologised for doubting Renwick and believing ill reports of him (Walker, *op.cit., i*, 106f).
18. Shields, *op.cit.*, in *Biographia Presbyteriana, ii*, 130.
19. Cowan, *op.cit.*, 129.
20. Shields, *op.cit.*, in *Biographia Presbyteriana, ii*, 91, 93. The family, with a father at its head, was a sacrosanct social unit. A sect which broke up families threatened to destroy society. The Cameronians understood this, and felt that it was a 'new question'. Renwick refused to give a general answer on the matter and dealt with it on an individual basis (*op.cit.*, 96f).

Chapter Twenty-Five:
Dancing At Holyrood

1. Mackenzie, *Works, i*, 3ff. Holland was the main source of artistic influence: Williams (*op.cit.*, 15) lists a number of Dutch painters and craftsmen who worked in 17th-century Sotland.
2. Drummond, *Letters*, 52.
3. Macky, *Memoirs*, 243.
4. Lang, *op.cit.*, 157.

5 Watson, *op.cit.*, Part *i*, 142ff.
6 *Hudibras*, by the English poet Samuel Butler, published between 1663 and 1678, is a satire on Presbyterians and Independents, much appreciated by Charles II and by the episcopalians. Cleland of course takes the opposite viewpoint.
7 *Oxford Book of Ballads*, 781.
8 NLS MS 3932, Robert Kirk.
9 Erskine, *op.cit.*, 90f.
10 See Ross, *Folklore of the Scottish Highlands*, Frazer, *The Golden Bough*, etc.
11 Jackson, *Restoration Scotland*, 39.
12 F. Marian McNeill; see Gordon, *Candie for the Foundling*, 203.
13 Eight knights formed the original order, all Catholics (including Perth and Melfort), except for the Earl of Arran and the Marquis of Atholl.
14 ODNB, Edward Corp, 'James Drummond'.
15 Burnet, *ii*, 348ff.
16 *Ibid.*
17 Quoted Ouston, in Dwyer, Mason, Murdoch, *New Perspectives*, 144.
18 H.M.C., *xi*, *vi*, 171, quoted in Lang, *op.cit.*, 287.
19 Quoted Wodrow, *History, iv*, 359f.
20 Wodrow, *History, iv*, 364.
21 Harris, *Revolution*, 158.
22 Quoted in Wodrow, *History, iv*, 360.
23 *Seafield Correspondence*, 29.
24 Burnet, *ii*, 301.
25 Erskine, *op.cit.*, 194.

Chapter Twenty-Six:
... before the Delivery come.

1 Brown, *Kingdom or Province?* refers to 'the nation's 2000 Catholics' (165). Alexander Leslie, emissary of the Congregation of Propaganda of the Faith in 1667, reckoned 12,000 communicants in the Highlands, 2,200 in the rest of the country (Bellsheim, *iv*, 132).
2 Wodrow, *History, iv*, 398.
3 Lauder, *Historical Notices, ii*, 783.
4 Erskine, *op.cit.*, 208.
5 Dunlop, *op.cit.*, 52f. The reference is to Sprat's widely circulated 'Account' of the plot.
6 Bateson, *op.cit.*, 150. Lauder, *Historical Notices, i*, 127.
7 Wodrow, *History, iv*, 417ff.
8 Shields, *op.cit.*, 168ff.
9 Wodrow, *History, iv*, 433.
10 *Ibid.*
11 Wodrow, *History, iv*, 437.
12 Walker, *Six Saints, i*, 7.
13 Shields, *op.cit.*, 144f.
14 *Ibid.*, vi.
15 *Drumlanrig Papers, ii*, 189, quoted in Lang, *op.cit.*, 283.

16. Kirkton (*op.cit.*, 450) quotes a letter from an unnamed informer to Lord Linlithgow in 1679: 'If the counsell would give money, I kno whom I could employ to travell through Clydesdale, and would give exact intelligence, but I fear the not allowing of it will be the ruine of this land… '
17. Lauder, *Historical Observes*, 249.
18. Wodrow, *History, iv,* 447.
19. It was not unusual for the extreme Presbyterians to be labelled as *agents provocateurs*, sent by the Jesuits to stir up trouble. An English-published *Vindication of the Presbyterians of Scotland from the Malicious Aspersions cast on them in a late Pamphlet written by Sir G. Mackenzie*, of 1692, claims to have it on good authority that James Renwick was 'a Romish priest' (quoted in Lang, *op.cit.*, 130n).
20. Wodrow, *History, iv,* 452.
21. *Ibid.*, 453–4.
22. Graham, *Stair Annals, i,* 126.
23. ODNB, E. Calvin Beisner, 'Sir James Stewart of Goodtrees'.
24. Gardiner, *op.cit.*, 166, 196, notes 'his penchant for meddling'. It was 1692 before he had cleared up his spillage and was appointed Lord Advocate.
25. Balcarres, *op.cit.*, 2.
26. Terry, *Claverhouse*, 231.

Chapter Twenty-Seven: Interregnum

1. Scott, *op.cit.*, 55.
2. Wodrow, *History, iv,* 465.
3. *Ibid.*, 468.
4. Burnet, *ii,* 411f. Harris in *Revolution* (369) says 'Plotter' Ferguson wrote it.
5. Quoted Wodrow, *iv,* 470ff.
6. See Jackson, *op.cit.*, 147. Back in 1659, Andrew Hay had noted, 'After supper I did read a little upon a little book by Mr Hobs *de corpore politico*' (Hay, *Diary*, 181).
7. Quoted in Terry, *Claverhouse*, 237f.
8. Story, *op.cit.* 156.
9. ODNB, Edward Corp, 'John Drummond'.
10. Wodrow, *History, iv,* 474.
11. See Scott, *Tales of a Grandfather*.
12. Wodrow, *History, iv,* 475.
13. See D. J. Patrick, 'Unconventional Procedure: Scottish Electoral Politics after the Revolution', in Brown & Mann, *op.cit.*, 211.
14. Balcarres, *op.cit.*, xvii.
15. Morer, *A Short Account*, 96.
16. Macaulay, *op.cit.*, 608f.
17. Drummond, *Letters*, 1ff.
18. Letter from Earl of Crawford to Carstares, 16 June 1691, in *Carstares State Papers*, 147.

19. Evelyn, *Diary*, iii, 285.
20. See list in Patrick, *op.cit.*, 242ff.
21. Burnet, *iii*, xx.
22. Scott, *op.cit.*, 68.

Chapter Twenty-Eight: The Revolution Settlement

1. Kishlansky, *A Monarchy Transformed*, 285.
2. Patrick, *op.cit.*, 208ff.
3. On 9 April 1689 Sir James Dalrymple wrote to Melville: '... the solid ground is, that the King having violated the constitution of the Kingdom in both its sacred and civil rights, the convention, as representing the body politic, did declare, that seeing he had violated his part of the mutual engagements, they were free of their part... seeing the violations were so high as to refuse, reject and renounce the government of the kingdom according to a true constitution, and to assume a despotic and arbitrary government, neither he nor any that come of him after that could have any title to reign' (*Leven & Melville Papers*, 8f).
4. Balcarres, *op.cit.*, 26.
5. Terry, *Claverhouse*, 256n.
6. Quoted in Scott, *op.cit.*, 78ff.
7. Balcarres, *op.cit.*, 27.
8. Dalrymple, *Memoirs*, *i*, Pt 1, 287.
9. Dickinson and Donaldson, *op.cit.*, 199.
10. *Leven & Melville Papers*, 4.
11. As Dickinson and Donaldson note (*op.cit.*, 200), the English Parliament considered that James had effectively abdicated; the Scottish Parliament deprived him of his crown.
12. *A.P.S., ix*, 37. The 'Claim of Right', quoted Dickinson and Donaldson, *op.cit.*, 200ff.
13. Dickinson and Donaldson, *op.cit.*, 207f.
14. Lang, *op.cit.*, 300f, quoting *Add. MSS*, 34, 516, f61–62.
15. *Leven & Melville Papers*, 128.
16. Macinnes, *Clanship*, 44.
17. Scott, *op.cit.*, 110.
18. Drummond, *Memoirs of Lochiel*, 237.
19. Story, *op.cit.*, 168.
20. Dickinson and Donaldson, *op.cit.*, 208f.
21. Wodrow, *History*, iv, 484n.
22. Cowan, *op.cit.*, 68f.
23. Story, *op.cit.*, 164.
24. Dickinson and Donaldson, *op.cit.*, 212.
25. *A.P.S., ix*, 104, quoted Dickinson and Donaldson, *op.cit.*, 213f.
26. Wodrow, *History*, iv, 484n.
27. An episcopalian pamphlet of 1690, *An Account of the Present Persecution of the Church of Scotland*, notes that on Sunday 28 April 1689, all ministers were required to proclaim and pray for William and Mary, or face

deprivation of their posts. One Falconer, a curate in Moray, had reluctantly decided to comply, when he found his normal congregation joined by Viscount Dundee. His consequent prayer for James VII resulted in his eventual 'outing'.

Chapter Twenty-Nine: Dark John Of The Battles

1. The first recorded ascent of Ben Nevis was in 1771. Among the gathering at Dalmucomir was surely the great bard Iain Lòm Macdonald, scourge of the Campbells.
2. Mackay, *Mackay*, 74f.
3. Letter to Melville, 1 June 1689, *Leven & Melville Papers*, 37.
4. Mackay, *Mackay*, 1ff.
5. Drummond, *Memoirs of Lochiel*, 278.
6. Ibid., 279. Dundee used his own funds to help finance his campaign, and his letter to Melfort of 27 June 1689 says also that 'my brother-in-law, Auldbar [Robert Young of Auldbar, husband of his sister Anne], and my wife found ways to get credit. For my own, nobody durst pay to a traitor' (Terry, *Claverhouse*, 311).
7. Terry, *Claverhouse*, 309ff.
8. *Leven & Melville Papers*, 222–5. Professor Brown (*Kingdom or Province?* 171) thinks Melfort was right to resist Dundee's 'extravagant claims' for aid.
9. Story, *op.cit.*, 187.
10. Kishlansky, *op.cit.*, 325.
11. *A.P.S., ix*, 133–4. Wodrow, *iv*, 484n.
12. Story, *op.cit.*, 180ff.
13. Grant, *The Old Scots Navy*, 3; Graham, *Maritime History*, 69.
14. Drummond, *Memoirs of Lochiel*, 257.
15. Terry, *Claverhouse*, 340n.
16. Drummond, *Memoirs of Lochiel*, 276.
17. Brown, *Kingdom or Province?* 170.
18. Copy of a letter written on 13 August 1689, bound into the NLS copy of Morer's *Short Account*.
19. Patrick Walker, *Biographia Presbyteriana*, i, 208–9. Ian Cowan notes that the first post-Revolution Cameronian meeting was at Douglas, on 31 January 1689, with around 300 armed men present. They agred to send a troop to protect the Convention of Estates against Jacobite attack. After long and heated debate at Douglas on 29 April, a minority agreed to support and serve in a regiment to 'resist popery and Prelacy, and arbitrary power; and to recover and establish the work of Reformation in Scotland' (Cowan, *op.cit.*, 143f).

20. Story, *op.cit.*, 173. Patrick Walker also complained about Richard Cameron's name being made contemptible by 'Drums and Pipes in the *Cameronian* March'.
21. Mackay, *Mackay*, 66. One wonders if the Council deliberately intended to expose the Cameronians to maximum danger in the hope of reducing their numbers. Sending them to Dunkeld was putting their head into the lion's mouth. Soon afterwards, they were sent out of Scotland to Flanders, to their great indignation.
22. Mackay, *Mackay*, 66.
23. Story, *op.cit.*, 193.
24. Erskine, *op.cit.*, 95.
25. Shields, *op.cit.*, 198.
26. Henderson, *op.cit.*, 189.

Chapter Thirty:
A Mirror-Scotland

1. *Leven and Melville Papers*, 580.
2. Usually assumed to be the work of 'Plotter' Ferguson.
3. Dalrymple, *Apology*, 2.
4. Mackay, *Stair*, 246.
5. Riley, *King William and the Scottish Politicians*, 23ff.
6. *Lockhart Papers, i*, 88. The same story is told about Sir James Stewart in Balcarres, *op.cit., iii*, 214n.
7. Mackay, *Stair*, 240.
8. Quoted in Dalrymple, *Memoirs, iii*, 54ff.
9. Story, *op.cit.*, 218.
10. *Leven and Melville Papers*, 568.
11. Story, *op.cit.*, 196ff.
12. Quoted in *ibid.*, 229.
13. Riley, *op.cit.*, 60f.
14. Letter to Lord Lothian, 27 February 1692, in Graham, *Stair Annals, i*, 179f.
15. *Carstares State Papers*, 143ff.
16. Brown, *Kingdom or Province?* 173.
17. Murray, *op.cit.*, 93.
18. Lenman, *Jacobite Clans*, 48.

Chapter Thirty-One:
'The Interest Of The State'

1. Macky, *Memoirs*, 199.
2. Mitchison, *History of Scotland*, 286.
3. Mitchell, *History of the Highlands*, 544.
4. *Ibid.*
5. Quoted in Mackay, *Stair*, 257.
6. Quoted in Prebble, *Glencoe*, 227.
7. Quoted in Mackay, *Stair*, 256; my italics.
8. Graham, *Stair Annals*, 162.
9. Macaulay, *op.cit., v*, 198.
10. See Graham, *Stair Annals, i*, 166.
11. Quoted in Dunlop, *op.cit.*, 90.

Chapter Thirty-Two: The Perils Of Atheism

1. Maidment *op.cit.*, 191. An anecdote in Murray's *Literary History of Galloway* (155) recounts an exchange between Lady Stair and Claverhouse, whose name was pronounced 'Clavers'. He made a derogatory reference to John Knox, to which she replied that: 'There is not, after all, so much difference between you and him, only he gained his point by "clavers", you by "knocks".'
2. Story, *op.cit.*, 237ff; Dunlop *op.cit.*, 87f.
3. Burnet, *iii*, 233.
4. Mackay, *Stair*, 261.
5. *State Trials, xiii*, 909.
6. *Ibid.*, 916.
7. Mackay, *Stair*, 263n.
8. Grant, *op.cit.*, 209f.
9. See Riley, *King William and the Scottish Politicians*.
10. *Carstares State Papers*, 289.
11. Story, *op.cit.*, 180f. Ten years later he wrote: 'I have no patron about court but the King himself, nor doe I seek any' (letter to Lord Seafield, 16 August 1700, in *Seafield Correspondence*, 311).
12. Macky, *Memoirs*, 210.
13. *Ibid.*
14. *Seafield Correspondence*, 96.
15. Lecky, *History of Rationalism*, 137f.
16. Hetherington, *History of the Church of Scotland, ii*, 222.
17. Bellsheim, *History of the Catholic Church in Scotland, iv*, 150.
18. Eric G. Forbes, 'Philosophy and Science Teaching in the 17th Century', in Donaldson, *Four Centuries*, 28ff.
19. Mackintosh, *op.cit.*, 392–3 and Note.
20. Watson, *op.cit.*, Part *iii*, 56. Lord Errol was the pub's ultimate landlord.
21. Drummond & Bulloch, *The Scottish Church*, 14f.
22. *State Trials, xiii*, 1274ff.
23. *Ibid.*, 917ff.
24. Hunter & Wootton, *Atheism from the Reformation to the Enlightenment*, 238.
25. Drummond & Bulloch, *op.cit.*, 14f.

Chapter Thirty-Three: The Silence Of Darien

1. Mathieson, *Scotland and the Union*, 28.
2. Lenman, *Economic History*, 50.
3. Mackintosh, *op.cit.*, 328.
4. Murdoch, *Network North*, 241.
5. The *African Merchant*, see Graham, *Maritime History*, 88. The last gold coins minted in Scots currency were made with gold from this voyage, see Bateson, *op.cit.*, 152.

6 *The Dreme of the Realme of Scotland*. Lindsay concluded that Scotland lacked 'Justice, Policie (good government) and Peace'.
7 Mathieson, *Scotland and the Union*, 41.
8 Letter of 14 July 1698 from Seafield to Carstares, *Carstares State Papers*, 390.
9 Letter to Lord Annandale, HMC Hope Johnstone 104, quoted in Dunlop, *op.cit.*, 96.
10 Dunlop, *op.cit.*, 96.
11 *Darien Papers*, 150.
12 Letter to Hugh Fraser from John Borland, John Campbell, and John Maxwell, *Darien Papers*, 157–9. Paterson's wife died in Darien.
13 Erskine, *Journal*, Appendix, 243.
14 Address to the Officers of the Company, 10 February 1700, *Darien Papers*, 269f.
15 *Darien Papers*, 264.
16 Macaulay, *op.cit.*, v, 231.
17 Seafield was proposing a bill for it in 1700; see letter of 7 November to Carstares, *Carstares State Papers*, 671f.
18 *Seafield Correspondence*, 241ff.
19 *Carstares State Papers*, 570.
20 Colonel Ferguson to Carstares, 15 June 1700, *Carstares State Papers*, 527.
21 Mathieson, *Scotland and the Union*, 31.
22 Murdoch (*op.cit.*, 241) estimates that between 18–25 per cent of 'the liquid capital available in Scotland' was lost.
23 Devine, *The Transformation of Rural Scotland*, 22f.
24 Gordon, *Candie for the Foundling*, 108.
25 Graham, *Social Life*, 151n.
26 Whatley, *The Scots and the Union*, 148.
27 Mitchison, *op.cit.*, 299. It was not an original idea; several Acts of Parliament in the previous century had allowed it. See Dickinson and Donaldson, *op.cit.*, 376, 383.
28 *Carstares State Papers*, 425.
29 *Seafield Correspondence*, 300f.
30 Whatley, *op.cit.*, 143, estimates that the population fell by 13 per cent to around a million.
31 Walker, 'Life of Mr Daniel [sic] Cargill', in *Biographia Presbyteriana*, ii, 25ff.

Chapter Thirty-Four: Questions Of Succession

1 *Carstares State Papers*, 539ff, 616.
2 By Lord Melville to Carstares, see Riley, *The Union of England and Scotland*, 35.
3 *Seafield Correspondence*, 331.
4 Whatley, *op.cit.*, 109.
5 *Carstares State Papers*, 709–11.

6 *Ibid.*, 633ff, 645f.
7 Grant, *op.cit.*, 336.
8 See Murdoch, *Network North*, 245ff. Scotland's economic return from this activity was perhaps substantial but has not been quantified.
9 Lockhart, *Letters*, 7.
10 Whatley, *op.cit.*, 185.
11 Letter of 2 August 1700 to Carstares, *Carstares State Papers*, 591.
12 Maidment, *op.cit.*, 258.
13 Story, *op.cit.*, 278, 282. In 1707 Carstares became minister of St Giles.
14 *Carstares State Papers*, 258. Seafield had opinions of his own when he chose to exercise them: as 26-year-old member for Cullen he was one of the handful to oppose the deprival of James VII in 1689, and in 1711 he would move repeal of the Union he had worked so hard to achieve.
15 John Robertson, 'An Elusive Sovereignty: The Union Debate in Scotland, 1698–1707', in Robertson, *A Union for Empire*, 205. See also Bowie, *Scottish Public Opinion and the Anglo-Scottish Union*, 67ff.

Chapter Thirty-Five: An Unruly Parliament

1 Mathieson, *Scotland and the Union*, 81.
2 Riley, *The Union of England and Scotland*, 49.
3 *A.P.S.*, xi, 136, c.3, quoted in Dickinson and Donaldson, 474ff.
4 Mackinnon, *The Union*, 130.
5 Riley, *The Union of England and Scotland*, 63.
6 *Carstares State Papers*, 720.
7 Grant, *op.cit.*, 255.
8 Mathieson, *Scotland and the Union*, 92; Riley, *The Union of England and Scotland*, 74.
9 Mackinnon, *op.cit.*, 170.
10 *Papers Relating to... the Company of Scotland*, xv; not the Thames as in Mathieson, *Scotland and the Union*, 133.
11 Robertson, *op.cit.*, 210.
12 *Ibid.*, 211.
13 *Jerviswood Papers*, 74.
14 Whatley, *op.cit.*, 217, suggests that from the middle of the year certain opposition politicians were inclining towards union as 'a better bet as a means of securing their political objectives.'
15 HMCR, Seafield MSS, 207, quoted in Riley, *The Union of England and Scotland*, 146.
16 Mathieson, *op.cit.*, 110.
17 Lockhart, *Letters*, 28.
18 'Memorial concerning the treaty', quoted in Riley, *The Union of England and Scotland*, 176.
19 Grant, *op.cit.*, 337.
20 Graham, *Stair Annals*, i, 211.

21 Dunlop, *op.cit.*, 116.
22 Mackinnon, *op.cit.*, 316.
23 Story, *op.cit.*, 299.
24 Quoted in Dunlop, *op.cit.*, 115.
25 Story, *op.cit.*, 301.
26 Dunlop, *op.cit.*, 115.
27 Ibid.

Chapter Thirty-Six: Forever After

1 Colonel Nathaniel Hooke, sent by Louis XIV. See Ferguson, *op.cit.*, 229.
2 *Jerviswood Papers*, 141–2. On 3 January 1706, he wrote to Roxburghe '... the Union is our onlie game' and that Tweeddale agreed (*Ibid.*, 170).
3 Bowie, *Scottish Public Opinion*, 103.
4 *Ibid.*, 95.
5 Whatley, *op.cit.*, 293, 307.
6 Bowie, *op.cit.*, 142ff.
7 Ferguson, *Scottish Social Sketches*, 58.
8 Mathieson, *Scotland and the Union*, 133.
9 *Ibid.*, 134f. Hooke's *Secret History* has much on Hamilton's vacillations.
10 *Lockhart Papers, i*, 193.
11 Riley, *The Union of England and Scotland*, 185.
12 HMCR Mar and Kellie MSS, *i*, 270, quoted in Riley, *The Union of England and Scotland*, 257.
13 James Johnston, writing in cipher to George Baillie, on 21 September 1706, *Jerviswood Papers*, 160. Ferguson, in *Scotland's Relations with England*, says 'To his contemporaries, Queensberry was simply a great unprincipled operator on the make' (187).
14 Whatley, *op.cit.*, 298ff.
15 Mackenzie, *Orain Iain Luim*, 223ff.
16 Mathieson, *Scotland and the Union*, 152.
17 ODNB, John R. Young, 'John Dalrymple'.
18 Mathieson, *op.cit.*, 152.
19 Macky, *Memoirs*, 212.
20 Letter of 1706, quoted by Robertson, 'The Union Debate in Scotland', in Robertson, *op.cit.*, 221.
21 Mackinnon, *The Union*, 334f.

Bibliography

APS   Acts of the Parliament of Scotland
HMC   Historical Manuscripts Commission
ODNB   *Oxford Dictionary of National Biography*
SHS   Scottish History Society

1   Contemporary Writings and Records

Argyll, Earl of, *Letters to John Duke of Lauderdale*. Bannatyne Club, Edinburgh, 1829

Baillie, George, *Correspondence, 1702–08*. Bannatyne Club, Edinburgh, 1842

Baillie, Robert, *Letters and Journals*, 3 vols. Bannatyne Club, Edinburgh, 1841–42

Balcarres, Colin, *Memoirs Touching the Revolution in Scotland*. Bannatyne Club, Edinburgh, 1841

Biographia Presbyteriana, 2 vols. Edinburgh, 1827

Brodie, Alexander, *Diary of Alexander Brodie of Brodie*. Spalding Club, Aberdeen, 1863

Burnet, Gilbert, *History of his own Time*. 6 vols., Oxford, 1833

Carstares State Papers, ed. Joseph McCormick. Edinburgh, 1774

Darien Papers, 1695–1700. Bannatyne Club, Edinburgh, 1849

Dalrymple, Sir James, *An Apology for Sir James Dalrymple of Stair* (1690). Bannatyne Club, Edinburgh, 1825

Dickinson, W. C., and Donaldson G. (eds.), *A Source Book of Scottish History*, vol iii, 1567–1707. London, 1954

Douglas, Robert, The Form and Order of the Coronation of Charles the Second. Aberdeen, 1651

Drummond, James, Earl of Perth, *Letters to His Sister*. Camden Society, London, 1845

Drummond, John, *Memoirs of Sir Ewen Cameron of Lochiel*. Abbotsford Club, Edinburgh, 1842

Erskine of Carnock, John, *Journal* (ed. Walter McLeod). SHS, Edinburgh, 1893

Evelyn, John, *Diary*. 4 vols, London, 1879

Firth, C. H. (ed.), *Scotland and the Protectorate*. SHS, Edinburgh, 1899

Gordon, James, *History of Scottish Affairs*, 3 vols. Spalding Club, Aberdeen, 1841

Gordon, Patrick, *Britane's Distemper*. Spalding Club, Aberdeen, 1844

Graham, John Murray, *Annals and Correspondence of the Viscount and First and Second Earls of Stair*. 2 vols., Edinburgh 1875

Grant, James (ed.), *The Old Scots Navy*. Naval Records Society, XLIV, London, 1914

Guthrie, James, *Two Speeches of Mr James Guthry Before the Parliament*. 1661

Guthry, Henry, *Memoirs of Henry Guthry, Bishop of Dunkeld*. Glasgow, 1747

Hay, Andrew, of Craignethan, *Diary, 1659–60* (ed. A. G. Reid). SHS, Edinburgh, 1901

Jerviswood Papers. Ballantyne Club, Edinburgh, 1842

Hooke, N., *Secret History of Col. Hooke's Negociations in Scotland in 1707*. Edinburgh, 1740

Johnston, Archibald, *Memento Quamdiu Vivas and Diary from 1632 to 1639*, (ed. G. M. Paul), Edinburgh 1911

Johnston, Archibald, *Diary of Sir Archibald Johnston of Wariston* (ed. D. H. Fleming), SHS, Edinburgh, 1911

Johnston, Archibald, *Diary of Sir Archibald Johnston of Wariston*, Vol iii, 1655–60, (ed. James D. Ogilvie). SHS, Edinburgh 1940

Kirk, Robert, *The Secret Commonwealth of Elves, Faunes and Fairies* (1691). London, 1815; new ed. New York 2006

Kirkton, James, *The Secret and True History of the Church of Scotland, from the Restoration to the Year 1678* (ed. C. K. Sharpe). Edinburgh, 1817

Lauder, Sir John, *Historical Notices of Scotish Affairs*, vols. i, ii. Bannatyne Club, Edinburgh, 1848

Lauder, Sir John, *Historical Observes*. Bannatyne Club, Edinburgh, 1840

Lauderdale Papers, 3 vols., (ed. O. Airy). Camden Society, London, 1885

Law, Robert, *Memorialls*. (ed. C. K. Sharpe). Edinburgh 1818

Leven and Melville Papers, 1689–91. Bannatyne Club, Edinburgh, 1843

Lockhart, George, *Letters* (ed. Daniel Szechi). SHS, Edinburgh, 1989

Lockhart Papers. 2 vols. London, 1817

Mackay, Hugh, *Memoirs of the War Carried on in Scotland and Ireland*. Maitland Club, Edinburgh, 1833

Mackenzie, Sir George, *Aretina*. Edinburgh, 1660

Mackenzie, Sir George, *Memoirs of the Affairs of Scotland from the Restoration of King Charles II*. Edinburgh, 1821

Mackenzie, Sir George, *Works* (ed. T. Ruddiman). 2 vols, Edinburgh, 1716–22

Macky, John, *Journey through Scotland*. London, 1732

Macky, John, *Memoirs of the Secret Services of John Macky, Esq*. London, 1733

McWard, Robert, *The Poor Man's Cup of Cold Water*. Edinburgh, 1678

Melville, James, *Diary, 1556–1601*. Bannatyne Club, Edinburgh, 1839

Morer, T., *A Short Account of Scotland, etc*. London, 1702

Nicoll, John, *A Diary of Public Transactions and Other Occurrences, Chiefly in Scotland, from January 1650 to June 1667*. Bannatyne Club, Edinburgh, 1836

Papers Relating to the Ships and Voyages of the Company of Scotland, 1696–1707 (ed. G. P. Insh), SHS, Edinburgh, 1924

Pepys, Samuel, *Diary*, 11 vols., London, 1972–83

Philip, James, *The Grameid* (1691). SHS, Edinburgh, 1888

Registers of the Privy Council of Scotland, 3rd series, vols. vi, ix, xi. Edinburgh, 1914–24

Seafield Correspondence, 1685–1708 (ed. James Grant). SHS, Edinburgh, 1912

Shields, Alexander, *A Hind Let Loose*. Amsterdam, 1687

Sinclair, George, *Satan's Invisible World Discovered*. New ed, Glasgow, 1789

Spalding, J., *Memorialls of the Troubles*, 2 vols. Maitland Club, Edinburgh, 1828–29

State Trials, Vol. XIII, London, 1812

Stewart, James, *Ius Populi Vindicatum*. 1670

Stewart, James and Stirling, James, *Naphtali*. Edinburgh, 1667

Turner, Sir James, *Memoirs of His Own Life and Times, 1632–1670*. Edinburgh, 1829

Walker, Patrick, *Six Saints of the Covenant*, 2 vols,. London 1901

Watson, James, *Choice Collection of Comic and Serious Scots Poems* (1706), ed. Harriet Harvey Wood. Edinburgh, 1977

Wodrow, Robert, *Analecta*, 4 vols. Maitland Club, Edinburgh, 1842

Wodrow, Robert, *History of the Sufferings of the Church of Scotland, from the Restoration to the Revolution* (1720). Glasgow, 1838

2   Other Works

Aldis, H. G., *List of Books Published in Scotland Before 1700*. Edinburgh, 1904

Allan, David, *Philosophy and Politics in Later Stuart Scotland*. Phantassie, 2000

Anderson, J., *Ladies of the Covenant*. Glasgow, 1851

Ash, Marinell, *This Noble Harbour*. Invergordon & Edinburgh, 1991

Bateson, J. D., *Coinage in Scotland*. London, 1997

Bellsheim, Alphons, *History of the Catholic Church in Scotland*. 4 vols. Edinburgh, 1890

Bowie, Karin, *Scottish Public Opinion and the Anglo-Scottish Union, 1699–1707*, Woodbridge, 2007

Brand, John, *Observations on Popular Antiquities*. London, 1877

Brown, K. M., *Bloodfeud in Scotland 1573–1625*. Edinburgh, 1986

Brown, K. M., *Kingdom or Province? Scotland and the Regal Union, 1603–1716*. Basingstoke, 1993

Brown, K. M., and Mann, A. J., *History of the Scottish Parliament, Vol ii, Parliament and Politics in Scotland, 1567–1707*. Edinburgh, 2005

Brown, P. Hume, *Early Travellers in Scotland*. Edinburgh, 1891

Buchan, John, *Montrose*. London, 1928

Buckle, Henry, *History of Civilisation in England*, 3 vols. London, 1904

Buckroyd, Julia, *Church and State in Scotland, 1660–1681*. Edinburgh, 1980

Burke, Peter, *Popular Culture in Early Modern Europe*. London, 1978

Cant, R. G., *The University of St Andrews*, 3rd ed. St Andrews, 1992

Carlyle, Thomas, *Letters and Speeches of Cromwell*. London, 1845

Chambers, Robert, *Biographical Dictionary of Eminent Scotsmen* (4 vols.). Edinburgh, 1835

Comrie, John D., *A History of Scottish Medicine*, 3 vols. London, 1932

Cowan, Ian B., *The Scottish Covenanters*. London, 1976

Dalrymple, J., *Memoirs of Great Britain and Ireland*, 3 vols. New edition, London 1790

Davidson, Neil, *Discovering the Scottish Revolution*. London, 2003

Defoe, Daniel, *History of the Union of Great Britain*. Edinburgh, 1709

Devine, T. M., *The Transformation of Rural Scotland, 1660–1815*. Edinburgh, 1994

Devine, T. M., *Scotland's Empire, 1600–1815*. London, 2003

Dodds, James, *The Fifty Years' Struggle of the Scottish Covenanters*. Edinburgh, 1860

Donaldson, Gordon, *Four Centuries of Edinburgh University Life*. Edinburgh, 1983

Donaldson, Gordon, *Scotland: James V to James VII*, Edinburgh, 1965

Donaldson, Gordon, *Scottish Church History*. Edinburgh, 1985

Donaldson, Gordon, and Morpeth, Ronald, *Dictionary of Scottish History*, Edinburgh 1977

Dow, F. D., *Cromwellian Scotland*, Edinburgh, 1979

Drummond, Andrew L., and Bulloch, James, *The Scottish Church, 1688–1843*. Edinburgh, 1973

Dunlop, A. I., *William Carstares and the Kirk by Law Established*. Edinburgh, 1967

Dwyer, J., Mason, R., Murdoch A. (eds), *New Perspectives on the Politics and Culture of Early Modern Scotland*. Edinburgh, 1982

Elder, John R., *The Highland Host of 1678*. Glasgow, 1914

Fergusson, R. F., *Scottish Social Sketches of the Seventeenth Century*. Stirling, 1907

Ferguson, William, *Scotland's Relations with England*. Edinburgh, 1977

Gardiner, Ginny, *The Scottish Exile Community in the Netherlands, 1660–1690*. Phantassie, 2004.

Gordon, Anne, *Candie for the Foundling*. Edinburgh, 1992

Graham, Eric J., *A Maritime History of Scotland, 1650–1790*. Phantassie, 2002

Graham, H. Grey, *The Social Life of Scotland in the Eighteenth Century*. 4th ed., London, 1937

Grainger, John D., *Cromwell Against the Scots*. Phantassie, 1997

Grant, I. F., *Highland Folk Ways*. London, 1961

Harris, Frances, *Transformations of Love*. Oxford, 2004

Harris, Tim, *Restoration: Charles II and his Kingdoms, 1660–1685*. London, 2005

Harris, Tim, *Revolution: The Crisis of the British Monarchy, 1685–1770*. London, 2006

Henderson, G.D., *Religious Life in Seventeenth-Century Scotland*. Cambridge, 1937

Hetherington, W. M., *History of the Church of Scotland*. 2 vols., Edinburgh, 1852

Hewison, J. K., *The Covenanters*, 2 vols. Glasgow, 1908

Hill Burton, John, *History of Scotland*, vols *vi*, *vii*. Edinburgh, 1870

Hill, Christopher, *God's Englishman*. London, 1970

Hill, Christopher, *The World Turned Upside Down*. London, 1972

Jackson, Clare, *Restoration Scotland, 1660-1690*. Woodbridge, 2003

Hook, A. (ed.), *History of Scottish Literature, vol. 2*. Aberdeen, 1987

Hopkins, P., *Glencoe and the End of the Highland War*. Edinburgh, 1986

Hunter, Michael, and Wootton, D. (eds.) *Atheism from the Reformation to the Enlightenment*. Oxford, 1992

Introduction to Scottish Legal History. Stair Society, Alva, 1958

Kishlansky, Mark, *A Monarchy Transformed: Britain 1603–1714*. London, 1996

Landsman, N. C., *Scotland and Its First American Colony, 1683–1765*. Princeton, NJ, 1985

Lang, Andrew, *Sir George Mackenzie, King's Advocate, of Rosehaugh: his Life and Times*. London, 1909

Laslett, Peter, *The world we have lost*. London, 1965

Lecky, J. H., *History of Rationalism in Europe*, 2 vols. London, 1865

Lee, Maurice, Jr., *The 'Inevitable' Union*. Phantassie, 2003

Lee, Maurice, Jr. (ed.) *Relation of the Wrongs Done to the Ladie Yester*, in SHS *Miscellany XIII*, Edinburgh, 2004

Lenman, Bruce, *An Economic History of Modern Scotland, 1660–1976*. London, 1977

Lenman, Bruce, *The Jacobite Clans of the Great Glen*. London, 1975

Lynch, Michael (ed.), *The Early Modern Town in Scotland*. London, 1987

Macaulay, Thomas, *The History of England, from the Accession of James II*. London, 1849–61

McCrie, Thomas, *The Story of the Church of Scotland*. Glasgow, 1874

Macdonald, Alan R., *The Jacobean Kirk, 1567–1625*. Aldershot, 1998

Macdonald, S., *The Witches of Fife*. Phantassie, 2002

Macdougall, N. (ed.), *Scotland and War: AD79–1918*. Edinburgh, 1991

Mackay, A. J., *A Memoir of Sir James Dalrymple, 1st Viscount Stair*. Edinburgh, 1873

Mackay, John, *Life of Lieutenant-General Hugh Mackay of Scoury*. Edinburgh, 1836

Mackenzie, Annie M. (ed.), *Orain Iain Luim*. Edinburgh, 1984

Mackenzie, W. C., *Life and Times of John Maitland, Duke of Lauderdale*. London, 1923

Makey, Walter, *The Church of the Covenant, 1637–1651*. Edinburgh, 1979

Macinnes, Allan I., *Charles I and the Making of the Covenanting Movement, 1625–41*. Edinburgh, 1991

Macinnes, Allan I., *Clanship, Commerce, and the House of Stuart, 1603–1788*. Phantassie, 1996

Mackinnon, James, *The Social and Industrial History of Scotland*. Glasgow, 1910

Mackinnon, John, *The Union of England and Scotland*. London, 1896

Mackintosh, John, *The History of Civilisation in Scotland*, vol. iii. Paisley, 1895

Maidment, J. (ed.), *A Book of Scotish Pasquils, 1568–1715*. Edinburgh, 1868

Masson, David, *The Life of John Milton*, vol. v. London, 1877

Mathew, David, *Scotland Under Charles I*. London, 1955

Mathieson, W. L., *Politics & Religion*, 2 vols, Edinburgh, 1902

Mathieson, W. L., *Scotland and the Union*. Glasgow, 1905

Maxwell-Stuart, P. G., *Witch Hunters*. Stroud, 2003

Millar, John, *James II: A Study in Kingship*. London 1978

Mitchell, Dugald, *History of the Highlands and Gaelic Scotland*. Paisley, 1900

Mitchison, Rosalind, *A History of Scotland*. London, 1970

Morrill, John (ed.), *The Scottish National Covenant in its British Context*. Edinburgh, 1990

Murdoch, Steve, *Network North: Scottish Kin, Commercial and Covert Associations in Northern Europe, 1603–1746*. Leiden, 2006

Murray, W. H., *Rob Roy MacGregor*. Edinburgh, 1982

Napier, Mark, *Memorials and Letters Illustrative of the Life and Times of Viscount Dundee*, 3 vols. London, 1859

Oxford Book of Ballads, ed. F. Quiller-Couch. Oxford, 1910

Oxford Dictionary of National Biography. Oxford, 2004

Parker, Geoffrey, *The Thirty Years' War*. London, 1984

Polson, Alexander, *Scottish Witchcraft Lore*. Inverness, 1932
Prebble, John, *Glencoe*. London, 1966
Riley, P. W. J., *King William and the Scottish Politicians*. Edinburgh, 1979
Riley, P. W. J., *The Union of England and Scotland*. Manchester, 1978
Royle, Trevor, *Civil War: The Wars of the Three Kingdoms, 1638–60*. London, 2004
Robertson, John (ed.), *A Union for Empire*. Cambridge, 1995
Salmond, James B. (ed.), *Veterum Laudes*. Edinburgh, 1950
Scott, A. M. S., *Bonnie Dundee*. Edinburgh, 1989
Scott-Moncrieff, George (ed.), *The Stones of Scotland*. London, 1938
Smout, T. C., *Scottish Trade on the Eve of Union, 1660–1707*. Edinburgh, 1963
Smout, T. C., *A History of the Scottish People, 1560–1830*. London, 1969
'Southern, A,' *Clavers: The Despot's Champion*. London, 1889
Stevenson, David, *Revolution and Counter-Revolution in Scotland, 1644–1651*. London, 1977
Stevenson, David (ed.), *The Government of Scotland Under the Covenanters, 1637–1651*. SHS, Edinburgh, 1982
Stevenson, David, *The Origins of Freemasonry: Scotland's Century, 1590–1710*. Cambridge, 1988
Stevenson, David, *Union, Revolution and Religion in Seventeenth-Century Scotland*. Aldershot, 1998
Stewart, Duncan, *The Covenanters of Teviotdale*. Galashiels, 1908
Story, Robert, *William Carstares: A Character and Career of the Revolutionary Epoch*. London, 1874
Symon, J. A., *Scottish Farming: Past and Present*. Edinburgh, 1959
Tawney, R. H., *Religion and the Rise of Capitalism*. London 1926
Terry, C. S., *John Graham of Claverhouse*. London, 1905
Terry, C. S., *The Scottish Parliament: Its Constitution and Procedure, 1603–1707*. Glasgow, 1905
Tobin, Terence, *Plays by Scots 1660–1800*. Iowa City, 1974
Trevelyan, G. M., *History of England*. London, 1927
Trevor-Roper, *Religion, the Reformation, and Social Change*. London, 1967
Veitch, A., *Richard Cameron: The Lion of the Covenant*. London, 1948

Watt, Hugh, *Recalling the Scottish Covenants*. London, 1946
Whatley, Christopher A., *The Scots and the Union*. Edinburgh, 2006
Williams, Julia, *Dutch Art and Scotland: A Reflection of Taste*. Edinburgh, 1992
Withers, C. W. J., *Gaelic Scotland: The Transformation of a Culture Region*. London, 1988
Woolrych, Austin, *Britain in Revolution, 1625–1660*. Oxford, 2002
Wormald, J. (ed.), *Scotland Revisited*. London, 1991
Yates, Frances, *The Art of Memory*. London, 1966
Young, J. R., *The Scottish Parliament, 1639–1661*. Edinburgh, 1996

Index

A

Aberdeen, 2, 10–11, 13, 18, 39, 42, 51–53, 68, 70–71, 161–165, 168–169, 173, 198, 205, 210, 353–354, 358
Aberdeen, George Gordon, Earl of, 155, 162
Aberfoyle, 207
Abernethy, 175
Act of Classes, 26, 30, 32–33, 247, 318–320
Advocates' Library, 242, 321
Agnew, Alexander, 43
Agnew, Sir Andrew, 158
Aikenhead, Thomas, 278, 322
Airlie, Earl of, 14
Airds Moss, 149, 316, 321
Alison, Isabel, 150
Alyth, 36
Amsterdam, 197, 280–281, 342, 355
Angus, Earl of, 255–256
Annandale, Earl of, 261
Anne, Queen, 145, 287, 292, 297, 302, 312
Apologetical Declaration and Admonitory Vindication, 180
Apologeticall Relation of the Particular Sufferings of Faithful Ministers and Professours of the Church of Scotland, 88
Apology for Sir James Dalrymple of Stair, President of the Session, by Himself, 261
Aretina, 60, 205, 320, 329, 354
Argyll, 68, 97, 198–200, 227
Argyll, Archibald Campbell, 10th Earl, first Duke of, 253, 267, 270, 275, 283, 295
Argyll, Archibald Campbell, eighth Earl, first Marquis of, 14, 19, 22, 31, 33–34, 36, 38, 57, 59, 61, 66, 69–70, 173, 320
Argyll, Archibald Campbell, ninth Earl of, 36, 84, 155, 165, 197–201
Argyll, John Campbell, second Duke of, 299, 301–302, 307, 309
Articles, Committee or Lords of the, 82, 109, 213
Atholl, John Murray, Earl and first Marquis of, 82, 128, 142, 198, 231, 239, 242, 256, 344
Atholl, John Murray, Earl of Tullibardine, later first Duke of, 276, 281, 283, 309, 315
Audace, L', 298

B

Badenoch, 243, 250
Baillie, George, of Jerviswood, 300
Baillie, Robert, of Jerviswood, 120, 179
Balcarres, Colin Lindsay, third Earl of, 36, 231
Ballads, 46, 206, 344, 359
Bank of Scotland, x, 280, 322
Barclay, Robert, 340
Bass Rock, 111, 114
Belhaven, John Hamilton, second Lord, 307
Benburb, 18, 319
Bergen, 112
Berwick, 111
Bishops' War, First, 11, 319
Bishops' War, Second, 13, 106, 319
Blackness Castle, 201
Blair Atholl, 253, 255
Blair Castle, 251, 253
Bogue, William, 164
Bothwell Bridge, 139, 140, 142–144, 147–149, 169–170, 180, 214, 220, 321, 339
Bourges, 54
Boyle, Roger, 41
Breadalbane, John Campbell, first Earl of, 267
Brechin, 2, 68
Brodie, Alexander, 43, 47, 53, 56, 72, 187, 353
Brown, John, of Priestfield, 71, 88, 194–195, 320
Brown, Rev. John, 71, 88, 90, 100, 167
Bruce, Andrew, of Earlshall, 131
Bruce, Sir William, 89, 143
Buchan, General Thomas, 265–266
Buchanan, George, 48, 229

INDEX

Burnet, Archbishop Alexander, 85, 100, 107
Burnet, Gilbert, 33, 38, 50–51, 57, 66, 70, 73–74, 85–86, 98, 101, 103, 145, 152, 197, 226–228, 235, 246, 272
Burntisland, 149, 202, 233
Butter, Peter, 278

C

Caelia's Country House and Closet, 96, 204, 328
Caerlaverock, 13
Cairncross, Alexander, 220
Callendar, Earl of, 115
Calvin, Jean, 5
Cameron, Michael, 148
Cameron of Lochiel, Ewen, 38, 165, 240, 253, 326, 353
Cameron, Richard, 23, 48, 51–52, 54, 88, 102, 119, 142, 144, 148–149, 335, 348, 360
Campbell, Captain Colin, 282
Campbell, George, of Cessnock, 165
Campbell, Robert, of Glenlyon, 268, 273
Campbeltown, 198
Campvere, 172
Canaries, Rev. James, 220
Cannon, Colonel Alexander, 252
Canongate, 174
Canons and Constitutions Eclesiasticall, 2
Carbisdale, 29
Cardross, Lady, 169
Cargill, Donald, 71, 132, 138, 144, 147, 150
Carmichael, William, 134
Carr, Lady Elizabeth, 28
Carstairs, Captain, 120–121
Carstairs, Rev. John, 30–31, 40, 50, 52, 66, 71, 91–93, 150
Carstares, William, 23, 48, 50, 52–53, 102, 109–111, 141, 161–162, 165–167, 175–177, 183–185, 190, 226, 228, 245–246, 252, 262, 264–265, 270, 272, 275–276, 282, 283–285, 289, 291–293, 298–300, 302–304, 311–312
Cassillis, John Kennedy, sixth Earl of, 206–207

Cathcart, 23, 129
Chambers, Robert, 310
Charles I, King, 1, 8, 12, 14–15, 97, 229, 319
Charles II, King, 28, 32–33, 56, 77–78, 126, 355
Christianity Not Mysterious, 278
Claverhouse, Graham of, see Graham, John,
Cleland, William, 137, 199, 205, 256
Clerke, William, 70
Cochrane, Lady Jean, 170
Cochrane, Sir John, 165, 170, 173, 180, 199
Cockburn, James, 208
Committee of Estates, 14, 19, 31–32, 36, 56, 316, 320
Company Trading to Africa and the Indies, 274, 322
Convention of Estates, 17, 237, 283, 316, 347
Copernicus, 53
Cowan, Ian, 167, 347
Crail, 58
Crawford, Earl of, 94, 259, 265, 345
Cromartie, George Mackenzie, first Earl of, see Mackenzie, George, of Tarbat
Cromdale, 265, 322
Cromwell, Oliver, 26, 29, 34, 37, 55
Culross, 64, 119
'Cumbernauld Band', 17
Cunningham, Alexander, 289

D

Dalkeith, 36, 104
Dalmellington, 130
Dalnaspidal, 37, 320
Dalrymple, James, first Viscount Stair, 23, 25, 29, 40–41, 52–53, 58, 75, 97, 102, 105, 108, 115, 143, 152–153, 155, 157, 165–166, 172, 216, 226, 228, 241, 245–246, 257, 260–261, 321, 346, 353, 358
Dalrymple, John, first Earl of Stair, 23, 48, 50–52, 54, 102, 106, 123, 155–157, 160, 165 269
Dalyell, Thomas, 89–91, 93, 146–147, 150, 171–172, 174, 177–178, 203

Danby, Earl of, 124
Danzig, 112
Defoe, Daniel, 289, 306, 310
Descartes, René, 53, 63, 277–278
Devine, David M., 80
Dick, Quintin, 130
Dick, William, 15
Dickson, David, 131
Douglas, 90
Douglas, James 162, 172, 188, 230, 317–318
Douglas, Lord George, 106
Douglas, Marquis of, 137
Douglas, Rev. Robert, 33, 58, 71
Douglas, William, first Duke of Queensberry, 109, 317–318
Drumclog, 137–138, 140, 142, 144, 206, 321
Drumlanrig, Lord, see Queensberry, second Duke of
Drummond, Alexander, of Balhaldie, 240
Drummond, James, see Perth, 4th Earl of
Drummond, John, Viscount Melfort, 54, 106, 111, 176, 179, 189, 199, 210–211, 334, 345
Drummond, William, 195, 203, 212
Dryden, John, 129
Dudhope Castle, 163, 170, 240
Dumbarton, 200
Dumbarton, George Douglas, first Earl of, 200, 231
Dumfries, 3, 13, 25, 32, 43, 90, 93, 103, 122, 131, 148, 158, 164, 274, 307
Dunbar, 31, 206, 320
Dunbar of Baldoon, 103
Dunblane, 68, 73, 135, 240
Duncanson, Major, 268
Dundee, ix, 23, 49, 171, 220, 236, 243–245
Dundee, John Graham, Viscount, see Graham, John,
Dundonald, William Cochrane, Earl of, 170
Dunfermline, Earl of, 244
Dunkeld, 68, 244, 253–256, 265, 322, 348, 354
Dunlop, William, 162, 172, 284
Dunottar Castle, 201, 330

Dysart, 79, 107, 274
Dysart, Elizabeth Murray, Countess of, see Lauderdale, Duchess of,

E

Edinburgh, 2, 10, 26, 35, 40, 47, 67, 78, 104, 106, 116, 123, 149, 176, 263
Edinburgh Castle, 33, 55, 58, 155, 160, 179, 234, 250
Edinburgh University, 23, 73, 151, 156, 177, 209
Elgin, 187, 244
Engagement, The, 19–21, 25–28, 49, 319
Errol, Countess of, 163, 205, 298
Errol, Earl of, 80, 163
Erskine, John, of Carnock, 169, 172, 199, 208, 257
Evelyn, John, 96, 235

F

Falkland, 23, 48, 51, 54, 88, 102, 119
Ferguson, Robert, 165–166
Fife, 3, 17, 23, 25, 33, 58, 79, 112, 119, 125, 134, 227, 233, 329, 358
Findlater, Earl of, 276
Fletcher, Andrew, of Saltoun, 285, 291, 294, 308
Fletcher, Sir John, 60
Flyting of Montgomery and Polwarth, 60
Forbes, John, 70, 205
Forrester, Sir Andrew, 166
Fort William, 265, 268
Fraser, Simon, 11th Lord Lovat, 297
Furgol, Edward M., 35

G

Galilei, Galileo, 53
Gaidhealtachd, see Highlands
Galloway, 13, 23, 25, 50, 69, 90, 93, 97, 115, 132, 147, 158, 160, 172, 182, 185–186, 331, 349
Gib, Muckle John, 151
Gibson, Walter and James, 172
Gillespie, George, 2
Girvan, 121
Glamis, 121
Glasgow, 11, 21, 23, 25, 41, 50, 52, 54, 64,

67, 69, 71, 79, 85, 88, 90, 93, 100–101, 113, 125, 131–132, 136–137, 149, 164, 172, 200, 219–220, 222, 231, 252, 277–278, 291, 307, 321, 330, 354–360
Glasgow University, 13, 52, 141, 262, 284, 303
Glen Coe, 82, 268, 270–273, 310, 322
Glencairn, William Cunningham, Earl of, 36, 55, 57, 85
Godolphin, Sidney, 292, 301, 309
Gordon, Commodore Thomas, 297–298, 302
Gordon, George, fourth Marquis of Huntly and first Duke of, 155, 162
Gordon, Lady Anne, 210
Gordon, Sir George, of Haddo, see Aberdeen, Earl of,
Gothenburg, 289
Gourock, 172
Graham, David, 195
Graham, Helen, 122, 147
Graham, James, see Montrose
Graham, John, of Claverhouse, 49–50, 54, 75, 88, 102, 106, 122–123, 131, 134–136, 139, 141, 144, 147, 154–155, 158–161, 163–164, 169–172, 177, 187–189, 193–195, 203, 220, 224, 227, 229–233, 235–236, 239–241, 243–245, 247–254
Graham, Sir James, 122
Grameid, 243, 355
Great Glen, 38, 82, 248, 265, 320, 358
Green, Captain Thomas, 299
Gregory, James, 53
Greyfriars' Church, 5, 262–263
Grierson, Sir Robert, of Lagg, 44–45, 182, 185, 193
Guthrie, James, 40, 66, 223
Guthrie, Rev. John, 101

H

Hackston, David, of Rathillet, 134, 139, 149
Haddington, 117, 163, 206
Hague, The, 29, 190, 227
Hamilton, 137
Hamilton, Anne, Duchess of, 143

Hamilton, James, third Marquis and first Duke of, 10–11, 15, 19, 91
Hamilton, James, fourth Duke of, 276, 289, 291–293, 300–302, 305–307, 316
Hamilton, Robert, 135–139
Hamilton, William, Earl of Lanark, then second Duke of, 19, 21, 316
Hamilton, William Douglas, third Duke of, 109, 114, 117, 120–121, 137, 142, 155, 177, 212, 232, 235, 238–240, 260, 264, 276
Harley, Robert, 293, 310
Harvey, Marion, 150
Hastings, Colonel, 255
Hatton, Lord, 81, 107, 123, 335
Hay, Andrew, 37, 327, 345
Henderson, Alexander, 3–4, 18
Heriot's Hospital, 156
Hickes, Doctor, 123
Highlands, 17–18, 31, 36–38, 41, 45, 49–50, 55, 79, 81–83, 112, 118, 121, 124, 156, 205, 209, 234, 240, 243, 248, 250–251, 253, 260, 265–266, 270, 275, 277, 290, 317, 320–321, 325, 344, 348, 359
Hill, Colonel, 268
Hind Let Loose, 94, 191, 218, 337, 355
Hobbes, Thomas, 57, 62, 77, 229
Hodges, James, 306
Holland, 29, 67, 71, 88–89, 142, 155, 160, 165, 172, 190, 197, 212, 214, 217–218, 224, 226, 249, 270
Holyrood Palace, 70, 143, 205, 209–210, 231
Home, Earl of, 186
Hume, Sir Patrick, of Polwarth, Earl of Marchmont, 199, 246
Huntly, George Gordon, second Marquis of, 18, 36, 125
Hyde, Edward, 56

I

Institutions of the Law of Scotland, 157, 184
Inveraray, 71, 199, 201, 268
Inverkeithing, 33, 320
Inverness, 38, 50, 186, 198, 244, 248, 250, 326, 339, 360

Ireland, 1, 15–16, 18, 28–29, 37, 80, 86, 97, 122, 141, 227, 239, 251, 319–320, 354, 356
Irongray, 74, 105
Irvine, James, 150
Ius Populi Vindicatum, 101, 224, 278, 333, 355

J

James VI, King, 1, 77, 98
James VII, King, 128, 133, 143, 145, 152, 228
Jesuits, 345
'Jock of Broad Scotland', see Agnew, Alexander
Johnston, Archibald, of Wariston, 3, 5, 33, 40, 43, 354
Johnston, James, 194, 264, 272, 281, 298–299, 352
Johnston, Margaret, 115
Johnston, Sir James, of Westerhall, 194
Jones, Colonel John, 38
Junto, The, 169

K

Kekewich, Elizabeth, 161
Kemnay, 277
Kenmure, Viscount, 193
Kid, Rev. John, 140
Killiecrankie, 253, 256, 322
Kincardine, Alexander Bruce, Earl of, 99, 108
King, Rev. John, 136
Kintore, John Keith, Earl of, 186
Kirk, Rev. Robert, 207–208
Kirkton, Rev. James, vi, 75, 114, 118, 120, 276
Kirkwall, 198
Knox, John, 14, 25, 105

L

La Rochelle, 112
Lagg, Laird of, see Grierson
Lambert, General, 33
Lanark, vi, 25, 93, 123, 125, 158
Lanark, Earl of, see Hamilton, William
Lang, Andrew, 96, 109, 117, 124, 179

Laud, William, Archbishop, 2
Lauder, Sir John, 121, 124
Lauderdale, Duchess of, 108, 163
Lauderdale, John Maitland, 2nd Earl, 1st Duke of, 19–20, 81, 84, 98, 102, 105, 112, 114–116, 123–124, 128–130, 135, 142–143, 145
Law, Rev. Robert, 41, 57, 149
Lawborrows, 125–126, 131, 143, 194, 321
Laws and Customes of Scotland in Matters Criminal 63, 124
Lecky, W. H., 276
Leiden, 160, 173, 217, 359
Leighton, Robert, 53–54, 73, 100–101, 105, 107, 141, 247, 337
Leith, 89, 111, 149, 186, 282, 299, 325
Leslie, Alexander, first Earl of Leven, 11, 21, 25, 344
Leslie, David, Lord Newark, 17, 21, 25, 29–30, 34
Leslie, John, Earl and Duke of Rothes, 57, 59, 88, 94, 98, 114, 125, 141, 145, 150
Life expectancy, 325
Lindsay, Sir David, 48, 135, 281, 290
Linlithgow, 25, 117, 141, 151, 182
Linlithgow, George Livingston, Earl of, 137, 141
Livingstone, Sir Thomas, 265, 267
Lockhart, George, of Carnwath, 116
Lockhart, Sir George, 60, 93, 115–116, 123, 142, 155, 212–213, 231, 261, 289, 302, 308, 310
Lockhart, Sir William, 106
Lorimer, William, 279
Lothian, Earl of, 28, 32, 38
Loudoun, John Campbell, first Earl of, 3, 19, 25, 27, 121

M

Macaulay, Thomas B., 233, 258, 269, 283
MacColla, Alastair, 17, 244
McCormick, Joseph, 272, 353
MacCrimmon, Patrick Mòr, 205
Macdonald, Iain Lòm, 309, 347
Macdonald of Glengarry, 36
Macdonald of Keppoch, 244, 250
MacGregor, Rob Roy, 49, 359

Machrihanish, 79
MacIan of Glencoe, 268–269
McIlwraith, Matthew, 195
Mackail, Matthew, 132
Mackay, General Hugh, 106, 359
Mackenzie, Colin, 171
Mackenzie, George, of Tarbat, first Earl of Cromartie, 84, 155, 221, 231, 234, 237, 243, 246, 248, 251, 307, 311–312
Mackenzie, Murdo, 72
Mackenzie, Sir George, of Rosehaugh, 23–24, 50–51, 54, 58–60, 70, 73–74, 93–96, 99, 103, 108–109, 115–117, 123–125, 128–129, 135, 142–143, 154, 160, 164, 167–168, 170, 173, 175–177, 183–185, 191, 196, 201, 205, 209, 213–214, 222, 224, 229, 234–234, 240, 242–243, 262–263
Macky, John, 205, 267, 275, 355
Mclauchlan, Margaret, 195
McWard, Rev. Robert, 67, 70–71, 90, 100, 110, 130–131, 142, 160, 167
Magus Muir, 134, 140
Mar, John Erskine, 10th Earl of, 208, 257
Mar, John Erskine, 11th Earl of, 309
Mary I, Queen, 56, 84, 143, 154
Mary II, Queen, 221, 242, 275
Mauchline Moor, 21
Maybole, 121, 132
Mein, James, 69
Meldrum, George, 279
Melfort, John Drummond, first Viscount, see Drummond, John
Melville, Andrew, 77
Melville, George, first Earl of, 241, 245
Menteith, William Graham, Earl of, 122
Middleton, John, Earl of, 31, 34, 37–38, 57–58, 66–67, 71, 84
Milroy, Gilbert, 186
Mitchell, James, 100, 114, 123, 179, 321
Moffat, 227
Monck, George, 34, 37, 40–41, 56
Monkland, Laird of, 173
Monmouth, Duke of, 128, 138, 165
Monro, Robert, 15, 25
Montgomery, Sir James, 245, 252, 260–261
Montrose, James Graham, third Earl, first Marquis of, 5, 17–18, 26, 29–30, 49, 93, 122, 147, 306
Moray, Alexander Stewart, fifth Earl of, 169, 185, 209
Moray, Sir Robert, 11, 39, 71, 96, 99, 108
Morer, Thomas, 51
Morgan, Colonel Thomas, 37
Morton, Rev. Andrew, 219
Munro, Sir George, of Culcairn, 186
Mure, William, of Caldwell, 91, 93
Murray, Lord John, 250–251, 253, 273, 276
Musselburgh, 111

N

Naphtali, 94–95, 97, 99, 101, 224, 321, 333–334, 355
National Covenant, xi, 1, 3, 5–7, 11–12, 17, 20, 28, 32, 39–40, 44, 68–69, 71, 77
Neo-Stoicism, 53, 61–63, 73
Newburn, 13
Nicoll, John, 29, 88
Nicolson, Thomas, 277
Nisbet, Sir John, 118
Nithsdale, Robert Maxwell, first Earl of, 13
Northern Band, 31–32, 317
Northesk, Earl of, 49

O

Oates, Titus, 133
O'Neill, Owen Roe, 18
Ogilvie, James, see Seafield
Orange, William of, see William II
Order of the Thistle, 209
Orkney, 29, 68, 100, 198, 274

P

Pacification of Berwick, 11, 315, 319
Paisley, 94, 101, 170–171, 359
Paterson, John, 222
Parliament: status of, 97
Paterson, Sir William, 177
Paterson, William, 274, 289, 293, 308
Payne, Neville, 262
Peden, Rev. Alexander, 139, 144, 202, 327
Peirson, Peter, 182
Pepys, Samuel, 99, 331

Perth, 32–34, 49, 244, 253, 255, 312
Perth Amboy, 340
Perth, James Drummond, fourth Earl of, ix, 23, 50–5, 128, 162, 173, 177, 210, 214, 230–234, 312, 321, 353
Philip, James, of Almerieclose, 243
Philiphaugh, 18, 31, 319
Poor Man's Cup of Cold Water, 130, 332, 336, 355
Popish Plot, 133, 317
Portland, Earl of, 245
Prayer Book, 2, 11, 69, 74, 319, 323
Preston, 21, 135, 316, 319
Privy Council, 2, 8, 15, 57, 63–64, 82–83, 85, 89, 94, 97–98, 105, 117, 120–121, 123–124, 129, 136, 140–141, 145, 156, 159–160, 164, 166, 168–169, 171, 174–182, 184–185, 187–188, 191, 193, 195, 213, 215–217, 231–233, 240, 251, 256, 267–268, 273–274, 279, 292, 299, 320, 323, 332, 335, 338, 341, 355
Protesters, 34, 36, 40–42, 45, 50, 67, 129, 263, 318, 320

Q

Quakers, 218, 327
Queensberry, James Douglas, second Duke of, 129, 173, 197, 235, 275–276, 292, 318
Queensberry, William Douglas, third Earl and first Duke of, 298

R

Ramsay, Sir Andrew, 91
Religious Stoic, The, 61
Remonstrants, 33–34, 129, 318, 320
Renwick, James, 131, 151, 161, 167, 180, 192, 221, 223, 279, 311, 315, 322, 337, 345
Resolutioners, 33, 40, 42
Ridpath, George, 294
Ripon, 13
Rose, Alexander, 246
Ross, 68, 96, 102, 164, 186, 327, 333, 344
Ross, Lord, 171, 262, 337
Rothes, John Leslie, seventh Earl and first Duke of, see Leslie, John

Rotterdam, 110, 142, 172, 270
Roxburghe, Earl of, 297, 300
Rullion Green, 91–92, 98, 102, 320
Rumbold, Colonel, 200
Russell, James, 134
Rutherford, Samuel, 3, 53, 87
Rutherglen, 136, 158
Rye House Plot, 166, 170, 176, 183, 318, 321

S

St Andrews, 6, 33, 50–53, 68, 85, 99, 120, 134, 136–137, 141, 149, 219, 277, 328, 356
Salt industry, 99
Sanquhar, 148, 150, 158, 173, 321
Satan's Invisible World Discovered, 64, 104, 327, 329, 355
School curriculum, 367
Scotch Presbyterian Eloquence Displayed, 46, 322, 327
Scott, Sir Walter, vi, 51, 103
Scott, Sir William, of Harden, 119
Scott-Moncrieff, George, 145
Scottish Navy, 274, 298, 302
Seafield, James Ogilvie, first Earl of, 79, 276, 281, 283–285, 289, 293, 298–300, 302, 311
Seaforth, Earl of, 24, 309, 325
Secret Commonwealth of Elves, Faunes and Fairies, 207, 354
Selkirk, Earl of, 109
Sempill, Francis, 205
Serfdom, 80, 146
Shaftesbury, Earl of, 128, 165, 170
Sharp, Archbishop James, 58, 67–68, 73, 89, 99, 115, 123, 140
Sheldon, Archbishop, 69
Shields, Alexander, 135, 181, 191, 218, 223, 258, 263, 282
Shorter Catechism, 47
Sibbald, Sir Robert, 210
Sinclair, George, 64
Smith, Margaret, 74
Smith, Walter, 144, 151
Solemn League and Covenant, 16–17, 19, 26, 28, 30, 34, 37, 40, 55, 68–69, 86, 132, 158, 319, 323, 332

Solitude Preferred to Public Employment, 94
Somers, Lord, 303
South Queensferry, 147
Spence, Rev. Mr., 174–175
Spinoza, Baruch, 62
Spottiswood, Archbishop John, 6
Stair, Lady, 75, 271
Stair, Viscount, see Dalrymple, James
Stair, Earl of, see Dalrymple, John
'Start', The, 32, 66
Stewart, James, of Goodtrees, 66, 94, 101, 111, 165, 224, 252, 262, 278, 345, 348
Stirling, 2, 21, 31, 33, 55, 66, 90, 125, 137, 150, 164, 171, 240, 303, 307
Stirling Castle, 233, 240–241, 341
Stirling, James, 94
Story, R. H., 97, 257
Stranraer, 242, 310
Strathaven, 136, 137
Strathmore, Patrick Lyon, first Earl of, 121
Sutherland, 106, 186, 235
Sutherland, William Gordon, Earl of, 79
Sweden, 1, 11, 112, 324
Sydserf, Thomas, 97

T
'Tables', The, 3
Tarbert, 198–199
Tawney, R. H., vi
Terry, C. S., 50, 187, 193
Thomson, Rev. William, 70
Tippermuir, 17, 23, 319
Tobermory, 198
Toland, John, 278
Tolbooth, Edinburgh, 167, 169
Treaty of Ripon, 315, 368
Treaty of Union, xi, 292, 301, 322
Treshnish Isles, 244
Trevelyan, G. M., 38
Tullibardine, Earl of, see Atholl, first Duke
Turner, Sir James, 38, 83, 89–90, 94, 122, 270
Tweed, River, 18, 97, 119
Tweeddale, John Hay, Earl of, 99, 102, 108, 271

U
United Societies, 151
Urquhart, Sir Thomas, 39

W
Walker, Patrick, 149, 286, 327, 347–348
Wallace, Captain, 231
Wallace, Colonel James, 90–92
Wallace, Hugh, 169
Weir, Jean, 104
Weir, Major Thomas, 104
Welsh, Rev. John, 92, 105, 119, 132, 138, 144
Wemyss, Earl of, 302
Western Remonstrance, 32, 34, 318, 320
Westminster, 16, 37, 69, 77, 86, 97, 167, 294, 304, 315, 318–319, 322
Whiggamores, 25, 31, 33, 92, 172, 318, 320
Whiggamores' Raid, 25, 238
Whitford, Walter, 2
Wigtown, 131, 152, 158, 195
William II, King, 106, 110, 122, 190, 217, 226–229, 270, 309, 322
Wilson, Margaret, 195
Windram, Lt-Col., 195
Witch-trials, 63, 104
Witt, Jacob de, 209
Wodrow, Robert, 113, 126, 139, 172, 194–195, 222
Worcester, 34, 56, 89, 316, 320
Worcester, 299–300, 322

Y
Yester, Lord, 108, 242

Luath Press Limited
committed to publishing well written books worth reading

LUATH PRESS takes its name from Robert Burns, whose little collie Luath (*Gael.*, swift or nimble) tripped up Jean Armour at a wedding and gave him the chance to speak to the woman who was to be his wife and the abiding love of his life. Burns called one of 'The Twa Dogs' Luath after Cuchullin's hunting dog in Ossian's *Fingal*. Luath Press was established in 1981 in the heart of Burns country, and is now based a few steps up the road from Burns' first lodgings on Edinburgh's Royal Mile.

Luath offers you distinctive writing with a hint of unexpected pleasures.

Most bookshops in the UK, the US, Canada, Australia, New Zealand and parts of Europe either carry our books in stock or can order them for you. To order direct from us, please send a £sterling cheque, postal order, international money order or your credit card details (number, address of cardholder and expiry date) to us at the address below. Please add post and packing as follows: UK – £1.00 per delivery address; overseas surface mail – £2.50 per delivery address; overseas airmail – £3.50 for the first book to each delivery address, plus £1.00 for each additional book by airmail to the same address. If your order is a gift, we will happily enclose your card or message at no extra charge.

Luath Press Limited
543/2 Castlehill
The Royal Mile
Edinburgh EH1 2ND
Scotland
Telephone: 0131 225 4326 (24 hours)
Fax: 0131 225 4324
email: sales@luath.co.uk
Website: www.luath.co.uk